Table of contents

Introduction 13
Slow Cooker Breakfast Recipes 13
Apple Crumble 13
Cinnamon Berries Oatmeal 13
Banana and Coconut Oatmeal 13
Sausage and Potato Mix 14
Coconut Quinoa 14
Breakfast Zucchini Oatmeal 14
Veggie Hash Brown Mix 14
Chocolate French Toast 14
Hash Brown and Bacon Casserole 15
Cranberry Quinoa 15
Cinnamon French Toast 15
Creamy Yogurt 15
Carrots Oatmeal 16
Breakfast Banana Bread 16
Thyme Hash Browns 16
Greek Breakfast Casserole 16
Maple Banana Oatmeal 16
Veggie Casserole 17
Chia Oatmeal 17
Mexican Eggs 17
Buttery Oatmeal 17
Apple Oatmeal 17
Ginger Raisins Oatmeal 18
Quinoa and Oats Mix 18
Apple and Chia Mix 18
Spiced Pumpkin Oatmeal 18
Pumpkin and Quinoa Mix 19
Quinoa Breakfast Bars 19
Cocoa and Berries Quinoa 19
Raspberry Oatmeal 19
Quinoa and Veggies Casserole 19
Artichoke Frittata 20
Cauliflower and Eggs Bowls 20
Spinach Frittata 20
Sausage and Eggs Mix 20
Veggie Omelet 20
Parmesan Quinoa 21
Hash Browns and Sausage Casserole 21
Broccoli Casserole 21
Vanilla Oats 21
Creamy Shrimp Bowls 22
Cheese ....
Peach ....
Egg ....
Hot ....
Butter 23
Potato and Ham Mix 23
Breakfast Stuffed Peppers 23
Spinach Frittata 24
Oats Granola 24
Chili Eggs Mix 24
Tropical Granola 24
Cheesy Eggs 24
Creamy Strawberries Oatmeal 25
Tomato and Zucchini Eggs Mix 25
Breakfast Potatoes 25
Chocolate Breakfast Bread 25
Hash Brown Mix 26
Almond and Quinoa Bowls 26
Bacon and Egg Casserole 26
Carrots Casserole 26
Breakfast Rice Pudding 27
Cranberry Maple Oatmeal 27
Apple Breakfast Rice 27
Mushroom Casserole 27
Quinoa and Banana Mix 27
Ginger Apple Bowls 28
Dates Quinoa 28
Granola Bowls 28
Cinnamon Quinoa 28
Squash Bowls 28
Quinoa and Apricots 28
Lamb and Eggs Mix 29
Blueberry Quinoa Oatmeal 29
Cauliflower Casserole 29
Lentils and Quinoa Mix 29
Beef Meatloaf 30
Butternut Squash Quinoa 30
Leek Casserole 30
Chia Seeds Mix 30
Eggs and Sweet Potato Mix 30
Chia Seeds and Chicken Breakfast 31
Pork and Eggplant Casserole 31
Chocolate Quinoa 31
Apple Spread 31

Chai Breakfast Quinoa 32
Cherries and Cocoa Oats................................ 32
Quinoa Breakfast Bake 32
Beans Salad 32
Mocha Latte Quinoa Mix 32
Peppers Rice Mix... 33
Breakfast Butterscotch Pudding.................... 33
Cashew Butter 33
French Breakfast Pudding 33
Pumpkin and Berries Bowls 33
Eggs and Sausage Casserole........................... 34
Quinoa and Chia Pudding.............................. 34
Cauliflower Rice Pudding 34
Beans Breakfast Bowls 34
Veggies Casserole 34
Basil Sausage and Broccoli Mix...................... 35
Arugula Frittata... 35
Zucchini and Cauliflower Eggs Mix 35
Mixed Egg and Sausage Scramble................. 35
Mushroom Quiche 36
Worcestershire Asparagus Casserole............ 36
Scallions Quinoa and Carrots Bowls............. 36
Peppers, Kale and Cheese Omelet................. 36
Ham Omelet... 37
Salmon Frittata 37
Peppers and Eggs Mix..................................... 37
Creamy Breakfast... 37
Baby Spinach Rice Mix.................................... 37
Brussels Sprouts Omelet 38
Herbed Egg Scramble...................................... 38
Chicken Frittata 38
Peas and Rice Bowls 38
Mushrooms Casserole 38
Asparagus Casserole 39
Carrot Pudding.. 39

Slow Cooker Lunch Recipes 40

Turkey Lunch 40
Seafood Soup 40
Lunch Roast 40
Sesame Salmon Bowls..................................... 40
Fajitas 41
Shrimp Stew 41
Teriyaki Pork 41
Garlic Shrimp and Spinach 41

Beef Stew 42
Ginger Salmon 42
Apple and Onion Lunch Roast 42
Creamy Cod Stew 42
Stuffed Peppers 43
Sweet Potato and Clam Chowder.................. 43
Beans and Pumpkin Chili 43
Maple Chicken Mix.. 43
Chicken and Peppers Mix............................... 44
Salsa Chicken.. 44
Chicken Tacos... 44
Turkey and Mushrooms 44
Orange Beef Dish 45
Indian Chicken and Tomato Mix................... 45
Chicken with Couscous................................... 45
Turkey and Figs.. 45
Pork Stew 46
Turkey and Walnuts.. 46
Seafood Stew.. 46
Slow Cooked Thyme Chicken........................ 46
Pork Sandwiches.. 46
Roasted Beef and Cauliflower 47
Peas and Ham Mix... 47
Soy Pork Chops 47
Beef and Veggie Stew...................................... 47
Pork and Cranberries 48
Onion Chicken.. 48
Lamb and Onion Stew..................................... 48
Beef Chili 48
Pork Roast and Olives..................................... 49
Moist Pork Loin.. 49
Beef Stew 49
Lunch Meatloaf 49
Beef and Celery Stew....................................... 49
Mexican Lunch Mix 50
Tomato Pasta Mix... 50
Sweet Turkey 50
Honey Lamb Roast 50
Beef Strips... 51
Worcestershire Beef Mix 51
BBQ Chicken Thighs....................................... 51
Chickpeas Stew 51
Fall Slow Cooker Roast 52
Lentils Soup 52

Creamy Chicken 52
Chicken Soup 52
Chicken Stew 53
Lime and Thyme Chicken.................................53
Lemon Chicken 53
Shrimp Gumbo 53
Chicken Noodle Soup..53
Squash and Chicken Soup 54
Lentils Soup 54
Pork Soup 54
Taco Soup 54
Mushroom Stew 55
Thai Chicken Soup...55
Beans Chili 55
Spinach and Mushroom Soup..........................55
Parsley Chicken Stew 56
Creamy Chicken Soup.......................................56
Mustard Short Ribs 56
Black Bean Soup..56
Creamy Brisket 57
Winter Veggie Stew 57
Mushroom Soup 57
Chickpeas Stew 57
Creamy Potato Soup 58
Lentils Curry 58
Chicken with Corn and Wild Rice...................58
Quinoa Chili..58
Mixed Pork and Beans......................................59
French Veggie Stew 59
Pork Chops and Butter Sauce.........................59
Beans and Rice 59
Chicken and Peach Mix....................................60
Black Beans Stew 60
Chicken Drumsticks and Buffalo Sauce.......60
Sweet Potato Stew 60
Mustard Pork Chops and Carrots 61
Minestrone Soup 61
Fennel Soup 61
Chili Cream 61
Artichoke Soup...61
Salmon and Cilantro Sauce..............................62
Beans and Mushroom Stew 62
Chili Salmon...62
Chicken and Eggplant Stew 62

Pulled Chicken 63
Turmeric Lentils Stew 63
Chicken Chili 63
Pork Chili 63
Salsa Chicken 64
Cinnamon Pork Ribs..64
Thai Chicken 64
Pork and Mushroom Stew 64
Turkey Chili 65
Pork and Tomatoes Mix 65
Turkey and Potatoes...65
Pesto Pork Shanks...65
Chicken Thighs Mix...66
Potato Stew 66
Chicken and Stew 66
Chicken and Rice...66
Chicken and Cabbage Mix................................67
Salmon Stew...67
Pork and Chorizo Lunch Mix...........................67
Paprika Pork and Chickpeas 67
Lamb Stew..67
Beef and Cabbage..68
Lamb Curry..68
Balsamic Beef Stew 68
Lamb and Bacon Stew 68
Beef Curry 69
Sweet Potato Soup 69
Chicken and Brussels Sprouts Mix.................69
White Beans Stew..69
Chickpeas Stew 70
Bulgur Chili..70
Eggplant Curry...70
Quinoa Chili..70
Beef and Artichokes Stew 71
Pumpkin Chili 71
Beef Soup 71
3 Bean Chili 71
Veggie Soup 72
Cod and Asparagus 72
Oregano Turkey Stew..72
Seafood Stew..72
Masala Beef Mix 73
Shrimp Stew 73

Slow Cooker Side Dish Recipes............73

Creamy Hash Brown Mix	73	Marjoram Rice Mix	83
Cheddar Potatoes Mix	73	Creamy Chipotle Sweet Potatoes	83
Broccoli Mix	73	Mashed Potatoes	83
Balsamic Cauliflower	74	Kale and Ham Mix	83
Bean Medley	74	Barley Mix	84
Italian Black Beans Mix	74	Sweet Potato Mash	84
Green Beans Mix	74	Lime Beans Mix	84
Butter Green Beans	75	Dill Cauliflower Mash	84
Corn and Bacon	75	Creamy Beans	84
Corn Sauté	75	Eggplant and Kale Mix	85
Peas and Carrots	75	Spinach Mix	85
Sage Peas	75	Thai Side Salad	85
Beans, Carrots and Spinach Salad	76	Bbq Beans	85
Tomato and Corn Mix	76	Rosemary Potatoes	86
Scalloped Potatoes	76	White Beans Mix	86
Dill Mushroom Sauté	76	Maple Brussels Sprouts	86
Sweet Potatoes with Bacon	77	Sweet Potato and Cauliflower Mix	86
Hot Zucchini Mix	77	Beets and Carrots	86
Cauliflower and Broccoli Mix	77	Cabbage Mix	87
Butternut Squash and Eggplant Mix	77	Italian Veggie Mix	87
Wild Rice Mix	78	Parsley Mushroom Mix	87
Carrots and Spinach Mix	78	Wild Rice and Barley Pilaf	87
Mashed Potatoes	78	Cinnamon Squash	87
Creamy Coconut Potatoes	78	Apples and Potatoes	88
Orange Glazed Carrots	78	Zucchini Mix	88
Sage Sweet Potatoes	79	Asparagus and Mushroom Mix	88
Creamy Risotto	79	Kale Mix	88
Veggie and Garbanzo Mix	79	Asparagus Mix	88
Garlic Risotto	79	Buttery Spinach	89
Cauliflower Pilaf	80	Chorizo and Cauliflower Mix	89
Red Curry Veggie Mix	80	Bacon Potatoes Mix	89
Squash Side Salad	80	Classic Veggies Mix	89
Rosemary Leeks	80	Cauliflower Mash	89
Mushrooms and Sausage Mix	80	Okra Side Dish	90
Mustard Brussels Sprouts	81	Veggie Mix	90
Glazed Baby Carrots	81	Okra Side Dish	90
Potatoes and Leeks Mix	81	Farro Mix	90
Spinach and Squash Side Salad	81	Okra Mix	91
Black Beans Mix	81	Cumin Quinoa Pilaf	91
Buttery Mushrooms	82	Stewed Okra	91
Orange Carrots Mix	82	Saffron Risotto	91
Cauliflower Rice and Spinach	82	Okra and Corn	91
Hot Lentils	82	Mint Farro Pilaf	92
Maple Sweet Potatoes	82	Roasted Beets	92

Parmesan Rice	92
Thyme Beets	92
Spinach Rice	92
Beets Side Salad	93
Mango Rice	93
Lemony Beets	93
Lemon Artichokes	93
Carrot and Beet Side Salad	93
Coconut Bok Choy	94
Cauliflower and Carrot Gratin	94
Italian Eggplant	94
Herbed Beets	94
Cabbage and Onion Mix	94
Summer Squash Mix	95
Balsamic Okra Mix	95
Veggie Side Salad	95
Garlic Carrots Mix	95
Italian Squash and Peppers Mix	95
Curry Broccoli Mix	96
Green Beans and Red Peppers	96
Rice and Corn	96
Garlic Butter Green Beans	96
Cauliflower and Potatoes Mix	96
Zucchini Casserole	97
Asparagus Mix	97
Nut and Berry Side Salad	97
Garlic Squash Mix	97
Blueberry and Spinach Salad	98
Baby Carrots and Parsnips Mix	98
Rice and Farro Pilaf	98
Lemon Kale Mix	98
Pink Rice	98
Brussels Sprouts and Cauliflower	99
Pumpkin Rice	99
Cabbage and Kale Mix	99
Rice and Veggies	99
Thyme Mushrooms and Corn	100
Farro	100
Veggie Medley	100
Mexican Rice	100
Paprika Green Beans and Zucchinis	100
Goat Cheese Rice	101
Tarragon Sweet Potatoes	101
Rice and Artichokes	101
Mustard Brussels Sprouts	101
Green Beans and Mushrooms	102
Parmesan Spinach Mix	102
Black Beans Mix	102
Minty Peas and Tomatoes	102
Rice and Beans	102
Savoy Cabbage Mix	103

Slow Cooker Snack Recipes 103

Tamale Dip	103
Spinach Spread	103
BBQ Chicken Dip	103
Artichoke Dip	104
Mexican Dip	104
Crab Dip	104
Tex Mex Dip	104
Lemon Shrimp Dip	105
Artichoke Dip	105
Squash Salsa	105
Taco Dip	105
Beans Spread	105
Lasagna Dip	106
Rice Snack Bowls	106
Beer and Cheese Dip	106
Cauliflower Spread	106
Queso Dip	106
Mushroom Dip	107
Crab Dip	107
Chickpeas Spread	107
Corn Dip	107
Spinach Dip	107
Candied Pecans	108
Dill Potato Salad	108
Chicken Bites	108
Stuffed Peppers Platter	108
Peanut Snack	109
Corn Dip	109
Apple Dip	109
Tomato and Mushroom Salsa	109
Beef and Chipotle Dip	109
Salsa Beans Dip	110
Sugary Chicken Wings	110
Pineapple and Tofu Salsa	110
Bean Dip	110
Chickpeas Salsa	110

Buffalo Meatballs	111
Creamy Mushroom Spread	111
Glazed Sausages	111
Bulgur and Beans Salsa	111
Cheesy Mix	111
Beets Salad	112
Cheeseburger Meatballs	112
Lentils Salsa	112
Caramel Corn	112
Tacos	113
Bourbon Sausage Bites	113
Almond Bowls	113
Curried Meatballs	113
Eggplant Salsa	113
Pizza Dip	114
Almond Spread	114
Sauerkraut Dip	114
Onion Dip	114
Spicy Dip	114
Nuts Bowls	115
Salsa Corn Dip	115
Eggplant Salad	115
Cheesy Corn Dip	115
Lentils Dip	115
White Bean Spread	116
Turkey Meatballs	116
Lentils Rolls	116
Stuffed Mushrooms	116
Eggplant Salsa	116
Paprika Cod Sticks	117
Veggie Spread	117
Macadamia Nuts Snack	117
Peas Dip	117
Salmon Bites	118
Hummus	118
Spinach and Walnuts Dip	118
Cashew Dip	118
Curry Pork Meatballs	118
Potato Salsa	119
Calamari Rings Bowls	119
Black Bean Salsa Salad	119
Shrimp Salad	119
Mushroom Dip	119
Chicken Salad	120
Beef Meatballs	120
Apple and Carrot Dip	120
Jalapeno Poppers	120
Sweet Potato Dip	121
Pecans Snack	121
Spinach, Walnuts and Calamari Salad	121
Apple Jelly Sausage Snack	121
Chicken Meatballs	121
Eggplant Dip	122
Cinnamon Pecans Snack	122
Lemon Peel Snack	122
Cajun Almonds and Shrimp Bowls	122
Fava Bean Dip	122
Broccoli Dip	123
Tamales	123
Walnuts Bowls	123
Tostadas	123
Cauliflower Bites	124
Mussels Salad	124
Beef Dip	124
Italian Mussels Salad	124
Zucchini Spread	125
Spicy Mussels	125
Beef Dip	125
Cheeseburger Dip	125
Eggplant Salsa	126
Onion Dip	126
Carrots Spread	126
Caramel Dip	126
Cauliflower Dip	126
Chicken Cordon Bleu Dip	127
Lentils Hummus	127
Fajita Dip	127
Spinach Dip	127
Simple Salsa	127
Peppers Salsa	128
Salsa Snack	128
Artichoke Dip	128
Onion Dip	128
Mushroom Salsa	129

Slow Cooker Poultry Recipes............129

Rotisserie Chicken	129
Garlic Chicken and Green Beans	129
Chicken and Dumplings	129

Oregano Turkey and Tomatoes	130
Balsamic Chicken	130
Mustard Chicken Mix	130
Buffalo Chicken	130
Lemon Turkey and Spinach	131
Alfredo Chicken	131
Paprika Chicken and Artichokes	131
Slow Cooked Chicken	131
Chives Chicken Wings	132
Parsley Turkey Breast	132
Lime Chicken Mix	132
Chicken Breasts	132
Chicken and Olives	133
Turkey Breast and Cranberries	133
Turkey, Tomato and Fennel Mix	133
Thyme Chicken	133
Chicken with Tomatoes and Eggplant Mix	133
Mediterranean Chicken	134
Chicken and Onions Mix	134
Chicken Chowder	134
Pesto Chicken Mix	134
Chicken Thighs Delight	135
Ginger Turkey Mix	135
Chicken with Peach and Orange Sauce	135
Turkey and Plums Mix	135
Flavored Chicken Thighs	136
Creamy Turkey Mix	136
Turkey Gumbo	136
Chicken and Apples Mix	136
Chinese Duck	136
Chicken and Endives	137
Turkey Wings and Veggies	137
Basil Chicken Wings	137
Turkey Wings and Sauce	137
Chicken and Broccoli	137
Chicken and Sauce	138
Rosemary Chicken	138
Chicken Wings and Mint Sauce	138
Chicken Curry	138
Lemony Chicken	139
Balsamic Turkey	139
Chicken and Paprika Sauce	139
Turkey and Scallions Mix	139
Chicken Thighs and Mushrooms	140
Parsley Chicken Mix	140
Creamy Duck Breast	140
Turkey Chili	140
Duck Breast and Veggies	140
Masala Turkey	141
Turkey Soup	141
Chicken and Beans	141
Slow Cooked Turkey Delight	141
Turkey and Corn	142
Turkey Curry	142
Coriander Turkey Mix	142
Chicken and Mustard Sauce	142
Turkey with Olives and Corn	142
Chicken Casserole	143
Dill Turkey and Peas	143
Chicken and Broccoli Casserole	143
Turkey with Rice	143
Red Chicken Soup	144
Italian Turkey	144
Citrus Chicken	144
Duck and Mushrooms	144
Chicken and Creamy Mushroom Sauce	145
Turkey and Tomato Sauce	145
Slow Cooker Chicken Breasts	145
Tomato Chicken and Chickpeas	145
Chicken and Sour Cream	145
Turkey with Leeks and Radishes	146
Chicken Stroganoff	146
Coconut Turkey	146
Pepperoni Chicken	146
Hot Chicken and Zucchinis	147
Creamy Spinach and Artichoke Chicken	147
Turkey with Radishes	147
Chicken Meatloaf	147
Chives Duck	148
Chicken and Green Onion Sauce	148
Cilantro Chicken and Eggplant Mix	148
Mushrooms Stuffed with Chicken	148
Chicken with Brussels Sprouts	149
Thai Peanut Chicken	149
Chicken and Mango Mix	149
Flavored Chicken Drumsticks	149
Turkey and Avocado	149

Chicken Thighs and Romano Cheese Mix 150
Chicken and Peppers 150
Slow Cooker Chicken Thighs 150
Chicken and Cabbage Mix 150
Chicken and Tomatillos 151
Lime Turkey and Chard 151
Duck and Potatoes 151
BBQ Turkey mix 151
Chicken Salad 152
Chicken and Asparagus 152
Sweet and Hot Chicken Wings 152
Lemon Turkey and Potatoes 152
Duck Chili 152
Turkey and Okra 153
Coca Cola Chicken 153
Mustard Duck Mix 153
Cuban Chicken 153
Orange Chicken Mix 154
Chicken and Lentils 154
Turkey and Carrots 154
Chicken and Chickpeas 154
Rosemary Chicken Thighs 155
Chicken and Sauce 155
Turkey and Kidney Beans 155
Goose Mix 155
Coriander and Turmeric Chicken 155
Goose and Sauce 156
Garlic Turkey 156
Chicken Liver Stew 156
Cumin Chicken Mix 156

Slow cooker Meat Recipes 157
Beef Roast 157
Pork Chops and Mango Mix 157
Short Ribs 157
Beef and Zucchinis Mix 157
Soy Pork Ribs 157
Pork and Olives Mix 158
Beef Chuck Roast 158
Pork and Soy Sauce Mix 158
Mexican Pork Roast 158
Beef and Sauce 159
Pork Chops and Pineapple Mix 159
Pork and Beans Mix 159

Pork Tenderloin and Apples 159
Beef with Spinach 159
Lamb Leg and Sweet Potatoes 160
Pork and Chilies Mix 160
Lamb Shanks 160
Mustard Ribs 160
Flavored Pork Roast 161
Beef and Corn Mix 161
Beef and Onions 161
Cider Beef Mix 161
Lamb Shoulder 161
Tarragon Pork Chops 162
Chinese Pork Shoulder 162
Honey Pork Chops 162
Roast and Pepperoncinis 162
Turmeric Lamb 163
Balsamic Beef Cheeks 163
Chili Lamb 163
Seasoned Beef 163
Beef and Red Onions Mix 163
Beef Soup 164
Pork and Okra 164
Thai Cocoa Pork 164
Chives Lamb 164
Herbed and Cinnamon Beef 165
Oregano Beef 165
Beef Brisket and Turnips Mix 165
Pork and Green Beans 165
Rich Lamb Shanks 165
Mint Lamb Chops 166
Lamb Leg and Mushrooms Mix 166
Beef and Artichokes 166
Smoky Lamb 166
Lamb and Potatoes 167
Sausage and Onion Jam 167
Lamb and Tomatoes Mix 167
French Lamb 167
Pork and Eggplant Mix 167
Jamaican Pork 168
Lemon Lamb 168
Pork Sirloin Salsa Mix 168
Rosemary Lamb with Olives 168
Beef Meatloaf 168
Nutmeg Lamb and Squash 169

Pork Loin and Cauliflower Rice 169
Lamb and Fennel Mix 169
Lamb and Spinach Salad 169
Creamy Lamb 170
Lamb Stew 170
Beef and Capers Sauce 170
Sausages and Celeriac Mash 170
Masala Beef and Sauce 171
Pork Belly and Applesauce 171
Lamb and Cabbage 171
Stuffed Pork 171
Pork and Lentils 171
Pork Rolls 172
Balsamic Lamb Mix 172
Tender Pork Chops 172
Beef and Endives 172
Worcestershire Pork Chops 173
Lamb and Lime Zucchinis 173
Rosemary Pork 173
Beef and Peas 173
Oregano Pork Chops 173
Maple Beef 174
Spicy Pork 174
Rosemary Beef 174
Beef Meatballs Casserole 174
Parsley and Chili Lamb 175
Beef Stuffed Squash 175
Cumin Pork Chops 175
Beef and Tzatziki 175
Paprika Lamb 176
German Beef Soup 176
Beef with Peas and Corn 176
Oregano Lamb 176
Lime Pork Chops 176
Lamb Casserole 177
Lamb with Capers 177
Lavender and Orange Lamb 177
Lamb and Zucchini Mix 177
Lamb and Orange Sauce 178
Beef and Peppers 178
Lamb and Mint Pesto 178
Cayenne Lamb Mix 178
Lamb and Fennel Mix 178
Cinnamon Lamb 179

Beef and Pancetta 179
Lamb and Kale 179
Veal Stew 179
Beef and Sprouts 180
Veal and Tomatoes 180
Veal Piccata 180
Pork Chops and Spinach 180
Sausage Mix 181
Green Curry Lamb 181
Cheesy Sausage Casserole 181
Oregano Lamb 181
Sausage Soup 181
Pesto Lamb Chops 182
Italian Sausage Soup 182
Beef with Green Beans and Cilantro 182
Beef Curry 182
Balsamic Lamb Chops 183
Flavored and Spicy Beef Mix 183
Creamy Beef 183
Walnut and Coconut Beef 183

Slow Cooker Fish Recipes 184
Salmon and Green Onions Mix 184
Lime Shrimp 184
Seafood Chowder 184
Chili Salmon 184
Asian Salmon Mix 184
Rosemary Shrimp 185
Shrimp Mix 185
Paprika Cod 185
Asian Steamed Fish 185
Spicy Tuna 185
Poached Cod and Pineapple Mix 186
Ginger Tuna 186
Chili Catfish 186
Chives Shrimp 186
Tuna Loin Mix 187
Coriander Salmon Mix 187
Creamy Sea Bass 187
Tuna and Green Beans 187
Flavored Cod Fillets 187
Cod and Corn 188
Shrimp and Baby Carrots Mix 188
Turmeric Salmon 188
Dill Trout 188

Sea Bass and Chickpeas	188
Fish Pie	189
Creamy Shrimp	189
Slow Cooked Haddock	189
Parsley Cod	189
Buttery Trout	190
Pesto Cod and Tomatoes	190
Easy Salmon and Kimchi Sauce	190
Orange Cod	190
Salmon Meatballs and Sauce	190
Garlic Sea Bass	191
Salmon and Caper Sauce	191
Tuna and Brussels Sprouts	191
Tabasco Halibut	191
Shrimp with Spinach	192
Creamy Salmon	192
Shrimp and Avocado	192
Chinese Cod	192
Chives Mackerel	192
Fish Mix	193
Dill Cod	193
Italian Barramundi and Tomato Relish	193
Shrimp and Mango Mix	193
Spicy Creole Shrimp	194
Balsamic Tuna	194
Sriracha Shrimp	194
Lime Trout Mix	194
Shrimp and Peas Soup	194
Creamy Tuna and Scallions	195
Calamari and Sauce	195
Cod and Mustard Sauce	195
Calamari and Shrimp	195
Shrimp and Pineapple Bowls	195
Clam Chowder	196
Lime Crab	196
Shrimp Salad	196
Hot Salmon and Carrots	196
Italian Clams	197
Shrimp and Eggplant	197
Orange Salmon	197
Sea Bass and Squash	197
Tuna and Chimichurri	197
Coconut Mackerel	198
Cider Clams	198
Salmon and Peas	198
Mustard Salmon	198
Chili Shrimp and Zucchinis	199
Salmon and Relish	199
Italian Shrimp	199
Mussels Soup	199
Basil Cod and Olives	199
Fish and Olives Mix	200
Indian Fish	200
Tuna and Fennel	200
Cod and Peas	200
Shrimp and Mushrooms	200
Salmon and Rice	201
Salmon and Berries	201
Milky Fish	201
Cod and Artichokes	201
Salmon and Raspberry Vinaigrette	202
Salmon, Tomatoes and Green Beans	202
Fish Pudding	202
Shrimp and Rice Mix	202
Jambalaya	202
Shrimp and Red Chard	203
Mushroom Tuna Mix	203
Chives Mussels	203
Chili Mackerel	203
Calamari and Sauce	204
Chinese Mackerel	204
Salmon Salad	204
Mackerel and Lemon	204
Walnut Tuna Mix	205
Mussels and Sausage Mix	205
Almond Shrimp and Cabbage	205
Mussels, Clams and Chorizo Mix	205
Indian Shrimp	205
Crab Legs	206
Shrimp, Tomatoes and Kale	206
Shrimp and Sausage Boil	206
Trout Bowls	206
Mushroom and Shrimp Curry	206
Calamari Curry	207
Dill Shrimp Mix	207
Balsamic Trout	207
Japanese Shrimp	207
Oregano Shrimp Bowls	207

Octopus and Veggies Mix	208
Salmon and Strawberries Mix	208
Mediterranean Octopus	208
Shrimp, Salmon and Tomatoes Mix	208
Stuffed Squid	209
Shrimp and Cauliflower Bowls	209
Flavored Squid	209
Cod and Broccoli	209
Cinnamon Trout	210

Slow Cooker Dessert Recipes 210

Pudding Cake	210
Cinnamon Apples	210
Peanut Butter Cake	210
Vanilla Pears	211
Blueberry Cake	211
Avocado Cake	211
Peach Pie	211
Coconut Cream	212
Sweet Strawberry Mix	212
Almond Rice Pudding	212
Sweet Plums	212
Cherry Bowls	212
Bananas and Sweet Sauce	212
Berry Cream	213
Orange Cake	213
Maple Pudding	213
Apples Stew	213
Chia and Orange Pudding	214
Pears and Sauce	214
Creamy Berries Mix	214
Vanilla Cookies	214
Apple Compote	214
Pumpkin Pie	215
Plums Stew	215
Strawberries Marmalade	215
Cinnamon Peach Mix	215
Rhubarb Marmalade	215
Strawberry Cake	215
Sweet Potato Pudding	216
Ginger Pears Mix	216
Cherry Jam	216
Raisin Cookies	216
Sweet Cookies	216
Blueberries Jam	217
Maple Pears	217
Orange Bowls	217
Stuffed Apples	217
Quinoa Pudding	217
Chocolate Cake	218
Chia and Avocado Pudding	218
Berry Cobbler	218
Almond and Cherries Pudding	218
Apple Bread	219
Vanilla Peach Cream	219
Banana Cake	219
Cinnamon Plums	219
Chocolate Pudding	219
Cardamom Apples	220
Cauliflower Pudding	220
Cherry and Rhubarb Mix	220
Chia Pudding	220
Peaches and Wine Sauce	220
Stewed Grapefruit	221
Apricot and Peaches Cream	221
Cocoa Cherry Compote	221
Vanilla Grapes Mix	221
Cashew Cake	221
Pomegranate and Mango Bowls	221
Lemon Pudding	222
Mandarin Cream	222
Lemon Jam	222
Cranberries Cream	222
Chocolate Cream	222
Buttery Pineapple	223
Coconut and Macadamia Cream	223
Strawberry and Orange Mix	223
Strawberry Pie	223
Maple Plums and Mango	223
Sweet Raspberry Mix	224
Cantaloupe Cream	224
Sweet Mascarpone Cream	224
Yogurt Cheesecake	224
Lemon Cream	224
Chocolate Mango Mix	225
Coconut Vanilla Cream	225
Lemon Jam	225
Avocado Pudding	225
Lemon Peach Mix	225

Coconut Pudding	226
Rhubarb Stew	226
Cocoa Cake	226
Strawberry and Blackberry Jam	226
Dark Chocolate Cream	226
Pear Cream	227
Mango Cream	227
Rhubarb Jam	227
Lime Cheesecake	227
Apricot Marmalade	227
Caramel Cream	228
Apple, Avocado and Mango Bowls	228
Ricotta Cream	228
Tomato Jam	228
Green Tea Pudding	228
Cinnamon and Chocolate Peaches	229
Sweet Lemon Mix	229
Coconut Jam	229
Banana Bread	229
Bread and Berries Pudding	229
Candied Lemon	230
Tapioca and Chia Pudding	230
Chocolate and Liquor Cream	230
Dates and Rice Pudding	230
Butternut Squash Sweet Mix	230
Almonds, Walnuts and Mango Bowls	230
Tapioca Pudding	231
Berries Salad	231
Fresh Cream Mix	231
Pears and Apples Bowls	231
Pears and Wine Sauce	231
Creamy Rhubarb and Plums Bowls	232
Pears and Grape Sauce	232
Greek Cream Cheese Pudding	232
Rice Pudding	232
Greek Cream	232
Orange Marmalade	233
Ginger Cream	233
Berry Marmalade	233
Bread and Quinoa Pudding	233
Pears Jam	233
Melon Pudding	234
Conclusion	234

Introduction

We know you are always looking for easier ways to cook your meals. We also know you are probably sick and tired of spending long hours in the kitchen cooking with so many pans and pots.

Well, now your search is over! We found the perfect kitchen tool you can use from now on! We are talking about the Slow cooker! These amazing pots allow you to cook some of the best dishes ever with minimum effort

Slow cookers cook your meals easier and a lot healthier! You don't need to be an expert in the kitchen to cook some of the most delicious, flavored, textured and rich dishes!

All you need is your Slow cooker and the right ingredients!

More and more people all over the world decide to make their work in the kitchen a lot more fun and a lot easier!

You can become one of these happy people who chose to purchase and to use a Slow cooker!

So, if you made the decision to use the Slow cooker from now on, all you need now is to get your hands on a copy of this magnificent cooking journal. This great cookbook you are about to discover will teach you how to cook the best slow cooked meals.

It will show you that you can make some amazing breakfasts, lunch dishes, side dishes, poultry, meat and fish dishes.

Finally yet importantly, this cookbook provides you some simple and sweet desserts.

This sounds pretty amazing, doesn't it?

Then, what are you waiting for? Get your Slow cooker and this cookbook and start cooking in a new and innovative way! It will be the best culinary experience of your life!

Have fun and a your delicious Slow cooker dishes!

Slow Cooker Breakfast Recipes

Apple Crumble
Preparation time: 10 minutes
Cooking time: 4 hours
Servings: 6

INGREDIENTS:

2 green apples, peeled, cored and sliced

½ cup granola
½ cup bran flakes
¼ cup apple juice
1/8 cup maple syrup
1 teaspoon cinnamon powder
2 tablespoons soft butter
½ teaspoon nutmeg, ground

DIRECTIONS:
In your Slow cooker, mix apples with granola, bran flakes, apple juice, maple syrup, cinnamon, butter and nutmeg, toss, cover, cook on Low for 4 hours, divide into bowls and serve for breakfast.

NUTRITION:
calories 363, fat 5, fiber 6, carbs 20, protein 6

Cinnamon Berries Oatmeal
Preparation time: 10 minutes
Cooking time: 6 hours
Servings: 2

INGREDIENTS:
1 cup old fashioned oats
3 cups almond milk
1 cup blackberries
½ cup Greek yogurt
½ teaspoon cinnamon powder
½ teaspoon vanilla extract

DIRECTIONS:
In your slow cooker, mix the oats with the milk, berries and the other ingredients, toss, put the lid on and cook on Low for 6 hours. Divide into bowls and serve for breakfast.

NUTRITION:
calories 932, fat 43, fiber 16.7, carbs 82.2, protein 24.3

Banana and Coconut Oatmeal
Preparation time: 10 minutes
Cooking time: 7 hours
Servings: 6

INGREDIENTS:
Cooking spray
2 bananas, sliced
1 cup steel cut oats
28 ounces canned coconut milk
½ cup water
1 tablespoon butter
2 tablespoons brown sugar
¼ teaspoon nutmeg, ground
½ teaspoon cinnamon powder
½ teaspoon vanilla extract
1 tablespoon flaxseed, ground

DIRECTIONS:
Grease your Slow cooker with cooking spray, add banana slices, oats, coconut milk, water, butter, sugar, cinnamon, butter, vanilla and flaxseed, toss a bit, cover and cook on Low for 7 hours. Divide into bowls and serve for breakfast.

NUTRITION:
calories 251, fat 6, fiber 8, carbs 16, protein 6

Sausage and Potato Mix
Preparation time: 10 minutes
Cooking time: 6 hours
Servings: 2

INGREDIENTS:
- 2 sweet potatoes, peeled and roughly cubed
- 1 green bell pepper, minced
- ½ yellow onion, chopped
- 4 ounces smoked andouille sausage, sliced
- 1 cup cheddar cheese, shredded
- ¼ cup Greek yogurt
- ¼ teaspoon basil, dried
- 1 cup chicken stock
- Salt and black pepper to the taste
- 1 tablespoon parsley, chopped

DIRECTIONS:
In your slow cooker, combine the potatoes with the bell pepper, sausage and the other ingredients, toss, put the lid on and cook on Low for 6 hours. Divide between plates and serve for breakfast.

NUTRITION:
calories 623, fat 35.7, fiber 7.6, carbs 53.1, protein 24.8

Coconut Quinoa
Preparation time: 10 minutes
Cooking time: 8 hours
Servings: 2

INGREDIENTS:
- ½ cup quinoa
- 2 cups coconut milk
- 1 tablespoon maple syrup
- 1 teaspoon vanilla extract
- 2 tablespoons raisins
- ¼ cup blackberries

DIRECTIONS:
In your slow cooker, mix the quinoa with the milk, maple syrup and the other ingredients, toss, put the lid on and cook on Low for 8 hours. Divide into 2 bowls and serve for breakfast.

NUTRITION:
calories 775, fat 60, fiber 9.7, carbs 56.5, protein 12

Breakfast Zucchini Oatmeal
Preparation time: 10 minutes
Cooking time: 8 hours
Servings: 4

INGREDIENTS:
- ½ cup steel cut oats
- 1 carrot, grated
- 1 and ½ cups coconut milk
- ¼ zucchini, grated
- A pinch of cloves, ground
- A pinch of nutmeg, ground
- ½ teaspoon cinnamon powder
- 2 tablespoons brown sugar
- ¼ cup pecans, chopped

DIRECTIONS:
In your Slow cooker, mix oats with carrot, milk, zucchini, cloves, nutmeg, cinnamon and sugar, stir, cover and cook on Low for 8 hours. Add pecans, toss, divide into bowls and serve.

NUTRITION:
calories 251, fat 6, fiber 8, carbs 19, protein 6

Veggie Hash Brown Mix
Preparation time: 10 minutes
Cooking time: 6 hours and 5 minutes
Servings: 2

INGREDIENTS:
- 1 tablespoon olive oil
- ½ cup white mushrooms, chopped
- ½ yellow onion, chopped
- ¼ teaspoon garlic powder
- ¼ teaspoon onion powder
- ¼ cup sour cream
- 10 ounces hash browns
- ¼ cup cheddar cheese, shredded
- Salt and black pepper to the taste
- ½ tablespoon parsley, chopped

DIRECTIONS:
Heat up a pan with the oil over medium heat, add the onion and mushrooms, stir and cook for 5 minutes. Transfer this to the slow cooker, add hash browns and the other ingredients, toss, put the lid on and cook on Low for 6 hours. Divide between plates and for breakfast.

NUTRITION:
calories 571, fat 35.6, fiber 5.4, carbs 54.9, protein 9.7

Chocolate French Toast
Preparation time: 10 minutes
Cooking time: 4 hours
Servings: 4

INGREDIENTS:
- Cooking spray
- 1 loaf of bread, cubed
- ¾ cup brown sugar
- 3 eggs
- 1 and ½ cups milk
- 1 teaspoon vanilla

extract
¾ cup chocolate chips

1 teaspoon cinnamon powder

DIRECTIONS:
Grease your Slow cooker with the cooking spray and arrange bread cubes inside. In a bowl, mix the eggs with milk, sugar, vanilla, cinnamon and chocolate chips, whisk well, add to the slow cooker, cover and cook on Low for 4 hours. Divide into bowls and serve for breakfast.

NUTRITION:
calories 261, fat 6, fiber 5, carbs 19, protein 6

Hash Brown and Bacon Casserole
Preparation time: 10 minutes
Cooking time: 3 hours
Servings: 2

INGREDIENTS:
5 ounces hash browns, shredded
2 bacon slices, cooked and chopped
¼ cup mozzarella cheese, shredded
2 eggs, whisked
¼ cup sour cream
1 tablespoon cilantro, chopped
1 tablespoon olive oil
A pinch of salt and black pepper

DIRECTIONS:
Grease your slow cooker with the oil, add the hash browns mixed with the eggs, sour cream and the other ingredients, toss, put the lid on and cook on High for 4 hours. Divide the casserole into bowls and serve.

NUTRITION:
calories 383, fat 26.9, fiber 2.3, carbs 26.6, protein 9.6

Cranberry Quinoa
Preparation time: 10 minutes
Cooking time: 2 hours
Servings: 4

INGREDIENTS:
3 cups coconut water
1 teaspoon vanilla extract
1 cup quinoa
3 teaspoons honey
1/8 cup almonds, sliced
1/8 cup coconut flakes
¼ cup cranberries, dried

DIRECTIONS:
In your Slow cooker, mix coconut water with vanilla, quinoa, honey, almonds, coconut flakes and cranberries, toss, cover and cook on High for 2 hours. Divide quinoa mix into bowls and serve.

NUTRITION:
calories 261, fat 7, fiber 8, carbs 18, protein

Cinnamon French Toast
Preparation time: 10 minutes
Cooking time: 4 hours
Servings: 2

INGREDIENTS:
½ French baguette, sliced
2 ounces cream cheese
1 tablespoon brown sugar
1 egg, whisked
3 tablespoons almond
milk
2 tablespoons honey
½ teaspoon cinnamon powder
1 tablespoon butter, melted
Cooking spray

DIRECTIONS:
Spread the cream cheese on all bread slices, grease your slow cooker with the cooking spray and arrange the slices in the pot. In a bowl, mix the egg with the cinnamon, almond milk and the remaining ingredients, whisk and pour over the bread slices. Put the lid on, cook on High for 4 hours, divide the mix between plates and serve for breakfast.

NUTRITION:
calories 316, fat 23.5, fiber 0.5, carbs 23.9, protein 5.6

Creamy Yogurt
Preparation time: 10 minutes
Cooking time: 10 hours
Servings: 8

INGREDIENTS:
3 teaspoons gelatin
½ gallon milk
7 ounces plain yogurt
1 and ½ tablespoons vanilla extract
½ cup maple syrup

DIRECTIONS:
Put the milk in your Slow cooker, cover and cook on Low for 3 hours. In a bowl, mix 1 cup of hot milk from the slow cooker with the gelatin, whisk well, pour into the slow cooker, cover and leave aside for 2 hours. Combine 1 cup of milk with the yogurt, whisk really well and pour into the pot. Also add vanilla and maple syrup, stir, cover and cook on Low for 7 more hours. Leave yogurt aside to cool down and serve it for breakfast.

NUTRITION:
calories 200, fat 4, fiber 5, carbs 10, protein 5

Carrots Oatmeal

Preparation time: 10 minutes
Cooking time: 8 hours
Servings: 2

INGREDIENTS:
½ cup old fashioned oats
1 cup almond milk
2 carrots, peeled and grated
½ teaspoon cinnamon powder
2 tablespoons brown sugar
¼ cup walnuts, chopped
Cooking spray

DIRECTIONS:
Grease your slow cooker with cooking spray, add the oats, milk, carrots and the other ingredients, toss, put the lid on and cook on Low for 8 hours. Divide the oatmeal into 2 bowls and serve.

NUTRITION:
calories 590, fat 40.7, fiber 9.1, carbs 49.9, protein 12

Breakfast Banana Bread

Preparation time: 10 minutes
Cooking time: 4 hours
Servings: 4

INGREDIENTS:
2 eggs
1 cup sugar
2 cups flour
½ cup butter
1 teaspoon baking powder
3 bananas, mashed
½ teaspoon baking soda

DIRECTIONS:
In a bowl, mix butter with sugar and eggs and whisk well. Add baking soda, baking powder, flour and bananas, stir really well and pour into a bread pan that fits your Slow cooker. Put the pan into your Slow cooker, cover and cook on Low for 4 hours. Slice and serve for breakfast.

NUTRITION:
calories 261, fat 9, fiber 6, carbs 20, protein 16

Thyme Hash Browns

Preparation time: 10 minutes
Cooking time: 4 hours
Servings: 2

INGREDIENTS:
Cooking spray
10 ounces hash browns
2 eggs, whisked
¼ cup heavy cream
¼ teaspoon thyme, dried
¼ teaspoon garlic powder
A pinch of salt and black pepper
½ cup mozzarella, shredded
1 tablespoon chives, chopped
1 tablespoon parsley, chopped

DIRECTIONS:
Grease your slow cooker with cooking spray, spread the hash browns on the bottom, add the eggs, cream and the other ingredients except the cheese and toss. Sprinkle the cheese on top, put the lid on and cook on High for 4 hours. Divide the mix between plates and serve for breakfast.

NUTRITION:
calories 516, fat 29.2, fiber 4.7, carbs 51.3, protein 12.3

Greek Breakfast Casserole

Preparation time: 10 minutes
Cooking time: 4 hours
Servings: 4

INGREDIENTS:
12 eggs, whisked
Salt and black pepper to the taste
½ cup milk
1 red onion, chopped
1 cup baby bell mushrooms, sliced
½ cup sun-dried tomatoes
1 teaspoon garlic, minced
2 cups spinach
½ cup feta cheese, crumbled

DIRECTIONS:
In a bowl, mix the eggs with salt, pepper and milk and whisk well. Add garlic, onion, mushrooms, spinach and tomatoes, toss well, pour this into your Slow cooker, sprinkle cheese all over, cover and cook on Low for 4 hours. Slice, divide between plates and serve for breakfast.

NUTRITION:
calories 325, fat 7, fiber 7, carbs 27, protein 18

Maple Banana Oatmeal

Preparation time: 10 minutes
Cooking time: 6 hours
Servings: 2

INGREDIENTS:
1/2 cup old fashioned oats
1 banana, mashed
½ teaspoon cinnamon powder
2 tablespoons maple syrup
2 cups almond milk
Cooking spray

DIRECTIONS:
Grease your slow cooker with the cooking spray, add the oats, banana and the other ingredients, stir, put the lid on and cook on Low for 6 hours. Divide into 2 bowls and serve for breakfast.

NUTRITION:
calories 815, fat 60.3, fiber 10.7, carbs 67, protein 11.1

Veggie Casserole
Preparation time: 10 minutes

Cooking time: 4 hours

Servings: 8

INGREDIENTS:
- 4 egg whites
- 8 eggs
- Salt and black pepper to the taste
- 2 teaspoons ground mustard
- ¾ cup milk
- 30 ounces hash browns
- 4 bacon strips, cooked and chopped
- 1 broccoli head, chopped
- 2 bell peppers, chopped
- Cooking spray
- 6 ounces cheddar cheese, shredded
- 1 small onion, chopped

DIRECTIONS:
In a bowl, mix the egg white with eggs, salt, pepper, mustard and milk and whisk really well. Grease your Slow cooker with the spray, add hash browns, broccoli, bell peppers and onion. Pour eggs mix, sprinkle bacon and cheddar on top, cover and cook on Low for 4 hours. Divide between plates and serve hot for breakfast.

NUTRITION:
calories 300, fat 4, fiber 8, carbs 18, protein 8

Chia Oatmeal
Preparation time: 10 minutes

Cooking time: 8 hours

Servings: 2

INGREDIENTS:
- 2 cups almond milk
- 1 cup steel cut oats
- 2 tablespoons butter, soft
- ½ teaspoon almond extract
- 2 tablespoons chia seeds

DIRECTIONS:
In your slow cooker, mix the oats with the chia seeds and the other ingredients, toss, put the lid on and cook on Low for 8 hours. Stir the oatmeal one more time, divide into 2 bowls and serve.

NUTRITION:
calories 812, fat 71.4, fiber 9.4, carbs 41.1, protein 11

Mexican Eggs
Preparation time: 10 minutes

Cooking time: 2 hours and 15 minutes

Servings: 8

INGREDIENTS:
- Cooking spray
- 10 eggs
- 12 ounces Monterey jack, shredded
- 1 cup half and half
- ½ teaspoon chili powder
- 1 garlic clove, minced
- A pinch of salt and black pepper
- 10 ounces taco sauce
- 4 ounces canned green chilies, chopped
- 8 corn tortillas

DIRECTIONS:
In a bowl, mix the eggs with half and half, 8 ounces of cheese, salt, pepper, chili powder, green chilies and garlic and whisk everything. Grease your Slow cooker with cooking spray, add eggs mix, cover and cook on Low for 2 hours. Spread taco sauce and the rest of the cheese all over, cover and cook on Low for 15 minutes more. Divide eggs on tortillas, wrap and serve for breakfast.

NUTRITION:
calories 312, fat 4, fiber 8, carbs 12, protein 5

Buttery Oatmeal
Preparation time: 10 minutes

Cooking time: 3 hours

Servings: 2

INGREDIENTS:
- Cooking spray
- 2 cups coconut milk
- 1 cup old fashioned oats
- 1 pear, cubed
- 1 apple, cored and cubed
- 2 tablespoons butter, melted

DIRECTIONS:
Grease your slow cooker with the cooking spray, add the milk, oats and the other ingredients, toss, put the lid on and cook on High for 3 hours. Divide the mix into bowls and serve for breakfast.

NUTRITION:
calories 1002, fat 74, fiber 18, carbs 93, protein 16.2

Apple Oatmeal
Preparation time: 10 minutes

Cooking time: 10 hours

Servings: 4

INGREDIENTS:
2 tablespoons butter, soft
¾ cup brown sugar
4 apples, cored, peeled and chopped
2 cups old-fashioned oats
1 and ½ tablespoons cinnamon powder
4 cups water

DIRECTIONS:
Spread butter in your Slow cooker. Add sugar, apples, oats, cinnamon and water, cover and cook on Low for 8 hours. Stir oatmeal, divide into bowls and serve for breakfast.

NUTRITION:
calories 282, fat 4, fiber 9, carbs 20, protein 5

Ginger Raisins Oatmeal
Preparation time: 10 minutes
Cooking time: 8 hours
Servings: 2

INGREDIENTS:
1 cup almond milk
½ cup steel cut oats
¼ cup raisins
½ teaspoon ginger, ground
1 tablespoon orange zest, grated
1 tablespoon orange juice
½ teaspoon vanilla extract
½ tablespoon honey

DIRECTIONS:
In your slow cooker, combine the milk with the oats, raisins and the other ingredients, toss, put the lid on and cook on Low for 8 hours. Divide into 2 bowls and serve for breakfast.

NUTRITION:
calories 435, fat 30.1, fiber 5.8, carbs 41.2, protein 6.2

Quinoa and Oats Mix
Preparation time: 10 minutes
Cooking time: 7 hours
Servings: 6

INGREDIENTS:
½ cup quinoa
1 and ½ cups steel cut oats
4 and ½ cups almond milk
2 tablespoons maple syrup
4 tablespoons brown sugar
1 and ½ teaspoons vanilla extract
Cooking spray

DIRECTIONS:
Grease your Slow cooker with cooking spray, add quinoa, oats, almond milk, maple syrup, sugar and vanilla extract, cover and cook on Low for 7 hours. Stir, divide into bowls and serve for breakfast.

NUTRITION:
calories 251, fat 8, fiber 8, carbs 20, protein 5

Apple and Chia Mix
Preparation time: 10 minutes
Cooking time: 8 hours
Servings: 2

INGREDIENTS:
¼ cup chia seeds
2 apples, cored and roughly cubed
1 cup almond milk
2 tablespoons maple syrup
1 teaspoon vanilla extract
½ tablespoon cinnamon powder
Cooking spray

DIRECTIONS:
Grease your slow cooker with the cooking spray, add the chia seeds, milk and the other ingredients, toss, put the lid on and cook on Low for 8 hours. Divide the mix into bowls and serve for breakfast.

NUTRITION:
calories 453, fat 29.3, fiber 8, carbs 51.1, protein 3.4

Spiced Pumpkin Oatmeal
Preparation time: 10 minutes
Cooking time: 9 hours
Servings: 4

INGREDIENTS:
Cooking spray
1 cup steel cut oats
½ cup milk
4 cups water
2 tablespoons brown sugar
½ cup pumpkin puree
½ teaspoon cinnamon powder
A pinch of cloves, ground
A pinch of ginger, grated
A pinch of allspice, ground
A pinch of nutmeg, ground

DIRECTIONS:
Grease your Slow cooker with cooking spray, add oats, milk, water, sugar, pumpkin puree, cinnamon, cloves, ginger, allspice and nutmeg, cover and cook on Low for 9 hours. Stir your oatmeal, divide into bowls and serve for breakfast.

NUTRITION:
calories 342, fat 5, fiber 8, carbs 20, protein 5

Pumpkin and Quinoa Mix

Preparation time: 10 minutes
Cooking time: 8 hours
Servings: 2

INGREDIENTS:
Cooking spray
½ cup quinoa
1 cup almond milk
1 tablespoon honey
¼ cup pumpkin puree
½ teaspoon vanilla extract
¼ teaspoon cinnamon powder

DIRECTIONS:
Grease your slow cooker with the cooking spray, add the quinoa, milk, honey and the other ingredients, stir, put the lid on and cook on Low for 7 hours. Divide the mix into bowls and serve for breakfast.

NUTRITION:
calories 242, fat 3, fiber 8, carbs 20, protein 7

Quinoa Breakfast Bars

Preparation time: 10 minutes
Cooking time: 4 hours
Servings: 8

INGREDIENTS:
2 tablespoons maple syrup
2 tablespoons almond butter, melted
Cooking spray
½ teaspoon cinnamon powder
1 cup almond milk
2 eggs
½ cup raisins
1/3 cup quinoa
1/3 cup almonds, roasted and chopped
1/3 cup dried apples, chopped
2 tablespoons chia seeds

DIRECTIONS:
In a bowl, mix almond butter with maple syrup, cinnamon, milk, eggs, quinoa, raisins, almonds, apples and chia seeds and stir really well. Grease your Slow cooker with the spray, line it with parchment paper, spread quinoa mix, cover and cook on Low for 4 hours. Leave mix aside to cool down, slice and serve for breakfast.

NUTRITION:
calories 300, fat 7, fiber 8, carbs 22, protein 5

Cocoa and Berries Quinoa

Preparation time: 10 minutes
Cooking time: 8 hours
Servings: 2

INGREDIENTS:
Cooking spray
1 cup quinoa
2 cups almond milk
¼ cup heavy cream
¼ cup blueberries
2 tablespoons cocoa powder
1 tablespoon brown sugar

DIRECTIONS:
Grease your slow cooker with the cooking spray, add the quinoa, berries and the other ingredients, toss, put the lid on and cook on Low for 8 hours. Divide into 2 bowls and serve for breakfast.

NUTRITION:
calories 200, fat 4, fiber 5, carbs 17, protein 5

Raspberry Oatmeal

Preparation time: 10 minutes
Cooking time: 8 hours
Servings: 4

INGREDIENTS:
2 cups water
1 tablespoon coconut oil
1 cup steel cut oats
1 tablespoon sugar
1 cup milk
½ teaspoon vanilla extract
1 cup raspberries
4 tablespoons walnuts, chopped

DIRECTIONS:
In your Slow cooker, mix oil with water, oats, sugar, milk, vanilla and raspberries, cover and cook on Low for 8 hours. Stir oatmeal, divide into bowls, sprinkle walnuts on top and serve for breakfast.

NUTRITION:
calories 200, fat 10, fiber 4, carbs 20, protein 4

Quinoa and Veggies Casserole

Preparation time: 10 minutes
Cooking time: 6 hours
Servings: 2

INGREDIENTS:
¼ cup quinoa
1 cup almond milk
2 eggs, whisked
1 tablespoon parsley, chopped
1 tablespoon chives, chopped
A pinch of salt and black pepper
¼ cup baby spinach
¼ cup cherry tomatoes, halved
2 tablespoons parmesan, shredded
Cooking spray

DIRECTIONS:
Grease your slow cooker with the cooking spray, add the quinoa mixed with he milk, eggs and the

other ingredients except the parmesan, toss and spread into the pot. Sprinkle the parmesan on top, put the lid on and cook on Low for 6 hours. Divide between plates and serve.

NUTRITION:
calories 251, fat 5, fiber 7, carbs 19, protein 11

Artichoke Frittata

Preparation time: 10 minutes

Cooking time: 3 hours

Servings: 4

INGREDIENTS:
- 14 ounces canned artichokes hearts, drained and chopped
- 12 ounces roasted red peppers, chopped
- 8 eggs, whisked
- ¼ cup green onions, chopped
- 4 ounces feta cheese, crumbled
- Cooking spray

DIRECTIONS:
Grease your Slow cooker with cooking spray and add artichokes, roasted peppers and green onions. Add eggs, sprinkle cheese all over, cover and cook on Low for 3 hours. Divide frittata between plates and serve.

NUTRITION:
calories 232, fat 7, fiber 9, carbs 17, protein 6

Cauliflower and Eggs Bowls

Preparation time: 10 minutes

Cooking time: 7 hours

Servings: 2

INGREDIENTS:
- Cooking spray
- 4 eggs, whisked
- A pinch of salt and black pepper
- ¼ teaspoon thyme, dried
- ½ teaspoon turmeric powder
- 1 cup cauliflower florets
- ½ small yellow onion, chopped
- 3 ounces breakfast sausages, sliced
- ½ cup cheddar cheese, shredded

DIRECTIONS:
Grease your slow cooker with cooking spray and spread the cauliflower florets on the bottom of the pot. Add the eggs mixed with salt, pepper and the other ingredients and toss. Put the lid on, cook on Low for 7 hours, divide between plates and serve for breakfast.

NUTRITION:
calories 261, fat 6, fiber 7, carbs 22, protein 6

Spinach Frittata

Preparation time: 10 minutes

Cooking time: 2 hours

Servings: 6

INGREDIENTS:
- 1 tablespoon olive oil
- 1 yellow onion, chopped
- 1 cup mozzarella cheese, shredded
- 3 egg whites
- 3 eggs
- 2 tablespoons milk
- Salt and black pepper to the taste
- 1 cup baby spinach
- 1 tomato, chopped

DIRECTIONS:
Grease your Slow cooker with the oil and spread onion, spinach and tomatoes on the bottom. In a bowl, mix the eggs with egg whites, milk, salt and pepper, whisk well and pour over the veggies from the pot. Sprinkle mozzarella all over, cover slow cooker, cook on Low for 2 hours, slice, divide between plates and serve for breakfast.

NUTRITION:
calories 200, fat 8, fiber 2, carbs 5, protein 12

Sausage and Eggs Mix

Preparation time: 10 minutes

Cooking time: 8 hours and 10 minutes

Servings: 2

INGREDIENTS:
- 4 eggs, whisked
- 1 red onion, chopped
- ¼ teaspoon rosemary, dried
- ½ teaspoon turmeric powder
- ½ pound pork sausage, sliced
- ½ tablespoon garlic powder
- 1 teaspoon basil, dried
- A pinch of salt and black pepper
- Cooking spray

DIRECTIONS:
Grease a pan with the cooking spray, heat it up over medium-high heat, add the onion and the pork sausage, toss and cook for 10 minutes. Transfer this to the slow cooker, also add the eggs mixed with the remaining ingredients, toss everything, put the lid on and cook on Low for 8 hours. Divide between plates and serve right away for breakfast.

NUTRITION:
calories 271, fat 7, fiber 8, carbs 20, protein 11

Veggie Omelet

Preparation time: 10 minutes

Cooking time: 2 hours

Servings: 4

INGREDIENTS:
- ½ cup milk
- 6 eggs
- Salt and black pepper to the taste
- A pinch of chili powder
- A pinch of garlic powder
- 1 red bell pepper, chopped
- 1 cup broccoli florets
- 1 yellow onion, chopped
- 1 garlic clove, minced
- 1 tablespoon cheddar cheese, shredded
- Cooking spray

DIRECTIONS:
In a bowl, mix the eggs with milk, salt, pepper, chili powder, garlic powder, broccoli, garlic, bell pepper and onion and whisk well. Grease your Slow cooker with cooking spray, add eggs mix, spread, cover slow cooker and cook on High for 2 hours. Slice omelet, divide it between plates and serve hot for breakfast.

NUTRITION:
calories 142, fat 7, fiber 1, carbs 8, protein 10

Parmesan Quinoa

Preparation time: 10 minutes

Cooking time: 6 hours

Servings: 2

INGREDIENTS:
- 1 cup quinoa
- 2 cups veggie stock
- 1 tablespoon chives, chopped
- 1 carrot, peeled and grated
- ½ cup parmesan, grated
- ¼ cup heavy cream
- Salt and black pepper to the taste
- Cooking spray

DIRECTIONS:
Grease your slow cooker with the cooking spray, add the quinoa mixed with the stock and the other ingredients except the parmesan and the cream, toss, put the lid on and cook on High for 3 hours. Add the remaining ingredients, toss the mix again, cook on High for 3 more hours, divide into bowls and serve for breakfast.

NUTRITION:
calories 261, fat 6, fiber 8, carbs 26, protein 11

Hash Browns and Sausage Casserole

Preparation time: 10 minutes

Cooking time: 4 hours

Servings: 12

INGREDIENTS:
- 30 ounces hash browns
- 1 pound sausage, browned and sliced
- 8 ounces mozzarella cheese, shredded
- 8 ounces cheddar cheese, shredded
- 6 green onions, chopped
- ½ cup milk
- 12 eggs
- Cooking spray
- Salt and black pepper to the taste

DIRECTIONS:
Grease your Slow cooker with cooking spray and add half of the hash browns, half of the sausage, half of the mozzarella, cheddar and green onions. In a bowl, mix the eggs with salt, pepper and milk and whisk well. Add half of the eggs mix into the slow cooker, then layer the remaining hash browns, sausages, mozzarella, cheddar and green onions. Top with the rest of the eggs, cover the slow cooker and cook on High for 4 hours. Divide between plates and serve hot.

NUTRITION:
calories 300, fat 3, fiber 7, carbs 10, protein 12

Broccoli Casserole

Preparation time: 10 minutes

Cooking time: 6 hours

Servings: 2

INGREDIENTS:
- 2 eggs, whisked
- 1 cup broccoli florets
- 2 cups hash browns
- ½ teaspoon coriander, ground
- ½ teaspoon rosemary, dried
- ½ teaspoon turmeric powder
- ½ teaspoon mustard powder
- A pinch of salt and black pepper
- 1 small red onion, chopped
- ½ red bell pepper, chopped
- 1 ounce cheddar cheese, shredded
- Cooking spray

DIRECTIONS:
Grease your slow cooker with the cooking spray, and spread hash browns, broccoli, bell pepper and the onion on the bottom of the pan. In a bowl, mix the eggs with the coriander and the other ingredients, whisk and pour over the broccoli mix in the pot. Put the lid on, cook on Low for 6 hours, divide between plates and serve for breakfast.

NUTRITION:
calories 261, fat 7, fiber 8, carbs 20, protein 11

Vanilla Oats

Preparation time: 10 minutes

Cooking time: 8 hours

Servings: 4

INGREDIENTS:
1 cup steel cut oats
2 teaspoons vanilla extract
2 cups vanilla almond milk
2 tablespoons maple syrup
2 teaspoons cinnamon powder
2 cups water
2 teaspoons flaxseed
Cooking spray
2 tablespoons blackberries

DIRECTIONS:
Grease your Slow cooker with the cooking spray and add oats, vanilla extract, almond milk, maple syrup, cinnamon, water and flaxseed, cover and cook on Low for 8 hours. Stir oats, divide into bowls, sprinkle blackberries on top and serve for breakfast.

NUTRITION:
calories 200, fat 3, fiber 6, carbs 9, protein 3

Creamy Shrimp Bowls

Preparation time: 10 minutes

Cooking time: 2 hours

Servings: 2

INGREDIENTS:
½ cup chicken stock
½ pound shrimp, peeled and deveined
1 carrot, peeled and cubed
½ cup baby spinach
¼ cup heavy cream
¼ tablespoon garlic powder
¼ tablespoon onion powder
¼ teaspoon rosemary, dried
A pinch of salt and black pepper
¼ cup cheddar cheese, shredded
1 ounce cream cheese
1 tablespoon chives, chopped

DIRECTIONS:
In your slow cooker, mix the shrimp with the stock, cream and the other ingredients, toss, put the lid on and cook on Low for 2 hours. Divide into bowls, and serve for breakfast.

NUTRITION:
calories 300, fat 7, fiber 12, carbs 20, protein 10

Cheesy Quiche

Preparation time: 10 minutes

Cooking time: 3 hours

Servings: 6

INGREDIENTS:
1 pie crust
1 cup ham, cooked and chopped
2 cups Swiss cheese, shredded
6 eggs
1 cup whipping cream
4 green onions, chopped
Salt and black pepper to the taste
A pinch of nutmeg, ground
Cooking spray

DIRECTIONS:
Grease your Slow cooker with cooking spray, add pie crust inside, cover and cook o High for 1 hour and 30 minutes. In a bowl, mix the eggs with salt, pepper, nutmeg and whipping cream and whisk well. Pour this into pie crust, sprinkle cheese, ham and green onions, cover slow cooker and cook on High for 1 hour and 30 minutes. Slice quiche, divide it between plates and serve for breakfast.

NUTRITION:
calories 300, fat 4, fiber 7, carbs 15, protein 5

Peach, Vanilla and Oats Mix

Preparation time: 10 minutes

Cooking time: 8 hours

Servings: 2

INGREDIENTS:
½ cup steel cut oats
2 cups almond milk
½ cup peaches, pitted and roughly chopped
½ teaspoon vanilla extract
1 teaspoon cinnamon powder

DIRECTIONS:
In your slow cooker, mix the oats with the almond milk, peaches and the other ingredients, toss, put the lid on and cook on Low for 8 hours. Divide into bowls and serve for breakfast right away.

NUTRITION:
calories 261, fat 5, fiber 8, carbs 18, protein 6

Egg Bake

Preparation time: 10 minutes

Cooking time: 8 hours

Servings: 8

INGREDIENTS:
20 ounces tater tots
2 yellow onions, chopped
6 ounces bacon, chopped
2 cups cheddar cheese, shredded
12 eggs
¼ cup parmesan, grated
1 cup milk
Salt and black pepper to the taste
4 tablespoons white flour
Cooking spray

DIRECTIONS:
Grease your Slow cooker with cooking spray and

layer half of the tater tots, onions, bacon, cheddar and parmesan. Continue layering the rest of the tater tots, bacon, onions, parmesan and cheddar. In a bowl, mix the eggs with milk, salt, pepper and flour and whisk well. Pour this into the slow cooker, cover and cook on Low for 8 hours. Slice, divide between plates and serve for breakfast.

NUTRITION:
calories 290, fat 9, fiber 1, carbs 9, protein 22

Hot Eggs Mix
Preparation time: 10 minutes
Cooking time: 2 hours
Servings: 2

INGREDIENTS:
Cooking spray
4 eggs, whisked
¼ cup sour cream
A pinch of salt and black pepper
½ teaspoon chili powder
½ teaspoon hot paprika
½ red bell pepper, chopped
½ yellow onion, chopped
2 cherry tomatoes, cubed
1 tablespoon parsley, chopped

DIRECTIONS:
In a bowl, mix the eggs with the cream, salt, pepper and the other ingredients except the cooking spray and whisk well. Grease your slow cooker with cooking spray, pour the eggs mix inside, spread, stir, put the lid on and cook on High for 2 hours. Divide the mix between plates and serve.

NUTRITION:
calories 162, fat 5, fiber 7, carbs 15, protein 4

Butternut Squash Oatmeal
Preparation time: 10 minutes
Cooking time: 8 hours
Servings: 6

INGREDIENTS:
½ cup almonds, soaked for 12 hours in water and drained
½ cup walnuts, chopped
2 apples, peeled, cored and cubed
1 butternut squash, peeled and cubed
½ teaspoon nutmeg, ground
1 teaspoon cinnamon powder
1 tablespoon sugar
1 cup milk

DIRECTIONS:
In your Slow cooker, mix almonds with walnuts, apples, squash, nutmeg, cinnamon, sugar and milk, cover and cook on Low for 8 hours. Stir oatmeal, divide into bowls and serve.

NUTRITION:
calories 178, fat 7, fiber 7, carbs 9, protein 4

Potato and Ham Mix
Preparation time: 10 minutes
Cooking time: 6 hours
Servings: 2

INGREDIENTS:
Cooking spray
4 eggs, whisked
½ cup red potatoes, peeled and grated
¼ cup heavy cream
¼ cup ham, chopped
1 tablespoon cilantro, chopped
½ teaspoon turmeric powder
Salt and black pepper to the taste

DIRECTIONS:
Grease your slow cooker with cooking spray, add the eggs, potatoes and the other ingredients, whisk, put the lid on and cook on High for 6 hours. Divide between plates and serve for breakfast.

NUTRITION:
calories 200, fat 4, fiber 6, carbs 12, protein 6

Breakfast Stuffed Peppers
Preparation time: 10 minutes
Cooking time: 4 hours
Servings: 3

INGREDIENTS:
3 bell peppers, halved and deseeded
Salt and black pepper to the taste
4 eggs
½ cup milk
2 tablespoons green onions, chopped
½ cup ham, chopped
¼ cup spinach, chopped
¾ cup cheddar cheese, shredded

DIRECTIONS:
In a bowl, mix the eggs with salt, pepper, green onion, milk, spinach, ham and half of the cheese and stir well. Line your Slow cooker with tin foil, divide eggs mix in each bell pepper half, arrange them all in the slow cooker, sprinkle the rest of the cheese all over them, cover and cook on Low for 4 hours. Divide peppers between plates and serve for breakfast.

NUTRITION:
calories 162, fat 4, fiber 1, carbs 6, protein 11

Spinach Frittata

Preparation time: 10 minutes
Cooking time: 5 hours and 10 minutes
Servings: 2

INGREDIENTS:
Cooking spray
1 cup baby spinach
1 cup cherry tomatoes, halved
3 spring onions, chopped
3 ounces roasted red peppers, drained and chopped
2 ounces mozzarella, shredded
4 eggs, whisked
½ teaspoon allspice, ground
A pinch of salt and black pepper

DIRECTIONS:
Grease a pan with the cooking spray, heat up over medium heat, add the spring onions and roasted peppers and cook for 10 minutes. Transfer the mix to the slow cooker, add the eggs mixed with the rest of the ingredients, toss, spread into the pot, put the lid on and cook on Low for 5 hours. Divide the frittata between plates and serve.

NUTRITION:
calories 251, fat 4, fiber 6, carbs 12, protein 5

Oats Granola

Preparation time: 10 minutes
Cooking time: 2 hours
Servings: 8

INGREDIENTS:
5 cups old-fashioned rolled oats
1/3 cup coconut oil
2/3 cup honey
½ cup almonds, chopped
½ cup peanut butter
1 tablespoon vanilla
2 teaspoons cinnamon powder
1 cup craisins
Cooking spray

DIRECTIONS:
Grease your Slow cooker with cooking spray, add oats, oil, honey, almonds, peanut butter, vanilla, craisins and cinnamon, toss just a bit, cover and cook on High for 2 hours, stirring every 30 minutes. Divide into bowls and serve for breakfast.

NUTRITION:
calories 200, fat 3, fiber 6, carbs 9, protein 4

Chili Eggs Mix

Preparation time: 10 minutes
Cooking time: 3 hours
Servings: 2

INGREDIENTS:
Cooking spray
3 spring onions, chopped
2 tablespoons sun dried tomatoes, chopped
1 ounce canned and roasted green chili pepper, chopped
½ teaspoon rosemary, dried
Salt and black pepper to the taste
3 ounces cheddar cheese, shredded
4 eggs, whisked
¼ cup heavy cream
1 tablespoon chives, chopped

DIRECTIONS:
Grease your slow cooker with cooking spray and mix the eggs with the chili peppers and the other ingredients except the cheese. Toss everything into the pot, sprinkle the cheese on top, put the lid on and cook on High for 3 hours. Divide between plates and serve.

NUTRITION:
calories 224, fat 4, fiber 7, carbs 18, protein 11

Tropical Granola

Preparation time: 10 minutes
Cooking time: 1 hour and 30 minutes
Servings: 6

INGREDIENTS:
1 cup almonds, sliced
4 cups old-fashioned oats
½ cup pecans, chopped
½ teaspoon ginger, ground
½ cup coconut oil
½ cup dried coconut
½ cup raisins
½ cup dried cherries
½ cup pineapple, dried

DIRECTIONS:
In your Slow cooker, mix oil with almonds, oats, pecans, ginger, coconut, raisins, cherries and pineapple, toss, cover, cook on High for 1 hour and 30 minutes, stir again, divide into bowls and serve for breakfast.

NUTRITION:
calories 172, fat 5, fiber 8, carbs 10, protein 4

Cheesy Eggs

Preparation time: 10 minutes
Cooking time: 3 hours
Servings: 2

INGREDIENTS:
4 eggs, whisked
¼ cup spring onions, chopped
1 tablespoon oregano, chopped
1 cup milk
2 ounces feta cheese, crumbled

A pinch of salt and black pepper

Cooking spray

DIRECTIONS:
In a bowl, combine the eggs with the spring onions and the other ingredients except the cooking spray and whisk. Grease your slow cooker with cooking spray, add eggs mix, stir, put the lid on and cook on Low for 3 hours. Divide between plates and serve for breakfast.

NUTRITION:
calories 214, fat 4, fiber 7, carbs 18, protein 5

Creamy Strawberries Oatmeal

Preparation time: 10 minutes

Cooking time: 8 hours

Servings: 8

INGREDIENTS:
6 cups water
2 cups milk
2 cups steel cut oats
1 cup Greek yogurt
1 teaspoon cinnamon powder
2 cups strawberries, halved
1 teaspoon vanilla extract

DIRECTIONS:
In your Slow cooker, mix water with milk, oats, yogurt, cinnamon, strawberries and vanilla, toss, cover and cook on Low for 8 hours. Divide into bowls and serve for breakfast.

NUTRITION:
calories 200, fat 4, fiber 6, carbs 8, protein 4

Tomato and Zucchini Eggs Mix

Preparation time: 10 minutes

Cooking time: 3 hours

Servings: 2

INGREDIENTS:
Cooking spray
4 eggs, whisked
2 spring onions, chopped
1 tablespoon basil, chopped
½ teaspoon turmeric powder
½ cup tomatoes, cubed
1 zucchini, grated
¼ teaspoon sweet paprika
A pinch of salt and black pepper
1 tablespoon parsley, chopped
2 tablespoons parmesan, grated

DIRECTIONS:
Grease your slow cooker with cooking spray, add the eggs mixed with the zucchini, tomatoes and the other ingredients except the cheese and stir well. Sprinkle the cheese, put the lid on and cook on High for 3 hours. Divide between plates and serve for breakfast right away.

NUTRITION:
calories 261, fat 5, fiber 7, carbs 19, protein 6

Breakfast Potatoes

Preparation time: 10 minutes

Cooking time: 4 hours

Servings: 8

INGREDIENTS:
3 potatoes, peeled and cubed
1 green bell pepper, chopped
1 red bell pepper, chopped
1 yellow onion, chopped
12 ounces smoked chicken sausage, sliced
1 and ½ cups cheddar cheese, shredded
¼ teaspoon oregano, dried
½ cup sour cream
¼ teaspoon basil, dried
10 ounces cream of chicken soup
2 tablespoons parsley, chopped
Salt and black pepper to the taste

DIRECTIONS:
In your Slow cooker, mix potatoes with red bell pepper, green bell pepper, sausage, onion, oregano, basil, cheese, salt, pepper and cream of chicken, cover and cook on Low for 4 hours. Add parsley, divide between plates and serve for breakfast.

NUTRITION:
calories 320, fat 5, fiber 7, carbs 10, protein 5

Chocolate Breakfast Bread

Preparation time: 10 minutes

Cooking time: 3 hours

Servings: 2

INGREDIENTS:
Cooking spray
1 cup almond flour
½ teaspoon baking soda
½ teaspoon cinnamon powder
1 tablespoon avocado oil
2 tablespoons maple syrup
2 eggs, whisked
1 tablespoon butter
½ tablespoon milk
½ teaspoon vanilla extract
½ cup dark chocolate, melted
2 tablespoons walnuts, chopped

DIRECTIONS:
In a bowl, mix the flour with the baking soda, cinnamon, oil and the other ingredients except the

cooking spray and stir well. Grease a loaf pan that fits the slow cooker with the cooking spray, pour the bread batter into the pan, put the pan in the slow cooker after you've lined it with tin foil, put the lid on and cook on High for 3 hours. Cool the sweet bread down, slice, divide between plates and serve for breakfast.

NUTRITION:
calories 200, fat 3, fiber 5, carbs 8, protein 4

Hash Brown Mix

Preparation time: 10 minutes

Cooking time: 3 hours

Servings: 6

INGREDIENTS:
3 tablespoons butter
½ cup sour cream
¼ cup mushrooms, sliced
¼ teaspoon garlic powder
¼ cup yellow onion, chopped
1 cup milk
3 tablespoons flour
20 ounces hash browns
Salt and black pepper to the taste
1 cup cheddar cheese, shredded
Cooking spray

DIRECTIONS:
Heat up a pan with the butter over medium-high heat, add mushrooms, onion and garlic powder, stir and cook for a few minutes. Add flour and whisk well. Add milk, stir really well and transfer everything to your Slow cooker greased with cooking spray. Add hash browns, salt, pepper, sour cream and cheese, toss, cover and cook on High for 3 hours. Divide between plates and serve for breakfast.

NUTRITION:
calories 262, fat 6, fiber 4, carbs 12, protein 6

Almond and Quinoa Bowls

Preparation time: 10 minutes

Cooking time: 5 hours

Servings: 2

INGREDIENTS:
1 cup quinoa
2 cups almond milk
2 tablespoons butter, melted
2 tablespoons brown sugar
A pinch of cinnamon powder
A pinch of nutmeg, ground
¼ cup almonds, sliced
Cooking spray

DIRECTIONS:
Grease your slow cooker with the cooking spray, add the quinoa, milk, melted butter and the other ingredients, toss, put the lid on and cook on Low for 5 hours. Divide the mix into bowls and serve for breakfast.

NUTRITION:
calories 211, fat 3, fiber 6, carbs 12, protein 5

Bacon and Egg Casserole

Preparation time: 10 minutes

Cooking time: 5 hours

Servings: 8

INGREDIENTS:
20 ounces hash browns
Cooking spray
8 ounces cheddar cheese, shredded
8 bacon slices, cooked and chopped
6 green onions, chopped
½ cup milk
12 eggs
Salt and black pepper to the taste
Salsa for serving

DIRECTIONS:
Grease your Slow cooker with cooking spray, spread hash browns, cheese, bacon and green onions and toss. In a bowl, mix the eggs with salt, pepper and milk and whisk really well. Pour this over hash browns, cover and cook on Low for 5 hours. Divide between plates and serve with salsa on top.

NUTRITION:
calories 300, fat 5, fiber 5, carbs 9, protein 5

Carrots Casserole

Preparation time: 10 minutes

Cooking time: 3 hours

Servings: 2

INGREDIENTS:
1 teaspoon ginger, ground
½ pound carrots, peeled and grated
2 eggs, whisked
½ teaspoon garlic powder
½ teaspoon rosemary, dried
Salt and black pepper to the taste
1 red onion, chopped
1 tablespoons parsley, chopped
2 garlic cloves, minced
½ tablespoon olive oil

DIRECTIONS:
Grease your slow cooker with the oil and mix the carrots with the eggs, ginger and the other ingredients inside. Toss, put the lid on, cook High for 3 hours, divide between plates and serve.

NUTRITION:
calories 218, fat 6, fiber 6, carbs 14, protein 5

Breakfast Rice Pudding

Preparation time: 10 minutes
Cooking time: 4 hours
Servings: 4

INGREDIENTS:
- 1 cup coconut milk
- 2 cups water
- 1 cup almond milk
- ½ cup raisins
- 1 cup brown rice
- 2 teaspoons vanilla extract
- 2 tablespoons flaxseed
- 1 teaspoon cinnamon powder
- 2 tablespoons coconut sugar
- Cooking spray

DIRECTIONS:
Grease your Slow cooker with the cooking spray, add coconut milk, water, almond milk, raisins, rice, vanilla, flaxseed and cinnamon, cover, cook on Low for 4 hours, stir, divide into bowls, sprinkle coconut sugar all over and serve.

NUTRITION:
calories 213, fat 3, fiber 6, carbs 10, protein 4

Cranberry Maple Oatmeal

Preparation time: 10 minutes
Cooking time: 6 hours
Servings: 2

INGREDIENTS:
- 1 cup almond milk
- ½ cup steel cut oats
- ½ cup cranberries
- ½ teaspoon vanilla extract
- 1 tablespoon maple syrup
- 1 tablespoon sugar

DIRECTIONS:
In your slow cooker, mix the oats with the berries, milk and the other ingredients, toss, put the lid on and cook on Low for 6 hours. Divide into bowls and serve for breakfast.

NUTRITION:
calories 200, fat 5, fiber 7, carbs 14, protein 4

Apple Breakfast Rice

Preparation time: 10 minutes
Cooking time: 7 hours
Servings: 4

INGREDIENTS:
- 4 apples, cored, peeled and chopped
- 2 tablespoons butter
- 2 teaspoons cinnamon powder
- 1 and ½ cups brown rice
- ½ teaspoon vanilla extract
- A pinch of nutmeg, ground
- 5 cups milk

DIRECTIONS:
Put the butter in your Slow cooker, add apples, cinnamon, rice, vanilla, nutmeg and milk, cover, cook on Low for 7 hours, stir, divide into bowls and serve for breakfast.

NUTRITION:
calories 214, fat 4, fiber 5, carbs 7, protein 4

Mushroom Casserole

Preparation time: 10 minutes
Cooking time: 5 hours
Servings: 2

INGREDIENTS:
- ½ cup mozzarella, shredded
- 2 eggs, whisked
- ½ tablespoon balsamic vinegar
- ½ tablespoon olive oil
- 4 ounces baby kale
- 1 red onion, chopped
- ¼ teaspoon oregano
- ½ pound white mushrooms, sliced
- Salt and black pepper to the taste
- Cooking spray

DIRECTIONS:
In a bowl, mix the eggs with the kale, mushrooms and the other ingredients except the cheese and cooking spray and stir well. Grease your slow cooker with cooking spray, add the mushroom mix, spread, sprinkle the mozzarella all over, put the lid on and cook on Low for 5 hours. Divide between plates and serve for breakfast.

NUTRITION:
calories 216, fat 6, fiber 8, carbs 12, protein 4

Quinoa and Banana Mix

Preparation time: 10 minutes
Cooking time: 6 hours
Servings: 8

INGREDIENTS:
- 2 cups quinoa
- 2 bananas, mashed
- 4 cups water
- 2 cups blueberries
- 2 teaspoons vanilla extract
- 2 tablespoons maple syrup
- 1 teaspoon cinnamon powder
- Cooking spray

DIRECTIONS:
Grease your Slow cooker with cooking spray, add quinoa, bananas, water, blueberries, vanilla, maple syrup and cinnamon, stir, cover and cook on Low for 6 hours. Stir again, divide into bowls and serve for breakfast.

NUTRITION:
calories 200, fat 4, fiber 6, carbs 12, protein 4

Ginger Apple Bowls

Preparation time: 10 minutes
Cooking time: 6 hours
Servings: 2

INGREDIENTS:
- 2 apples, cored, peeled and cut into medium chunks
- 1 tablespoon sugar
- 1 tablespoon ginger, grated
- 1 cup heavy cream
- ¼ teaspoon cinnamon powder
- ½ teaspoon vanilla extract
- ¼ teaspoon cardamom, ground

DIRECTIONS:
In your slow cooker, combine the apples with the sugar, ginger and the other ingredients, toss, put the lid on and cook on Low for 6 hours. Divide into bowls and serve for breakfast.

NUTRITION:
calories 201, fat 3, fiber 7, carbs 19, protein 4

Dates Quinoa

Preparation time: 10 minutes
Cooking time: 3 hours
Servings: 4

INGREDIENTS:
- 1 cup quinoa
- 4 medjol dates, chopped
- 3 cups milk
- 1 apple, cored and chopped
- ¼ cup pepitas
- 2 teaspoons cinnamon powder
- 1 teaspoon vanilla extract
- ¼ teaspoon nutmeg, ground

DIRECTIONS:
In your Slow cooker, mix quinoa with dates, milk, apple, pepitas, cinnamon, nutmeg and vanilla, stir, cover and cook on High for 3 hours. Stir again, divide into bowls and serve.

NUTRITION:
calories 241, fat 4, fiber 4, carbs 10, protein 3

Granola Bowls

Preparation time: 10 minutes
Cooking time: 4 hours
Servings: 2

INGREDIENTS:
- ½ cup granola
- ¼ cup coconut cream
- 2 tablespoons brown sugar
- 2 tablespoons cashew butter
- 1 teaspoon cinnamon powder
- ½ teaspoon nutmeg, ground

DIRECTIONS:
In your slow cooker, mix the granola with the cream, sugar and the other ingredients, toss, put the lid on and cook on Low for 4 hours. Divide into bowls and serve for breakfast.

NUTRITION:
calories 218, fat 6, fiber 9, carbs 17, protein 6

Cinnamon Quinoa

Preparation time: 10 minutes
Cooking time: 4 hours
Servings: 4

INGREDIENTS:
- 1 cup quinoa
- 2 cups milk
- 2 cups water
- ¼ cup stevia
- 1 teaspoon cinnamon powder
- 1 teaspoon vanilla extract

DIRECTIONS:
In your Slow cooker, mix quinoa with milk, water, stevia, cinnamon and vanilla, stir, cover, cook on Low for 3 hours and 30 minutes, stir, cook for 30 minutes more, divide into bowls and serve for breakfast.

NUTRITION:
calories 172, fat 4, fiber 3, carbs 8, protein 2

Squash Bowls

Preparation time: 10 minutes
Cooking time: 6 hours
Servings: 2

INGREDIENTS:
- 2 tablespoons walnuts, chopped
- 2 cups squash, peeled and cubed
- ½ cup coconut cream
- ½ teaspoon cinnamon powder
- ½ tablespoon sugar

DIRECTIONS:
In your slow cooker, mix the squash with the nuts and the other ingredients, toss, put the lid on and cook on Low for 6 hours. Divide into bowls and serve.

NUTRITION:
calories 140, fat 1, fiber 2, carbs 2, protein 5

Quinoa and Apricots

Preparation time: 10 minutes
Cooking time: 10 hours
Servings: 6

INGREDIENTS:
¾ cup quinoa
¾ cup steel cut oats
2 tablespoons honey
1 cup apricots, chopped
6 cups water
1 teaspoon vanilla extract
¾ cup hazelnuts, chopped

DIRECTIONS:
In your Slow cooker, mix quinoa with oats honey, apricots, water, vanilla and hazelnuts, stir, cover and cook on Low for 10 hours. Stir quinoa mix again, divide into bowls and serve for breakfast.

NUTRITION:
calories 200, fat 3, fiber 5, carbs 8, protein 6

Lamb and Eggs Mix

Preparation time: 10 minutes
Cooking time: 6 hours
Servings: 2

INGREDIENTS:
1 pound lamb meat, ground
4 eggs, whisked
1 tablespoon basil, chopped
½ teaspoon cumin powder
1 tablespoon chili powder
1 red onion, chopped
1 tablespoon olive oil
A pinch of salt and black pepper

DIRECTIONS:
Grease the slow cooker with the oil and mix the lamb with the eggs, basil and the other ingredients inside. Toss, put the lid on, cook on Low for 6 hours, divide into bowls and serve for breakfast.

NUTRITION:
calories 220, fat 2, fiber 2, carbs 6, protein 2

Blueberry Quinoa Oatmeal

Preparation time: 10 minutes
Cooking time: 8 hours
Servings: 4

INGREDIENTS:
½ cup quinoa
1 cup steel cut oats
1 teaspoon vanilla extract
5 cups water
Zest of 1 lemon, grated
1 teaspoon vanilla extract
2 tablespoons flaxseed
1 tablespoon butter, melted
3 tablespoons maple syrup
1 cup blueberries

DIRECTIONS:
In your Slow cooker, mix butter with quinoa, water, oats, vanilla, lemon zest, flaxseed, maple syrup and blueberries, stir, cover and cook on Low for 8 hours. Divide into bowls and serve for breakfast.

NUTRITION:
calories 189, fat 5, fiber 5, carbs 20, protein 5

Cauliflower Casserole

Preparation time: 10 minutes
Cooking time: 5 hours
Servings: 2

INGREDIENTS:
1 pound cauliflower florets
3 eggs, whisked
1 red onion, sliced
½ teaspoon sweet paprika
½ teaspoon turmeric powder
1 garlic clove, minced
A pinch of salt and black pepper
Cooking spray

DIRECTIONS:
Spray your slow cooker with the cooking spray, and mix the cauliflower with the eggs, onion and the other ingredients inside. Put the lid on, cook on Low for 5 hours, divide between 2 plates and serve for breakfast.

NUTRITION:
calories 200, fat 3, fiber 6, carbs 13, protein 8

Lentils and Quinoa Mix

Preparation time: 10 minutes
Cooking time: 8 hours
Servings: 6

INGREDIENTS:
3 garlic cloves, minced
1 yellow onion, chopped
1 celery stalk, chopped
2 red bell peppers, chopped
12 ounces canned tomatoes, chopped
4 cups veggie stock
1 cup lentils
14 ounces pinto beans
2 tablespoons chili powder
½ cup quinoa
1 tablespoons oregano, chopped
2 teaspoon cumin, ground

DIRECTIONS:
In your Slow cooker, mix garlic with the onion, celery, bell peppers, tomatoes, stock, lentils, pinto beans, chili powder, quinoa, oregano and cumin, stir, cover, cook on Low for 8 hours, divide between plates and serve for breakfast

NUTRITION:
calories 231, fat 4, fiber 5, carbs 16, protein 4

Beef Meatloaf

Preparation time: 10 minutes
Cooking time: 4 hours
Servings: 2

INGREDIENTS:
1 red onion, chopped
1 pound beef stew meat, ground
½ teaspoon chili powder
1 egg, whisked
½ teaspoon olive oil
½ teaspoon sweet paprika
2 tablespoons white flour
½ teaspoon oregano, chopped
½ tablespoon basil, chopped
A pinch of salt and black pepper
½ teaspoon marjoram, dried

DIRECTIONS:
In a bowl, mix the beef with the onion, chili powder and the other ingredients except the oil, stir well and shape your meatloaf. Grease a loaf pan that fits your slow cooker with the oil, add meatloaf mix into the pan, put it in your slow cooker, put the lid on and cook on Low for 4 hours. Slice and serve for breakfast.

NUTRITION:
calories 200, fat 6, fiber 12, carbs 17, protein 10

Butternut Squash Quinoa

Preparation time: 10 minutes
Cooking time: 6 hours
Servings: 6

INGREDIENTS:
1 yellow onion, chopped
1 tablespoon olive oil
3 garlic cloves, minced
2 teaspoons oregano, dried
1 and ½ pound chicken breasts, skinless, boneless and chopped
2 teaspoons parsley, dried
2 teaspoons curry powder
½ teaspoon chili flakes
Salt and black pepper to the taste
1 butternut squash, peeled and cubed
2/3 cup quinoa
12 ounces canned tomatoes, chopped
4 cups veggie stock

DIRECTIONS:
In your Slow cooker, mix onion with oil, garlic, oregano, chicken, parsley, curry powder, chili, squash, quinoa, salt, pepper, tomatoes and stock, stir, cover and cook on Low for 6 hours. Divide into bowls and serve for breakfast.

NUTRITION:
calories 231, fat 4, fiber 6, carbs 20, protein 5

Leek Casserole

Preparation time: 10 minutes
Cooking time: 4 hours
Servings: 2

INGREDIENTS:
1 cup leek, chopped
Cooking spray
½ cup mozzarella, shredded
1 garlic clove, minced
4 eggs, whisked
1 cup beef sausage, chopped
1 tablespoon cilantro, chopped

DIRECTIONS:
Grease the slow cooker with the cooking spray and mix the leek with the mozzarella and the other ingredients inside. Toss, spread into the pot, put the lid on and cook on Low for 4 hours. Divide between plates and serve for breakfast.

NUTRITION:
calories 232, fat 4, fiber 8, carbs 17, protein 4

Chia Seeds Mix

Preparation time: 10 minutes
Cooking time: 8 hours
Servings: 4

INGREDIENTS:
1 cup steel cut oats
1 cup water
3 cups almond milk
2 tablespoons chia seeds
¼ cup pomegranate seeds
¼ cup dried blueberries
¼ cup almonds, sliced

DIRECTIONS:
In your Slow cooker, mix oats with water, almond milk, chia seeds, pomegranate ones, blueberries and almonds, stir, cover and cook on Low for 8 hours. Stir again, divide into bowls and serve for breakfast.

NUTRITION:
calories 200, fat 3, fiber 7, carbs 16, protein 3

Eggs and Sweet Potato Mix

Preparation time: 10 minutes
Cooking time: 6 hours
Servings: 2

INGREDIENTS:
½ red onion, chopped
½ green bell pepper, chopped
2 sweet potatoes, peeled and grated
½ red bell pepper, chopped
1 garlic clove, minced

½ teaspoon olive oil
4 eggs, whisked
1 tablespoon chives, chopped
A pinch of red pepper, crushed
A pinch of salt and black pepper

DIRECTIONS:
In a bowl, mix the eggs with the onion, bell peppers and the other ingredients except the oil and whisk well. Grease your slow cooker with the oil, add the eggs and potato mix, spread, put the lid on and cook on Low for 6 hours. Divide everything between plates and serve.

NUTRITION:
calories 261, fat 6, fiber 6, carbs 16, protein 4

Chia Seeds and Chicken Breakfast
Preparation time: 10 minutes
Cooking time: 3 hours
Servings: 4

INGREDIENTS:
1 pound chicken breasts, skinless, boneless and cubed
½ teaspoon basil, dried
¾ cup flaxseed, ground
¼ cup chia seeds
¼ cup parmesan, grated
½ teaspoon oregano, chopped
Salt and black pepper to the taste
2 eggs
2 garlic cloves, minced

DIRECTIONS:
In a bowl, mix flaxseed with chia seeds, parmesan, salt, pepper, oregano, garlic and basil and stir. Put the eggs in a second bowl and whisk them well. Dip chicken in eggs mix, then in chia seeds mix, put them in your Slow cooker after you've greased it with cooking spray, cover and cook on High for 3 hours. Serve them right away for a Sunday breakfast.

NUTRITION:
calories 212, fat 3, fiber 4, carbs 17, protein 4

Pork and Eggplant Casserole
Preparation time: 10 minutes
Cooking time: 6 hours
Servings: 2

INGREDIENTS:
1 red onion, chopped
1 eggplant, cubed
½ pound pork stew meat, ground
3 eggs, whisked
½ teaspoon chili powder
½ teaspoon garam masala
1 tablespoon sweet paprika
1 teaspoon olive oil

DIRECTIONS:
In a bowl, mix the eggs with the meat, onion, eggplant and the other ingredients except the oil and stir well. Grease your slow cooker with oil, add the pork and eggplant mix, spread into the pot, put the lid on and cook on Low for 6 hours. Divide the mix between plates and serve for breakfast.

NUTRITION:
calories 261, fat 7, fiber 6, carbs 16, protein 7

Chocolate Quinoa
Preparation time: 10 minutes
Cooking time: 6 hours
Servings: 4

INGREDIENTS:
1 cup quinoa
1 cup coconut milk
1 cup milk
2 tablespoons cocoa powder
3 tablespoons maple syrup
4 dark chocolate squares, chopped

DIRECTIONS:
In your Slow cooker, mix quinoa with coconut milk, milk, cocoa powder, maple syrup and chocolate, stir, cover and cook on Low for 6 hours. Stir quinoa mix again, divide into bowls and serve.

NUTRITION:
calories 215, fat 5, fiber 8, carbs 17, protein 4

Apple Spread
Preparation time: 10 minutes
Cooking time: 4 hours
Servings: 2

INGREDIENTS:
2 apples, cored, peeled and pureed
½ cup coconut cream
2 tablespoons apple cider
2 tablespoons sugar
¼ teaspoon cinnamon powder
½ teaspoon lemon juice
¼ teaspoon ginger, grated

DIRECTIONS:
In your slow cooker, mix the apple puree with the cream, sugar and the other ingredients, whisk, put the lid on and cook on High for 4 hours. Blend using an immersion blender, cool down and serve for breakfast.

NUTRITION:
calories 172, fat 3, fiber 3, carbs 8, protein 3

Chai Breakfast Quinoa

Preparation time: 10 minutes
Cooking time: 6 hours
Servings: 2

INGREDIENTS:
- 1 cup quinoa
- 1 egg white
- 2 cups milk
- ¼ teaspoon vanilla extract
- 1 and ½ tablespoons brown sugar
- ¼ teaspoon cardamom, ground
- ¼ teaspoon ginger, grated
- ¼ teaspoon cinnamon powder
- ¼ teaspoon vanilla extract
- ¼ teaspoon nutmeg, ground
- 1 tablespoons coconut flakes

DIRECTIONS:
In your Slow cooker, mix quinoa with egg white, milk, vanilla, sugar, cardamom, ginger, cinnamon, vanilla and nutmeg, stir a bit, cover and cook on Low for 6 hours. Stir, divide into bowls and serve for breakfast with coconut flakes on top.

NUTRITION:
calories 211, fat 4, fiber 6, carbs 10, protein 4

Cherries and Cocoa Oats

Preparation time: 10 minutes
Cooking time: 7 hours
Servings: 2

INGREDIENTS:
- 1 cup almond milk
- ½ cup steel cut oats
- 1 tablespoon cocoa powder
- ½ cup cherries, pitted
- 2 tablespoons sugar
- ¼ teaspoon vanilla extract

DIRECTIONS:
In your slow cooker, mix the almond milk with the cherries and the other ingredients, toss, put the lid on and cook on Low for 7 hours. Divide into 2 bowls and serve for breakfast.

NUTRITION:
calories 150, fat 1, fiber 2, carbs 6, protein 5

Quinoa Breakfast Bake

Preparation time: 10 minutes
Cooking time: 7 hours
Servings: 4

INGREDIENTS:
- 1 cup quinoa
- 4 tablespoons olive oil
- 2 cups water
- ½ cup dates, chopped
- 3 bananas, chopped
- ¼ cup coconut, shredded
- 2 teaspoons cinnamon powder
- 2 tablespoons brown sugar
- 1 cup walnuts, toasted and chopped

DIRECTIONS:
Put the oil in your Slow cooker, add quinoa, water, dates, bananas, coconut, cinnamon, brown sugar and walnuts, stir, cover and cook on Low for 7 hours. Divide into bowls and serve for breakfast.

NUTRITION:
calories 241, fat 4, fiber 8, carbs 16, protein 6

Beans Salad

Preparation time: 10 minutes
Cooking time: 6 hours
Servings: 2

INGREDIENTS:
- 1 cup canned black beans, drained
- 1 cup canned red kidney beans, drained
- 1 cup baby spinach
- 2 spring onions, chopped
- ½ red bell pepper, chopped
- ¼ teaspoon turmeric powder
- ½ teaspoon garam masala
- ¼ cup veggie stock
- A pinch of cumin, ground
- A pinch of chili powder
- A pinch of salt and black pepper
- ½ cup salsa

DIRECTIONS:
In your slow cooker, mix the beans with the spinach, onions and the other ingredients, toss, put the lid on and cook on High for 6 hours. Divide the mix into bowls and serve for breakfast.

NUTRITION:
calories 130, fat 4, fiber 2, carbs 5, protein 4

Mocha Latte Quinoa Mix

Preparation time: 10 minutes
Cooking time: 6 hours
Servings: 4

INGREDIENTS:
- 1 cup hot coffee
- 1 cup quinoa
- 1 cup coconut water
- ¼ cup chocolate chips
- ½ cup coconut cream

DIRECTIONS:
In your Slow cooker, mix quinoa with coffee, coconut water and chocolate chips, cover and cook

on Low for 6 hours. Stir, divide into bowls, spread coconut cream all over and serve for breakfast.

NUTRITION:
calories 251, fat 4, fiber 7, carbs 15, protein 4

Peppers Rice Mix

Preparation time: 10 minutes
Cooking time: 3 hours
Servings: 2

INGREDIENTS:
½ cup brown rice
1 cup chicken stock
2 spring onions, chopped
½ orange bell pepper, chopped
½ red bell pepper, chopped
½ green bell pepper, chopped
2 ounces canned green chilies, chopped
½ cup canned black beans, drained
½ cup mild salsa
½ teaspoon sweet paprika
½ teaspoon lime zest, grated
A pinch of salt and black pepper

DIRECTIONS:
In your slow cooker, mix the rice with the stock, spring onions and the other ingredients, toss, put the lid on and cook on High for 3 hours. Divide the mix into bowls and serve for breakfast.

NUTRITION:
calories 140, fat 2, fiber 2, carbs 5, protein 5

Breakfast Butterscotch Pudding

Preparation time: 10 minutes
Cooking time: 1 hour and 40 minutes
Servings: 6

INGREDIENTS:
4 ounces butter, melted
2 ounces brown sugar
7 ounces flour
¼ pint milk
1 teaspoon vanilla extract
Zest of ½ lemon, grated
2 tablespoons maple syrup
Cooking spray
1 egg

DIRECTIONS:
In a bowl, mix butter with sugar, milk, vanilla, lemon zest, maple syrup and eggs and whisk well. Add flour and whisk really well again. Grease your Slow cooker with cooking spray, add pudding mix, spread, cover and cook on High for 1 hour and 30 minutes. Divide between plates and serve for breakfast.

NUTRITION:
calories 271, fat 5, fiber 5, carbs 17, protein 4

Cashew Butter

Preparation time: 10 minutes
Cooking time: 4 hours
Servings: 2

INGREDIENTS:
1 cup cashews, soaked overnight, drained and blended
½ cup coconut cream
¼ teaspoon cinnamon powder
1 teaspoon lemon zest, grated
2 tablespoons sugar
A pinch of ginger, ground

DIRECTIONS:
In your slow cooker, mix the cashews with the cream and the other ingredients, whisk, put the lid on and cook on High for 4 hours. Blend using an immersion blender, divide into jars, and serve for breakfast cold.

NUTRITION:
calories 143, fat 2, fiber 3, carbs 3, protein 4

French Breakfast Pudding

Preparation time: 10 minutes
Cooking time: 1 hour and 30 minutes
Servings: 4

INGREDIENTS:
3 egg yolks
6 ounces double cream
1 teaspoon vanilla extract
2 tablespoons caster sugar

DIRECTIONS:
In a bowl, mix the egg yolks with sugar and whisk well. Add cream and vanilla extract, whisk well, pour into your 4 ramekins, place them in your Slow cooker, add some water to the slow cooker, cover and cook on High for 1 hour and 30 minutes. Leave aside to cool down and serve.

NUTRITION:
calories 261, fat 5, fiber 6, carbs 15, protein 2

Pumpkin and Berries Bowls

Preparation time: 10 minutes
Cooking time: 4 hours
Servings: 2

INGREDIENTS:
½ cup coconut cream
1 and ½ cups pumpkin, peeled and cubed
1 cup blackberries

2 tablespoons maple syrup
¼ teaspoon nutmeg, ground
½ teaspoon vanilla extract

DIRECTIONS:
In your slow cooker, combine the pumpkin with the berries, cream and the other ingredients, toss, put the lid on and cook on Low for 4 hours. Divide into bowls and serve for breakfast!

NUTRITION:
calories 120, fat 2, fiber 2, carbs 4, protein 2

Eggs and Sausage Casserole
Preparation time: 10 minutes
Cooking time: 8 hours
Servings: 4

INGREDIENTS:
8 eggs, whisked
1 yellow onion, chopped
1 pound pork sausage, chopped
2 teaspoons basil, dried
1 tablespoon garlic powder
Salt and black pepper to the taste
1 yellow bell pepper, chopped
1 teaspoon olive oil

DIRECTIONS:
Grease your Slow cooker with the olive oil, add eggs, onion, pork sausage, basil, garlic powder, salt, pepper and yellow bell pepper, toss, cover and cook on Low for 8 hours. Slice, divide between plates and serve for breakfast.

NUTRITION:
calories 301, fat 4, fiber 4, carbs 14, protein 7

Quinoa and Chia Pudding
Preparation time: 10 minutes
Cooking time: 6 hours
Servings: 2

INGREDIENTS:
1 cup coconut cream
2 tablespoons chia seeds
½ cup almond milk
1 tablespoon sugar
½ cup quinoa, rinsed
½ teaspoon vanilla extract

DIRECTIONS:
In your slow cooker, mix the cream with the chia seeds and the other ingredients, toss, put the lid on and cook on Low for 6 hours. Divide into 2 bowls and serve for breakfast.

NUTRITION:
calories 120, fat 2, fiber 1, carbs 6, protein 4

Cauliflower Rice Pudding
Preparation time: 10 minutes
Cooking time: 2 hours
Servings: 2

INGREDIENTS:
¼ cup maple syrup
3 cups almond milk
1 cup cauliflower rice
2 tablespoons vanilla extract

DIRECTIONS:
Put cauliflower rice in your Slow cooker, add maple syrup, almond milk and vanilla extract, stir, cover and cook on High for 2 hours. Stir your pudding again, divide into bowls and serve for breakfast.

NUTRITION:
calories 240, fat 2, fiber 2, carbs 15, protein 5

Beans Breakfast Bowls
Preparation time: 10 minutes
Cooking time: 3 hours and 10 minutes
Servings: 2

INGREDIENTS:
2 spring onions, chopped
½ green bell pepper, chopped
½ red bell pepper, chopped
½ yellow onion, chopped
5 ounces canned black beans, drained
5 ounces canned red kidney beans, drained
5 ounces canned pinto beans, drained
½ cup corn
½ teaspoon turmeric powder
1 teaspoons chili powder
½ teaspoon hot sauce
A pinch of salt and black pepper
1 tablespoon olive oil

DIRECTIONS:
Heat up a pan with the oil over medium-high heat, add the spring onions, bell peppers and the onion, sauté for 10 minutes and transfer to the slow cooker. Add the beans and the other ingredients, toss, put the lid on and cook on High for 3 hours. Divide the mix into bowls and serve for breakfast.

NUTRITION:
calories 240, fat 4, fiber 2, carbs 6, protein 9

Veggies Casserole
Preparation time: 10 minutes
Cooking time: 4 hours
Servings: 8

INGREDIENTS:
8 eggs
4 egg whites
2 teaspoons mustard
¾ cup almond milk
A pinch of salt and black pepper
2 red bell peppers, chopped
1 yellow onion, chopped
1 teaspoon sweet paprika
4 bacon strips, chopped
6 ounces cheddar cheese, shredded
Cooking spray

DIRECTIONS:
In a bowl, mix the eggs with egg whites, mustard, milk, salt, pepper and sweet paprika and whisk well. Grease your Slow cooker with cooking spray and spread bell peppers, bacon and onion on the bottom. Add mixed eggs, sprinkle cheddar all over, cover and cook on Low for 4 hours. Divide between plates and serve for breakfast.

NUTRITION:
calories 262, fat 6, fiber 3, carbs 15, protein 7

Basil Sausage and Broccoli Mix
Preparation time: 10 minutes
Cooking time: 8 hours and 10 minutes
Servings: 2

INGREDIENTS:
4 eggs, whisked
1 yellow onion, chopped
2 spring onions, chopped
1 cup pork sausage, chopped
1 cup broccoli florets
2 teaspoons basil, dried
A pinch of salt and black pepper
A drizzle of olive oil

DIRECTIONS:
Heat up a pan with the oil over medium-high heat, add the yellow onion and the sausage, toss, cook for 10 minutes and transfer to the slow cooker. Add the eggs and the other ingredients, toss, put the lid on and cook on Low for 8 hours. Divide between plates and serve for breakfast.

NUTRITION:
calories 251, fat 4, fiber 4, carbs 6, protein 7

Arugula Frittata
Preparation time: 10 minutes
Cooking time: 4 hours
Servings: 4

INGREDIENTS:
8 eggs
Salt and black pepper to the taste
½ cup milk
1 teaspoon oregano, dried
4 cups baby arugula
1 and ¼ cup roasted red peppers, chopped
½ cup red onion, chopped
¾ cup goat cheese, crumbled
Cooking spray

DIRECTIONS:
In a bowl, mix the eggs with milk, oregano, salt and pepper and whisk well. Grease your Slow cooker with cooking spray and spread roasted peppers, onion and arugula. Add eggs mix, sprinkle goat cheese all over, cover, cook on Low for 4 hours, divide frittata between plates and serve for breakfast.

NUTRITION:
calories 269, fat 3, fiber 6, carbs 15, protein 4

Zucchini and Cauliflower Eggs Mix
Preparation time: 10 minutes
Cooking time: 6 hours
Servings: 2

INGREDIENTS:
2 spring onions, chopped
A pinch of salt and black pepper
4 eggs, whisked
½ cup cauliflower florets
1 zucchini, grated
¼ cup cheddar cheese, shredded
¼ cup whipping cream
1 tablespoon chives, chopped
Cooking spray

DIRECTIONS:
Grease the slow cooker with the cooking spray and mix the eggs with the spring onions, cauliflower and the other ingredients inside. Put the lid on and cook on Low for 6 hours. Divide the mix between plates and serve for breakfast.

NUTRITION:
calories 211, fat 7, fiber 4, carbs 5, protein 5

Mixed Egg and Sausage Scramble
Preparation time: 10 minutes
Cooking time: 6 hours
Servings: 6

INGREDIENTS:
12 eggs
14 ounces sausages, sliced
1 cup milk
16 ounces cheddar cheese, shredded
A pinch of salt and black pepper
1 teaspoon basil, dried
1 teaspoon oregano, dried
Cooking spray

DIRECTIONS:
Grease your Slow cooker with cooking spray, spread sausages on the bottom, crack eggs, add

milk, basil, oregano, salt and pepper, whisk a bit, sprinkle cheddar all over, cover and cook on Low for 6 hours. Divide egg and sausage scramble between plates and serve.

NUTRITION:
calories 267, fat 4, fiber 5, carbs 12, protein 9

Mushroom Quiche
Preparation time: 10 minutes
Cooking time: 6 hours
Servings: 2

INGREDIENTS:
2 cups baby Bella mushrooms, chopped
½ cup cheddar cheese, shredded
4 eggs, whisked
½ cup heavy cream
1 tablespoon basil, chopped
2 tablespoons chives, chopped
A pinch of salt and black pepper
½ cup almond flour
¼ teaspoons baking soda
Cooking spray

DIRECTIONS:
In a bowl, mix the eggs with the cream, flour and the other ingredients except the cooking spray and stir well. Grease the slow cooker with the cooking spray, pour the quiche mix, spread well, put the lid on and cook on High for 6 hours. Slice the quiche, divide between plates and serve for breakfast.

NUTRITION:
calories 211, fat 6, fiber 6, carbs 6, protein 10

Worcestershire Asparagus Casserole
Preparation time: 10 minutes
Cooking time: 5 hours
Servings: 4

INGREDIENTS:
2 pounds asparagus spears, cut into 1-inch pieces
1 cup mushrooms, sliced
1 teaspoon olive oil
Salt and black pepper to the taste
2 cups coconut milk
1 teaspoon Worcestershire sauce
5 eggs, whisked

DIRECTIONS:
Grease your Slow cooker with the oil and spread asparagus and mushrooms on the bottom. In a bowl, mix the eggs with milk, salt, pepper and Worcestershire sauce, whisk, pour into the slow cooker, toss everything, cover and cook on Low for 6 hours. Divide between plates and serve right away for breakfast.

NUTRITION:
calories 211, fat 4, fiber 4, carbs 8, protein 5

Scallions Quinoa and Carrots Bowls
Preparation time: 10 minutes
Cooking time: 4 hours
Servings: 2

INGREDIENTS:
1 cup quinoa
2 cups veggie stock
4 scallions, chopped
2 carrots, peeled and grated
1 tablespoon olive oil
A pinch of salt and
black pepper
3 eggs, whisked
2 tablespoons cheddar cheese, grated
2 tablespoons heavy cream

DIRECTIONS:
In a bowl mix the eggs with the cream, cheddar, salt and pepper and whisk. Grease the slow cooker with the oil, add the quinoa, scallions, carrots and the stock, stir, put the lid on and cook on Low for 2 hours. Add the eggs mix, stir the whole thing, cook on Low for 2 more hours, divide into bowls and serve for breakfast.

NUTRITION:
calories 172, fat 5, fiber 4, carbs 6, protein 8

Peppers, Kale and Cheese Omelet
Preparation time: 10 minutes
Cooking time: 3 hours
Servings: 4

INGREDIENTS:
1 teaspoon olive oil
7 ounces roasted red peppers, chopped
6 ounces baby kale
Salt and black pepper to the taste
6 ounces feta cheese, crumbled
¼ cup green onions, sliced
7 eggs, whisked

DIRECTIONS:
In a bowl, mix the eggs with cheese, kale, red peppers, green onions, salt and pepper, whisk well, pour into the Slow cooker after you've greased it with the oil, cover, cook o Low for 3 hours, divide between plates and serve right away.

NUTRITION:
calories 231, fat 7, fiber 4, carbs 7, protein 14

Ham Omelet

Preparation time: 10 minutes
Cooking time: 3 hours
Servings: 2

INGREDIENTS:

Cooking spray
4 eggs, whisked
1 tablespoon sour cream
2 spring onions, chopped
1 small yellow onion, chopped
½ cup ham, chopped
½ cup cheddar cheese, shredded
1 tablespoon chives, chopped
A pinch of salt and black pepper

DIRECTIONS:

Grease your slow cooker with the cooking spray and mix the eggs with the sour cream, spring onions and the other ingredients inside. Toss the mix, spread into the pot, put the lid on and cook on High for 3 hours. Divide the mix between plates and serve for breakfast right away.

NUTRITION:
calories 192, fat 6, fiber 5, carbs 6, protein 12

Salmon Frittata

Preparation time: 10 minutes
Cooking time: 3 hours and 40 minutes
Servings: 3

INGREDIENTS:

4 eggs, whisked
½ teaspoon olive oil
2 tablespoons green onions, chopped
Salt and black pepper to the taste
4 ounces smoked salmon, chopped

DIRECTIONS:

Drizzle the oil in your Slow cooker, add eggs, salt and pepper, whisk, cover and cook on Low for 3 hours. Add salmon and green onions, toss a bit, cover, cook on Low for 40 minutes more and divide between plates. Serve right away for breakfast.

NUTRITION:
calories 220, fat 10, fiber 2, carbs 15, protein 7

Peppers and Eggs Mix

Preparation time: 10 minutes
Cooking time: 4 hours
Servings: 2

INGREDIENTS:

4 eggs, whisked
½ teaspoon coriander, ground
½ teaspoon rosemary, dried
2 spring onions, chopped
1 red bell pepper, cut into strips
1 green bell pepper, cut into strips
1 yellow bell pepper, cut into strips
¼ cup heavy cream
½ teaspoon garlic powder
A pinch of salt and black pepper
1 teaspoon sweet paprika
Cooking spray

DIRECTIONS:

Grease your slow cooker with the cooking spray, and mix the eggs with the coriander, rosemary and the other ingredients into the pot. Put the lid on, cook on Low for 4 hours, divide between plates and serve for breakfast.

NUTRITION:
calories 172, fat 6, fiber 3, carbs 6, protein 7

Creamy Breakfast

Preparation time: 5 minutes
Cooking time: 3 hours
Servings: 1

INGREDIENTS:

1 teaspoon cinnamon powder
½ teaspoon nutmeg, ground
½ cup almonds, chopped
1 teaspoon sugar
1 and ½ cup heavy cream
¼ teaspoon cardamom, ground
¼ teaspoon cloves, ground

DIRECTIONS:

In your Slow cooker, mix cream with cinnamon, nutmeg, almonds, sugar, cardamom and cloves, stir, cover, cook on Low for 3 hours, divide into bowls and serve for breakfast

NUTRITION:
calories 250, fat 12, fiber 4, carbs 8, protein 16

Baby Spinach Rice Mix

Preparation time: 10 minutes
Cooking time: 6 hours
Servings: 4

INGREDIENTS:

¼ cup mozzarella, shredded
½ cup baby spinach
½ cup wild rice
1 and ½ cups chicken stock
½ teaspoon turmeric powder
½ teaspoon oregano, dried
A pinch of salt and black pepper
3 scallions, minced
¾ cup goat cheese, crumbled

DIRECTIONS:
In your slow cooker, mix the rice with the stock, turmeric and the other ingredients, toss, put the lid on and cook on Low for 6 hours. Divide the mix into bowls and serve for breakfast.

NUTRITION:
calories 165, fat 1.2, fiber 3.5, carbs 32.6, protein 7.6

Brussels Sprouts Omelet
Preparation time: 10 minutes
Cooking time: 4 hours
Servings: 4

INGREDIENTS:

4 eggs, whisked	2 garlic cloves, minced
Salt and black pepper to the taste	12 ounces Brussels sprouts, sliced
1 tablespoon olive oil	2 ounces bacon, chopped
2 green onions, minced	

DIRECTIONS:
Drizzle the oil on the bottom of your Slow cooker and spread Brussels sprouts, garlic, bacon, green onions, eggs, salt and pepper, toss, cover and cook on Low for 4 hours. Divide between plates and serve right away for breakfast.

NUTRITION:
calories 240, fat 7, fiber 4, carbs 7, protein 13

Herbed Egg Scramble
Preparation time: 10 minutes
Cooking time: 6 hours
Servings: 2

INGREDIENTS:

4 eggs, whisked	chopped
¼ cup heavy cream	1 tablespoon rosemary, chopped
¼ cup mozzarella, shredded	A pinch of salt and black pepper
1 tablespoon chives, chopped	Cooking spray
1 tablespoon oregano,	

DIRECTIONS:
Grease your slow cooker with the cooking spray, and mix the eggs with the cream, herbs and the other ingredients inside. Stir well, put the lid on, cook for 6 hours on Low, stir once again, divide between plates and serve.

NUTRITION:
calories 203, fat 15.7, fiber 1.7, carbs 3.8, protein 12.8

Chicken Frittata
Preparation time: 10 minutes
Cooking time: 3 hours
Servings: 2

INGREDIENTS:

½ cup chicken, cooked and shredded	and crumbled
1 teaspoon mustard	4 eggs
1 tablespoon mayonnaise	1 small avocado, pitted, peeled and chopped
1 tomato, chopped	Salt and black pepper to the taste
2 bacon slices, cooked	

DIRECTIONS:
In a bowl, mix the eggs with salt, pepper, chicken, avocado, tomato, bacon, mayo and mustard, toss, transfer to your Slow cooker, cover and cook on Low for 3 hours. Divide between plates and serve for breakfast

NUTRITION:
calories 300, fat 32, fiber 6, carbs 15, protein 25

Peas and Rice Bowls
Preparation time: 10 minutes
Cooking time: 6 hours
Servings: 2

INGREDIENTS:

¼ cup peas	ground
1 cup wild rice	½ teaspoon allspice, ground
2 cups veggie stock	A pinch of salt and black pepper
¼ cup heavy cream	
1 tablespoon dill, chopped	¼ cup cheddar cheese, shredded
3 spring onions, chopped	1 teaspoon olive oil
½ teaspoon coriander,	

DIRECTIONS:
Grease the slow cooker with the oil, add the rice, peas, stock and the other ingredients except the dill and heavy cream, stir, put the lid on and cook on Low for 3 hours. Add the remaining ingredients, stir the mix, put the lid back on, cook on Low for 3 more hours, divide into bowls and serve for breakfast.

NUTRITION:
calories 442, fat 13.6, fiber 6.8, carbs 66, protein 17.4

Mushrooms Casserole
Preparation time: 10 minutes
Cooking time: 4 hours
Servings: 4

INGREDIENTS:
1 teaspoon lemon zest, grated
10 ounces goat cheese, cubed
1 tablespoon lemon juice
1 tablespoon apple cider vinegar
1 tablespoon olive oil
2 garlic cloves, minced
10 ounces spinach, torn
½ cup yellow onion, chopped
½ teaspoon basil, dried
8 ounces mushrooms, sliced
Salt and black pepper to the taste
Cooking spray

DIRECTIONS:
Spray your Slow cooker with cooking spray, arrange cheese cubes on the bottom and add lemon zest, lemon juice, vinegar, olive oil, garlic, spinach, onion, basil, mushrooms, salt and pepper. Toss well, cover, cook on Low for 4 hours, divide between plates and serve for breakfast right away.

NUTRITION:
calories 276, fat 6, fiber 5, carbs 7, protein 4

Asparagus Casserole

Preparation time: 10 minutes
Cooking time: 5 hours
Servings: 2

INGREDIENTS:
1 pound asparagus spears, cut into medium pieces
1 red onion, sliced
4 eggs, whisked
½ cup cheddar cheese, shredded
¼ cup heavy cream
1 tablespoon chives, chopped
A drizzle of olive oil
A pinch of salt and black pepper

DIRECTIONS:
Grease your slow cooker with the oil, and mix the eggs with the asparagus, onion and the other ingredients except the cheese into the pot. Sprinkle the cheese all over, put the lid on and cook on Low for 5 hours. Divide between plates and serve right away for breakfast.

NUTRITION:
calories 359, fat 24, fiber 6, carbs 15.5, protein 24.1

Carrot Pudding

Preparation time: 10 minutes
Cooking time: 8 hours
Servings: 4

INGREDIENTS:
4 carrots, grated
1 and ½ cups milk
A pinch of nutmeg, ground
A pinch of cloves, ground
½ teaspoon cinnamon powder
2 tablespoons maple syrup
¼ cup walnuts, chopped
1 teaspoon vanilla extract

DIRECTIONS:
In your Slow cooker, mix carrots with milk, cloves, nutmeg, cinnamon, maple syrup, walnuts and vanilla extract, stir, cover and cook on Low for 8 hours. Divide into bowls and serve for breakfast.

NUTRITION:
calories 215, fat 4, fiber 4, carbs 7, protein 7

Slow Cooker Lunch Recipes

Turkey Lunch

Preparation time: 10 minutes
Cooking time: 4 hours and 20 minutes
Servings: 12

INGREDIENTS:
- ½ teaspoon thyme, dried
- ½ teaspoon garlic powder
- Salt and black pepper to the taste
- 2 turkey breast halves, boneless
- 1/3 cup water
- 1 cup grape juice
- 2 cups raspberries
- 2 apples, peeled and chopped
- 2 cups blueberries
- A pinch of red pepper flakes, crushed
- ¼ teaspoon ginger powder

DIRECTIONS:
In your Slow cooker, mix water with salt, pepper, thyme and garlic powder and stir. Add turkey breast halves, toss, cover and cook on Low for 4 hours. Meanwhile, heat up a pan over medium-high heat, add grape juice, apples, raspberries, blueberries, pepper flakes and ginger, stir, bring to a simmer, cook for 20 minutes and take off heat. Divide turkey between plates, drizzle berry sauce all over and serve for lunch.

NUTRITION:
calories 215, fat 2, fiber 3, carbs 12, protein 26

Seafood Soup

Preparation time: 10 minutes
Cooking time: 8 hours
Servings: 2

INGREDIENTS:
- 2 cups chicken stock
- 1 cup coconut milk
- 1 sweet potato, cubed
- ½ yellow onion, chopped
- 1 bay leaf
- 1 carrot, peeled and sliced
- ½ tablespoon thyme, dried
- Salt and black pepper to the taste
- ½ pounds salmon fillets, skinless, boneless cubed
- 12 shrimp, peeled and deveined
- 1 tablespoon chives, chopped

DIRECTIONS:
In your slow cooker, mix the carrot with the sweet potato, onion and the other ingredients except the salmon, shrimp and chives, toss, put the lid on and cook on Low for 6 hours. Add the rest of the ingredients, toss, put the lid on and cook on Low for 2 more hours. Divide the soup into bowls and serve for lunch.

NUTRITION:
calories 354, fat 10, fiber 4, carbs 17, protein 12

Lunch Roast

Preparation time: 10 minutes
Cooking time: 8 hours
Servings: 8

INGREDIENTS:
- 2 pounds beef chuck roast
- Salt and black pepper to the taste
- 1 yellow onion, chopped
- 2 teaspoons olive oil
- 8 ounces tomato sauce
- ¼ cup lemon juice
- ¼ cup water
- ¼ cup ketchup
- ¼ cup apple cider vinegar
- 1 tablespoons Worcestershire sauce
- 2 tablespoons brown sugar
- ½ teaspoon mustard powder
- ½ teaspoons paprika

DIRECTIONS:
In your Slow cooker, mix beef with salt, pepper, onion oil, tomato sauce, lemon juice, water, ketchup, vinegar, Worcestershire sauce, sugar, mustard and paprika, toss well, cover and cook on Low for 8 hours. Slice roast, divide between plates, drizzle cooking sauce all over and serve for lunch.

NUTRITION:
calories 243, fat 12, fiber 2, carbs 10, protein 23

Sesame Salmon Bowls

Preparation time: 10 minutes
Cooking time: 3 hours
Servings: 2

INGREDIENTS:
- 2 salmon fillets, boneless and roughly cubed
- 1 cup cherry tomatoes, halved
- 3 spring onions, chopped
- 1 cup baby spinach
- ½ cup chicken stock
- Salt and black pepper to the taste
- 2 tablespoons balsamic vinegar
- 2 tablespoons lemon juice
- 1 teaspoon sesame seeds

DIRECTIONS:
In your slow cooker, mix the salmon with the cherry tomatoes, spring onions and the other ingredients, toss gently, put the lid on and cook on Low for 3 hours. Divide everything into bowls and serve.

NUTRITION:
calories 230, fat 4, fiber 2, carbs 7, protein 6

Fajitas

Preparation time: 10 minutes
Cooking time: 3 hours
Servings: 8

INGREDIENTS:
- 1 and ½ pounds beef sirloin, cut into thin strips
- 2 tablespoons lemon juice
- 2 tablespoons olive oil
- 1 garlic clove, minced
- 1 and ½ teaspoon cumin, ground
- Salt and black pepper to the taste
- ½ teaspoon chili powder
- A pinch of red pepper flakes, crushed
- 1 red bell pepper, cut into thin strips
- 1 yellow onion, cut into thin strips
- 8 mini tortillas

DIRECTIONS:
Heat up a pan with the oil over medium-high heat, add beef strips, brown them for a few minutes and transfer to your Slow cooker. Add lemon juice, garlic, cumin, salt, pepper, chili powder and pepper flakes to the slow cooker as well, cover and cook on High for 2 hours. Add bell pepper and onion, stir and cook on High for 1 more hour. Divide beef mix between your mini tortillas and serve for lunch.

NUTRITION:
calories 220, fat 9, fiber 2, carbs 14, protein 20

Shrimp Stew

Preparation time: 10 minutes
Cooking time: 3 hours
Servings: 2

INGREDIENTS:
- 1 garlic clove, minced
- 1 red onion, chopped
- 1 cup canned tomatoes, crushed
- 1 cup veggie stock
- ½ teaspoon turmeric powder
- 1 pound shrimp, peeled and deveined
- ½ teaspoon coriander, ground
- ½ teaspoon thyme, dried
- ½ teaspoon basil, dried
- A pinch of salt and black pepper
- A pinch of red pepper flakes

DIRECTIONS:
In your slow cooker, mix the onion with the garlic, shrimp and the other ingredients, toss, put the lid on and cook on High for 3 hours. Divide the stew into bowls and serve.

NUTRITION:
calories 313, fat 4.2, fiber 2.5, carbs 13.2, protein 53.3

Teriyaki Pork

Preparation time: 10 minutes
Cooking time: 7 hours
Servings: 8

INGREDIENTS:
- 2 tablespoons sugar
- 2 tablespoons soy sauce
- ¾ cup apple juice
- 1 teaspoon ginger powder
- 1 tablespoon white vinegar
- Salt and black pepper to the taste
- ¼ teaspoon garlic powder
- 3 pounds pork loin roast, halved
- 7 teaspoons cornstarch
- 3 tablespoons water

DIRECTIONS:
In your Slow cooker, mix apple juice with sugar, soy sauce, vinegar, ginger, garlic powder, salt, pepper and pork loin, toss well, cover and cook on Low for 7 hours. Transfer cooking juices to a small pan, heat up over medium-high heat, add cornstarch mixed with water, stir well, cook for 2 minutes until it thickens and take off heat. Slice roast, divide between plates, drizzle sauce all over and serve for lunch.

NUTRITION:
calories 247, fat 8, fiber 1, carbs 9, protein 33

Garlic Shrimp and Spinach

Preparation time: 10 minutes
Cooking time: 2 hours
Servings: 2

INGREDIENTS:
- 1 pound shrimp, peeled and deveined
- 1 cup baby spinach
- ½ teaspoon sweet paprika
- ½ cup chicken stock
- 1 garlic clove, minced
- 2 jalapeno peppers, chopped
- Cooking spray
- 1 teaspoon coriander, ground
- ½ teaspoon rosemary, dried
- A pinch of sea salt and black pepper

DIRECTIONS:
Grease the slow cooker with the oil, add the shrimp, spinach and the other ingredients, toss, put the lid on and cook on High for 2 hours. Divide everything between plates and serve for lunch.

NUTRITION:
calories 200, fat 4, fiber 6, carbs 16, protein 4

Beef Stew

Preparation time: 10 minutes
Cooking time: 7 hours and 30 minutes
Servings: 5

INGREDIENTS:
- 2 potatoes, peeled and cubed
- 1 pound beef stew meat, cubed
- 11 ounces tomato juice
- 14 ounces beef stock
- 2 celery ribs, chopped
- 2 carrots, chopped
- 3 bay leaves
- 1 yellow onion, chopped
- Salt and black pepper to the taste
- ½ teaspoon chili powder
- ½ teaspoon thyme, dried
- 1 tablespoon water
- 2 tablespoons cornstarch
- ½ cup peas
- ½ cup corn

DIRECTIONS:
In your Slow cooker, mix potatoes with beef, tomato juice, stock, ribs, carrots, bay leaves, onion, salt, pepper, chili powder and thyme, stir, cover and cook on Low for 7 hours. Add cornstarch mixed with water, peas and corn, stir, cover and cook on Low for 30 minutes more. Divide into bowls and serve for lunch.

NUTRITION:
calories 273, fat 7, fiber 6, carbs 30, protein 22

Ginger Salmon

Preparation time: 10 minutes
Cooking time: 3 hours
Servings: 2

INGREDIENTS:
- 2 salmon fillets, boneless
- 1 tablespoon olive oil
- 1 tablespoon balsamic vinegar
- 1 tablespoon ginger, grated
- A pinch of nutmeg, ground
- A pinch of cloves, ground
- A pinch of salt and black pepper
- 1 teaspoon onion powder
- ½ teaspoon cayenne pepper
- ¼ cup chicken stock

DIRECTIONS:
Grease the slow cooker with the oil and arrange the salmon fillets inside. Add the vinegar, ginger and the other ingredients, rub gently, put the lid on and cook on Low for 3 hours. Divide the fish between plates and serve with a side salad for lunch.

NUTRITION:
calories 315, fat 18.4, fiber 0.6, carbs 3.6, protein 35.1

Apple and Onion Lunch Roast

Preparation time: 10 minutes
Cooking time: 5 hours
Servings: 8

INGREDIENTS:
- 1 beef sirloin roast, halved
- Salt and black pepper to the taste
- 1 cup water
- ½ teaspoon soy sauce
- 1 apple, cored and quartered
- ¼ teaspoon garlic powder
- ½ teaspoon Worcestershire sauce
- 1 yellow onion, cut into medium wedges
- 2 tablespoons water
- 2 tablespoons cornstarch
- 1/8 teaspoon browning sauce
- Cooking spray

DIRECTIONS:
Grease a pan with the cooking spray, heat it up over medium-high heat, add roast, brown it for a few minutes on each side and transfer to your Slow cooker. Add salt, pepper, soy sauce, garlic powder, Worcestershire sauce, onion and apple, cover and cook on Low for 6 hours. Transfer cooking juices from the slow cooker to a pan, heat it up over medium heat, add cornstarch, water and browning sauce, stir well, cook for a few minutes and take off heat. Slice roast, divide between plates, drizzle sauce all over and serve for lunch.

NUTRITION:
calories 242, fat 8, fiber 1, carbs 8, protein 34

Creamy Cod Stew

Preparation time: 10 minutes
Cooking time: 3 hours
Servings: 2

INGREDIENTS:
- ½ pound cod fillets, boneless and cubed
- 2 spring onions, chopped
- ¼ cup heavy cream
- 1 carrot, sliced
- 1 zucchini, cubed
- 1 tomato, cubed
- 1 cup chicken stock
- 1 tablespoon olive oil
- 1 green bell pepper, chopped
- 1 tablespoon chives, chopped
- A pinch of salt and black pepper

DIRECTIONS:
In your slow cooker, combine the fish with the

spring onions, carrot and the other ingredients except the cream, toss gently, put the lid on and cook on High for 2 hours and 30 minutes. Add the cream, toss gently, put the lid back on, cook the stew on Low for 30 minutes more, divide into bowls and serve.

NUTRITION:
calories 175, fat 13.3, fiber 3.4, carbs 14, protein 3.3

Stuffed Peppers
Preparation time: 10 minutes
Cooking time: 4 hours
Servings: 4

INGREDIENTS:
- 15 ounces canned black beans, drained
- 4 sweet red peppers, tops and seeds discarded
- 1 cup pepper jack cheese, shredded
- 1 yellow onion, chopped
- ¾ cup salsa
- ½ cup corn
- 1/3 cup white rice
- ½ teaspoon cumin, ground
- 1 and ½ teaspoons chili powder

DIRECTIONS:
In a bowl, mix black beans with cheese, salsa, onion, corn, rice, cumin and chili powder and stir well. Stuff peppers with this mix, place them in your Slow cooker, cover and cook on Low for 4 hours. Divide between plates and serve them for lunch.

NUTRITION:
calories 317, fat 10, fiber 8, carbs 43, protein 12

Sweet Potato and Clam Chowder
Preparation time: 10 minutes
Cooking time: 3 hours and 30 minutes
Servings: 2

INGREDIENTS:
- 1 small yellow onion, chopped
- 1 carrot, chopped
- 1 red bell pepper, cubed
- 6 ounces canned clams, chopped
- 1 sweet potato, chopped
- 2 cups chicken stock
- ½ cup coconut milk
- 1 teaspoon Worcestershire sauce

DIRECTIONS:
In your slow cooker, mix the onion with the carrot, clams and the other ingredients, toss, put the lid on and cook on High for 3 hours. Divide the chowder into bowls and serve for lunch.

NUTRITION:
calories 288, fat 15.3, fiber 5.9, carbs 36.4, protein 5

Beans and Pumpkin Chili
Preparation time: 10 minutes
Cooking time: 4 hours
Servings: 10

INGREDIENTS:
- 1 yellow bell pepper, chopped
- 1 yellow onion, chopped
- 3 garlic cloves, minced
- 2 tablespoons olive oil
- 3 cups chicken stock
- 30 ounces canned black beans, drained
- 14 ounces pumpkin, cubed
- 2 and ½ cups turkey meat, cooked and cubed
- 2 teaspoons parsley, dried
- 1 and ½ teaspoon oregano, dried
- 2 teaspoons chili powder
- 1 and ½ teaspoon cumin, ground
- Salt and black pepper to the taste

DIRECTIONS:
Heat up a pan with the oil over medium-high heat, add bell pepper, onion and garlic, stir, cook for a few minutes and transfer to your Slow cooker. Add stock, beans, pumpkin, turkey, parsley, oregano, chili powder, cumin, salt and pepper, stir, cover and cook on Low for 4 hours. Divide into bowls and serve right away for lunch.

NUTRITION:
calories 200, fat 5, fiber 7, carbs 20, protein 15

Maple Chicken Mix
Preparation time: 10 minutes
Cooking time: 6 hours
Servings: 2

INGREDIENTS:
- 2 spring onions, chopped
- 1 pound chicken breast, skinless and boneless
- 2 garlic cloves, minced
- 1 tablespoon maple syrup
- A pinch of salt and black pepper
- ½ cup chicken stock
- ½ cup tomato sauce
- 1 tablespoon chives, chopped
- 1 teaspoon basil, dried

DIRECTIONS:
In your slow cooker mix the chicken with the garlic, maple syrup and the other ingredients, toss, put the lid on and cook on Low for 6 hours. Divide the mix between plates and serve for lunch.

NUTRITION:
calories 200, fat 3, fiber 3, carbs 17, protein 6

Chicken and Peppers Mix

Preparation time: 10 minutes
Cooking time: 4 hours
Servings: 6

INGREDIENTS:
24 ounces tomato sauce
¼ cup parmesan, grated
1 yellow onion, chopped
2 garlic cloves, minced
1 teaspoon basil, dried
1 teaspoon oregano, dried
Salt and black pepper to the taste
6 chicken breast halves, skinless and boneless
½ green bell pepper, chopped
½ yellow bell pepper, chopped
½ red bell pepper, chopped

DIRECTIONS:
In your Slow cooker, mix tomato sauce with parmesan, onion, garlic, basil, oregano, salt, pepper, chicken, green bell pepper, yellow bell pepper and red bell pepper, toss, cover and cook on Low for 4 hours. Divide between plates and serve for lunch.

NUTRITION:
calories 221, fat 6, fiber 3, carbs 16, protein 26

Salsa Chicken

Preparation time: 10 minutes
Cooking time: 8 hours
Servings: 2

INGREDIENTS:
7 ounces mild salsa
1 pound chicken breast, skinless, boneless and cubed
1 small yellow onion, chopped
½ teaspoon coriander, ground
½ teaspoon rosemary, dried
1 green bell pepper, chopped
Cooking spray
1 tablespoon cilantro, chopped
1 red bell pepper, chopped
1 tablespoon chili powder

DIRECTIONS:
Grease the slow cooker with the cooking spray and mix the chicken with the salsa, onion and the other ingredients inside. Put the lid on, cook on Low for 8 hours, divide into bowls and serve for lunch.

NUTRITION:
calories 240, fat 3, fiber 7, carbs 17, protein 8

Chicken Tacos

Preparation time: 10 minutes
Cooking time: 5 hours
Servings: 16

INGREDIENTS:
2 mangos, peeled and chopped
2 tomatoes, chopped
1 and ½ cups pineapple chunks
1 red onion, chopped
2 small green bell peppers, chopped
1 tablespoon lime juice
2 green onions, chopped
1 teaspoon sugar
4 pounds chicken breast halves, skinless
Salt and black pepper to the taste
32 taco shells, warm
¼ cup cilantro, chopped
¼ cup brown sugar

DIRECTIONS:
In a bowl, mix mango with pineapple, red onion, tomatoes, bell peppers, green onions and lime juice and toss. Put chicken in your Slow cooker, add salt, pepper and sugar and toss. Add mango mix, cover and cook on Low for 5 hours. Transfer chicken to a cutting board, cool it down, discard bones and shred meat. Divide meat and mango mix between taco shells and serve them for lunch.

NUTRITION:
calories 246, fat 7, fiber 2, carbs 25, protein 21

Turkey and Mushrooms

Preparation time: 10 minutes
Cooking time: 7 hours and 10 minutes
Servings: 2

INGREDIENTS:
1 red onion, sliced
2 garlic cloves, minced
1 pound turkey breast, skinless, boneless and cubed
1 tablespoon olive oil
1 teaspoon oregano, dried
1 teaspoon basil, dried
A pinch of red pepper flakes
1 cup mushrooms, sliced
¼ cup chicken stock
½ cup canned tomatoes, chopped
A pinch of salt and black pepper

DIRECTIONS:
Heat up a pan with the oil over medium-high heat, add the onion, garlic and the meat, brown for 10 minutes and transfer to the slow cooker. Add the oregano, basil and the other ingredients, toss, put the lid on and cook on Low for 7 hours. Divide into bowls and serve for lunch.

NUTRITION:
calories 240, fat 4, fiber 6, carbs 18, protein 10

Orange Beef Dish

Preparation time: 10 minutes
Cooking time: 5 hours
Servings: 5

INGREDIENTS:
1 pound beef sirloin steak, cut into medium strips
2 and ½ cups shiitake mushrooms, sliced
1 yellow onion, cut into medium wedges
3 red hot chilies, dried
¼ cup brown sugar
¼ cup orange juice
¼ cup soy sauce
2 tablespoons cider vinegar
1 tablespoon cornstarch
1 tablespoon ginger, grated
1 tablespoon sesame oil
1 cup snow peas
2 garlic cloves, minced
1 tablespoon orange zest, grated

DIRECTIONS:
In your Slow cooker, mix steak strips with mushrooms, onion, chilies, sugar, orange juice, soy sauce, vinegar, cornstarch, ginger, oil, garlic and orange zest, toss, cover and cook on Low for 4 hours and 30 minutes. Add snow peas, cover, cook on Low for 30 minutes more, divide between plates and serve.

NUTRITION:
calories 310, fat 7, fiber 4, carbs 26, protein 33

Indian Chicken and Tomato Mix

Preparation time: 10 minutes
Cooking time: 6 hours
Servings: 2

INGREDIENTS:
1 cup cherry tomatoes, halved
1 pound chicken breast, skinless, boneless and cubed
1 red onion, sliced
1 tablespoons garam masala
1 garlic clove, minced
½ small yellow onion, chopped
½ teaspoon ginger powder
A pinch of salt and cayenne pepper
½ teaspoon sweet paprika
2 tablespoons chives, chopped

DIRECTIONS:
In your slow cooker, mix the chicken with the tomatoes, onion and the other ingredients, toss, put the lid on and cook on Low for 6 hours. Divide into bowls and serve right away.

NUTRITION:
calories 259, fat 3, fiber 7, carbs 17, protein 14

Chicken with Couscous

Preparation time: 10 minutes
Cooking time: 3 hours
Servings: 6

INGREDIENTS:
2 sweet potatoes, peeled and cubed
1 sweet red peppers, chopped
1 and ½ pounds chicken breasts, skinless and boneless
13 ounces canned stewed tomatoes
Salt and black pepper to the taste
¼ cup raisins
¼ teaspoon cinnamon powder
¼ teaspoon cumin, ground
For the couscous:
1 cup whole wheat couscous
1 cup water
Salt to the taste

DIRECTIONS:
In your Slow cooker, mix potatoes with red peppers, chicken, tomatoes, salt, pepper, raisins, cinnamon and cumin, toss, cover, cook on Low for 3 hours and shred meat using 2 forks. Meanwhile, heat up a pan with the water over medium-high heat, add salt, bring water to a boil, add couscous, stir, leave aside covered for 10 minutes and fluff with a fork. Divide chicken mix between plates, add couscous on the side and serve.

NUTRITION:
calories 351, fat 4, fiber 7, carbs 45, protein 30

Turkey and Figs

Preparation time: 10 minutes
Cooking time: 8 hours
Servings: 2

INGREDIENTS:
1 pound turkey breast, boneless, skinless and sliced
½ cup black figs, halved
1 red onion, sliced
½ cup tomato sauce
½ teaspoon onion powder
¼ teaspoon garlic powder
1 tablespoon basil, chopped
½ teaspoon chili powder
¼ cup white wine
½ teaspoon thyme, dried
¼ teaspoon sage, dried
½ teaspoon paprika, dried
A pinch of salt and black pepper

DIRECTIONS:
In your slow cooker, mix the turkey breast with the figs, onion and the other ingredients, toss, put the lid on and cook on Low for 8 hours. Divide between plates and serve.

NUTRITION:
calories 220, fat 5, fiber 8, carbs 18, protein 15

Pork Stew

Preparation time: 10 minutes
Cooking time: 5 hours
Servings: 8

INGREDIENTS:

2 pork tenderloins, cubed
Salt and black pepper to the taste
2 carrots, sliced
1 yellow onion, chopped
2 celery ribs, chopped
2 tablespoons tomato paste
3 cups beef stock
1/3 cup plums, dried, pitted and chopped
1 rosemary spring
1 thyme spring
2 bay leaves
4 garlic cloves, minced
1/3 cup green olives, pitted and sliced
1 tablespoon parsley, chopped

DIRECTIONS:
In your Slow cooker, mix pork with salt, pepper, carrots, onion, celery, tomato paste, stock, plums, rosemary, thyme, bay leaves, garlic, olives and parsley, cover and cook on Low for 5 hours. Discard thyme, rosemary and bay leaves, divide stew into bowls and serve for lunch.

NUTRITION:
calories 200, fat 4, fiber 2, carbs 8, protein 23

Turkey and Walnuts

Preparation time: 10 minutes
Cooking time: 8 hours
Servings: 2

INGREDIENTS:

1 pound turkey breast, skinless, boneless and sliced
½ cup scallions, chopped
2 tablespoons walnuts, chopped
1 tablespoon lemon juice
¼ cup veggie stock
½ teaspoon chili powder
1 tablespoon olive oil
1 tablespoon rosemary, chopped
Salt and black pepper to the taste

DIRECTIONS:
In your slow cooker, mix the turkey with the scallions, walnuts and the other ingredients, toss, put the lid on and cook on Low for 8 hours. Divide everything between plates and serve.

NUTRITION:
calories 264, fat 4, fiber 6, carbs 15, protein 15

Seafood Stew

Preparation time: 10 minutes
Cooking time: 4 hours and 30 minutes
Servings: 8

INGREDIENTS:

8 ounces clam juice
2 yellow onions, chopped
28 ounces canned tomatoes, chopped
6 ounces tomato paste
3 celery ribs, chopped
½ cup white wine
1 tablespoon red vinegar
5 garlic cloves, minced
1 tablespoon olive oil
1 teaspoon Italian seasoning
1 bay leaf
1 pound haddock fillets, boneless and cut into medium pieces
½ teaspoon sugar
1 pound shrimp, peeled and deveined
6 ounces crabmeat
6 ounces canned clams
2 tablespoons parsley, chopped

DIRECTIONS:
In your Slow cooker, mix tomatoes with onions, clam juice, tomato paste, celery, wine, vinegar, garlic, oil, seasoning, sugar and bay leaf, stir, cover and cook on Low for 4 hours. Add shrimp, haddock, crabmeat and clams, cover, cook on Low for 30 minutes more, divide into bowls and serve with parsley sprinkled on top.

NUTRITION:
calories 205, fat 4, fiber 4, carbs 14, protein 27

Slow Cooked Thyme Chicken

Preparation time: 10 minutes
Cooking time: 7 hours
Servings: 2

INGREDIENTS:

1 pound chicken legs
1 tablespoon thyme, chopped
2 garlic cloves, minced
½ cup chicken stock
1 carrot, chopped
½ yellow onion, chopped
A pinch of salt and white pepper
Juice of ½ lemon

DIRECTIONS:
In your slow cooker, mix the chicken legs with the thyme, garlic and the other ingredients, toss, put the lid on and cook on Low for 7 hours. Divide between plates and serve.

NUTRITION:
calories 320, fat 4, fiber 7, carbs 16, protein 6

Pork Sandwiches

Preparation time: 10 minutes
Cooking time: 8 hours
Servings: 12

INGREDIENTS:
1 tablespoon steak seasoning
1 tablespoon fennel seeds
A pinch of cayenne pepper
Salt and black pepper to the taste
3 pounds pork shoulder butt, boneless
2 green bell peppers, chopped
1 tablespoon olive oil
2 yellow onions, chopped
14 ounces canned tomatoes, chopped
12 hamburger buns, split

DIRECTIONS:
In your Slow cooker, mix pork butt with steak seasoning, fennel, cayenne, salt, pepper, bell peppers, oil, onions and tomatoes, toss, cover and cook on Low for 8 hours, Shred meat using 2 forks, divide the whole mix between your hamburger buns and serve for lunch.

NUTRITION:
calories 288, fat 8, fiber 5, carbs 28, protein 25

Roasted Beef and Cauliflower

Preparation time: 10 minutes

Cooking time: 8 hours

Servings: 2

INGREDIENTS:
1 pound beef chuck roast, sliced
1 cup cauliflower florets
½ cup tomato sauce
½ cup veggie stock
½ tablespoon olive oil
2 garlic cloves, minced
½ carrot, roughly chopped
1 celery rib, roughly chopped
A pinch of salt and black pepper to the taste
1 tablespoon parsley, chopped

DIRECTIONS:
In your slow cooker, mix the roast with the cauliflower, tomato sauce and the other ingredients, toss, put the lid on and cook on Low for 8 hours. Divide between plates and serve.

NUTRITION:
calories 340, fat 5, fiber 7, carbs 18, protein 22

Peas and Ham Mix

Preparation time: 10 minutes

Cooking time: 5 hours

Servings: 12

INGREDIENTS:
½ cup ham, cooked and chopped
16 ounces black-eyed peas
1 yellow onion, chopped
1 red bell pepper, chopped
5 bacon strips, cooked and crumbled
1 jalapeno pepper, chopped
2 garlic cloves, minced
1 teaspoon cumin, ground
Salt and black pepper to the taste
A pinch of cayenne pepper
6 cups water
1 tablespoon cilantro, chopped

DIRECTIONS:
In your Slow cooker, mix ham with peas, onion, bell pepper, bacon, jalapeno, garlic, cumin, salt, pepper, cayenne and water, toss, cover and cook on Low for 5 hours. Add cilantro, stir, divide into bowls and serve for lunch.

NUTRITION:
calories 170, fat 3, fiber 6, carbs 26, protein 13

Soy Pork Chops

Preparation time: 10 minutes

Cooking time: 7 hours

Servings: 2

INGREDIENTS:
1 pound pork chops
2 tablespoons sugar
2 tablespoons soy sauce
½ cup beef stock
1 tablespoon balsamic vinegar
1 tablespoon cilantro, chopped

DIRECTIONS:
In your slow cooker, mix the pork chops with the soy sauce and the other ingredients, toss, put the lid on and cook on Low for 7 hours. Divide everything between plates and serve.

NUTRITION:
calories 345, fat 5, fiber 7, carbs 17, protein 14

Beef and Veggie Stew

Preparation time: 10 minutes

Cooking time: 6 hours and 30 minutes

Servings: 8

INGREDIENTS:
3 potatoes, cubed
1 and ½ pound beef chuck roast, boneless and cubed
10 ounces canned tomato soup
1 and ½ cup baby carrots
3 and ¾ cups water
1 celery rib, chopped
1 yellow onion, chopped
2 tablespoons Worcestershire sauce
1 garlic clove, minced
Salt and black pepper to the taste
1 teaspoon sugar
2 cups peas
¼ cup cornstarch

DIRECTIONS:
In your Slow cooker, mix potatoes with beef cubes, tomato soup, baby carrots, 3 cups water, celery, onion, Worcestershire sauce, garlic, salt, pepper and sugar, stir, cover and cook on Low for 6 hours. Add cornstarch mixed with the rest of the water and the peas, stir, cover and cook on Low for 30 minutes more. Divide into bowls and serve for lunch.

NUTRITION:
calories 287, fat 4, fiber 5, carbs 31, protein 20

Pork and Cranberries
Preparation time: 10 minutes
Cooking time: 8 hours
Servings: 2

INGREDIENTS:
1 pound pork tenderloin, roughly cubed
½ cup cranberries
½ cup red wine
½ teaspoon sweet paprika
½ teaspoon chili powder
1 tablespoon maple syrup

DIRECTIONS:
In your slow cooker, mix the pork with the cranberries, wine and the other ingredients, toss, put the lid on and cook on Low for 8 hours. Divide between plates and serve.

NUTRITION:
calories 400, fat 12, fiber 8, carbs 18, protein 20

Onion Chicken
Preparation time: 10 minutes
Cooking time: 6 hours
Servings: 2

INGREDIENTS:
1 small yellow onion, chopped
2 carrots, sliced
1 cup green beans
½ celery rib, chopped
2 chicken breast halves, boneless and skinless
2 small red potatoes, halved
2 bacon strips, cooked and crumbled
Salt and black pepper to the taste
¾ cup water
¼ teaspoon basil, dried
¼ teaspoon thyme, dried

DIRECTIONS:
In your Slow cooker, mix onion with carrots, green beans, celery, chicken, red potatoes, bacon, salt, pepper, water, basil and thyme, cover and cook on Low for 6 hours. Divide between plates and serve for lunch.

NUTRITION:
calories 304, fat 7, fiber 5, carbs 20, protein 37

Lamb and Onion Stew
Preparation time: 10 minutes
Cooking time: 8 hours
Servings: 2

INGREDIENTS:
1 pound lamb meat, cubed
1 red onion, sliced
3 spring onions, sliced
Salt and black pepper to the taste
1 tablespoon olive oil
½ teaspoon rosemary, dried
¼ teaspoon thyme, dried
1 cup water
½ cup baby carrots, peeled
½ cup tomato sauce
1 tablespoon cilantro, chopped

DIRECTIONS:
In your slow cooker, mix the lamb with the onion, spring onions and the other ingredients, toss, put the lid on and cook on Low for 8 hours. Divide the stew between plates and serve hot.

NUTRITION:
calories 350, fat 8, fiber 3, carbs 14, protein 16

Beef Chili
Preparation time: 10 minutes
Cooking time: 6 hours
Servings: 8

INGREDIENTS:
3 chipotle chili peppers in adobo sauce, chopped
2 pounds beef steak, cubed
1 yellow onion, chopped
2 garlic cloves, minced
1 tablespoon chili powder
Salt and black pepper to the taste
45 canned tomato puree
½ teaspoon cumin, ground
14 ounces beef stock
2 tablespoons cilantro, chopped

DIRECTIONS:
In your Slow cooker, chipotle chilies with beef, onion, garlic, chili powder, salt, pepper, tomato puree, cumin and stock, stir, cover and cook on Low for 6 hours. Add cilantro, stir, divide into bowls and serve for lunch.

NUTRITION:
calories 230, fat 8, fiber 2, carbs 12, protein 25

Pork Roast and Olives

Preparation time: 10 minutes

Cooking time: 6 hours

Servings: 2

INGREDIENTS:
1 pound pork roast, sliced
½ cup black olives, pitted and halved
½ cup kalamata olives, pitted and halved
2 medium carrots, chopped
½ cup tomato sauce
1 small yellow onion, chopped
2 garlic cloves, minced
1 bay leaf
Salt and black pepper to the taste

DIRECTIONS:
In your slow cooker, mix the pork roast with the olives and the other ingredients, toss, put the lid on and cook on High for 6 hours. Divide everything between plates and serve.

NUTRITION:
calories 360, fat 4, fiber 3, carbs 17, protein 27

Moist Pork Loin

Preparation time: 10 minutes

Cooking time: 5 hours

Servings: 8

INGREDIENTS:
3 pound pork loin roast
1 teaspoon onion powder
1 teaspoon mustard powder
2 cups chicken stock
2 tablespoons olive oil
¼ cup cornstarch
¼ cup water

DIRECTIONS:
In your Slow cooker, mix pork with onion powder, mustard powder, stock and oil, cover and cook on Low for 5 hours. Transfer roast to a cutting board, slice and divide between plates. Transfer cooking juices to a pan and heat it up over medium heat. Add water and cornstarch, stir, cook until it thickens, drizzle over roast and serve for lunch.

NUTRITION:
calories 300, fat 11, fiber 1, carbs 10, protein 34

Beef Stew

Preparation time: 10 minutes

Cooking time: 6 hours and 10 minutes

Servings: 2

INGREDIENTS:
1 tablespoon olive oil
1 red onion, chopped
1 carrot, peeled and sliced
1 pound beef meat, cubed
½ cup beef stock
½ cup canned tomatoes, chopped
2 tablespoons tomato sauce
2 tablespoons balsamic vinegar
2 garlic cloves, minced
½ cup black olives, pitted and sliced
1 tablespoon rosemary, chopped
Salt and black pepper to the taste

DIRECTIONS:
Heat up a pan with the oil over medium-high heat, add the meat, brown for 10 minutes and transfer to your slow cooker. Add the rest of the ingredients, toss, put the lid on and cook on High for 6 hours. Divide between plates and serve right away!

NUTRITION:
calories 370, fat 14, fiber 6, carbs 26, protein 38

Lunch Meatloaf

Preparation time: 10 minutes

Cooking time: 4 hours

Servings: 8

INGREDIENTS:
½ cup breadcrumbs

1 yellow onion, chopped

1 green bell pepper, chopped
2 eggs, whisked
2 tablespoons brown mustard
½ cup chili sauce
Salt and black pepper to the taste
4 garlic cloves, minced
¼ teaspoon oregano, dried
2 pounds beef meat, ground
¼ teaspoon basil, dried
Cooking spray

DIRECTIONS:
In a bowl, mix beef with onion, breadcrumbs, bell pepper, mustard, chili sauce, eggs, salt, pepper, garlic, oregano and basil and stir well. Line your Slow cooker with tin foil, grease with cooking spray, add beef meat, shape your meatloaf with your hands, cover and cook on Low for 4 hours. Divide between plates and serve for lunch.

NUTRITION:
calories 253, fat 11, fiber 1, carbs 12, protein 25

Beef and Celery Stew

Preparation time: 10 minutes

Cooking time: 8 hours

Servings: 2

INGREDIENTS:
½ cup beef stock
1 pound beef stew meat, cubed
1 cup celery, cubed
½ cup tomato sauce
2 carrots, chopped
½ cup mushrooms, halved
½ red onion, roughly chopped
½ tablespoon olive oil
Salt and black pepper to the taste
¼ cup red wine
1 tablespoon parsley, chopped

DIRECTIONS:
In your slow cooker, mix the beef with the stock, celery and the other ingredients, toss, put the lid on and cook on Low for 8 hours. Divide the stew into bowls and serve.

NUTRITION:
calories 433, fat 20, fiber 4, carbs 14, protein 39

Mexican Lunch Mix

Preparation time: 10 minutes
Cooking time: 7 hours
Servings: 12

INGREDIENTS:
12 ounces beer
¼ cup flour
2 tablespoons tomato paste
1 jalapeno pepper, chopped
1 bay leaf
4 teaspoons Worcestershire sauce
2 teaspoons red pepper flakes, crushed
1 and ½ teaspoons cumin, ground
2 teaspoons chili powder
Salt and black pepper to the taste
2 garlic cloves, minced
½ teaspoon sweet paprika
½ teaspoon red vinegar
3 pounds pork shoulder butter, cubed
2 potatoes, chopped
1 yellow onion, chopped

DIRECTIONS:
In your Slow cooker, mix pork with potatoes, onion, beef, flour, tomato paste, jalapeno, bay leaf, Worcestershire sauce, pepper flakes, cumin, chili powder, garlic, paprika and vinegar, toss, cover and cook on Low for 7 hours. Divide between plates and serve for lunch.

NUTRITION:
calories 261, fat 12, fiber 2, carbs 16, protein 21

Tomato Pasta Mix

Preparation time: 10 minutes
Cooking time: 6 hours
Servings: 2

INGREDIENTS:
½ pound beef stew meat, ground
1 red onion, chopped
½ teaspoon sweet paprika
½ teaspoon chili powder
Salt and black pepper to the taste
½ teaspoon basil, dried
½ teaspoon parsley, dried
14 ounces canned tomatoes, chopped
1 cup chicken stock
1 cup short pasta

DIRECTIONS:
In your slow cooker, mix the beef with the onion, paprika and the other ingredients except the pasta, toss, put the lid on and cook on Low for 5 hours and 30 minutes. Add the pasta, stir, put the lid on again and cook on Low for 30 minutes more. Divide everything between plates and serve.

NUTRITION:
calories 300, fat 6, fiber 8, carbs 18, protein 17

Sweet Turkey

Preparation time: 8 hours
Cooking time: 3 hours and 30 minutes
Servings: 12

INGREDIENTS:
14 ounces chicken stock
¼ cup brown sugar
½ cup lemon juice
¼ cup lime juice
¼ cup sage, chopped
¼ cup cider vinegar
2 tablespoons mustard
¼ cup olive oil
1 tablespoon marjoram, chopped
1 teaspoon sweet paprika
Salt and black pepper to the taste
1 teaspoon garlic powder
2 turkey breast halves, boneless and skinless

DIRECTIONS:
In your blender, mix stock with brown sugar, lemon juice, lime juice, sage, vinegar, mustard, oil, marjoram, paprika, salt, pepper and garlic powder and pulse well. Put turkey breast halves in a bowl, add blender mix, cover and leave aside in the fridge for 8 hours. Transfer everything to your Slow cooker, cover and cook on High for 3 hours and 30 minutes. Divide between plates and serve for lunch.

NUTRITION:
calories 219, fat 4, fiber 1, carbs 5, protein 36

Honey Lamb Roast

Preparation time: 10 minutes
Cooking time: 7 hours
Servings: 2

INGREDIENTS:
1 pound lamb roast, sliced
3 tablespoons honey
½ tablespoon basil, dried
½ tablespoons oregano, dried
1 tablespoon garlic, minced
1 tablespoon olive oil
Salt and black pepper to the taste
½ cup beef stock

DIRECTIONS:
In your slow cooker, mix the lamb roast with the honey, basil and the other ingredients, toss well, put the lid on and cook on Low for 7 hours. Divide everything between plates and serve.

NUTRITION:
calories 374, fat 6, fiber 8, carbs 29, protein 6

Beef Strips
Preparation time: 10 minutes
Cooking time: 6 hours
Servings: 4

INGREDIENTS:
½ pound baby mushrooms, sliced
1 yellow onion, chopped
1 pound beef sirloin steak, cubed
Salt and black pepper to the taste
1/3 cup red wine
2 teaspoons olive oil
2 cups beef stock
1 tablespoon Worcestershire sauce

DIRECTIONS:
In your Slow cooker, mix beef strips with onion, mushrooms, salt, pepper, wine, olive oil, beef stock and Worcestershire sauce, toss, cover and cook on Low for 6 hours. Divide between plates and serve for lunch.

NUTRITION:
calories 212, fat 7, fiber 1, carbs 8, protein 26

Worcestershire Beef Mix
Preparation time: 10 minutes
Cooking time: 8 hours
Servings: 2

INGREDIENTS:
1 pound beef stew meat, cubed
1 teaspoon chili powder
Salt and black pepper to the taste
1 cup beef stock
1 and ½ tablespoons Worcestershire sauce
1 teaspoon garlic, minced
2 ounces cream cheese, soft
Cooking spray

DIRECTIONS:
Grease your slow cooker with the cooking spray, and mix the beef with the stock and the other ingredients inside. Put the lid on, cook on Low for 8 hours, divide between plates and serve.

NUTRITION:
calories 372, fat 6, fiber 9, carbs 18, protein 22

BBQ Chicken Thighs
Preparation time: 10 minutes
Cooking time: 5 hours
Servings: 6

INGREDIENTS:
6 chicken thighs, skinless and boneless
1 yellow onion, chopped
½ teaspoon poultry seasoning
14 ounces canned tomatoes, chopped
8 ounces tomato sauce
½ cup bbq sauce
1 teaspoon garlic powder
¼ cup orange juice
½ teaspoon hot pepper sauce
¾ teaspoon oregano, dried
Salt and black pepper to the taste

DIRECTIONS:
In your Slow cooker, mix chicken with onion, poultry seasoning, tomatoes, tomato sauce, bbq sauce, garlic powder, orange juice, pepper sauce, oregano, salt and pepper, toss, cover and cook on Low for 5 hours. Divide between plates and serve with the sauce drizzled on top.

NUTRITION:
calories 211, fat 9, fiber 2, carbs 12, protein 23

Chickpeas Stew
Preparation time: 10 minutes
Cooking time: 6 hours
Servings: 2

INGREDIENTS:
½ tablespoon olive oil
1 red onion, chopped
2 garlic cloves, minced
1 red chili pepper, chopped
¼ cup carrots, chopped
6 ounces canned tomatoes, chopped
6 ounces canned chickpeas, drained
½ cup chicken stock
1 bay leaf
½ teaspoon coriander, ground
A pinch of red pepper flakes
½ tablespoon parsley, chopped
Salt and black pepper to the taste

DIRECTIONS:
In your slow cooker, mix the chickpeas with the

onion, garlic and the other ingredients, toss, put the lid on and cook on Low for 6 hours. Divide into bowls and serve.

NUTRITION:
calories 462, fat 7, fiber 9, carbs 30, protein 17

Fall Slow Cooker Roast
Preparation time: 10 minutes
Cooking time: 6 hours
Servings: 6

INGREDIENTS:
2 sweet potatoes, cubed
2 carrots, chopped
2 pounds beef chuck roast, cubed
¼ cup celery, chopped
1 tablespoon canola oil
2 garlic cloves, minced
1 yellow onion, chopped
1 tablespoon flour
1 tablespoon brown sugar
1 tablespoon sugar
1 teaspoon cumin, ground
Salt and black pepper to the taste
¾ teaspoon coriander, ground
½ teaspoon oregano, dried
1 teaspoon chili powder
1/8 teaspoon cinnamon powder
¾ teaspoon orange peel grated
15 ounces tomato sauce

DIRECTIONS:
In your Slow cooker, mix potatoes with carrots, beef cubes, celery, oil, garlic, onion, flour, brown sugar, sugar, cumin, salt pepper, coriander, oregano, chili powder, cinnamon, orange peel and tomato sauce, stir, cover and cook on Low for 6 hours. Divide into bowls and serve for lunch.

NUTRITION:
calories 278, fat 12, fiber 2, carbs 16, protein 25

Lentils Soup
Preparation time: 10 minutes
Cooking time: 4 hours
Servings: 2

INGREDIENTS:
2 garlic cloves, minced
1 carrot, chopped
1 red onion, chopped
3 cups veggie stock
1 cup brown lentils
½ teaspoon cumin, ground
1 bay leaf
1 tablespoon lime juice
1 tablespoon cilantro, chopped
Salt and black pepper to the taste

DIRECTIONS:
In your slow cooker, mix the lentils with the garlic, carrot and the other ingredients, toss, put the lid on and cook on High for 4 hours. Ladle the soup into bowls and serve.

NUTRITION:
calories 361, fat 7, fiber 7, carbs 16, protein 5

Creamy Chicken
Preparation time: 10 minutes
Cooking time: 8 hours and 30 minutes
Servings: 6

INGREDIENTS:
10 ounces canned cream of chicken soup
Salt and black pepper to the taste
A pinch of cayenne pepper
3 tablespoons flour
1 pound chicken breasts, skinless, boneless and cubed
1 celery rib, chopped
½ cup green bell pepper, chopped
¼ cup yellow onion, chopped
10 ounces peas
2 tablespoons pimientos, chopped

DIRECTIONS:
In your Slow cooker, mix cream of chicken with salt, pepper, cayenne and flour and whisk well. Add chicken, celery, bell pepper and onion, toss, cover and cook on Low for 8 hours. Add peas and pimientos, stir, cover and cook on Low for 30 minutes more. Divide into bowls and serve for lunch.

NUTRITION:
calories 200, fat 3, fiber 4, carbs 16, protein 17

Chicken Soup
Preparation time: 10 minutes
Cooking time: 7 hours
Servings: 2

INGREDIENTS:
½ pound chicken breast, skinless, boneless and cubed
3 cups chicken stock
1 red onion, chopped
1 garlic clove, minced
½ celery stalk, chopped
¼ teaspoon chili powder
¼ teaspoon sweet paprika
A pinch of salt and black pepper
A pinch of cayenne pepper
1 tablespoon lemon juice
½ tablespoon chives, chopped

DIRECTIONS:
In your slow cooker, mix the chicken with the stock, onion and the other ingredients, toss, put the lid on and cook on Low for 7 hours. Divide into bowls and serve right away.

NUTRITION:
calories 351, fat 6, fiber 7, carbs 17, protein 16

Chicken Stew

Preparation time: 10 minutes
Cooking time: 8 hours
Servings: 6

INGREDIENTS:

32 ounces chicken stock
3 spicy chicken sausage links, cooked and sliced
28 ounces canned tomatoes, chopped
1 yellow onion, chopped
1 cup lentils
1 carrot, chopped
2 garlic cloves, minced
1 celery rib, chopped
½ teaspoon thyme, dried
Salt and black pepper to the taste

DIRECTIONS:

In your Slow cooker, mix stock with sausage, tomatoes, onion, lentils, carrot, garlic, celery, thyme, salt and pepper, stir, cover and cook on Low for 8 hours. Divide into bowls and serve for lunch.

NUTRITION:
calories 231, fat 4, fiber 12, carbs 31, protein 15

Lime and Thyme Chicken

Preparation time: 10 minutes
Cooking time: 6 hours
Servings: 2

INGREDIENTS:

1 pound chicken thighs, boneless and skinless
Juice of 1 lime
1 tablespoon lime zest, grated
2 teaspoons olive oil
½ cup tomato sauce
2 garlic cloves, minced
1 tablespoon thyme, chopped
Salt and black pepper to the taste

DIRECTIONS:

In your slow cooker, mix the chicken with the lime juice, zest and the other ingredients, toss, put the lid on and cook on High for 6 hours. Divide between plates and serve right away.

NUTRITION:
calories 324, fat 7, fiber 8, carbs 20, protein 17

Lemon Chicken

Preparation time: 10 minutes
Cooking time: 5 hours
Servings: 6

INGREDIENTS:

6 chicken breast halves, skinless and bone in
Salt and black pepper to the taste
1 teaspoon oregano, dried
¼ cup water
2 tablespoons butter
3 tablespoons lemon juice
2 garlic cloves, minced
1 teaspoon chicken bouillon granules
2 teaspoons parsley, chopped

DIRECTIONS:

In your Slow cooker, mix chicken with salt, pepper, water, butter, lemon juice, garlic and chicken granules, stir, cover and cook on Low for 5 hours. Add parsley, stir, divide between plates and serve for lunch.

NUTRITION:
calories 336, fat 10, fiber 1, carbs 1, protein 46

Shrimp Gumbo

Preparation time: 10 minutes
Cooking time: 2 hours
Servings: 2

INGREDIENTS:

1 pound shrimp, peeled and deveined
½ pound pork sausage, sliced
1 red onion, chopped
½ green bell pepper, chopped
1 red chili pepper, minced
½ teaspoon cumin, ground
½ teaspoon coriander, ground
Salt and black pepper to the taste
1 cup tomato sauce
½ cup chicken stock
½ tablespoon Cajun seasoning
½ teaspoon oregano, dried

DIRECTIONS:

In your slow cooker, mix the shrimp with the sausage, onion and the other ingredients, toss, put the lid on and cook on High for 2 hours. Divide into bowls and serve.

NUTRITION:
calories 721, fat 36.7, fiber 3.7, carbs 18.2, protein 76.6

Chicken Noodle Soup

Preparation time: 10 minutes
Cooking time: 6 hours and 15 minutes
Servings: 4

INGREDIENTS:

1 and ½ pound chicken breast, boneless,

skinless and cubed
1 yellow onion, chopped
3 carrots, chopped
2 celery stalks, chopped
3 garlic cloves minced
2 bay leaves
1 cup water
6 cups chicken stock
1 teaspoon Italian seasoning
2 cup cheese tortellini
1 tablespoon parsley, chopped

DIRECTIONS:

In your Slow cooker, mix chicken with onion, carrots, celery, garlic, bay leaves, water, stock and seasoning, stir, cover and cook on Low for 6 hours. Add tortellini, stir, cover, cook on Low for 15 minutes more, ladle into bowls and serve for lunch.

NUTRITION:

calories 231, fat 3, fiber 4, carbs 17, protein 22

Squash and Chicken Soup

Preparation time: 10 minutes

Cooking time: 6 hours

Servings: 2

INGREDIENTS:

½ pound chicken thighs, skinless, boneless and cubed
½ small yellow onion, chopped
½ red bell pepper, chopped
½ green bell pepper, chopped
3 cups chicken stock
½ cup butternut squash, peeled and cubed
2 ounces canned green chilies, chopped
½ teaspoon oregano, dried
A pinch of salt and black pepper
½ tablespoon lime juice
1 tablespoon cilantro, chopped

DIRECTIONS:

In your slow cooker, mix the chicken with the onion, bell pepper and the other ingredients, toss, put the lid on and cook on High for 6 hours. Ladle the soup into bowls and serve.

NUTRITION:

calories 365, fat 11.2, fiber 10.2, carbs 31.4, protein 38

Lentils Soup

Preparation time: 10 minutes

Cooking time: 6 hours

Servings: 6

INGREDIENTS:

1 yellow onion, chopped
6 carrots, sliced
1 yellow bell pepper, chopped
4 garlic cloves, minced
A pinch of cayenne pepper
3 cups red lentils
4 cups chicken stock
Salt and black pepper to the taste
2 cups water
1 teaspoon lemon zest, grated
1 teaspoon lemon juice
1 tablespoon rosemary, chopped

DIRECTIONS:

In your Slow cooker, mix onion with carrots, bell pepper, garlic, cayenne, lentils, stock, salt, pepper and water, stir, cover and cook on Low for 6 hours. Add lemon zest, lemon juice and rosemary, stir, ladle into bowls and serve for lunch.

NUTRITION:

calories 281, fat 4, fiber 3, carbs 38, protein 17

Pork Soup

Preparation time: 10 minutes

Cooking time: 6 hours

Servings: 2

INGREDIENTS:

½ cup canned black beans, drained and rinsed
1 pound pork stew meat, cubed
3 cups beef stock
1 small red bell pepper, chopped
1 yellow onion, chopped
1 teaspoon Italian seasoning
½ tablespoon olive oil
Salt and black pepper to the taste
½ cup canned tomatoes, crushed
1 tablespoon basil, chopped

DIRECTIONS:

In your slow cooker, mix the pork with the beans, stock and the other ingredients, toss, put the lid on and cook on Low for 6 hours. Divide into bowls and serve.

NUTRITION:

calories 758, fat 27.9, fiber 9.9, carbs 42.1, protein 82.6

Taco Soup

Preparation time: 10 minutes

Cooking time: 6 hours

Servings: 4

INGREDIENTS:

1 tablespoon olive oil
4 red bell peppers, chopped
1 yellow onion, chopped
2 pounds beef, ground
2 tablespoons chili powder
2 tablespoons cumin, ground

Salt and black pepper to the taste
1 teaspoon cinnamon powder
1 teaspoon sweet paprika
½ teaspoon onion powder
½ teaspoon garlic powder
A pinch of cayenne pepper
24 ounces beef stock
28 ounces canned tomatoes, chopped
8 ounces canned green chilies, chopped
6 ounces coconut milk

DIRECTIONS:
In your Slow cooker, mix oil with bell peppers, onion, beef, chili powder, cumin, salt, pepper, cinnamon, paprika, onion powder, garlic powder, cayenne, stock, tomatoes chilies and coconut milk, stir well, cover and cook on Low for 6 hours. Ladle into bowls and serve for lunch.

NUTRITION:
calories 403, fat 12, fiber 4, carbs 14, protein 45

Mushroom Stew

Preparation time: 10 minutes

Cooking time: 6 hours

Servings: 2

INGREDIENTS:
1 pound white mushrooms, sliced
2 carrots, peeled and cubed
1 red onion, chopped
1 tablespoon olive oil
1 tablespoon balsamic vinegar
½ cup tomato sauce
Salt and black pepper to the taste
1 cup veggie stock
1 tablespoon basil, chopped

DIRECTIONS:
In your slow cooker, mix the mushrooms with the onion and the other ingredients, toss, put the lid on and cook on Low for 6 hours. Divide the stew into bowls and serve.

NUTRITION:
calories 400, fat 15, fiber 4, carbs 25, protein 14

Thai Chicken Soup

Preparation time: 10 minutes

Cooking time: 7 hours

Servings: 4

INGREDIENTS:
1 pound chicken breasts, skinless and boneless
1 cup wild rice
1 tablespoon olive oil
1 sweet potato, peeled and cubed
1 cup butternut squash, peeled and cubed
1 zucchini, chopped
1 green apple, cored and chopped
1 yellow onion, chopped
1 tablespoon ginger, grated
¼ cup red curry paste
4 garlic cloves, minced
2 tablespoons brown sugar
2 tablespoons fish sauce
2 tablespoons soy sauce
1 tablespoon basil, dried
1 teaspoon cumin, ground
Salt and black pepper to the taste
28 ounces coconut milk
5 cups chicken stock

DIRECTIONS:
In your Slow cooker, mix chicken with rice, oil, sweet potato, squash, zucchini, apple, onion, ginger, curry paste, garlic, sugar, fish, soy sauce, basil, cumin, salt, pepper, coconut milk and stock, stir, cover and cook on Low for 7 hours. Transfer meat to a cutting board, shred using 2 forks, return to slow cooker, stir, ladle soup into bowls and serve for lunch.

NUTRITION:
calories 300, fat 4, fiber 6, carbs 28, protein 17

Beans Chili

Preparation time: 10 minutes

Cooking time: 3 hours

Servings: 2

INGREDIENTS:
½ red bell pepper, chopped
½ green bell pepper, chopped
1 garlic clove, minced
½ cup yellow onion, chopped
½ cup roasted tomatoes, crushed
1 cup canned red kidney beans, drained
1 cup canned white beans, drained
1 cup canned black beans, drained
½ cup corn
Salt and black pepper to the taste
1 tablespoon chili powder
1 cup veggie stock

DIRECTIONS:
In your slow cooker, mix the peppers with the beans and the other ingredients, toss, put the lid on and cook on High for 3 hours. Divide into bowls and serve right away.

NUTRITION:
calories 400, fat 14, fiber 5, carbs 29, protein 22

Spinach and Mushroom Soup

Preparation time: 10 minutes

Cooking time: 3 hours

Servings: 6

INGREDIENTS:
2/3 cup yellow onion, chopped
16 ounces baby spinach
3 tablespoons butter
Salt and black pepper to the taste
5 cups veggie stock
3 garlic cloves, minced
½ teaspoon Italian seasoning
1 and ½ cups half and half
¼ teaspoon thyme, dried
16 ounces cheese tortellini
2 teaspoons garlic powder
3 cups mushrooms, sliced
½ cup parmesan, grated

DIRECTIONS:
Heat up a pan with the butter over medium-high heat, add onion, garlic, mushrooms and spinach, stir and cook for a few minutes. Transfer to your Slow cooker, add salt, pepper, stock, Italian seasoning, half and half, thyme, garlic powder and parmesan, cover and cook on High for 2 hours and 30 minutes. Add tortellini, stir, cover, cook on High for 30 minutes more, ladle into bowls and serve for lunch.

NUTRITION:
calories 231, fat 5, fiber 6, carbs 14, protein 5

Parsley Chicken Stew

Preparation time: 10 minutes

Cooking time: 4 hours

Servings: 2

INGREDIENTS:
1 tablespoon olive oil
Salt and black pepper to the taste
2 spring onions, chopped
1 carrot, peeled and sliced
¼ cup chicken stock
1 pound chicken breast, skinless, boneless sand cubed
½ cup tomato sauce
1 tablespoon parsley, chopped

DIRECTIONS:
In your slow cooker, mix the chicken with the spring onions and the other ingredients, toss, put the lid on and cook on High for 4 hours. Divide into bowls and serve.

NUTRITION:
calories 453, fat 15, fiber 5, carbs 20, protein 20

Creamy Chicken Soup

Preparation time: 10 minutes

Cooking time: 6 hours

Servings: 6

INGREDIENTS:
2 chicken breasts, skinless and boneless
1 cup yellow corn
1 cup peas
1 celery stalk, chopped
1 cup carrots, chopped
2 gold potatoes, cubed
4 ounces cream cheese, soft
1 yellow onion, chopped
4 cups chicken stock
2 teaspoons garlic powder
3 cups heavy cream
Salt and black pepper to the taste

DIRECTIONS:
In your Slow cooker, mix chicken with corn, peas, carrots, potatoes, celery, cream cheese, onion, garlic powder, stock, heavy cream, salt and pepper, stir, cover and cook on Low for 6 hours. Transfer chicken to a cutting board, shred meat using2 forks, return to the slow cooker, stir, ladle soup into bowls and serve for lunch.

NUTRITION:
calories 300, fat 6, fiber 5, carbs 20, protein 22

Mustard Short Ribs

Preparation time: 10 minutes

Cooking time: 8 hours

Servings: 2

INGREDIENTS:
2 beef short ribs, bone in and cut into individual ribs
Salt and black pepper to the taste
½ cup BBQ sauce
1 tablespoon mustard
1 tablespoon green onions, chopped

DIRECTIONS:
In your slow cooker, mix the ribs with the sauce and the other ingredients, toss, put the lid on and cook on Low for 8 hours. Divide the mix between plates and serve.

NUTRITION:
calories 284, fat 7, 4, carbs 18, protein 20

Black Bean Soup

Preparation time: 10 minutes

Cooking time: 6 hours

Servings: 6

INGREDIENTS:
1 pound black beans
2 celery stalks, chopped
2 garlic cloves, minced
1 yellow onion, chopped
2 carrots, chopped
1 tablespoon chili powder
1 cup salsa
1 teaspoon oregano,

dried
½ tablespoon cumin, ground
2 cups water
4 cups veggie stock

DIRECTIONS:
In your Slow cooker, mix beans with celery, garlic, onion, carrots, chili powder, salsa, oregano, cumin, water and stock, stir, cover and cook on Low for 6 hours. Blend soup using an immersion blender, ladle into bowls and serve for lunch.

NUTRITION:
calories 300, fat 4, fiber 7, carbs 20, protein 16

Creamy Brisket

Preparation time: 10 minutes

Cooking time: 8 hours

Servings: 2

INGREDIENTS:
1 tablespoon olive oil
1 shallot, chopped
2 garlic cloves, mined
1 pound beef brisket
Salt and black pepper to the taste
¼ cup beef stock
3 tablespoons heavy cream
1 tablespoon parsley, chopped

DIRECTIONS:
In your slow cooker, mix the brisket with the oil and the other ingredients, toss, put the lid on and cook on Low for 8 hours. Transfer the beef to a cutting board, slice, divide between plates and serve with the sauce drizzled all over.

NUTRITION:
calories 400, fat 10, fiber 4, carbs 15, protein 20

Winter Veggie Stew

Preparation time: 10 minutes

Cooking time: 4 hours

Servings: 8

INGREDIENTS:
1 yellow onion, chopped
1 teaspoon olive oil
2 red potatoes, chopped
Salt and black pepper to the taste
1 tablespoon sugar
1 tablespoon curry powder
1 tablespoon ginger, grated
3 garlic cloves, minced
30 ounces canned chickpeas, drained
1 green bell pepper, chopped
2 cups chicken stock
1 red bell pepper, chopped
1 cauliflower head, florets separated
28 ounces canned tomatoes, chopped
1 cup coconut milk
10 ounces baby spinach

DIRECTIONS:
In your slow cooker, mix oil with onion, potatoes, salt, pepper, sugar, curry powder, ginger, garlic, chickpeas, red and green bell pepper, stock, cauliflower, tomatoes, spinach and milk, stir, cover and cook on High for 4 minutes. Stir your stew again, divide into bowls and serve for lunch.

NUTRITION:
calories 319, fat 10, fiber 13, carbs 45, protein 14

Mushroom Soup

Preparation time: 10 minutes

Cooking time: 4 hours

Servings: 2

INGREDIENTS:
1 small yellow onion, chopped
1 carrot, chopped
1 small red bell pepper, chopped
1 green bell pepper, chopped
1 pound mushrooms, sliced
1 garlic clove, minced
½ teaspoon Italian seasoning
Salt and black pepper to the taste
3 cups chicken stock
½ cup half and half
1 tablespoon chives, chopped

DIRECTIONS:
In your slow cooker, mix the mushrooms with the onion, carrot and the other ingredients, toss, put the lid on and cook on High for 4 hours. Divide into bowls and serve.

NUTRITION:
calories 453, fat 14, fiber 6, carbs 28, protein 33

Chickpeas Stew

Preparation time: 10 minutes

Cooking time: 4 hours and 10 minutes

Servings: 6

INGREDIENTS:
1 yellow onion, chopped
1 tablespoon ginger, grated
1 tablespoon olive oil
6 ounces canned chickpeas, drained
4 garlic cloves, minced
Salt and black pepper to the taste
2 red Thai chilies, chopped
½ teaspoon turmeric powder
2 tablespoons garam masala
4 ounces tomato paste
2 cups chicken stock
2 tablespoons cilantro, chopped

DIRECTIONS:
Heat up a pan with the oil over medium-high

heat, add ginger and onions, stir and cook for 4-5 minutes. Add garlic, salt, pepper, Thai chilies, garam masala and turmeric, stir, cook for 2 minutes more and transfer everything to your slow cooker. Add stock, chickpeas and tomato paste, stir, cover and cook on Low for 4 hours. Add cilantro, stir, divide into bowls and serve for lunch.

NUTRITION:
calories 225, fat 7, fiber 4, carbs 14, protein 7

Creamy Potato Soup

Preparation time: 10 minutes

Cooking time: 5 hours

Servings: 2

INGREDIENTS:
1 small yellow onion, chopped
3 cups chicken stock
½ pound red potatoes, peeled and cubed
1 teaspoon turmeric powder
½ cup heavy whipping cream
2 ounces cream cheese, cubed
1 tablespoon chives, chopped

DIRECTIONS:
In your slow cooker, mix the potatoes with the stock, onion and the other ingredients, toss, put the lid on and cook on High for 5 hours. Divide into bowls and serve.

NUTRITION:
calories 372, fat 15, fiber 4, carbs 20, protein 22

Lentils Curry

Preparation time: 10 minutes

Cooking time: 8 hours

Servings: 16

INGREDIENTS:
4 garlic cloves, minced
4 cups brown lentils
2 yellow onions, chopped
1 tablespoon ginger, grated
4 tablespoons olive oil
1 tablespoon garam masala
4 tablespoons red curry paste
2 teaspoons sugar
1 and ½ teaspoons turmeric powder
A pinch of salt and black pepper
45 ounces canned tomato puree
½ cup coconut milk
1 tablespoon cilantro, chopped

DIRECTIONS:
In your slow cooker, mix lentils with onions, garlic, ginger, oil, curry paste, garam masala, turmeric, salt, pepper, sugar and tomato puree, stir, cover and cook on Low for 7 hours and 20 minutes. Add coconut milk and cilantro, stir, cover, cook on Low for 40 minutes, divide into bowls and serve for lunch.

NUTRITION:
calories 268, fat 5, fiber 4, carbs 18, protein 6

Chicken with Corn and Wild Rice

Preparation time: 10 minutes

Cooking time: 6 hours

Servings: 2

INGREDIENTS:
1 pound chicken breast, skinless, boneless and cubed
1 cup wild rice
1 cup chicken stock
1 tablespoon tomato paste
Salt and black pepper to the taste
¼ teaspoon cumin, ground
3 ounces canned roasted tomatoes, chopped
¼ cup corn
2 tablespoons cilantro, chopped

DIRECTIONS:
In your slow cooker, mix the chicken with the rice, stock and the other ingredients, toss, put the lid on and cook on Low for 6 hours. Divide everything between plates and serve.

NUTRITION:
calories 372, fat 12, fiber 5, carbs 20, protein 25

Quinoa Chili

Preparation time: 10 minutes

Cooking time: 3 hours

Servings: 4

INGREDIENTS:
15 ounces canned black beans, drained
2 and ¼ cups veggie stock
½ cup quinoa
14 ounces canned tomatoes, chopped
¼ cup red bell pepper, chopped
1 carrot, sliced
¼ cup green bell pepper, chopped
2 garlic cloves, minced
½ chili pepper, chopped
½ cup corn
2 teaspoons chili powder
1 small yellow onion, chopped
Salt and black pepper to the taste
1 teaspoon oregano, dried
1 teaspoon cumin, ground

DIRECTIONS:
In your slow cooker, mix black beans with stock, quinoa, tomatoes, red and green bell pepper, carrot, garlic, chili, chili powder, onion, salt, pepper, oregano, cumin and corn, stir, cover and cook on High for 3 hours. Divide chili into bowls and serve for lunch.

NUTRITION:
calories 291, fat 7, fiber 4, carbs 28, protein 8

Mixed Pork and Beans

Preparation time: 10 minutes

Cooking time: 8 hours

Servings: 2

INGREDIENTS:
- 1 cup canned black beans, drained
- 1 cup green beans, trimmed and halved
- ½ pound pork shoulder, cubed
- Salt and black pepper to the taste
- 3 garlic cloves, minced
- ½ yellow onion, chopped
- ½ cup beef stock
- ¼ tablespoon balsamic vinegar
- 1 tablespoon olive oil

DIRECTIONS:
In your slow cooker, mix the beans with the pork and the other ingredients, toss, put the lid on and cook on Low for 8 hours. Divide everything between plates and serve.

NUTRITION:
calories 453, fat 10, fiber 12, carbs 20, protein 36

French Veggie Stew

Preparation time: 10 minutes

Cooking time: 9 hours

Servings: 6

INGREDIENTS:
- 2 yellow onions, chopped
- 1 eggplant, sliced
- 4 zucchinis, sliced
- 2 garlic cloves, minced
- 2 green bell peppers, cut into medium strips
- 6 ounces canned tomato paste
- 2 tomatoes, cut into medium wedges
- 1 teaspoon oregano, dried
- 1 teaspoon sugar
- 1 teaspoon basil, dried
- Salt and black pepper to the taste
- 2 tablespoons parsley, chopped
- ¼ cup olive oil
- A pinch of red pepper flakes, crushed

DIRECTIONS:
In your Slow cooker, mix oil with onions, eggplant, zucchinis, garlic, bell peppers, tomato paste, basil, sugar, oregano, salt and pepper, cover and cook on Low for 9 hours. Add pepper flakes and parsley, stir gently, divide into bowls and serve for lunch.

NUTRITION:
calories 269, fat 7, fiber 6, carbs 17, protein 4

Pork Chops and Butter Sauce

Preparation time: 10 minutes

Cooking time: 7 hours

Servings: 2

INGREDIENTS:
- ½ pound pork loin chops
- 2 tablespoons butter
- 2 scallions, chopped
- 1 cup beef stock
- 1 garlic clove, minced
- ¼ teaspoon thyme, dried
- Salt and black pepper to the taste
- ¼ cup heavy cream
- ¼ tablespoon cornstarch
- ½ teaspoon basil, dried

DIRECTIONS:
In your slow cooker, mix the pork chops with the butter, scallions and the other ingredients, toss, put the lid on and cook on Low for 7 hours. Divide everything between plates and serve.

NUTRITION:
calories 453, fat 16, fiber 8, carbs 7, protein 27

Beans and Rice

Preparation time: 10 minutes

Cooking time: 3 hours

Servings: 6

INGREDIENTS:
- 1 pound pinto beans, dried
- 1/3 cup hot sauce
- Salt and black pepper to the taste
- 1 tablespoon garlic, minced
- 1 teaspoon garlic powder
- ½ teaspoon cumin, ground
- 1 tablespoon chili powder
- 3 bay leaves
- ½ teaspoon oregano, dried
- 1 cup white rice, cooked

DIRECTIONS:
In your slow cooker, mix pinto beans with hot sauce, salt, pepper, garlic, garlic powder, cumin, chili powder, bay leaves and oregano, stir, cover and cook on High for 3 hours. Divide rice between plates, add pinto beans on top and serve for lunch

NUTRITION:
calories 381, fat 7, fiber 12, carbs 35, protein 10

Chicken and Peach Mix
Preparation time: 10 minutes
Cooking time: 6 hours
Servings: 2

INGREDIENTS:
1 pound chicken breast, skinless and boneless
1 cup peaches, cubed
½ tablespoon avocado oil
½ cup chicken stock
1 tablespoon balsamic vinegar
½ teaspoon garlic, minced
¼ cup cherry tomatoes, halved
1 tablespoon basil, chopped

DIRECTIONS:
In your slow cooker, mix the chicken with the peaches, oil and the other ingredients, toss, put the lid on and cook on Low for 6 hours. Divide everything between plates and serve.

NUTRITION:
calories 300, fat 7, fiber 8, carbs 20, protein 39

Black Beans Stew
Preparation time: 10 minutes
Cooking time: 6 hours and 20 minutes
Servings: 6

INGREDIENTS:
1 yellow onion, chopped
1 tablespoon olive oil
1 red bell pepper, chopped
1 jalapeno, chopped
2 garlic cloves, minced
1 teaspoon ginger, grated
½ teaspoon cumin
½ teaspoon allspice, ground
½ teaspoon oregano, dried
30 ounces canned black beans, drained
½ teaspoon sugar
1 cup chicken stock
Salt and black pepper
3 cups brown rice, cooked
2 mangoes, peeled and chopped

DIRECTIONS:
Heat up a pan with the oil over medium-high heat, add onion, stir and cook for 3-4 minutes, Add garlic, ginger and jalapeno, stir, cook for 3 minutes more and transfer to your slow cooker. Add red bell pepper, cumin, allspice, oregano, black beans, sugar, stock, salt and pepper, stir, cover and cook on Low for 6 hours. Add rice and mangoes, stir, cover, cook on Low for 10 minutes more, divide between plates and serve.

NUTRITION:
calories 490, fat 6, fiber 20, carbs 80, protein 17

Chicken Drumsticks and Buffalo Sauce
Preparation time: 10 minutes
Cooking time: 8 hours
Servings: 2

INGREDIENTS:
1 pound chicken drumsticks
2 tablespoons buffalo wing sauce
½ cup chicken stock
2 tablespoons honey
1 teaspoon lemon juice
Salt and black pepper to the taste

DIRECTIONS:
In your slow cooker, mix the chicken with the sauce and the other ingredients, toss, put the lid on and cook on Low for 8 hours. Divide everything between plates and serve.

NUTRITION:
calories 361, fat 7, fiber 8, carbs 18, protein 22

Sweet Potato Stew
Preparation time: 10 minutes
Cooking time: 8 hours
Servings: 8

INGREDIENTS:
1 yellow onion, chopped
½ cup red beans, dried
2 red bell peppers, chopped
2 tablespoons ginger, grated
4 garlic cloves, minced
2 pounds sweet, peeled and cubed
3 cups chicken stock
14 ounces canned tomatoes, chopped
2 jalapeno peppers, chopped
Salt and black pepper to the taste
½ teaspoon cumin, ground
½ teaspoon coriander, ground
¼ teaspoon cinnamon powder
¼ cup peanuts, roasted and chopped
Juice of ½ lime

DIRECTIONS:
In your slow cooker, mix onion with red beans, red bell peppers, ginger, garlic, potatoes, stock, tomatoes, jalapenos, salt, pepper, cumin, coriander and cinnamon, stir, cover and cook on Low for 8 hours. Divide into bowls, divide peanuts on top, drizzle lime juice and serve for lunch.

NUTRITION:
calories 259, fat 8, fiber 7, carbs 42, protein 8

Mustard Pork Chops and Carrots

Preparation time: 10 minutes
Cooking time: 4 hours
Servings: 2

INGREDIENTS:
1 tablespoon butter
1 pound pork chops, bone in
2 carrots, sliced
1 cup beef stock
½ tablespoon honey
½ tablespoon lime juice
1 tablespoon lime zest, grated

DIRECTIONS:
In your slow cooker, mix the pork chops with the butter and the other ingredients, toss, put the lid on and cook on High for 4 hours. Divide between plate sand serve.

NUTRITION:
calories 300, fat 8, fiber 10, carbs 16, protein 16

Minestrone Soup

Preparation time: 10 minutes
Cooking time: 4 hours
Servings: 8

INGREDIENTS:
2 zucchinis, chopped
3 carrots, chopped
1 yellow onion, chopped
1 cup green beans, halved
3 celery stalks, chopped
4 garlic cloves, minced
10 ounces canned garbanzo beans
1 pound lentils, cooked
4 cups veggie stock
28 ounces canned tomatoes, chopped
1 teaspoon curry powder
½ teaspoon garam masala
½ teaspoon cumin, ground
Salt and black pepper to the taste

DIRECTIONS:
In your slow cooker, mix zucchinis with carrots, onion, green beans, celery, garlic, garbanzo beans, lentils, stock, tomatoes, salt, pepper, cumin, curry powder and garam masala, stir, cover, cook on High for 4 hours, ladle into bowls and serve for lunch.

NUTRITION:
calories 273, fat 12, fiber 7, carbs 34, protein 10

Fennel Soup

Preparation time: 10 minutes
Cooking time: 4 hours
Servings: 2

INGREDIENTS:
2 fennel bulbs, sliced
½ cup tomatoes, crushed
1 red onion, sliced
1 leek, chopped
2 cups veggie stock
½ teaspoon cumin, ground
1 tablespoon dill, chopped
½ tablespoon olive oil
Salt and black pepper to the taste

DIRECTIONS:
In your slow cooker, mix the fennel with the tomatoes, onion and the other ingredients, toss, put the lid on and cook on High for 4 hours. Ladle into bowls and serve hot.

NUTRITION:
calories 132, fat 2, fiber 5, carbs 11, protein 3

Chili Cream

Preparation time: 10 minutes
Cooking time: 6 hours
Servings: 6

INGREDIENTS:
2 jalapeno chilies, chopped
1 cup yellow onion, chopped
1 tablespoon olive oil
4 poblano chilies, chopped
4 Anaheim chilies, chopped
3 cups corn
6 cups veggie stock
½ bunch cilantro, chopped
Salt and black pepper to the taste

DIRECTIONS:
In your slow cooker, mix jalapenos with onion, oil, poblano chilies, Anaheim chilies, corn and stock, stir, cover and cook on Low for 6 hours. Add cilantro, salt and pepper, stir, transfer to your blender, pulse well, divide into bowls and serve for lunch.

NUTRITION:
calories 209, fat 5, fiber 5, carbs 33, protein 5

Artichoke Soup

Preparation time: 10 minutes
Cooking time: 5 hours
Servings: 2

INGREDIENTS:
2 cups canned artichoke hearts, drained and halved
1 small carrot, chopped
1 small yellow onion, chopped
1 garlic clove, minced
¼ teaspoon oregano, dried
¼ teaspoon rosemary,

dried
A pinch of red pepper flakes
A pinch of garlic powder
1 tablespoon cilantro, chopped
A pinch of salt and black pepper
3 cups chicken stock
1 tablespoon tomato paste

DIRECTIONS:
In your slow cooker, mix the artichokes with the carrot, onion and the other ingredients, toss, put the lid on and cook on Low for 5 hours. Ladle into bowls and serve.

NUTRITION:
calories 362, fat 3, fiber 5, carbs 16, protein 5

Salmon and Cilantro Sauce
Preparation time: 10 minutes
Cooking time: 2 hours and 30 minutes
Servings: 4

INGREDIENTS:
2 garlic cloves, minced
4 salmon fillets, boneless
¾ cup cilantro, chopped
3 tablespoons lime juice
1 tablespoon olive oil
Salt and black pepper to the taste

DIRECTIONS:
Grease your Slow cooker with the oil, add salmon fillets inside skin side down, also add garlic, cilantro, lime juice, salt and pepper, cover and cook on Low for 2 hours and 30 minutes. Divide salmon fillets on plates, drizzle the cilantro sauce all over and serve for lunch.

NUTRITION:
calories 200, fat 3, fiber 2, carbs 14, protein 8

Beans and Mushroom Stew
Preparation time: 10 minutes
Cooking time: 8 hours
Servings: 2

INGREDIENTS:
Cooking spray
½ green bell pepper, chopped
½ red bell pepper, chopped
½ red onion, chopped
2 garlic cloves, minced
1 cup tomatoes, cubed
1 cup veggie stock
Salt and black pepper
to the taste
1 cup white mushrooms, sliced
1 cup canned kidney beans, drained
½ teaspoon turmeric powder
½ teaspoon coriander, ground
1 tablespoon parsley, chopped
½ tablespoon Cajun seasoning

DIRECTIONS:
Grease the slow cooker with the cooking spray and mix the bell peppers with the onion, garlic and the other ingredients into the pot. Put the lid on, cook on Low for 8 hours, divide into bowls and serve.

NUTRITION:
calories 272, fat 4, fiber 7, carbs 19, protein 7

Chili Salmon
Preparation time: 10 minutes
Cooking time: 2 hours
Servings: 2

INGREDIENTS:
2 medium salmon fillets, boneless
A pinch of nutmeg, ground
A pinch of cloves, ground
A pinch of ginger powder
Salt and black pepper to the taste
2 teaspoons sugar
1 teaspoon onion powder
¼ teaspoon chipotle chili powder
½ teaspoon cayenne pepper
½ teaspoon cinnamon, ground
1/8 teaspoon thyme, dried

DIRECTIONS:
In a bowl, mix salmon fillets with nutmeg, cloves, ginger, salt, coconut sugar, onion powder, chili powder, cayenne black pepper, cinnamon and thyme, toss, transfer fish to 2 tin foil pieces, wrap, add to your Slow cooker, cover and cook on Low for 2 hours. Unwrap fish, divide between plates and serve with a side salad for lunch.

NUTRITION:
calories 220, fat 4, fiber 2, carbs 7, protein 4

Chicken and Eggplant Stew
Preparation time: 10 minutes
Cooking time: 8 hours
Servings: 2

INGREDIENTS:
1 cup tomato paste
½ cup chicken stock
1 pound chicken breast, skinless, boneless and cubed
2 eggplants, cubed
1 small red onion, chopped
1 red bell pepper, chopped
½ teaspoon rosemary, dried

½ tablespoon smoked paprika
1 teaspoon cumin, ground
Cooking spray
Salt and black pepper to the taste
Juice of ½ lemon
½ tablespoon parsley, chopped

DIRECTIONS:
In your slow cooker, mix the chicken with the stock, tomato paste and the other ingredients, toss, put the lid on and cook on Low for 8 hours. Divide into bowls and serve for lunch.

NUTRITION:
calories 261, fat 4, fiber 6, carbs 14, protein 7

Pulled Chicken

Preparation time: 10 minutes
Cooking time: 6 hours
Servings: 2

INGREDIENTS:
2 tomatoes, chopped
2 red onions, chopped
2 chicken breasts, skinless and boneless
2 garlic cloves, minced
1 tablespoon maple syrup
1 teaspoon chili powder
1 teaspoon basil, dried
3 tablespoons water
1 teaspoon cloves, ground

DIRECTIONS:
In your Slow cooker, mix onion with tomatoes, chicken, garlic, maple syrup, chili powder, basil, water and cloves, toss well, cover and cook on Low for 6 hours. Shred chicken, divide it along with the veggies between plates and serve for lunch.

NUTRITION:
calories 220, fat 3, fiber 3, carbs 14, protein 6

Turmeric Lentils Stew

Preparation time: 10 minutes
Cooking time: 5 hours
Servings: 2

INGREDIENTS:
2 cups veggie stock
½ cup canned red lentils, drained
1 carrot, sliced
1 eggplant, cubed
½ cup tomatoes, chopped
1 red onion, chopped
1 garlic clove, minced
1 teaspoon turmeric powder
¼ tablespoons ginger, grated
½ teaspoons mustard seeds
¼ teaspoon sweet paprika
½ cup tomato paste
1 tablespoon dill, chopped
Salt and black pepper to the taste

DIRECTIONS:
In your slow cooker, combine the lentils with the stock, tomatoes, eggplant and the other ingredients, toss, put the lid on, cook on High for 5 hours, divide into bowls and serve.

NUTRITION:
calories 303, fat 4, fiber 8, carbs 12, protein 4

Chicken Chili

Preparation time: 10 minutes
Cooking time: 7 hours
Servings: 4

INGREDIENTS:
16 ounces salsa
8 chicken thighs
1 yellow onion, chopped
16 ounces canned tomatoes, chopped
1 red bell pepper, chopped
2 tablespoons chili powder

DIRECTIONS:
Put the salsa in your slow cooker, add chicken, onion, tomatoes, bell pepper and chili powder, stir, cover, cook on Low for 7 hours, divide into bowls and serve for lunch.

NUTRITION:
calories 250, fat 3, fiber 3, carbs 14, protein 8

Pork Chili

Preparation time: 10 minutes
Cooking time: 10 hours
Servings: 2

INGREDIENTS:
1 pound pork stew meat, cubed
1 red onion, sliced
1 carrot, sliced
1 teaspoon sweet paprika
½ teaspoon cumin, ground
1 cup tomato paste
1 cup veggie stock
2 tablespoons chili powder
2 teaspoons cayenne pepper
1 tablespoon red pepper flakes
A pinch of salt and black pepper
1 red bell pepper, chopped
1 yellow bell pepper, chopped
1 tablespoon chives, chopped

DIRECTIONS:
In your slow cooker, mix the pork meat with the onion, carrot and the other ingredients, toss, put

the lid on and cook on Low for 10 hours. Divide the mix into bowls and serve.

NUTRITION:
calories 261, fat 7, fiber 4, carbs 8, protein 18

Salsa Chicken

Preparation time: 10 minutes
Cooking time: 7 hours
Servings: 4

INGREDIENTS:
4 chicken breasts, skinless and boneless
½ cup veggie stock
Salt and black pepper to the taste
16 ounces salsa
1 and ½ tablespoons parsley, dried
1 teaspoon garlic powder
½ tablespoon cilantro, chopped
1 teaspoon onion powder
½ tablespoons oregano, dried
½ teaspoon paprika, smoked
1 teaspoon chili powder
½ teaspoon cumin, ground

DIRECTIONS:
Put the stock in your slow cooker, add chicken breasts, add salsa, parsley, garlic powder, cilantro, onion powder, oregano, paprika, chili powder, cumin, salt and black pepper to the taste, stir, cover and cook on Low for 7 hours. Divide chicken between plates, drizzle the sauces on top and serve for lunch.

NUTRITION:
calories 270, fat 4, fiber 2, carbs 14, protein 9

Cinnamon Pork Ribs

Preparation time: 10 minutes
Cooking time: 8 hours
Servings: 2

INGREDIENTS:
2 pounds baby back pork ribs
1 tablespoon cinnamon powder
2 tablespoons olive oil
½ teaspoon allspice, ground
A pinch of salt and black pepper
½ teaspoon garlic powder
1 tablespoon balsamic vinegar
½ cup beef stock
1 tablespoon tomato paste

DIRECTIONS:
In your slow cooker, mix the pork ribs with the cinnamon, the oil and the other ingredients, toss, put the lid on and cook on Low for 8 hours. Divide ribs between plates and serve for lunch with a side salad.

NUTRITION:
calories 312, fat 7, fiber 7, carbs 8, protein 18

Thai Chicken

Preparation time: 10 minutes
Cooking time: 4 hours
Servings: 6

INGREDIENTS:
1 and ½ pound chicken breast, boneless, skinless and cubed
1 tablespoon olive oil
3 tablespoons soy sauce
2 tablespoons flour
Salt and black pepper to the taste
1 tablespoon ketchup
2 tablespoons white vinegar
1 teaspoon ginger, grated
2 tablespoons sugar
½ cup cashews, chopped
2 garlic cloves, minced
1 green onion, chopped

DIRECTIONS:
Put chicken pieces in a bowl, season with salt, black pepper, add flour and toss well. Heat up a pan with the oil over medium-high heat, add chicken, cook for 5 minutes and transfer to your slow cooker. Add soy sauce, ketchup, vinegar, ginger, sugar and garlic, stir well, cover, cook on Low for 4 hours, add cashews and green onion, stir, divide into bowls and serve for lunch.

NUTRITION:
calories 200, fat 3, fiber 2, carbs 13, protein 12

Pork and Mushroom Stew

Preparation time: 10 minutes
Cooking time: 7 hours
Servings: 2

INGREDIENTS:
2 tablespoons olive oil
1 garlic clove, minced
1 red onion, sliced
2 pounds pork stew meat, cubed
1 cup mushrooms, sliced
1 cup tomato paste
A pinch of salt and black pepper
1 teaspoon oregano, dried
1 teaspoon rosemary, dried
½ teaspoon nutmeg, ground
1 and ½ cups veggie stock
1 tablespoon chives, chopped

DIRECTIONS:
Grease the slow cooker with the oil, add the meat, onion, garlic and the other ingredients, toss, put

the lid on and cook on Low for 7 hours. Divide into bowls and serve for lunch.

NUTRITION:
calories 345, fat 7, fiber 5, carbs 14, protein 32

Turkey Chili

Preparation time: 10 minutes
Cooking time: 4 hours
Servings: 8

INGREDIENTS:

1 red bell pepper, chopped
2 pounds turkey meat, ground
28 ounces canned tomatoes, chopped
1 red onion, chopped
1 green bell pepper, chopped
4 tablespoons tomato paste
1 tablespoon oregano, dried
3 tablespoon chili powder
3 tablespoons cumin, ground
Salt and black pepper to the taste

DIRECTIONS:
Heat up a pan over medium-high heat, add turkey, brown it for a few minutes, transfer to your slow cooker, add red and green bell pepper, onion, tomatoes, tomato paste, chili powder, oregano, cumin, salt and black pepper to the taste, stir, cover and cook on High for 4 hours. Divide into bowls and serve for lunch.

NUTRITION:
calories 225, fat 6, fiber 4, carbs 15, protein 18

Pork and Tomatoes Mix

Preparation time: 10 minutes
Cooking time: 8 hours
Servings: 2

INGREDIENTS:

1 and ½ pounds pork stew meat, cubed
1 cup cherry tomatoes, halved
1 cup tomato paste
1 tablespoon rosemary, chopped
½ teaspoon sweet paprika
½ teaspoon coriander, ground
A pinch of salt and black pepper
1 tablespoon chives, chopped

DIRECTIONS:
In your Crockpot, combine the meat with the tomatoes, tomato paste and the other ingredients, toss, put the lid on and cook on Low for 8 hours. Divide between plates and serve for lunch.

NUTRITION:
calories 352, fat 8, fiber 4, carbs 10, protein 27

Turkey and Potatoes

Preparation time: 10 minutes
Cooking time: 8 hours
Servings: 4

INGREDIENTS:

3 pounds turkey breast, skinless and boneless
1 cup cranberries, chopped
2 sweet potatoes, chopped
½ cup raisins
½ cup walnuts, chopped
1 sweet onion, chopped
2 tablespoons lemon juice
1 cup sugar
1 teaspoon ginger, grated
½ teaspoon nutmeg, ground
1 teaspoon cinnamon powder
½ cup veggie stock
1 teaspoon poultry seasoning
Salt and black pepper to the taste
3 tablespoons olive oil

DIRECTIONS:
Heat up a pan with the oil over medium-high heat, add cranberries, walnuts, raisins, onion, lemon juice, sugar, ginger, nutmeg, cinnamon, stock and black pepper, stir well and bring to a simmer. Place turkey breast in your slow cooker, add sweet potatoes, cranberries mix and poultry seasoning, cover and cook on Low for 8 hours. Slice turkey breast and divide between plates, add sweet potatoes, drizzle sauce from the slow cooker and serve for lunch.

NUTRITION:
calories 264, fat 4, fiber 6, carbs 8, protein 15

Pesto Pork Shanks

Preparation time: 10 minutes
Cooking time: 7 hours
Servings: 2

INGREDIENTS:

1 and ½ pounds pork shanks
1 tablespoon olive oil
2 tablespoons basil pesto
1 red onion, sliced
1 cup beef stock
½ cup tomato paste
4 garlic cloves, minced
1 tablespoon oregano, chopped
Zest and juice of 1 lemon
A pinch of salt and black pepper

DIRECTIONS:
In your slow cooker, mix the pork shanks with

the oil, pesto and the other ingredients, toss, put the lid on and cook on Low for 7 hours. Divide everything between plates and serve for lunch.

NUTRITION:
calories 372, fat 7, fiber 5, carbs 12, protein 37

Chicken Thighs Mix

Preparation time: 10 minutes
Cooking time: 6 hours
Servings: 6

INGREDIENTS:
- 2 and ½ pounds chicken thighs, skinless and boneless
- 1 and ½ tablespoon olive oil
- 2 yellow onions, chopped
- 1 teaspoon cinnamon powder
- ¼ teaspoon cloves, ground
- ¼ teaspoon allspice, ground
- Salt and black pepper to the taste
- A pinch of saffron
- A handful pine nuts
- A handful mint, chopped

DIRECTIONS:
In a bowl, mix oil with onions, cinnamon, allspice, cloves, salt, pepper and saffron, whisk and transfer to your slow cooker. Add the chicken, toss well, cover and cook on Low for 6 hours. Sprinkle pine nuts and mint on top before serving,

NUTRITION:
calories 223, fat 3, fiber 2, carbs 6, protein 13

Potato Stew

Preparation time: 10 minutes
Cooking time: 5 hours and 5 minutes
Servings: 4

INGREDIENTS:
- ½ tablespoon olive oil
- 1 pound gold potatoes, peeled and cut into wedges
- 1 red onion, sliced
- 1 cup tomato paste
- ½ cup beef stock
- 1 carrot, sliced
- 1 red bell pepper, cubed
- 4 garlic cloves, minced
- 1 teaspoon sweet paprika
- 1 tablespoon chives, chopped

DIRECTIONS:
Heat up a pan with the oil over medium-high heat, add the onion and garlic, sauté for 5 minutes and transfer to the slow cooker. Add the potatoes and the other ingredients, toss, put the lid on and cook on Low for 5 hours. Divide the stew into bowls and serve for lunch.

NUTRITION:
calories 273, fat 6, fiber 7, carbs 10, protein 17

Chicken and Stew

Preparation time: 10 minutes
Cooking time: 5 hours
Servings: 4

INGREDIENTS:
- 4 chicken breasts, skinless and boneless
- 6 Italian sausages, sliced
- 5 garlic cloves, minced
- 1 white onion, chopped
- 1 teaspoon Italian seasoning
- A drizzle of olive oil
- 1 teaspoon garlic powder
- 29 ounces canned tomatoes, chopped
- 15 ounces tomato sauce
- 1 cup water
- ½ cup balsamic vinegar

DIRECTIONS:
Put chicken and sausage slices in your slow cooker, add garlic, onion, Italian seasoning, oil, tomatoes, tomato sauce, garlic powder, water and the vinegar, cover and cook on High for 5 hours. Stir the stew, divide between plates and serve for lunch

NUTRITION:
calories 267, fat 4, fiber 3, carbs 15, protein 13

Chicken and Rice

Preparation time: 10 minutes
Cooking time: 6 hours
Servings: 2

INGREDIENTS:
- 1 pound chicken breast, skinless, boneless and cubed
- 1 red onion, sliced
- 2 spring onions, chopped
- Cooking spray
- 1 cup wild rice
- 2 cups chicken stock
- ½ teaspoon garam masala
- ½ teaspoon turmeric powder
- 1 tablespoon cilantro, chopped
- A pinch of salt and black pepper

DIRECTIONS:
Grease the slow cooker with the cooking spray, add the chicken, rice, onion and the other ingredients, toss, put the lid on and cook on Low for 6 hours. Divide the mix into bowls and serve for lunch.

NUTRITION:
calories 362, fat 8, fiber 8, carbs 10, protein 26

Chicken and Cabbage Mix

Preparation time: 10 minutes
Cooking time: 5 hours and 20 minutes
Servings: 6

INGREDIENTS:
6 garlic cloves, minced
4 scallions, sliced
1 cup veggie stock
1 tablespoon olive oil
2 teaspoons sugar
1 tablespoon soy sauce
1 teaspoon ginger, minced
2 pounds chicken thighs, skinless and boneless
2 cups cabbage, shredded

DIRECTIONS:
In your Slow cooker, mix stock with oil, scallions, garlic, sugar, soy sauce, ginger and chicken, stir, cover and cook on Low for 5 hours. Transfer chicken to plates, add cabbage to the slow cooker, cover, cook on High for 20 minutes more, add next to the chicken and serve for lunch.

NUTRITION:
calories 240, fat 3, fiber 4, carbs 14, protein 10

Salmon Stew

Preparation time: 10 minutes
Cooking time: 2 hours
Servings: 4

INGREDIENTS:
1 pound salmon fillets, boneless and roughly cubed
1 cup chicken stock
½ cup tomato paste
½ red onion, sliced
1 carrot, sliced
1 sweet potato, peeled and cubed
1 tablespoon cilantro, chopped
Cooking spray
½ cup mild salsa
2 garlic cloves, minced
A pinch of salt and black pepper

DIRECTIONS:
In your slow cooker, mix the fish with the stock, tomato paste, onion and the other ingredients, toss gently, put the lid on and cook on Low for 2 hours Divide the mix into bowls and serve for lunch.

NUTRITION:
calories 292, fat 6, fiber 7, carbs 12, protein 22

Pork and Chorizo Lunch Mix

Preparation time: 10 minutes
Cooking time: 4 hours
Servings: 8

INGREDIENTS:
1 pound chorizo, ground
1 pound pork, ground
3 tablespoons olive oil
1 tomato, chopped
1 avocado, pitted, peeled and chopped
Salt and black pepper to the taste
1 small red onion, chopped
2 tablespoons enchilada sauce

DIRECTIONS:
Heat up a pan with the oil over medium-high heat, add pork, stir, brown for a couple of minutes, transfer to your slow cooker, add salt, pepper, chorizo, onion and enchilada sauce, stir, cover and cook on Low for 4 hours. Divide between plates and serve with chopped tomato and avocado on top.

NUTRITION:
calories 300, fat 12, fiber 3, carbs 15, protein 17

Paprika Pork and Chickpeas

Preparation time: 10 minutes
Cooking time: 10 hours
Servings: 2

INGREDIENTS:
1 red onion, sliced
1 pound pork stew meat, cubed
1 cup canned chickpeas, drained
1 cup beef stock
1 cup tomato paste
½ teaspoon sweet paprika
½ teaspoon turmeric powder
A pinch of salt and black pepper
1 tablespoon hives, chopped

DIRECTIONS:
In your slow cooker, mix the onion with the meat, chickpeas, stock and the other ingredients, toss, put the lid on and cook on Low for 10 hours. Divide the mix between plates and serve for lunch.

NUTRITION:
calories 322, fat 6, fiber 6, carbs 9, protein 22

Lamb Stew

Preparation time: 10 minutes
Cooking time: 8 hours
Servings: 4

INGREDIENTS:
1 and ½ pounds lamb meat, cubed
¼ cup flour
Salt and black pepper to the taste
2 tablespoons olive oil
1 teaspoon rosemary, dried

1 onion, sliced
½ teaspoon thyme, dried
2 cups water
1 cup baby carrots
2 cups sweet potatoes, chopped

DIRECTIONS:
In a bowl, mix lamb with flour and toss. Heat up a pan with the oil over medium-high heat, add meat, brown it on all sides and transfer to your slow cooker. Add onion, salt, pepper, rosemary, thyme, water, carrots and sweet potatoes, cover and cook on Low for 8 hours. Divide lamb stew between plates and serve for lunch

NUTRITION:
calories 350, fat 8, fiber 3, carbs 20, protein 16

Beef and Cabbage

Preparation time: 10 minutes

Cooking time: 8 hours

Servings: 2

INGREDIENTS:
1 pound beef stew meat, cubed
1 cup green cabbage, shredded
1 cup red cabbage, shredded
1 carrot, grated
½ cup water
1 cup tomato paste
½ teaspoon sweet paprika
1 tablespoon chives, chopped
A pinch of salt and black pepper

DIRECTIONS:
In your slow cooker, mix the beef with the cabbage, carrot and the other ingredients, toss, put the lid on and cook on Low for 8 hours. Divide the mix between plates and serve for lunch.

NUTRITION:
calories 251, fat 6, fiber 7, carbs 12, protein 6

Lamb Curry

Preparation time: 10 minutes

Cooking time: 4 hours

Servings: 4

INGREDIENTS:
1 and ½ tablespoons sweet paprika
3 tablespoons curry powder
Salt and black pepper to the taste
2 pounds lamb meat, cubed
2 tablespoons olive oil
3 carrots, chopped
4 celery stalks, chopped
1 onion, chopped
4 celery stalks, chopped
1 cup chicken stock
4 garlic cloves minced
1 cup coconut milk

DIRECTIONS:
Heat up a pan with the oil over medium-high heat, add lamb meat, brown it on all sides and transfer to your slow cooker. Add stock, onions, celery and carrots to the slow cooker and stir everything gently. In a bowl, mix paprika with a pinch of salt, black pepper and curry powder and stir. Add spice mix to the cooker, also add coconut milk, cover, cook on High for 4 hours, divide into bowls and serve for lunch.

NUTRITION:
calories 300, fat 4, fiber 4, carbs 16, protein 13

Balsamic Beef Stew

Preparation time: 10 minutes

Cooking time: 6 hours

Servings: 2

INGREDIENTS:
1 pound beef stew meat, cubed
1 teaspoon sweet paprika
1 red onion, sliced
½ cup mushrooms, sliced
1 carrot, peeled and cubed
½ cup tomatoes, cubed
1 tablespoon balsamic vinegar
A pinch of salt and black pepper
1 teaspoon onion powder
1 teaspoon thyme, dried
1 cup beef stock
1 tablespoon cilantro, chopped

DIRECTIONS:
In your slow cooker, mix the beef with the paprika, onion, mushrooms and the other ingredients except the cilantro, toss, put the lid on and cook on Low for 6 hours. Divide into bowls and serve with the cilantro, sprinkled on top.

NUTRITION:
calories 322, fat 5, fiber 7, carbs 9, protein 16

Lamb and Bacon Stew

Preparation time: 10 minutes

Cooking time: 7 hours and 10 minutes

Servings: 6

INGREDIENTS:
2 tablespoons flour
2 ounces bacon, cooked and crumbled
1 and ½ pounds lamb loin, chopped
Salt and black pepper to the taste
1 garlic clove, minced
1 cup yellow onion, chopped
3 and ½ cups veggie stock
1 cup carrots, chopped
1 cup celery, chopped

2 cups sweet potatoes, chopped
chopped
1 tablespoon thyme, 1 bay leaf
2 tablespoons olive oil

DIRECTIONS:
Put lamb meat in a bowl, add flour, salt and pepper and toss to coat. Heat up a pan with the oil over medium-high heat, add lamb, brown for 5 minutes on each side and transfer to your slow cooker. Add onion, garlic, bacon, carrots, potatoes, bay leaf, stock, thyme and celery to the slow cooker as well, stir gently, cover and cook on Low for 7 hours. Discard bay leaf, stir your stew, divide into bowls and serve for lunch

NUTRITION:
calories 360, fat 5, fiber 3, carbs 16, protein 17

Beef Curry

Preparation time: 10 minutes

Cooking time: 6 hours

Servings: 2

INGREDIENTS:
1 pound beef stew meat
4 garlic cloves, minced
1 red onion, sliced
2 carrots, grated
1 tablespoon ginger, grated
2 tablespoons yellow curry paste
2 cups coconut milk
A pinch of salt and black pepper

DIRECTIONS:
In your slow cooker, mix the beef with the garlic, onion and the other ingredients, toss, put the lid on and cook on Low for 6 hours. Divide the curry into bowls and serve for lunch.

NUTRITION:
calories 352, fat 6, fiber 7, carbs 9, protein 18

Sweet Potato Soup

Preparation time: 10 minutes

Cooking time: 5 hours and 20 minutes

Servings: 6

INGREDIENTS:
5 cups veggie stock
3 sweet potatoes, peeled and chopped
2 celery stalks, chopped
1 cup yellow onion, chopped
1 cup milk
1 teaspoon tarragon, dried
2 garlic cloves, minced
2 cups baby spinach
8 tablespoons almonds, sliced
Salt and black pepper to the taste

DIRECTIONS:
In your slow cooker, mix stock with potatoes, celery, onion, milk, tarragon, garlic, salt and pepper, stir, cover and cook on High for 5 hours. Blend soup using an immersion blender, add spinach and almonds, toss, cover and leave aside for 20 minutes. Divide soup into bowls and serve for lunch.

NUTRITION:
calories 301, fat 5, fiber 4, carbs 12, protein 5

Chicken and Brussels Sprouts Mix

Preparation time: 10 minutes

Cooking time: 6 hours

Servings: 2

INGREDIENTS:
1 pound chicken breast, skinless, boneless and cubed
1 red onion, sliced
1 cup Brussels sprouts, trimmed and halved
1 cup chicken stock
½ cup tomato paste
A pinch of salt and black pepper
1 garlic clove, crushed
1 tablespoon thyme, chopped
1 tablespoon rosemary, chopped

DIRECTIONS:
In your slow cooker, mix the chicken with the onion, sprouts and the other ingredients, toss, put the lid on and cook on Low for 6 hours. Divide the mix between plates and serve for lunch.

NUTRITION:
calories 261, fat 7, fiber 6, carbs 8, protein 26

White Beans Stew

Preparation time: 10 minutes

Cooking time: 4 hours

Servings: 10

INGREDIENTS:
2 pounds white beans dried
3 celery stalks, chopped
2 carrots, chopped
1 bay leaf
1 yellow onion, chopped
3 garlic cloves, minced
1 teaspoon rosemary, dried
1 teaspoon oregano, dried
1 teaspoon thyme, dried
10 cups water
Salt and black pepper to the taste
28 ounces canned tomatoes, chopped
6 cups chard, chopped

DIRECTIONS:
In your slow cooker, mix white beans with celery,

carrots, bay leaf, onion, garlic, rosemary, oregano, thyme, water, salt, pepper, tomatoes and chard, cover and cook o High for 4 hours. Stir, divide into bowls and serve for lunch,

NUTRITION:
calories 341, fat 8, fiber 12, carbs 20, protein 6

Chickpeas Stew
Preparation time: 10 minutes
Cooking time: 3 hours
Servings: 4

INGREDIENTS:
2 cups canned chickpeas, drained and rinsed
1 cup tomato sauce
½ cup chicken stock
1 red onion, sliced
2 garlic cloves, minced
1 tablespoon thyme, chopped
½ teaspoon turmeric powder
½ teaspoon garam masala
2 carrots, chopped
3 celery stalks, chopped
2 tablespoons parsley, chopped
A pinch of salt and black pepper

DIRECTIONS:
In your slow cooker, mix the chickpeas with the tomato sauce, chicken stock and the other ingredients, toss, put the lid on and cook on High for 3 hours. Divide into bowls and serve for lunch.

NUTRITION:
calories 300, fat 4, fiber 7, carbs 9, protein 22

Bulgur Chili
Preparation time: 10 minutes
Cooking time: 8 hours
Servings: 4

INGREDIENTS:
2 cups white mushrooms, sliced
¾ cup bulgur, soaked in 1 cup hot water for 15 minutes and drained
2 cups yellow onion, chopped
½ cup red bell pepper, chopped
1 cup veggie stock
2 garlic cloves, minced
1 cup strong brewed coffee
14 ounces canned kidney beans, drained
14 ounces canned pinto beans, drained
2 tablespoons sugar
2 tablespoons chili powder
1 tablespoon cocoa powder
1 teaspoon oregano, dried
2 teaspoons cumin, ground
1 bay leaf
Salt and black pepper to the taste

DIRECTIONS:
In your Slow cooker, mix mushrooms with bulgur, onion, bell pepper, stock, garlic, coffee, kidney and pinto beans, sugar, chili powder, cocoa, oregano, cumin, bay leaf, salt and pepper, stir gently, cover and cook on Low for 12 hours. Discard bay leaf, divide chili into bowls and serve for lunch.

NUTRITION:
calories 351, fat 4, fiber 6, carbs 20, protein 4

Eggplant Curry
Preparation time: 10 minutes
Cooking time: 3 hours
Servings: 2

INGREDIENTS:
2 tablespoons olive oil
1 pound eggplant, cubed
2 tablespoons red curry paste
1 cup coconut milk
½ cup veggie stock
1 teaspoon turmeric powder
½ teaspoon rosemary, dried
4 kaffir lime leaves

DIRECTIONS:
In your slow cooker, mix the eggplant with the oil, curry paste and the other ingredients, toss, put the lid on and cook on High for 3 hours. Discard lime leaves, divide the curry into bowls and serve for lunch.

NUTRITION:
calories 281, fat 7, fiber 6, carbs 8, protein 22

Quinoa Chili
Preparation time: 10 minutes
Cooking time: 6 hours
Servings: 6

INGREDIENTS:
2 cups veggie stock
½ cup quinoa
30 ounces canned black beans, drained
28 ounces canned tomatoes, chopped
1 green bell pepper, chopped
1 yellow onion, chopped
2 sweet potatoes, cubed
1 tablespoon chili powder
2 tablespoons cocoa powder
2 teaspoons cumin, ground
Salt and black pepper to the taste
¼ teaspoon smoked paprika

DIRECTIONS:
In your slow cooker, mix stock with quinoa, black beans, tomatoes, bell pepper, onion, sweet

potatoes, chili powder, cocoa, cumin, paprika, salt and pepper, stir, cover and cook on High for 6 hours. Divide into bowls and serve for lunch.

NUTRITION:
calories 342, fat 6, fiber 7, carbs 18, protein 4

Beef and Artichokes Stew

Preparation time: 10 minutes
Cooking time: 4 hours
Servings: 2

INGREDIENTS:
1 pound beef stew meat, cubed
1 cup canned artichoke hearts, halved
1 cup beef stock
1 red onion, sliced
1 cup tomato sauce
½ teaspoon rosemary, dried
½ teaspoon coriander, ground
1 teaspoon garlic powder
A drizzle of olive oil
A pinch of salt and black pepper
1 tablespoon chives, chopped

DIRECTIONS:
Grease the slow cooker with the oil and mix the beef with the artichokes, stock and the other ingredients inside. Toss, put the lid on and cook on High for 4 hours. Divide the stew into bowls and serve.

NUTRITION:
calories 322, fat 5, fiber 4, carbs 12, protein 22

Pumpkin Chili

Preparation time: 10 minutes
Cooking time: 5 hours
Servings: 6

INGREDIENTS:
1 cup pumpkin puree
30 ounces canned kidney beans, drained
30 ounces canned roasted tomatoes, chopped
2 cups water
1 cup red lentils, dried
1 cup yellow onion, chopped
1 jalapeno pepper, chopped
1 tablespoon chili powder
1 tablespoon cocoa powder
½ teaspoon cinnamon powder
2 teaspoons cumin, ground
A pinch of cloves, ground
Salt and black pepper to the taste
2 tomatoes, chopped

DIRECTIONS:
In your Slow cooker, mix pumpkin puree with kidney beans, roasted tomatoes, water, lentils, onion, jalapeno, chili powder, cocoa, cinnamon, cumin, cloves, salt and pepper, stir, cover and cook on High for 5 hours. Divide into bowls, top with chopped tomatoes and serve for lunch.

NUTRITION:
calories 266, fat 6, fiber 4, carbs 12, protein 4

Beef Soup

Preparation time: 10 minutes
Cooking time: 5 hours
Servings: 2

INGREDIENTS:
1 pound beef stew meat, cubed
3 cups beef stock
½ cup tomatoes, cubed
1 red onion, chopped
1 green bell pepper, chopped
1 carrot, cubed
A pinch of salt and black pepper
½ tablespoon oregano, dried
¼ teaspoon chili pepper
2 tablespoon tomato paste
1 jalapeno, chopped
1 tablespoon cilantro, chopped

DIRECTIONS:
In your slow cooker, mix the beef with the stock, tomatoes and the other ingredients, toss, put the lid on and cook on Low for 5 hours. Divide the soup into bowls and serve for lunch.

NUTRITION:
calories 391, fat 6, fiber 7, carbs 8, protein 27

3 Bean Chili

Preparation time: 10 minutes
Cooking time: 8 hours
Servings: 6

INGREDIENTS:
15 ounces canned kidney beans, drained
30 ounces canned chili beans in sauce
15 ounces canned black beans, drained
2 green bell peppers, chopped
30 ounces canned tomatoes, crushed
2 tablespoons chili powder
2 yellow onions, chopped
2 garlic cloves, minced
1 teaspoon oregano, dried
1 tablespoon cumin, ground
Salt and black pepper to the taste

DIRECTIONS:
In your Slow cooker, mix kidney beans with chili

beans, black beans, bell peppers, tomatoes, chili powder, onion, garlic, oregano, cumin, salt and pepper, stir, cover and cook on Low for 8 hours. Divide into bowls and serve for lunch.

NUTRITION:
calories 314, fat 6, fiber 5, carbs 14, protein 4

Veggie Soup

Preparation time: 10 minutes
Cooking time: 4 hours
Servings: 2

INGREDIENTS:
½ pound gold potatoes, peeled and roughly cubed
1 carrot, sliced
1 zucchini, cubed
1 eggplant, cubed
1 cup tomatoes, cubed
4 cups veggie stock
A pinch of salt and black pepper
3 tablespoons tomato paste
1 sweet onion, chopped
1 tablespoon lemon juice
1 tablespoon chives, chopped

DIRECTIONS:
In your slow cooker, mix the potatoes with the carrot, zucchini and the other ingredients, toss, put the lid on and cook on Low for 4 hours. Divide the soup into bowls and serve.

NUTRITION:
calories 392, fat 7, fiber 8, carbs 12, protein 28

Cod and Asparagus

Preparation time: 10 minutes
Cooking time: 2 hours
Servings: 4

INGREDIENTS:
4 cod fillets, boneless
1 bunch asparagus
12 tablespoons lemon juice
Salt and black pepper to the taste
2 tablespoons olive oil

DIRECTIONS:
Divide cod fillets between tin foil pieces, top each with asparagus spears, lemon juice, lemon pepper and oil and wrap them. Arrange wrapped fish in your Slow cooker, cover and cook on High for 2 hours. Unwrap fish, divide it and asparagus between plates and serve for lunch.

NUTRITION:
calories 202, fat 3, fiber 6, carbs 7, protein 3

Oregano Turkey Stew

Preparation time: 10 minutes
Cooking time: 8 hours
Servings: 2

INGREDIENTS:
1 pound turkey breast, skinless, boneless and cubed
1 carrot, peeled and sliced
3 tomatoes, cubed
1 red onion, chopped
2 garlic cloves, minced
½ teaspoon sweet paprika
½ teaspoon chili powder
1 cup chicken stock
2 tablespoons tomato paste
1 teaspoon cumin powder
1 teaspoon oregano, dried
A pinch of salt and black pepper

DIRECTIONS:
In your slow cooker, mix the turkey with the carrot, tomatoes, onion and the other ingredients, toss, put the lid on and cook on Low for 8 hours. Divide the stew into bowls and serve for lunch.

NUTRITION:
calories 328, fat 6, fiber 8, carbs 12, protein 28

Seafood Stew

Preparation time: 10 minutes
Cooking time: 7 hours
Servings: 4

INGREDIENTS:
28 ounces canned tomatoes, crushed
4 cups veggie stock
3 garlic cloves, minced
1 pound sweet potatoes, cubed
½ cup yellow onion, chopped
2 pounds mixed seafood
1 teaspoon thyme, dried
1 teaspoon cilantro, dried
1 teaspoon basil, dried
Salt and black pepper to the taste
A pinch of red pepper flakes, crushed

DIRECTIONS:
In your Slow cooker, mix tomatoes with stock, garlic, sweet potatoes, onion, thyme, cilantro, basil, salt, pepper and pepper flakes, stir, cover and cook on Low for 6 hours. Add seafood, stir, cover, cook on High for 1 more hour, divide stew into bowls and serve for lunch.

NUTRITION:
calories 270, fat 4, fiber 4, carbs 12, protein 3

Masala Beef Mix

Preparation time: 10 minutes

Cooking time: 5 hours

Servings: 2

INGREDIENTS:
- 1 pound beef roast meat, cubed
- 1 red onion, sliced
- 1 eggplant, cubed
- 2 tablespoons olive oil
- 1 teaspoon black mustard seeds
- A pinch of salt and black pepper
- 1 tablespoon lemon zest, grated
- 2 tablespoons lemon juice
- 1 tablespoon garam masala
- 1 tablespoons coriander powder
- 1 teaspoon turmeric powder
- ½ teaspoon black peppercorns, ground
- ½ cup beef stock

DIRECTIONS:
In your slow cooker, mix the meat with the onion, eggplant, oil, mustard seeds and the other ingredients, toss, put the lid on and cook on High for 5 hours. Divide the mix between plates and serve for lunch with a side salad.

NUTRITION:
calories 300, fat 4, fiber 6, carbs 9, protein 22

Shrimp Stew

Preparation time: 10 minutes

Cooking time: 4 hours and 30 minutes

Servings: 8

INGREDIENTS:
- 29 ounces canned tomatoes, chopped
- 2 yellow onions, chopped
- 2 celery ribs, chopped
- ½ cup fish stock
- 4 garlic cloves, minced
- 1 tablespoon red vinegar
- 2 tablespoons olive oil
- 3 pounds shrimp, peeled and deveined
- 6 ounces canned clams
- 2 tablespoons cilantro, chopped

DIRECTIONS:
In your Slow cooker, mix tomatoes with onion, celery, stock, vinegar and oil, stir, cover and cook on Low for 4 hours. Add shrimp, clams and cilantro, stir, cover, cook on Low for 30 minutes more, divide into bowls and serve for lunch.

NUTRITION:
calories 255, fat 4, fiber 3, carbs 14, protein 26

Slow Cooker Side Dish Recipes

Creamy Hash Brown Mix

Preparation time: 10 minutes

Cooking time: 3 hours

Servings: 12

INGREDIENTS:
- 2 pounds hash browns
- 1 and ½ cups milk
- 10 ounces cream of chicken soup
- 1 cup cheddar cheese, shredded
- ½ cup butter, melted
- Salt and black pepper to the taste
- ¾ cup cornflakes, crushed

DIRECTIONS:
In a bowl, mix hash browns with milk, cream of chicken, cheese, butter, salt and pepper, stir, transfer to your Slow cooker, cover and cook on Low for 3 hours. Add cornflakes, divide between plates and serve as a side dish.

NUTRITION:
calories 234, fat 12, fiber 2, carbs 22, protein 6

Cheddar Potatoes Mix

Preparation time: 10 minutes

Cooking time: 3 hours

Servings: 2

INGREDIENTS:
- ½ pound gold potatoes, peeled and cut into wedges
- 2 ounces heavy cream
- ½ teaspoon turmeric powder
- ½ teaspoon rosemary, dried
- ¼ cup cheddar cheese, shredded
- 1 tablespoon butter, melted
- Cooking spray
- A pinch of salt and black pepper

DIRECTIONS:
Grease your slow cooker with the cooking spray, add the potatoes, cream, turmeric and the other ingredients, toss, put the lid on and cook on High for 3 hours. Divide between plates and serve as a side dish.

NUTRITION:
calories 300, fat 14, fiber 6, carbs 22, protein 6

Broccoli Mix

Preparation time: 10 minutes

Cooking time: 2 hours

Servings: 10

INGREDIENTS:
6 cups broccoli florets
1 and ½ cups cheddar cheese, shredded
10 ounces canned cream of celery soup
½ teaspoon Worcestershire sauce
¼ cup yellow onion, chopped
Salt and black pepper to the taste
1 cup crackers, crushed
2 tablespoons soft butter

DIRECTIONS:
In a bowl, mix broccoli with cream of celery soup, cheese, salt, pepper, onion an Worcestershire sauce, toss and transfer to your Slow cooker. Add butter, toss again, sprinkle crackers, cover and cook on High for 2 hours. Serve as a side dish.

NUTRITION:
calories 159, fat 11, fiber 1, carbs 11, protein 6

Balsamic Cauliflower

Preparation time: 10 minutes

Cooking time: 5 hours

Servings: 2

INGREDIENTS:
2 cups cauliflower florets
½ cup veggie stock
1 tablespoon balsamic vinegar
1 tablespoon lemon zest, grated
2 spring onions, chopped
¼ teaspoon sweet paprika
Salt and black pepper to the taste
1 tablespoon dill, chopped

DIRECTIONS:
In your slow cooker, mix the cauliflower with the stock, vinegar and the other ingredients, toss, put the lid on and cook on Low for 5 hours. Divide the cauliflower mix between plates and serve.

NUTRITION:
calories 162, fat 11, fiber 2, carbs 11, protein 5

Bean Medley

Preparation time: 10 minutes

Cooking time: 5 hours

Servings: 12

INGREDIENTS:
2 celery ribs, chopped
1 and ½ cups ketchup
1 green bell pepper, chopped
1 yellow onion, chopped
1 sweet red pepper, chopped
½ cup brown sugar
½ cup Italian dressing
½ cup water
1 tablespoon cider vinegar
2 bay leaves
16 ounces kidney beans, drained
Salt and black pepper to the taste
15 ounces canned black-eyed peas, drained
15 ounces canned northern beans, drained
15 ounces canned corn, drained
15 ounces canned lima beans, drained
15 ounces canned black beans, drained

DIRECTIONS:
In your Slow cooker, mix celery with ketchup, red and green bell pepper, onion, sugar, Italian dressing, water, vinegar, bay leaves, kidney beans, black-eyed peas, northern beans, corn, lima beans and black beans, stir, cover and cook on Low for 5 hours. Divide between plates and serve as a side dish.

NUTRITION:
calories 255, fat 4, fiber 9, carbs 45, protein 6

Italian Black Beans Mix

Preparation time: 10 minutes

Cooking time: 5 hours

Servings: 2

INGREDIENTS:
2 tablespoons tomato paste
Cooking spray
2 cups black beans
¼ cup veggie stock
1 red onion, sliced
Cooking spray
1 teaspoon Italian seasoning
½ celery rib, chopped
½ red bell pepper, chopped
½ sweet red pepper, chopped
¼ teaspoon mustard seeds
Salt and black pepper to the taste
2 ounces canned corn, drained
1 tablespoon cilantro, chopped

DIRECTIONS:
Grease the slow cooker with the cooking spray, and mix the beans with the stock, onion and the other ingredients inside. Put the lid on, cook on Low for 5 hours, divide between plates and serve as a side dish.

NUTRITION:
calories 255, fat 6, fiber 7, carbs 38, protein 7

Green Beans Mix

Preparation time: 10 minutes

Cooking time: 2 hours

Servings: 12

INGREDIENTS:
16 ounces green beans
½ cup brown sugar
½ cup butter, melted
¾ teaspoon soy sauce
Salt and black pepper to the taste

DIRECTIONS:
In your Slow cooker, mix green beans with sugar, butter, soy sauce, salt and pepper, stir, cover and cook on Low for 2 hours. Divide between plates and serve as a side dish.

NUTRITION:
calories 176, fat 4, fiber 7, carbs 14, protein 4

Butter Green Beans
Preparation time: 10 minutes
Cooking time: 2 hours
Servings: 2

INGREDIENTS:
1 pound green beans, trimmed and halved
2 tablespoons butter, melted
½ cup veggie stock
1 teaspoon rosemary, dried
1 tablespoon chives, chopped
Salt and black pepper to the taste
¼ teaspoon soy sauce

DIRECTIONS:
In your slow cooker, combine the green beans with the melted butter, stock and the other ingredients, toss, put the lid on and cook on Low for 2 hours. Divide between plates and serve as a side dish.

NUTRITION:
calories 236, fat 6, fiber 8, carbs 10, protein 6

Corn and Bacon
Preparation time: 10 minutes
Cooking time: 4 hours
Servings: 20

INGREDIENTS:
10 cups corn
24 ounces cream cheese, cubed
½ cup milk
½ cup melted butter
½ cup heavy cream
¼ cup sugar
A pinch of salt and black pepper
4 bacon strips, cooked and crumbled
2 tablespoons green onions, chopped

DIRECTIONS:
In your Slow cooker, mix corn with cream cheese, milk, butter, cream, sugar, salt, pepper, bacon and green onions, cover and cook on Low for 4 hours. Stir the corn, divide between plates and serve as a side dish.

NUTRITION:
calories 259, fat 20, fiber 2, carbs 18, protein 5

Corn Sauté
Preparation time: 10 minutes
Cooking time: 2 hours
Servings: 2

INGREDIENTS:
3 cups corn
2 tablespoon whipping cream
1 carrot, peeled and grated
1 tablespoon chives, chopped
2 tablespoons butter, melted
Salt and black pepper to the taste
2 bacon strips, cooked and crumbled
1 tablespoon green onions, chopped

DIRECTIONS:
In your slow cooker, combine the corn with the cream, carrot and the other ingredients, toss, put the lid on and cook on Low for 2 hours. Divide between plates, and serve.

NUTRITION:
calories 261, fat 11, fiber 3, carbs 17, protein 6

Peas and Carrots
Preparation time: 10 minutes
Cooking time: 5 hours
Servings: 12

INGREDIENTS:
1 yellow onion, chopped
1 pound carrots, sliced
16 ounces peas
¼ cup melted butter
¼ cup water
¼ cup honey
4 garlic cloves, minced
A pinch of salt and black pepper
1 teaspoon marjoram, dried

DIRECTIONS:
In your Slow cooker, mix onion with carrots, peas, butter, water, honey, garlic, salt, pepper and marjoram, cover and cook on Low for 5 hours. Stir peas and carrots mix, divide between plates and serve as a side dish.

NUTRITION:
calories 105, fat 4, fiber 3, carbs 16, protein 4

Sage Peas
Preparation time: 10 minutes
Cooking time: 2 hours
Servings: 2

INGREDIENTS:
1 pound peas
1 red onion, sliced
½ cup veggie stock
½ cup tomato sauce
2 garlic cloves, minced
¼ teaspoon sage, dried
Salt and black pepper to the taste
1 tablespoon dill, chopped

DIRECTIONS:
In your slow cooker, combine the peas with the onion, stock and the other ingredients, toss, put the lid on and cook on Low for 2 hours. Divide between plates and serve as a side dish.

NUTRITION:
calories 100, fat 4, fiber 3, carbs 15, protein 4

Beans, Carrots and Spinach Salad
Preparation time: 10 minutes
Cooking time: 7 hours
Servings: 6

INGREDIENTS:
1 and ½ cups northern beans
1 yellow onion, chopped
5 carrots, chopped
2 garlic cloves, minced
½ teaspoon oregano, dried
Salt and black pepper to the taste
4 and ½ cups chicken stock
5 ounces baby spinach
2 teaspoons lemon peel, grated
1 avocado, peeled, pitted and chopped
3 tablespoons lemon juice
¾ cup feta cheese, crumbled
1/3 cup pistachios, chopped

DIRECTIONS:
In your Slow cooker, mix beans with onion, carrots, garlic, oregano, salt, pepper and stock, stir, cover and cook on Low for 7 hours. Drain beans and veggies, transfer them to a salad bowl, add baby spinach, lemon peel, avocado, lemon juice, pistachios and cheese, toss, divide between plates and serve as a side dish.

NUTRITION:
calories 300, fat 8, fiber 14, carbs 43, protein 16

Tomato and Corn Mix
Preparation time: 10 minutes
Cooking time: 4 hours
Servings: 2

INGREDIENTS:
1 red onion, sliced
2 spring onions, chopped
1 cup corn
1 cup tomatoes, cubed
1 tablespoon olive oil
½ red bell pepper, chopped
½ cup tomato sauce
¼ teaspoon sweet paprika
½ teaspoon cumin, ground
1 tablespoon chives, chopped
Salt and black pepper to the taste

DIRECTIONS:
Heat up a pan with the oil over medium-high heat, add the onion, spring onions and bell pepper and cook for 10 minutes. Transfer the mix to the slow cooker, add the corn and the other ingredients, toss, put the lid on and cook on Low for 4 hours. Divide the mix between plates and serve as a side dish.

NUTRITION:
calories 312, fat 4, fiber 6, carbs 12, protein 6

Scalloped Potatoes
Preparation time: 10 minutes
Cooking time: 6 hours
Servings: 6

INGREDIENTS:
Cooking spray
2 and ½ pounds gold potatoes, sliced
10 ounces canned cream of potato soup
1 yellow onion, roughly chopped
8 ounces sour cream
1 cup Gouda cheese, shredded
½ cup blue cheese, crumbled
½ cup parmesan, grated
½ cup chicken stock
Salt and black pepper to the taste
1 tablespoon chives, chopped

DIRECTIONS:
Grease your Slow cooker with cooking spray and arrange potato slices on the bottom. Add cream of potato soup, onion, sour cream, Gouda cheese, blue cheese, parmesan, stock, salt and pepper, cover and cook on Low for 6 hours. Add chives, divide between plates and serve as a side dish.

NUTRITION:
calories 306, fat 14, fiber 4, carbs 33, protein 12

Dill Mushroom Sauté
Preparation time: 10 minutes
Cooking time: 3 hours
Servings: 2

INGREDIENTS:
1 pound white mushrooms, halved

1 tablespoon olive oil
1 red onion, sliced
1 carrot, peeled and grated
2 green onions, chopped
1 garlic clove, minced
1 cup beef stock
½ cup tomato sauce
1 tablespoon dill, chopped

DIRECTIONS:
Grease the slow cooker with the oil and mix the mushrooms with the onion, carrot and the other ingredients inside. Put the lid on, cook on Low for 3 hours, divide between plates and serve as a side dish.

NUTRITION:
calories 200, fat 6, fiber 4, carbs 28, protein 5

Sweet Potatoes with Bacon
Preparation time: 10 minutes
Cooking time: 5 hours
Servings: 6

INGREDIENTS:
4 pounds sweet potatoes, peeled and sliced
3 tablespoons brown sugar
½ cup orange juice
½ teaspoon sage, dried
½ teaspoon thyme, dried
4 bacon slices, cooked and crumbled
2 tablespoons soft butter

DIRECTIONS:
Arrange sweet potato slices in your Slow cooker, add sugar, orange juice, sage, thyme, butter and bacon, cover and cook on Low for 5 hours. Divide between plates and serve them as a side dish.

NUTRITION:
calories 200, fat 4, fiber 4, carbs 30, protein 4

Hot Zucchini Mix
Preparation time: 10 minutes
Cooking time: 2 hours
Servings: 2

INGREDIENTS:
¼ cup carrots, grated
1 pound zucchinis, roughly cubed
1 teaspoon hot paprika
½ teaspoon chili powder
2 spring onions, chopped
½ tablespoon olive oil
½ teaspoon curry powder
1 garlic clove, minced
½ teaspoon ginger powder
A pinch of salt and black pepper
1 tablespoon cilantro, chopped

DIRECTIONS:
In your slow cooker, mix the carrots with the zucchinis, paprika and the other ingredients, toss, put the lid on and cook on Low for 2 hours. Divide between plates and serve as a side dish.

NUTRITION:
calories 200, fat 5, fiber 7, carbs 28, protein 4

Cauliflower and Broccoli Mix
Preparation time: 10 minutes
Cooking time: 7 hours
Servings: 10

INGREDIENTS:
4 cups broccoli florets
4 cups cauliflower florets
7 ounces Swiss cheese, torn
14 ounces Alfredo sauce
1 yellow onion, chopped
Salt and black pepper to the taste
1 teaspoon thyme, dried
½ cup almonds, sliced

DIRECTIONS:
In your Slow cooker, mix broccoli with cauliflower, cheese, sauce, onion, salt, pepper and thyme, stir, cover and cook on Low for 7 hours. Add almonds, divide between plates and serve as a side dish.

NUTRITION:
calories 177, fat 7, fiber 2, carbs 10, protein 7

Butternut Squash and Eggplant Mix
Preparation time: 10 minutes
Cooking time: 4 hours
Servings: 2

INGREDIENTS:
1 butternut squash, peeled and roughly cubed
1 eggplant, roughly cubed
1 red onion, chopped
Cooking spray
½ cup veggie stock
¼ cup tomato paste
½ tablespoon parsley, chopped
Salt and black pepper to the taste
2 garlic cloves, minced

DIRECTIONS:
Grease the slow cooker with the cooking spray and mix the squash with the eggplant, onion and the other ingredients inside. Put the lid on and cook on Low for 4 hours. Divide between plates and serve as a side dish.

NUTRITION:
calories 114, fat 4, fiber 4, carbs 18, protein 4

Wild Rice Mix

Preparation time: 10 minutes
Cooking time: 6 hours
Servings: 16

INGREDIENTS:
45 ounces chicken stock
1 cup carrots, sliced
2 and ½ cups wild rice
4 ounces mushrooms, sliced
2 tablespoons butter, soft
Salt and black pepper to the taste
2 teaspoons marjoram, dried
2/3 cup dried cherries
2/3 cup green onions, chopped
½ cup pecans, chopped

DIRECTIONS:
In your Slow cooker, mix stock with carrots, rice, mushrooms, butter, salt, pepper and marjoram, cover and cook on Low for 6 hours. Add cherries, green onions and pecans, toss, divide between plates and serve as a side dish.

NUTRITION:
calories 169, fat 6, fiber 4, carbs 27, protein 5

Carrots and Spinach Mix

Preparation time: 10 minutes
Cooking time: 2 hours
Servings: 2

INGREDIENTS:
2 carrots, sliced
1 small yellow onion, chopped
Salt and black pepper to the taste
¼ teaspoon oregano, dried
½ teaspoon sweet paprika
2 ounces baby spinach
1 cup veggie stock
1 tablespoons lemon juice
2 tablespoons pistachios, chopped

DIRECTIONS:
In your slow cooker, mix the spinach with the carrots, onion and the other ingredients, toss, put the lid on and cook on Low for 2 hours. Divide everything between plates and serve.

NUTRITION:
calories 219, fat 8, fiber 14, carbs 15, protein 17

Mashed Potatoes

Preparation time: 10 minutes
Cooking time: 4 hours
Servings: 12

INGREDIENTS:
3 pounds gold potatoes, peeled and cubed
1 bay leaf
6 garlic cloves, minced
28 ounces chicken stock
1 cup milk
¼ cup butter
Salt and black pepper to the taste

DIRECTIONS:
In your Slow cooker, mix potatoes with bay leaf, garlic, salt, pepper and stock, cover and cook on Low for 4 hours. Drain potatoes, mash them, mix with butter and milk, blend really, divide between plates and serve as a side dish.

NUTRITION:
calories 135, fat 4, fiber 2, carbs 22, protein 4

Creamy Coconut Potatoes

Preparation time: 10 minutes
Cooking time: 4 hours
Servings: 2

INGREDIENTS:
½ pound gold potatoes, halved and sliced
2 scallions, chopped
1 tablespoon avocado oil
2 ounces coconut milk
¼ cup veggie stock
Salt and black pepper to the taste
1 tablespoons parsley, chopped

DIRECTIONS:
In your slow cooker, mix the potatoes with the scallions and the other ingredients, toss, put the lid on and cook on High for 4 hours. Divide the mix between plates and serve.

NUTRITION:
calories 306, fat 14, fiber 4, carbs 15, protein 12

Orange Glazed Carrots

Preparation time: 10 minutes
Cooking time: 8 hours
Servings: 10

INGREDIENTS:
3 pounds carrots, cut into medium chunks
1 cup orange juice
2 tablespoons orange peel, grated
½ cup orange marmalade
½ cup veggie stock
¼ cup white wine
1 tablespoon tapioca, crushed
¼ cup parsley, chopped
3 tablespoons butter
Salt and black pepper to the taste

DIRECTIONS:
In your Slow cooker, mix carrots with orange juice,

orange peel, marmalade, stock, wine, tapioca, parsley, butter, salt and pepper, cover and cook on Low for 8 hours. Toss carrots, divide between plates and serve as a side dish.

NUTRITION:
calories 160, fat 4, fiber 4, carbs 31, protein 3

Sage Sweet Potatoes

Preparation time: 10 minutes

Cooking time: 3 hours

Servings: 2

INGREDIENTS:
- ½ pound sweet potatoes, thinly sliced
- 1 tablespoon sage, chopped
- 2 tablespoons orange juice
- A pinch of salt and black pepper
- ½ cup veggie stock
- ½ tablespoon olive oil

DIRECTIONS:
In your slow cooker, mix the potatoes with the sage and the other ingredients, toss, put the lid on and cook on High for 3 hours. Divide between plates and serve as a side dish.

NUTRITION:
calories 189, fat 4, fiber 4, carbs 17, protein 4

Creamy Risotto

Preparation time: 10 minutes

Cooking time: 1 hour

Servings: 4

INGREDIENTS:
- 4 ounces mushrooms, sliced
- ½ quart veggie stock
- 1 teaspoon olive oil
- 2 tablespoons porcini mushrooms
- 2 cups white rice
- A small bunch of parsley, chopped

DIRECTIONS:
In your Slow cooker, mix mushrooms with stock, oil, porcini mushrooms and rice, stir, cover and cook on High for 1 hour. Add parsley, stir, divide between plates and serve as a side dish.

NUTRITION:
calories 346, fat 3, fiber 4, carbs 35, protein 10

Cauliflower and Almonds Mix

Preparation time: 10 minutes

Cooking time: 3 hours

Servings: 2

INGREDIENTS:
- 2 cups cauliflower florets
- 2 ounces tomato paste
- 1 small yellow onion, chopped
- 1 tablespoon chives, chopped
- Salt and black pepper to the taste
- 1 tablespoon almonds, sliced

DIRECTIONS:
In your slow cooker, mix the cauliflower with the tomato paste and the other ingredients, toss, put the lid on and cook on High for 3 hours. Divide between plates and serve as a side dish.

NUTRITION:
calories 177, fat 12, fiber 7, carbs 20, protein 7

Veggie and Garbanzo Mix

Preparation time: 10 minutes

Cooking time: 6 hours

Servings: 4

INGREDIENTS:
- 15 ounces canned garbanzo beans, drained
- 3 cups cauliflower florets
- 1 cup green beans
- 1 cup carrot, sliced
- 14 ounces veggie stock
- ½ cup onion, chopped
- 2 teaspoons curry powder
- ¼ cup basil, chopped
- 14 ounces coconut milk

DIRECTIONS:
In your Slow cooker, mix beans with cauliflower, green beans, carrot, onion, stock, curry powder, basil and milk, stir, cover and cook on Low for 6 hours. Stir veggie mix again, divide between plates and serve as a side dish.

NUTRITION:
calories 219, fat 5, fiber 8, carbs 32, protein 7

Garlic Risotto

Preparation time: 10 minutes

Cooking time: 2 hours

Servings: 2

INGREDIENTS:
- 1 small shallot, chopped
- 1 cup wild rice
- 1 cup chicken stock
- 1 tablespoons olive oil
- 2 garlic cloves, minced
- Salt and black pepper to the taste
- 2 tablespoons cilantro, chopped

DIRECTIONS:
In your slow cooker, mix the rice with the stock, shallot and the other ingredients, toss, put the lid

on and cook on High for 2 hours Divide between plates and serve as a side dish.

NUTRITION:
calories 204, fat 7, fiber 3, carbs 17, protein 7

Cauliflower Pilaf

Preparation time: 10 minutes
Cooking time: 3 hours
Servings: 6

INGREDIENTS:
1 cup cauliflower rice
6 green onions, chopped
3 tablespoons ghee, melted
2 garlic cloves, minced
½ pound Portobello mushrooms, sliced
2 cups warm water
Salt and black pepper to the taste

DIRECTIONS:
In your Slow cooker, mix cauliflower rice with green onions, melted ghee, garlic, mushrooms, water, salt and pepper, stir well, cover and cook on Low for 3 hours. Divide between plates and serve as a side dish.

NUTRITION:
calories 200, fat 5, fiber 3, carbs 14, protein 4

Red Curry Veggie Mix

Preparation time: 10 minutes
Cooking time: 3 hours
Servings: 2

INGREDIENTS:
2 zucchinis, cubed
1 eggplant, cubed
½ cup button mushrooms, quartered
1 small red sweet potatoes, chopped
½ cup veggie stock
1 garlic cloves, minced
¼ tablespoon Thai red curry paste
¼ tablespoon ginger, grated
Salt and black pepper to the taste
2 tablespoons coconut milk

DIRECTIONS:
In your slow cooker, mix the zucchinis with the eggplant and the other ingredients, toss, put the lid on and cook on Low for 3 hours. Divide between plates and serve as a side dish.

NUTRITION:
calories 169, fat 2, fiber 2, carbs 15, protein 6

Squash Side Salad

Preparation time: 10 minutes
Cooking time: 4 hours
Servings: 8

INGREDIENTS:
1 tablespoon olive oil
1 cup carrots, chopped
1 yellow onion, chopped
1 teaspoon sugar
1 and ½ teaspoons curry powder
1 garlic clove, minced
1 big butternut squash, peeled and cubed
A pinch of sea salt and black pepper
¼ teaspoon ginger, grated
½ teaspoon cinnamon powder
3 cups coconut milk

DIRECTIONS:
In your Slow cooker, mix oil with carrots, onion, sugar, curry powder, garlic, squash, salt, pepper, ginger, cinnamon and coconut milk, stir well, cover and cook on Low for 4 hours. Stir, divide between plates and serve as a side dish.

NUTRITION:
calories 200, fat 4, fiber 4, carbs 17, protein 4

Rosemary Leeks

Preparation time: 10 minutes
Cooking time: 3 hours
Servings: 2

INGREDIENTS:
½ tablespoon olive oil
½ leeks, sliced
½ cup tomato sauce
2 garlic cloves, minced
Salt and black pepper to the taste
¼ tablespoon rosemary, chopped

DIRECTIONS:
In your slow cooker, mix the leeks with the oil, sauce and the other ingredients, toss, put the lid on, cook on High for 3 hours, divide between plates and serve as a side dish.

NUTRITION:
calories 202, fat 2, fiber 6, carbs 18, protein 8

Mushrooms and Sausage Mix

Preparation time: 10 minutes
Cooking time: 2 hours and 30 minutes
Servings: 12

INGREDIENTS:
½ cup butter, melted
1 pound pork sausage, ground
½ pound mushrooms, sliced
6 celery ribs, chopped
2 yellow onions, chopped
2 garlic cloves, minced
1 tablespoon sage, chopped
1 cup cranberries, dried
½ cup cauliflower florets, chopped
½ cup veggie stock

DIRECTIONS:
Heat up a pan with the butter over medium-high heat, add sausage, stir, cook for a couple of minutes and transfer to your Slow cooker. Add mushrooms, celery, onion, garlic, sage, cranberries, cauliflower and stock, stir, cover and cook on High for 2 hours and 30 minutes. Divide between plates and serve as a side dish.

NUTRITION:
calories 200, fat 3, fiber 6, carbs 9, protein 4

Mustard Brussels Sprouts

Preparation time: 10 minutes

Cooking time: 3 hours

Servings: 2

INGREDIENTS:
½ pounds Brussels sprouts, trimmed and halved
A pinch of salt and black pepper
2 tablespoons mustard
½ cup veggie stock
1 tablespoons olive oil
2 tablespoons maple syrup
1 tablespoon thyme, chopped

DIRECTIONS:
In your slow cooker, mix the sprouts with the mustard and the other ingredients, toss, put the lid on and cook on Low for 3 hours. Divide between plates and serve as a side dish.

NUTRITION:
calories 170, fat 4, fiber 4, carbs 14, protein 6

Glazed Baby Carrots

Preparation time: 10 minutes

Cooking time: 6 hours

Servings: 6

INGREDIENTS:
½ cup peach preserves
½ cup butter, melted
2 pounds baby carrots
2 tablespoon sugar
1 teaspoon vanilla extract
A pinch of salt and
black pepper
A pinch of nutmeg, ground
½ teaspoon cinnamon powder
2 tablespoons water

DIRECTIONS:
Put baby carrots in your Slow cooker, add butter, peach preserves, sugar, vanilla, salt, pepper, nutmeg, cinnamon and water, toss well, cover and cook on Low for 6 hours. Divide between plates and serve as a side dish.

NUTRITION:
calories 283, fat 14, fiber 4, carbs 28, protein 3

Potatoes and Leeks Mix

Preparation time: 10 minutes

Cooking time: 4 hours

Servings: 2

INGREDIENTS:
2 leeks, sliced
½ pound sweet potatoes, cut into medium wedges
½ cup veggie stock
½ tablespoon balsamic vinegar
1 tablespoon chives, chopped
½ teaspoon pumpkin pie spice

DIRECTIONS:
In your slow cooker, mix the leeks with the potatoes and the other ingredients, toss, put the lid on and cook on High for 4 hours. Divide between plates and serve as a side dish.

NUTRITION:
calories 351, fat 8, fiber 5, carbs 48, protein 7

Spinach and Squash Side Salad

Preparation time: 10 minutes

Cooking time: 4 hours

Servings: 12

INGREDIENTS:
3 pounds butternut squash, peeled and cubed
1 yellow onion, chopped
2 teaspoons thyme, chopped
3 garlic cloves, minced
A pinch of salt and black pepper
10 ounces veggie stock
6 ounces baby spinach

DIRECTIONS:
In your Slow cooker, mix squash cubes with onion, thyme, salt, pepper and stock, stir, cover and cook on Low for 4 hours. Transfer squash mix to a bowl, add spinach, toss, divide between plates and serve as a side dish.

NUTRITION:
calories 100, fat 1, fiber 4, carbs 18, protein 4

Black Beans Mix

Preparation time: 10 minutes

Cooking time: 6 hours

Servings: 2

INGREDIENTS:
½ pound black beans, soaked overnight and

drained
A pinch of salt and black pepper
½ cup veggie stock
½ tablespoon lime juice
2 tablespoons cilantro, chopped
2 tablespoons pine nuts

DIRECTIONS:
In your slow cooker, mix the beans with the stock and the other ingredients, toss, put the lid on and cook on Low for 6 hours. Divide everything between plates and serve.

NUTRITION:
calories 200, fat 3, fiber 4, carbs 7, protein 5

Buttery Mushrooms
Preparation time: 10 minutes
Cooking time: 4 hours
Servings: 6

INGREDIENTS:
1 yellow onion, chopped
1 pounds mushrooms, halved
½ cup butter, melted
1 teaspoon Italian seasoning
Salt and black pepper to the taste
1 teaspoon sweet paprika

DIRECTIONS:
In your Slow cooker, mix mushrooms with onion, butter, Italian seasoning, salt, pepper and paprika, toss, cover and cook on Low for 4 hours. Divide between plates and serve as a side dish.

NUTRITION:
calories 120, fat 6, fiber 1, carbs 8, protein 4

Orange Carrots Mix
Preparation time: 10 minutes
Cooking time: 6 hours
Servings: 2

INGREDIENTS:
½ pound carrots, sliced
A pinch of salt and black pepper
½ tablespoon olive oil
½ cup orange juice
½ teaspoon orange rind, grated

DIRECTIONS:
In your slow cooker, mix the carrots with the oil and the other ingredients, toss, put the lid on and cook on Low for 6 hours. Divide between plates and serve as a side dish.

NUTRITION:
calories 140, fat 2, fiber 2, carbs 7, protein 6

Cauliflower Rice and Spinach
Preparation time: 10 minutes
Cooking time: 3 hours
Servings: 8

INGREDIENTS:
2 garlic cloves, minced
2 tablespoons butter, melted
1 yellow onion, chopped
¼ teaspoon thyme, dried
3 cups veggie stock
20 ounces spinach, chopped
6 ounces coconut cream
Salt and black pepper to the taste
2 cups cauliflower rice

DIRECTIONS:
Heat up a pan with the butter over medium heat, add onion, stir and cook for 4 minutes. Add garlic, thyme and stock, stir, cook for 1 minute more and transfer to your Slow cooker. Add spinach, coconut cream, cauliflower rice, salt and pepper, stir a bit, cover and cook on High for 3 hours. Divide between plates and serve as a side dish.

NUTRITION:
calories 200, fat 4, fiber 4, carbs 8, protein 2

Hot Lentils
Preparation time: 10 minutes
Cooking time: 6 hours
Servings: 2

INGREDIENTS:
1 tablespoon thyme, chopped
½ tablespoon olive oil
1 cup canned lentils, drained
½ cup veggie stock
2 garlic cloves, minced
1 tablespoon cider vinegar
2 tablespoons tomato paste
1 tablespoon rosemary, chopped

DIRECTIONS:
In your slow cooker, mix the lentils with the thyme and the other ingredients, toss, put the lid on and cook on Low for 6 hours. Divide between plates and serve as a side dish.

NUTRITION:
calories 200, fat 2, fiber 4, carbs 7, protein 8

Maple Sweet Potatoes
Preparation time: 10 minutes
Cooking time: 5 hours
Servings: 10

INGREDIENTS:
8 sweet potatoes, halved and sliced
1 cup walnuts, chopped
½ cup cherries, dried and chopped
½ cup maple syrup
¼ cup apple juice
A pinch of salt

DIRECTIONS:
Arrange sweet potatoes in your slow cooker, add walnuts, dried cherries, maple syrup, apple juice and a pinch of salt, toss a bit, cover and cook on Low for 5 hours. Divide between plates and serve as a side dish.

NUTRITION:
calories 271, fat 6, fiber 4, carbs 26, protein 6

Marjoram Rice Mix
Preparation time: 10 minutes
Cooking time: 6 hours
Servings: 2

INGREDIENTS:
1 cup wild rice
2 cups chicken stock
1 carrot, peeled and grated
2 tablespoons marjoram, chopped
1 tablespoon olive oil
A pinch of salt and black pepper
1 tablespoon green onions, chopped

DIRECTIONS:
In your slow cooker, mix the rice with the stock and the other ingredients, toss, put the lid on and cook on Low for 6 hours. Divide between plates and serve.

NUTRITION:
calories 200, fat 2, fiber 3, carbs 7, protein 5

Creamy Chipotle Sweet Potatoes
Preparation time: 10 minutes
Cooking time: 4 hours
Servings: 10

INGREDIENTS:
1 sweet onion, chopped
2 tablespoons olive oil
¼ cup parsley, chopped
2 shallots, chopped
2 teaspoons chipotle pepper, crushed
Salt and black pepper
4 big sweet potatoes, shredded
8 ounces coconut cream
16 ounces bacon, cooked and chopped
½ teaspoon sweet paprika
Cooking spray

DIRECTIONS:
Heat up a pan with the oil over medium-high heat, add shallots and onion, stir, cook for 6 minutes and transfer to a bowl. Add parsley, chipotle pepper, salt, pepper, sweet potatoes, coconut cream, paprika and bacon, stir, pour everything in your Slow cooker after you've greased it with some cooking spray, cover, cook on Low for 4 hours, leave aside to cool down a bit, divide between plates and serve as a side dish.

NUTRITION:
calories 260, fat 14, fiber 6, carbs 20, protein 15

Mashed Potatoes
Preparation time: 10 minutes
Cooking time: 6 hours
Servings: 2

INGREDIENTS:
1 pound gold potatoes, peeled and cubed
2 garlic cloves, chopped
1 cup milk
1 cup water
2 tablespoons butter
A pinch of salt and white pepper

DIRECTIONS:
In your slow cooker, mix the potatoes with the water, salt and pepper, put the lid on and cook on Low for 6 hours. Mash the potatoes, add the rest of the ingredients, whisk and serve.

NUTRITION:
calories 135, fat 4, fiber 2, carbs 10, protein 4

Kale and Ham Mix
Preparation time: 10 minutes
Cooking time: 6 hours
Servings: 6

INGREDIENTS:
8 ounces ham hock slices
1 and ½ cups water
1 cup chicken stock
12 cups kale leaves, torn
A pinch of salt and cayenne pepper
2 tablespoons olive oil
1 yellow onion, chopped
2 tablespoons apple cider vinegar
Cooking spray

DIRECTIONS:
Put ham in a heatproof bowl, add the water and the stock, cover and microwave for 3 minutes. Heat up a pan with the oil over medium-high heat, add onion, stir and cook for 5 minutes. Drain ham and add it to your slow cooker, add onions, kale, salt, cayenne and vinegar, toss, cover and cook on Low for 6 hours. Divide between plates and serve as a side dish.

NUTRITION:
calories 200, fat 4, fiber 7, carbs 10, protein 3

Barley Mix

Preparation time: 10 minutes

Cooking time: 6 hours

Servings: 2

INGREDIENTS:
- 1 red onion, sliced
- ½ teaspoon sweet paprika
- ½ teaspoon turmeric powder
- 1 cup barley
- 1 cup veggie stock
- A pinch of salt and black pepper
- 1 garlic clove, minced

DIRECTIONS:
In your slow cooker, mix the barley with the onion, paprika and the other ingredients, toss, put the lid on and cook on Low for 6 hours. Divide between plates and serve as a side dish.

NUTRITION:
calories 160, fat 3, fiber 7, carbs 13, protein 7

Sweet Potato Mash

Preparation time: 10 minutes

Cooking time: 5 hours

Servings: 6

INGREDIENTS:
- 2 pounds sweet potatoes, peeled and sliced
- 1 tablespoon cinnamon powder
- 1 cup apple juice
- 1 teaspoon nutmeg, ground
- ¼ teaspoon cloves, ground
- ½ teaspoon allspice
- 1 tablespoon butter, melted

DIRECTIONS:
In your Slow cooker, mix sweet potatoes with cinnamon, apple juice, nutmeg, cloves and allspice, stir, cover and cook on Low for 5 hours. Mash using a potato masher, add butter, whisk well, divide between plates and serve as a side dish.

NUTRITION:
calories 111, fat 2, fiber 2, carbs 16, protein 3

Lime Beans Mix

Preparation time: 10 minutes

Cooking time: 8 hours

Servings: 2

INGREDIENTS:
- ½ pound lima beans, soaked for 6 hours and drained
- 1 tablespoon olive oil
- 2 scallions, chopped
- 1 carrot, chopped
- 2 tablespoons tomato paste
- 1 garlic cloves, minced
- A pinch of salt and black pepper to the taste
- 3 cups water
- A pinch of red pepper, crushed
- 2 tablespoons parsley, chopped

DIRECTIONS:
In your slow cooker, mix the beans with the scallions, oil and the other ingredients, toss, put the lid on and cook on Low for 8 hours. Divide between plates and serve as a side dish/

NUTRITION:
calories 160, fat 3, fiber 7, carbs 9, protein 12

Dill Cauliflower Mash

Preparation time: 10 minutes

Cooking time: 5 hours

Servings: 6

INGREDIENTS:
- 1 cauliflower head, florets separated
- 1/3 cup dill, chopped
- 6 garlic cloves
- 2 tablespoons butter, melted
- A pinch of salt and black pepper

DIRECTIONS:
Put cauliflower in your Slow cooker, add dill, garlic and water to cover cauliflower, cover and cook on High for 5 hours. Drain cauliflower and dill, add salt, pepper and butter, mash using a potato masher, whisk well and serve as a side dish.

NUTRITION:
calories 187, fat 4, fiber 5, carbs 12, protein 3

Creamy Beans

Preparation time: 10 minutes

Cooking time: 2 hours

Servings: 2

INGREDIENTS:
- 2 ounces green beans, trimmed and halved
- 2 tablespoons hot sauce
- 2 tablespoons heavy cream
- ½ cup coconut milk
- ¼ teaspoon cumin, ground
- ¼ tablespoon chili powder

DIRECTIONS:
In your slow cooker, mix the beans with the hot

sauce and the other ingredients, toss, put the lid on and cook on Low for 2 hours. Divide between plates and serve right away as a side dish.

NUTRITION:
calories 230, fat 4, fiber 6, carbs 8, protein 10

Eggplant and Kale Mix

Preparation time: 10 minutes
Cooking time: 2 hours
Servings: 6

INGREDIENTS:
- 14 ounces canned roasted tomatoes and garlic
- 4 cups eggplant, cubed
- 1 yellow bell pepper, chopped
- 1 red onion, cut into medium wedges
- 4 cups kale leaves
- 2 tablespoons olive oil
- 1 teaspoon mustard
- 3 tablespoons red vinegar
- 1 garlic clove, minced
- Salt and black pepper to the taste
- ½ cup basil, chopped

DIRECTIONS:
In your Slow cooker, mix the eggplant with tomatoes, bell pepper and onion, toss, cover and cook on High for 2 hours. Add kale, toss, cover slow cooker and leave aside for now. In a bowl, mix oil with vinegar, mustard, garlic, salt and pepper and whisk well. Add this over eggplant mix, also add basil, toss, divide between plates and serve as a side dish.

NUTRITION:
calories 251, fat 9, fiber 6, carbs 34, protein 8

Spinach Mix

Preparation time: 10 minutes
Cooking time: 1 hour
Servings: 2

INGREDIENTS:
- 1 pound baby spinach
- ½ cup cherry tomatoes, halved
- ½ tablespoon olive oil
- ½ cup veggie stock
- 1 small yellow onion, chopped
- ¼ teaspoon coriander, ground
- ¼ teaspoon cumin, ground
- ¼ teaspoon garam masala
- ¼ teaspoon chili powder
- Salt and black pepper to the taste

DIRECTIONS:
In your slow cooker, mix the spinach with the tomatoes, oil and the other ingredients, toss, put the lid on and cook on High for 1 hour. Divide between plates and serve as a side dish.,

NUTRITION:
calories 270, fat 4, fiber 6, carbs 8, protein 12

Thai Side Salad

Preparation time: 10 minutes
Cooking time: 3 hours
Servings: 8

INGREDIENTS:
- 8 ounces yellow summer squash, peeled and roughly chopped
- 12 ounces zucchini, halved and sliced
- 2 cups button mushrooms, quartered
- 1 red sweet potatoes, chopped
- 2 leeks, sliced
- 2 tablespoons veggie stock
- 2 garlic cloves, minced
- 2 tablespoon Thai red curry paste
- 1 tablespoon ginger, grated
- 1/3 cup coconut milk
- ¼ cup basil, chopped

DIRECTIONS:
In your Slow cooker, mix zucchini with summer squash, mushrooms, red pepper, leeks, garlic, stock, curry paste, ginger, coconut milk and basil, toss, cover and cook on Low for 3 hours. Stir your Thai mix one more time, divide between plates and serve as a side dish.

NUTRITION:
calories 69, fat 2, fiber 2, carbs 8, protein 2

Bbq Beans

Preparation time: 10 minutes
Cooking time: 8 hours
Servings: 2

INGREDIENTS:
- ¼ pound navy beans, soaked overnight and drained
- 1 cup bbq sauce
- 1 tablespoon sugar
- 1 tablespoon ketchup
- 1 tablespoon water
- 1 tablespoon apple cider vinegar
- 1 tablespoon olive oil
- 1 tablespoon soy sauce

DIRECTIONS:
In your slow cooker, mix the beans with the sauce, sugar and the other ingredients, toss, put the lid on and cook on Low for 8 hours. Divide between plates and serve as a side dish.

NUTRITION:
calories 430, fat 7, fiber 8, carbs 15, protein 19

Rosemary Potatoes

Preparation time: 10 minutes
Cooking time: 3 hours
Servings: 12

INGREDIENTS:
2 tablespoons olive oil
3 pounds new potatoes, halved
7 garlic cloves, minced
1 tablespoon rosemary, chopped
A pinch of salt and black pepper

DIRECTIONS:
In your Slow cooker, mix oil with potatoes, garlic, rosemary, salt and pepper, toss, cover and cook on High for 3 hours. Divide between plates and serve as a side dish.

NUTRITION:
calories 102, fat 2, fiber 2, carbs 18, protein 2

White Beans Mix

Preparation time: 10 minutes
Cooking time: 6 hours
Servings: 4

INGREDIENTS:
1 celery stalk, chopped
2 garlic cloves, minced
1 carrot, chopped
1 cup veggie stock
½ cup canned tomatoes, crushed
½ teaspoon chili powder
½ tablespoon Italian seasoning
15 ounces canned white beans, drained
1 tablespoon parsley, chopped

DIRECTIONS:
In your slow cooker, mix the beans with the celery, garlic and the other ingredients, toss, put the lid on and cook on Low for 6 hours. Divide the mix between plates and serve.

NUTRITION:
calories 223, fat 3, fiber 7, carbs 10, protein 7

Maple Brussels Sprouts

Preparation time: 10 minutes
Cooking time: 3 hours
Servings: 12

INGREDIENTS:
1 cup red onion, chopped
2 pounds Brussels sprouts, trimmed and halved
Salt and black pepper to the taste
¼ cup apple juice
3 tablespoons olive oil
¼ cup maple syrup
1 tablespoon thyme, chopped

DIRECTIONS:
In your slow cooker, mix Brussels sprouts with onion, salt, pepper and apple juice, toss, cover and cook on Low for 3 hours. In a bowl, mix maple syrup with oil and thyme, whisk really well, add over Brussels sprouts, toss well, divide between plates and serve as a side dish.

NUTRITION:
calories 100, fat 4, fiber 4, carbs 14, protein 3

Sweet Potato and Cauliflower Mix

Preparation time: 10 minutes
Cooking time: 4 hours
Servings: 2

INGREDIENTS:
2 sweet potatoes, peeled and cubed
1 cup cauliflower florets
½ cup coconut milk
1 teaspoons sriracha sauce
A pinch of salt and black pepper
½ tablespoon sugar
1 tablespoon red curry paste
3 ounces white mushrooms, roughly chopped
2 tablespoons cilantro, chopped

DIRECTIONS:
In your slow cooker, mix the sweet potatoes with the cauliflower and the other ingredients, toss, put the lid on and cook on Low for 4 hours. Divide between plates and serve as a side dish.

NUTRITION:
calories 200, fat 3, fiber 5, carbs 15, protein 12

Beets and Carrots

Preparation time: 10 minutes
Cooking time: 7 hours
Servings: 8

INGREDIENTS:
2 tablespoons stevia
¾ cup pomegranate juice
2 teaspoons ginger, grated
2 and ½ pounds beets, peeled and cut into wedges
12 ounces carrots, cut into medium wedges

DIRECTIONS:
In your Slow cooker, mix beets with carrots, ginger, stevia and pomegranate juice, toss, cover and cook on Low for 7 hours. Divide between plates and serve as a side dish.

NUTRITION:
calories 125, fat 0, fiber 4, carbs 28, protein 3

Cabbage Mix

Preparation time: 10 minutes
Cooking time: 6 hours
Servings: 2

INGREDIENTS:

1 pound red cabbage, shredded
1 apple, peeled, cored and roughly chopped
A pinch of salt and black pepper to the taste
¼ cup chicken stock
1 tablespoon mustard
½ tablespoon olive oil

DIRECTIONS:

In your slow cooker, mix the cabbage with the apple and the other ingredients, toss, put the lid on and cook on Low for 6 hours. Divide between plates and serve as a side dish.

NUTRITION:

calories 200, fat 4, fiber 2, carbs 8, protein 6

Italian Veggie Mix

Preparation time: 10 minutes
Cooking time: 6 hours
Servings: 8

INGREDIENTS:

38 ounces canned cannellini beans, drained
1 yellow onion, chopped
¼ cup basil pesto
19 ounces canned fava beans, drained
4 garlic cloves, minced
1 and ½ teaspoon Italian seasoning, dried and crushed
1 tomato, chopped
15 ounces already cooked polenta, cut into medium pieces
2 cups spinach
1 cup radicchio, torn

DIRECTIONS:

In your Slow cooker, mix cannellini beans with fava beans, basil pesto, onion, garlic, Italian seasoning, polenta, tomato, spinach and radicchio, toss, cover and cook on Low for 6 hours. Divide between plates and serve as a side dish.

NUTRITION:

calories 364, fat 12, fiber 10, carbs 45, protein 21

Parsley Mushroom Mix

Preparation time: 10 minutes
Cooking time: 4 hours
Servings: 2

INGREDIENTS:

1 pound brown mushrooms, halved
2 garlic cloves, minced
A pinch of basil, dried
A pinch of oregano, dried
½ cup veggie stock
Salt and black pepper to the taste
1 tablespoon olive oil
1 tablespoon parsley, chopped

DIRECTIONS:

In your slow cooker, mix the mushrooms with the garlic, basil and the other ingredients, toss, put the lid on and cook on Low for 4 hours. Divide everything between plates and serve.

NUTRITION:

calories 122, fat 6, fiber 1, carbs 8, protein 5

Wild Rice and Barley Pilaf

Preparation time: 10 minutes
Cooking time: 7 hours
Servings: 12

INGREDIENTS:

½ cup wild rice
½ cup barley
2/3 cup wheat berries
27 ounces veggie stock
2 cups baby lima beans
1 red bell pepper, chopped
1 yellow onion, chopped
1 tablespoon olive oil
A pinch of salt and black pepper
1 teaspoon sage, dried and crushed
4 garlic cloves, minced

DIRECTIONS:

In your Slow cooker, mix rice with barley, wheat berries, lima beans, bell pepper, onion, oil, salt, pepper, sage and garlic, stir, cover and cook on Low for 7 hours. Stir one more time, divide between plates and serve as a side dish.

NUTRITION:

calories 168, fat 5, fiber 4, carbs 25, protein 6

Cinnamon Squash

Preparation time: 10 minutes
Cooking time: 4 hours
Servings: 2

INGREDIENTS:

1 acorn squash, peeled and cut into medium wedges
1 cup coconut cream
A pinch of cinnamon powder
A pinch of salt and black pepper

DIRECTIONS:

In your slow cooker, mix the squash with the cream and the other ingredients, toss, put the lid on and cook on Low for 4 hours. Divide between plates and serve as a side dish.

NUTRITION:
calories 230, fat 3, fiber 3, carbs 10, protein 2

Apples and Potatoes

Preparation time: 10 minutes
Cooking time: 7 hours
Servings: 10

INGREDIENTS:
2 green apples, cored and cut into wedges
3 pounds sweet potatoes, peeled and cut into medium wedges
1 cup coconut cream
½ cup dried cherries
1 cup apple butter
1 and ½ teaspoon pumpkin pie spice

DIRECTIONS:
In your Slow cooker, mix sweet potatoes with green apples, cream, cherries, apple butter and spice, toss, cover and cook on Low for 7 hours. Toss, divide between plates and serve as a side dish.

NUTRITION:
calories 351, fat 8, fiber 5, carbs 48, protein 2

Zucchini Mix

Preparation time: 10 minutes
Cooking time: 6 hours
Servings: 2

INGREDIENTS:
1 pound zucchinis, sliced
½ teaspoon Italian seasoning
½ teaspoon sweet paprika
Salt and black pepper
½ cup heavy cream
½ teaspoon garlic powder
1 tablespoon olive oil

DIRECTIONS:
In your slow cooker, mix the zucchinis with the seasoning, paprika and the other ingredients, toss, put the lid on and cook on Low for 6 hours. Divide between plates and serve as a side dish.

NUTRITION:
calories 170, fat 2, fiber 4, carbs 8, protein 5

Asparagus and Mushroom Mix

Preparation time: 10 minutes
Cooking time: 5 hours
Servings: 4

INGREDIENTS:
2 pounds asparagus spears, cut into medium pieces
1 cup mushrooms, sliced
A drizzle of olive oil
Salt and black pepper to the taste
2 cups coconut milk
1 teaspoon Worcestershire sauce
5 eggs, whisked

DIRECTIONS:
Grease your Slow cooker with the oil and spread asparagus and mushrooms on the bottom. In a bowl, mix the eggs with milk, salt, pepper and Worcestershire sauce, whisk, pour into the slow cooker, toss everything, cover and cook on Low for 6 hours. Divide between plates and serve as a side dish.

NUTRITION:
calories 211, fat 4, fiber 4, carbs 6, protein 5

Kale Mix

Preparation time: 10 minutes
Cooking time: 2 hours
Servings: 2

INGREDIENTS:
1 pound baby kale
½ tablespoon tomato paste
½ cup chicken stock
½ teaspoon chili powder
A pinch of salt and black pepper
1 tablespoon olive oil
1 small yellow onion, chopped
1 tablespoon apple cider vinegar

DIRECTIONS:
In your slow cooker, mix the kale with the tomato paste, stock and the other ingredients, toss, put the lid on and cook on Low for 2 hours. Divide between plates and serve as a side dish.

NUTRITION:
calories 200, fat 4, fiber 7, carbs 10, protein 3

Asparagus Mix

Preparation time: 10 minutes
Cooking time: 6 hours
Servings: 4

INGREDIENTS:
10 ounces cream of celery
12 ounces asparagus, chopped
2 eggs, hard-boiled, peeled and sliced
1 cup cheddar cheese, shredded
1 teaspoon olive oil

DIRECTIONS:
Grease your Slow cooker with the oil, add cream of celery and cheese to the slow cooker and stir. Add asparagus and eggs, cover and cook on Low for 6 hours. Divide between plates and serve as a side dish.

NUTRITION:
calories 241, fat 5, fiber 4, carbs 5, protein 12

Buttery Spinach

Preparation time: 10 minutes
Cooking time: 2 hours
Servings: 2

INGREDIENTS:
1 pound baby spinach
1 cup heavy cream
½ teaspoon turmeric powder
A pinch of salt and black pepper
½ teaspoon garam masala
2 tablespoons butter, melted

DIRECTIONS:
In your slow cooker, mix the spinach with the cream and the other ingredients, toss, put the lid on and cook on Low for 2 hours. Divide between plates and serve as a side dish.

NUTRITION:
calories 230, fat 12, fiber 2, carbs 9, protein 12

Chorizo and Cauliflower Mix

Preparation time: 10 minutes
Cooking time: 5 hours
Servings: 4

INGREDIENTS:
1 pound chorizo, chopped
12 ounces canned green chilies, chopped
1 yellow onion, chopped
½ teaspoon garlic powder
Salt and black pepper to the taste
1 cauliflower head, riced
2 tablespoons green onions, chopped

DIRECTIONS:
Heat up a pan over medium heat, add chorizo and onion, stir, brown for a few minutes and transfer to your Slow cooker. Add chilies, garlic powder, salt, pepper, cauliflower and green onions, toss, cover and cook on Low for 5 hours. Divide between plates and serve as a side dish.

NUTRITION:
calories 350, fat 12, fiber 4, carbs 6, protein 20

Bacon Potatoes Mix

Preparation time: 10 minutes
Cooking time: 6 hours
Servings: 2

INGREDIENTS:
2 sweet potatoes, peeled and cut into wedges
1 tablespoon balsamic vinegar
½ tablespoon sugar
A pinch of salt and black pepper
¼ teaspoon sage, dried
A pinch of thyme, dried
1 tablespoon olive oil
½ cup veggie stock
2 bacon slices, cooked and crumbled

DIRECTIONS:
In your slow cooker, mix the potatoes with the vinegar, sugar and the other ingredients, toss, put the lid on and cook on Low for 6 hours Divide between plates and serve as a side dish.

NUTRITION:
calories 209, fat 4, fiber 4, carbs 29, protein 4

Classic Veggies Mix

Preparation time: 10 minutes
Cooking time: 3 hours
Servings: 4

INGREDIENTS:
1 and ½ cups red onion, cut into medium chunks
1 cup cherry tomatoes, halved
2 and ½ cups zucchini, sliced
2 cups yellow bell pepper, chopped
1 cup mushrooms, sliced
2 tablespoons basil, chopped
1 tablespoon thyme, chopped
½ cup olive oil
½ cup balsamic vinegar

DIRECTIONS:
In your Slow cooker, mix onion pieces with tomatoes, zucchini, bell pepper, mushrooms, basil, thyme, oil and vinegar, toss to coat everything, cover and cook on High for 3 hours. Divide between plates and serve as a side dish.

NUTRITION:
calories 150, fat 2, fiber 2, carbs 6, protein 5

Cauliflower Mash

Preparation time: 10 minutes
Cooking time: 5 hours
Servings: 2

INGREDIENTS:
1 pound cauliflower florets
½ cup heavy cream
1 tablespoon dill, chopped
2 garlic cloves, minced
1 tablespoons butter, melted
A pinch of salt and black pepper

DIRECTIONS:
In your slow cooker, mix the cauliflower with the cream and the other ingredients, toss, put the lid on and cook on High for 5 hours. Mash the mix, whisk, divide between plates and serve.

NUTRITION:
calories 187, fat 4, fiber 5, carbs 7, protein 3

Okra Side Dish
Preparation time: 10 minutes
Cooking time: 3 hours
Servings: 4

INGREDIENTS:
2 cups okra, sliced
1 and ½ cups red onion, roughly chopped
1 cup cherry tomatoes, halved
2 and ½ cups zucchini, sliced
2 cups red and yellow bell peppers, sliced
1 cup white mushrooms, sliced
½ cup olive oil
½ cup balsamic vinegar
2 tablespoons basil, chopped
1 tablespoon thyme, chopped

DIRECTIONS:
In your Slow cooker, mix okra with onion, tomatoes, zucchini, bell peppers, mushrooms, basil and thyme. In a bowl mix oil with vinegar, whisk well, add to the slow cooker, cover and cook on High for 3 hours. Divide between plates and serve as a side dish.

NUTRITION:
calories 233, fat 12, fiber 4, carbs 8, protein 4

Veggie Mix
Preparation time: 10 minutes
Cooking time: 5 hours
Servings: 2

INGREDIENTS:
1 eggplant, cubed
1 cup cherry tomatoes, halved
1 small zucchini, halved and sliced
½ red bell pepper, chopped
½ cup tomato sauce
1 carrot, peeled and cubed
1 sweet potato, peeled and cubed
A pinch of red pepper flakes, crushed
1 tablespoon basil, chopped
1 tablespoon parsley, chopped
A pinch of salt and black pepper
½ cup veggie stock
1 tablespoon capers
1 tablespoon red wine vinegar

DIRECTIONS:
In your slow cooker, mix the eggplant with the tomatoes, zucchini and the other ingredients, toss, put the lid on and cook on Low for 5 hours. Divide between plates and serve as a side dish.

NUTRITION:
calories 100, fat 1, fiber 2, carbs 7, protein 5

Okra Side Dish
Preparation time: 10 minutes
Cooking time: 4 hours
Servings: 4

INGREDIENTS:
1 pound okra, sliced
1 tomato, chopped
6 ounces tomato sauce
1 cup water
Salt and black pepper to the taste
1 yellow onion, chopped
2 garlic cloves, minced

DIRECTIONS:
In your Slow cooker, mix okra with tomato, tomato sauce, water, salt, pepper, onion and garlic, stir, cover and cook on Low for 4 hours. Divide between plates and serve as a side dish.

NUTRITION:
calories 211, fat 4, fiber 6, carbs 17, protein 3

Farro Mix
Preparation time: 10 minutes
Cooking time: 4 hours
Servings: 2

INGREDIENTS:
2 scallions, chopped
2 garlic cloves, minced
1 tablespoon olive oil
1 cup whole grain farro
2 cups chicken stock
Salt and black pepper to the taste
½ tablespoon parsley, chopped
1 tablespoon cherries, dried

DIRECTIONS:
In your slow cooker, mix the farro with the scallions, garlic and the other ingredients, toss, put the lid on and cook on Low for 4 hours. Divide between plates and serve as a side dish.

NUTRITION:
calories 152, fat 4, fiber 5, carbs 20, protein 4

Okra Mix

Preparation time: 10 minutes
Cooking time: 8 hours
Servings: 4

INGREDIENTS:
2 garlic cloves, minced
1 yellow onion, chopped
14 ounces tomato sauce
1 teaspoon sweet paprika
2 cups okra, sliced
Salt and black pepper to the taste

DIRECTIONS:
In your Slow cooker, mix garlic with the onion, tomato sauce, paprika, okra, salt and pepper, cover and cook on Low for 8 hours. Divide between plates and serve as a side dish.

NUTRITION:
calories 200, fat 6, fiber 5, carbs 10, protein 4

Cumin Quinoa Pilaf

Preparation time: 10 minutes
Cooking time: 2 hours
Servings: 2

INGREDIENTS:
1 cup quinoa
2 teaspoons butter, melted
Salt and black pepper to the taste
1 teaspoon turmeric powder
2 cups chicken stock
1 teaspoon cumin, ground

DIRECTIONS:
Grease your slow cooker with the butter, add the quinoa and the other ingredients, toss, put the lid on and cook on High for 2 hours Divide between plates and serve as a side dish.

NUTRITION:
calories 152, fat 3, fiber 6, carbs 8, protein 4

Stewed Okra

Preparation time: 10 minutes
Cooking time: 3 hours
Servings: 4

INGREDIENTS:
2 cups okra, sliced
2 garlic cloves, minced
6 ounces tomato sauce
1 red onion, chopped
A pinch of cayenne peppers
1 teaspoon liquid smoke
Salt and black pepper to the taste

DIRECTIONS:
In your Slow cooker, mix okra with garlic, onion, cayenne, tomato sauce, liquid smoke, salt and pepper, cover, cook on Low for 3 hours. Divide between plates and serve as a side dish.

NUTRITION:
calories 182, fat 3, fiber 6, carbs 8, protein 3

Saffron Risotto

Preparation time: 10 minutes
Cooking time: 2 hours
Servings: 2

INGREDIENTS:
½ tablespoon olive oil
¼ teaspoon saffron powder
1 cup Arborio rice
2 cups veggie stock
A pinch of salt and black pepper
A pinch of cinnamon powder
1 tablespoon almonds, chopped

DIRECTIONS:
In your slow cooker, mix the rice with the stock and the other ingredients, toss, put the lid on and cook on High for 2 hours. Divide between plates and serve as a side dish.

NUTRITION:
calories 251, fat 4, fiber 7, carbs 29, protein 4

Okra and Corn

Preparation time: 10 minutes
Cooking time: 8 hours
Servings: 4

INGREDIENTS:
3 garlic cloves, minced
1 small green bell pepper, chopped
1 small yellow onion, chopped
1 cup water
16 ounces okra, sliced
2 cups corn
1 and ½ teaspoon smoked paprika
28 ounces canned tomatoes, crushed
1 teaspoon oregano, dried
1 teaspoon thyme, dried
1 teaspoon marjoram, dried
A pinch of cayenne pepper
Salt and black pepper to the taste

DIRECTIONS:
In your Slow cooker, mix garlic with bell pepper, onion, water, okra, corn, paprika, tomatoes,

oregano, thyme, marjoram, cayenne, salt and pepper, cover, cook on Low for 8 hours, divide between plates and serve as a side dish.

NUTRITION:
calories 182, fat 3, fiber 6, carbs 8, protein 5

Mint Farro Pilaf

Preparation time: 10 minutes

Cooking time: 4 hours

Servings: 2

INGREDIENTS:
- ½ tablespoon balsamic vinegar
- ½ cup whole grain farro
- A pinch of salt and black pepper
- 1 cup chicken stock
- ½ tablespoon olive oil
- 1 tablespoon green onions, chopped
- 1 tablespoon mint, chopped

DIRECTIONS:
In your slow cooker, mix the farro with the vinegar and the other ingredients, toss, put the lid on and cook on Low for 4 hours. Divide between plates and serve.

NUTRITION:
calories 162, fat 3, fiber 6, carbs 9, protein 4

Roasted Beets

Preparation time: 10 minutes

Cooking time: 4 hours

Servings: 5

INGREDIENTS:
- 10 small beets
- 5 teaspoons olive oil
- A pinch of salt and black pepper

DIRECTIONS:
Divide each beet on a tin foil piece, drizzle oil, season them with salt and pepper, rub well, wrap beets, place them in your Slow cooker, cover and cook on High for 4 hours. Unwrap beets, cool them down a bit, peel, slice and serve them as a side dish.

NUTRITION:
calories 100, fat 2, fiber 2, carbs 4, protein 5

Parmesan Rice

Preparation time: 10 minutes

Cooking time: 2 hours and 30 minutes

Servings: 2

INGREDIENTS:
- 1 cup rice
- 2 cups chicken stock
- 1 tablespoon olive oil
- 1 red onion, chopped
- 1 tablespoon lemon juice
- Salt and black pepper to the taste
- 1 tablespoon parmesan, grated

DIRECTIONS:
In your slow cooker, mix the rice with the stock, oil and the other ingredients, toss, put the lid on and cook on High for 2 hours and 30 minutes. Divide between plates and serve as a side dish.

NUTRITION:
calories 162, fat 4, fiber 6, carbs 29, protein 6

Thyme Beets

Preparation time: 10 minutes

Cooking time: 6 hours

Servings: 8

INGREDIENTS:
- 12 small beets, peeled and sliced
- ¼ cup water
- 4 garlic cloves, minced
- 2 tablespoons olive oil
- 1 teaspoon thyme, dried
- Salt and black pepper to the taste
- 1 tablespoon fresh thyme, chopped

DIRECTIONS:
In your Slow cooker, mix beets with water, garlic, oil, dried thyme, salt and pepper, cover and cook on Low for 6 hours. Divide beets on plates, sprinkle fresh thyme all over and serve as a side dish.

NUTRITION:
66, fat 4, fiber 1, carbs 8, protein 1

Spinach Rice

Preparation time: 10 minutes

Cooking time: 2 hours

Servings: 2

INGREDIENTS:
- 2 scallions, chopped
- 1 tablespoon olive oil
- 1 cup Arborio rice
- 1 cup chicken stock
- 6 ounces spinach, chopped
- Salt and black pepper to the taste
- 2 ounces goat cheese, crumbled

DIRECTIONS:
In your slow cooker, mix the rice with the stock and the other ingredients, toss, put the lid on and cook on High for 2 hours. Divide between plates and serve as a side dish.

NUTRITION:
calories 300, fat 10, fiber 6, carbs 20, protein 14

Beets Side Salad

Preparation time: 10 minutes

Cooking time: 7 hours

Servings: 12

INGREDIENTS:
- 5 beets, peeled and sliced
- ¼ cup balsamic vinegar
- 1/3 cup honey
- 1 tablespoon rosemary, chopped
- 2 tablespoons olive oil
- Salt and black pepper to the taste
- 2 garlic cloves, minced

DIRECTIONS:
In your Slow cooker, mix beets with vinegar, honey, oil, salt, pepper, rosemary and garlic, cover and cook on Low for 7 hours. Divide between plates and serve as a side dish.

NUTRITION:
calories 70, fat 3, fiber 2, carbs 17, protein 3

Mango Rice

Preparation time: 10 minutes

Cooking time: 2 hours

Servings: 2

INGREDIENTS:
- 1 cup rice
- 2 cups chicken stock
- ½ cup mango, peeled and cubed
- Salt and black pepper to the taste
- 1 teaspoon olive oil

DIRECTIONS:
In your slow cooker, mix the rice with the stock and the other ingredients, toss, put the lid on and cook on High for 2 hours. Divide between plates and serve as a side dish.

NUTRITION:
calories 152, fat 4, fiber 5, carbs 18, protein 4

Lemony Beets

Preparation time: 10 minutes

Cooking time: 8 hours

Servings: 6

INGREDIENTS:
- 6 beets, peeled and cut into medium wedges
- 2 tablespoons honey
- 2 tablespoons olive oil
- 2 tablespoons lemon juice
- Salt and black pepper to the taste
- 1 tablespoon white vinegar
- ½ teaspoon lemon peel, grated

DIRECTIONS:
In your Slow cooker, mix beets with honey, oil, lemon juice, salt, pepper, vinegar and lemon peel, cover and cook on Low for 8 hours. Divide between plates and serve as a side dish.

NUTRITION:
calories 80, fat 3, fiber 4, carbs 8, protein 4

Lemon Artichokes

Preparation time: 10 minutes

Cooking time: 3 hours

Servings: 2

INGREDIENTS:
- 1 cup veggie stock
- 2 medium artichokes, trimmed
- 1 tablespoon lemon juice
- 1 tablespoon lemon zest, grated
- Salt to the taste

DIRECTIONS:
In your slow cooker, mix the artichokes with the stock and the other ingredients, toss, put the lid on and cook on Low for 3 hours. Divide artichokes between plates and serve as a side dish.

NUTRITION:
calories 100, fat 2, fiber 5, carbs 10, protein 4

Carrot and Beet Side Salad

Preparation time: 10 minutes

Cooking time: 7 hours

Servings: 6

INGREDIENTS:
- ½ cup walnuts, chopped
- ¼ cup lemon juice
- ½ cup olive oil
- 1 shallot, chopped
- 1 teaspoon Dijon mustard
- 1 tablespoon brown sugar
- Salt and black pepper to the taste
- 2 beets, peeled and cut into wedges
- 2 carrots, peeled and sliced
- 1 cup parsley
- 5 ounces arugula

DIRECTIONS:
In your Slow cooker, mix beets with carrots, salt, pepper, sugar, mustard, shallot, oil, lemon juice and walnuts, cover and cook on Low for 7 hours. Transfer everything to a bowl, add parsley and arugula, toss, divide between plates and serve as a side dish.

NUTRITION:
calories 100, fat 3, fiber 3, carbs 7, protein 3

Coconut Bok Choy

Preparation time: 10 minutes
Cooking time: 1 hour
Servings: 2

INGREDIENTS:
1 pound bok choy, torn
½ cup chicken stock
½ teaspoon chili powder
1 garlic clove, minced
1 teaspoon ginger, grated
1 tablespoon coconut oil
Salt to the taste

DIRECTIONS:
In your slow cooker, mix the bok choy with the stock and the other ingredients, toss, put the lid on and cook on High for 1 hour. Divide between plates and serve as a side dish.

NUTRITION:
calories 100, fat 1, fiber 2, carbs 7, protein 4

Cauliflower and Carrot Gratin

Preparation time: 10 minutes
Cooking time: 7 hours
Servings: 12

INGREDIENTS:
16 ounces baby carrots
6 tablespoons butter, soft
1 cauliflower head, florets separated
Salt and black pepper to the taste
1 yellow onion, chopped
1 teaspoon mustard powder
1 and ½ cups milk
6 ounces cheddar cheese, grated
½ cup breadcrumbs

DIRECTIONS:
Put the butter in your Slow cooker, add carrots, cauliflower, onion, salt, pepper, mustard powder and milk and toss. Sprinkle cheese and breadcrumbs all over, cover and cook on Low for 7 hours. Divide between plates and serve as a side dish.

NUTRITION:
calories 182, fat 4, fiber 7, carbs 9, protein 4

Italian Eggplant

Preparation time: 10 minutes
Cooking time: 2 hours
Servings: 2

INGREDIENTS:
2 small eggplants, roughly cubed
½ cup heavy cream
Salt and black pepper to the taste
1 tablespoon olive oil
A pinch of hot pepper flakes
2 tablespoons oregano, chopped

DIRECTIONS:
In your slow cooker, mix the eggplants with the cream and the other ingredients, toss, put the lid on and cook on High for 2 hours. Divide between plates and serve as a side dish.

NUTRITION:
calories 132, fat 4, fiber 6, carbs 12, protein 3

Herbed Beets

Preparation time: 10 minutes
Cooking time: 7 hours
Servings: 4

INGREDIENTS:
6 medium assorted-color beets, peeled and cut into wedges
2 tablespoons balsamic vinegar
2 tablespoons olive oil
2 tablespoons chives, chopped
1 tablespoon tarragon, chopped
Salt and black pepper to the taste
1 teaspoon orange peel, grated

DIRECTIONS:
In your Slow cooker, mix beets with vinegar, oil, chives, tarragon, salt, pepper and orange peel, cover and cook on Low for 7 hours. Divide between plates and serve as a side dish.

NUTRITION:
calories 144, fat 3, fiber 1, carbs 17, protein 3

Cabbage and Onion Mix

Preparation time: 10 minutes
Cooking time: 2 hours
Servings: 2

INGREDIENTS:
1 and ½ cups green cabbage, shredded
1 cup red cabbage, shredded
1 tablespoon olive oil
1 red onion, sliced
2 spring onions, chopped
½ cup tomato paste
¼ cup veggie stock
2 tomatoes, chopped
2 jalapenos, chopped
1 tablespoon chili powder
1 tablespoon chives, chopped
A pinch of salt and black pepper

DIRECTIONS:
Grease your slow cooker with the oil and mix the cabbage with the onion, spring onions and the other ingredients inside. Toss, put the lid on and cook on High for 2 hours. Divide between plates and serve as a side dish.

NUTRITION:
calories 211, fat 3, fiber 3, carbs 6, protein 8

Summer Squash Mix

Preparation time: 10 minutes

Cooking time: 2 hours

Servings: 4

INGREDIENTS:
- ¼ cup olive oil
- 2 tablespoons basil, chopped
- 2 tablespoons balsamic vinegar
- 2 garlic cloves, minced
- 2 teaspoons mustard
- Salt and black pepper to the taste
- 3 summer squash, sliced
- 2 zucchinis, sliced

DIRECTIONS:
In your Slow cooker, mix squash with zucchinis, salt, pepper, mustard, garlic, vinegar, basil and oil, toss a bit, cover and cook on High for 2 hours. Divide between plates and serve as a side dish.

NUTRITION:
calories 179, fat 13, fiber 2, carbs 10, protein 4

Balsamic Okra Mix

Preparation time: 10 minutes

Cooking time: 2 hours

Servings: 4

INGREDIENTS:
- 2 cups okra, sliced
- 1 cup cherry tomatoes, halved
- 1 tablespoon olive oil
- ½ teaspoon turmeric powder
- ½ cup canned tomatoes, crushed
- 2 tablespoons balsamic vinegar
- 2 tablespoons basil, chopped
- 1 tablespoon thyme, chopped

DIRECTIONS:
In your slow cooker, mix the okra with the tomatoes, crushed tomatoes and the other ingredients, toss, put the lid on and cook on High for 2 hours. Divide between plates and serve as a side dish.

NUTRITION:
calories 233, fat 12, fiber 4, carbs 8, protein 4

Veggie Side Salad

Preparation time: 10 minutes

Cooking time: 2 hours

Servings: 4

INGREDIENTS:
- 2 garlic cloves, minced
- ½ cup olive oil
- ¼ cup basil, chopped
- Salt and black pepper to the taste
- 1 red bell pepper, chopped
- 1 eggplant, roughly chopped
- 1 summer squash, cubed
- 1 Vidalia onion, cut into wedges
- 1 zucchini, sliced
- 1 green bell pepper, chopped

DIRECTIONS:
In your Slow cooker, mix red bell pepper with green one, squash, zucchini, eggplant, onion, salt, pepper, basil, oil and garlic, toss gently, cover and cook on High for 2 hours. Divide between plates and serve as a side dish.

NUTRITION:
calories 165, fat 11, fiber 3, carbs 15, protein 2

Garlic Carrots Mix

Preparation time: 10 minutes

Cooking time: 4 hours

Servings: 2

INGREDIENTS:
- 1 pound carrots, sliced
- 2 garlic cloves, minced
- 1 red onion, chopped
- 1 tablespoon olive oil
- ½ cup tomato sauce
- A pinch of salt and black pepper
- ½ teaspoon oregano, dried
- 2 teaspoons lemon zest, grated
- 1 tablespoon lemon juice
- 1 tablespoon chives, chopped

DIRECTIONS:
In your slow cooker, mix the carrots with the garlic, onion and the other ingredients, toss, put the lid on and cook on Low for 4 hours. Divide the mix between plates and serve.

NUTRITION:
calories 219, fat 8, fiber 4, carbs 8, protein 17

Italian Squash and Peppers Mix

Preparation time: 10 minutes

Cooking time: 1 hour and 30 minutes

Servings: 4

INGREDIENTS:
- 12 small squash, peeled and cut into wedges
- 2 red bell peppers, cut into wedges
- 2 green bell peppers, cut into wedges
- 1/3 cup Italian dressing
- 1 red onion, cut into wedges
- Salt and black pepper to the taste
- 1 tablespoon parsley, chopped

DIRECTIONS:
In your Slow cooker, mix squash with red bell peppers, green bell peppers, salt, pepper and Italian dressing, cover and cook on High for 1 hour and 30 minutes. Add parsley, toss, divide between plates and serve as a side dish.

NUTRITION:
calories 80, fat 2, fiber 3, carbs 11, protein 2

Curry Broccoli Mix
Preparation time: 10 minutes
Cooking time: 3 hours
Servings: 2

INGREDIENTS:
- 1 pound broccoli florets
- 1 cup tomato paste
- 1 tablespoon red curry paste
- 1 red onion, sliced
- ½ teaspoon Italian seasoning
- 1 teaspoon thyme, dried
- Salt and black pepper to the taste
- ½ tablespoon cilantro, chopped

DIRECTIONS:
In your slow cooker, mix the broccoli with the curry paste, tomato paste and the other ingredients, toss, put the lid on and cook on Low for 3 hours. Divide the mix between plates and serve as a side dish.

NUTRITION:
calories 177, fat 12, fiber 2, carbs 7, protein 7

Green Beans and Red Peppers
Preparation time: 10 minutes
Cooking time: 2 hours
Servings: 2

INGREDIENTS:
- 2 cups green beans, halved
- 1 red bell pepper, cut into strips
- Salt and black pepper to the taste
- 1 tablespoon olive oil
- 1 and ½ tablespoon honey mustard

DIRECTIONS:
In your Slow cooker, mix green beans with bell pepper, salt, pepper, oil and honey mustard, toss, cover and cook on High for 2 hours. Divide between plates and serve as a side dish.

NUTRITION:
calories 50, fat 0, fiber 4, carbs 8, protein 2

Rice and Corn
Preparation time: 10 minutes
Cooking time: 6 hours
Servings: 2

INGREDIENTS:
- 2 cups veggie stock
- 1 cup wild rice
- 1 cup corn
- 3 spring onions, chopped
- 1 tablespoon olive oil
- 2 teaspoons rosemary, dried
- ½ teaspoon garam masala
- Salt and black pepper to the taste
- 1 tablespoon cilantro, chopped

DIRECTIONS:
In your slow cooker, mix the stock with the rice, corn and the other ingredients, toss, put the lid on and cook on Low for 6 hours. Divide between plates and serve as a side dish.

NUTRITION:
calories 169, fat 5, fiber 3, carbs 8, protein 5

Garlic Butter Green Beans
Preparation time: 10 minutes
Cooking time: 2 hours
Servings: 6

INGREDIENTS:
- 22 ounces green beans
- 2 garlic cloves, minced
- ¼ cup butter, soft
- 2 tablespoons parmesan, grated

DIRECTIONS:
In your Slow cooker, mix green beans with garlic, butter and parmesan, toss, cover and cook on High for 2 hours. Divide between plates, sprinkle parmesan all over and serve as a side dish.

NUTRITION:
calories 60, fat 4, fiber 1, carbs 3, protein 1

Cauliflower and Potatoes Mix
Preparation time: 10 minutes
Cooking time: 4 hours
Servings: 2

INGREDIENTS:
- 1 cup cauliflower florets
- ½ pound sweet potatoes, peeled and cubed
- 1 cup veggie stock
- ½ cup tomato sauce
- 1 tablespoon chives, chopped
- Salt and black pepper to the taste
- 1 teaspoon sweet paprika

DIRECTIONS:
In your slow cooker, mix the cauliflower with the potatoes, stock and the other ingredients, toss, put the lid on and cook on High for 4 hours. Divide between plates and serve as a side dish.

NUTRITION:
calories 135, fat 5, fiber 1, carbs 7, protein 3

Zucchini Casserole

Preparation time: 10 minutes
Cooking time: 2 hours
Servings: 10

INGREDIENTS:
- 7 cups zucchini, sliced
- 2 cups crackers, crushed
- 2 tablespoons melted butter
- 1/3 cup yellow onion, chopped
- 1 cup cheddar cheese, shredded
- 1 cup chicken stock
- 1/3 cup sour cream
- Salt and black pepper to the taste
- 1 tablespoon parsley, chopped
- Cooking spray

DIRECTIONS:
Grease your Slow cooker with cooking spray and arrange zucchini and onion in the pot. Add melted butter, stock, sour cream, salt and pepper and toss. Add cheese mixed with crackers, cover and cook on High for 2 hours. Divide zucchini casserole on plates, sprinkle parsley all over and serve as a side dish.

NUTRITION:
calories 180, fat 6, fiber 1, carbs 14, protein 4

Asparagus Mix

Preparation time: 10 minutes
Cooking time: 2 hours
Servings: 2

INGREDIENTS:
- 1 pound asparagus, trimmed and halved
- 1 red onion, sliced
- 2 garlic cloves, minced
- 1 cup veggie stock
- 1 tablespoon lemon juice
- A pinch of salt and black pepper
- ¼ cup parsley, chopped

DIRECTIONS:
In your slow cooker, mix the asparagus with the onion, garlic and the other ingredients, toss, put the lid on and cook on High for 2 hours. Divide between plates and serve as a side dish.

NUTRITION:
calories 159, fat 4, fiber 4, carbs 6, protein 2

Nut and Berry Side Salad

Preparation time: 10 minutes
Cooking time: 1 hour
Servings: 4

INGREDIENTS:
- 2 cups strawberries, halved
- 2 tablespoons mint, chopped
- 1/3 cup raspberry vinegar
- 2 tablespoons honey
- 1 tablespoon canola oil
- Salt and black pepper to the taste
- 4 cups spinach, torn
- ½ cup blueberries
- ¼ cup walnuts, chopped
- 1 ounce goat cheese, crumbled

DIRECTIONS:
In your Slow cooker, mix strawberries with mint, vinegar, honey, oil, salt, pepper, spinach, blueberries and walnuts, cover and cook on High for 1 hour. Divide salad on plates, sprinkle cheese on top and serve as a side dish.

NUTRITION:
calories 200, fat 12, fiber 4, carbs 17, protein 15

Garlic Squash Mix

Preparation time: 10 minutes
Cooking time: 3 hours
Servings: 2

INGREDIENTS:
- 1 pound butternut squash, peeled and cubed
- 2 spring onions, chopped
- 1 cup veggie stock
- ½ teaspoon red pepper flakes, crushed
- ½ teaspoon turmeric powder
- A pinch of salt and black pepper
- 3 garlic cloves, minced

DIRECTIONS:
In your slow cooker, mix the squash with the garlic, stock and the other ingredients, toss, put the lid on and cook on Low for 3 hours. Divide squash mix between plates and serve as a side dish.

NUTRITION:
calories 196, fat 3, fiber 7, carbs 8, protein 7

Blueberry and Spinach Salad

Preparation time: 10 minutes
Cooking time: 1 hour
Servings: 3

INGREDIENTS:
¼ cup pecans, chopped
½ teaspoon sugar
2 teaspoons maple syrup
1 tablespoon white vinegar
2 tablespoons orange juice
1 tablespoon olive oil
4 cups spinach
2 oranges, peeled and cut into segments
1 cup blueberries

DIRECTIONS:
In your Slow cooker, mix pecans with sugar, maple syrup, vinegar, orange juice, oil, spinach, oranges and blueberries, toss, cover and cook on High for 1 hour. Divide between plates and serve as a side dish.

NUTRITION:
calories 140, fat 4, fiber 3, carbs 10, protein 3

Baby Carrots and Parsnips Mix

Preparation time: 10 minutes
Cooking time: 6 hours
Servings: 2

INGREDIENTS:
1 tablespoon avocado oil
1 pound baby carrots, peeled
½ pound parsnips, peeled and cut into sticks
1 teaspoon sweet paprika
½ cup tomato paste
½ cup veggie stock
½ teaspoon chili powder
A pinch of salt and black pepper
2 garlic cloves, minced
1 tablespoon dill, chopped

DIRECTIONS:
Grease the slow cooker with the oil and mix the carrots with the parsnips, paprika and the other ingredients inside. Toss, put the lid on and cook on Low for 6 hours. Divide everything between plates and serve as a side dish.

NUTRITION:
calories 273, fat 7, fiber 5, carbs 8, protein 12

Rice and Farro Pilaf

Preparation time: 10 minutes
Cooking time: 5 hours
Servings: 12

INGREDIENTS:
1 shallot, chopped
1 teaspoon garlic, minced
A drizzle of olive oil
1 and ½ cups whole grain farro
¾ cup wild rice
6 cups chicken stock
Salt and black pepper to the taste
1 tablespoon parsley and sage, chopped
½ cup hazelnuts, toasted and chopped
¾ cup cherries, dried

DIRECTIONS:
In your Slow cooker, mix oil with garlic, shallot, farro, rice, stock, salt, pepper, sage and parsley, hazelnuts and cherries, toss, cover and cook on Low for 5 hours. Divide between plates and serve as a side dish.

NUTRITION:
calories 120, fat 2, fiber 7, carbs 20, protein 3

Lemon Kale Mix

Preparation time: 10 minutes
Cooking time: 2 hours
Servings: 2

INGREDIENTS:
1 yellow bell pepper, chopped
1 red bell pepper, chopped
1 tablespoon olive oil
1 red onion, sliced
4 cups baby kale
1 teaspoon lemon zest, grated
1 tablespoon lemon juice
½ cup veggie stock
1 garlic clove, minced
A pinch of salt and black pepper
1 tablespoon basil, chopped

DIRECTIONS:
In your slow cooker, mix the kale with the oil, onion, bell peppers and the other ingredients, toss, put the lid on and cook on Low for 2 hours. Divide the mix between plates and serve as a side dish.

NUTRITION:
calories 251, fat 9, fiber 6, carbs 7, protein 8

Pink Rice

Preparation time: 10 minutes
Cooking time: 5 hours
Servings: 8

INGREDIENTS:
1 teaspoon salt
2 and ½ cups water
2 cups pink rice

DIRECTIONS:
Put the rice in your Slow cooker add water and

salt, stir, cover and cook on Low for 5 hours Stir rice a bit, divide it between plates and serve as a side dish.

NUTRITION:
calories 120, fat 3, fiber 3, carbs 16, protein 4

Brussels Sprouts and Cauliflower
Preparation time: 10 minutes
Cooking time: 4 hours
Servings: 2

INGREDIENTS:
- 1 cup Brussels sprouts, trimmed and halved
- 1 cup cauliflower florets
- 1 tablespoon olive oil
- 1 cup veggie stock
- 2 tablespoons tomato paste
- 1 teaspoon chili powder
- ½ teaspoon ginger powder
- A pinch of salt and black pepper
- 1 tablespoon thyme, chopped

DIRECTIONS:
In your slow cooker, mix the Brussels sprouts with the cauliflower, oil, stock and the other ingredients, toss, put the lid on and cook on Low for 4 hours. Divide the mix between plates and serve as a side dish.

NUTRITION:
calories 100, fat 4, fiber 4, carbs 8, protein 3

Pumpkin Rice
Preparation time: 10 minutes
Cooking time: 5 hours
Servings: 4

INGREDIENTS:
- 2 ounces olive oil
- 1 small yellow onion, chopped
- 2 garlic cloves, minced
- 12 ounces risotto rice
- 4 cups chicken stock
- 6 ounces pumpkin puree
- ½ teaspoon nutmeg, ground
- 1 teaspoon thyme, chopped
- ½ teaspoon ginger, grated
- ½ teaspoon cinnamon powder
- ½ teaspoon allspice, ground
- 4 ounces heavy cream

DIRECTIONS:
In your Slow cooker, mix oil with onion, garlic, rice, stock, pumpkin puree, nutmeg, thyme, ginger, cinnamon and allspice, stir, cover and cook on Low for 4 hours and 30 minutes. Add cream, stir, cover, cook on Low for 30 minutes more, divide between plates and serve as a side dish.

NUTRITION:
calories 251, fat 4, fiber 3, carbs 30, protein 5

Cabbage and Kale Mix
Preparation time: 10 minutes
Cooking time: 2 hours
Servings: 2

INGREDIENTS:
- 1 red onion, sliced
- 1 cup green cabbage, shredded
- 1 cup baby kale
- ½ cup canned tomatoes, crushed
- ½ teaspoon hot paprika
- ½ teaspoon Italian seasoning
- A pinch of salt and black pepper
- 1 tablespoon dill, chopped

DIRECTIONS:
In your slow cooker, mix the cabbage with the kale, onion and the other ingredients, toss, put the lid on and cook on High for 2 hours. Divide between plates and serve right away as a side dish.

NUTRITION:
calories 200, fat 4, fiber 2, carbs 8, protein 6

Rice and Veggies
Preparation time: 6 minutes
Cooking time: 5 hours
Servings: 4

INGREDIENTS:
- 2 cups basmati rice
- 1 cup mixed carrots, peas, corn and green beans
- 2 cups water
- ½ teaspoon green chili, minced
- ½ teaspoon ginger, grated
- 3 garlic cloves, minced
- 2 tablespoons butter
- 1 cinnamon stick
- 1 tablespoon cumin seeds
- 2 bay leaves
- 3 whole cloves
- 5 black peppercorns
- 2 whole cardamoms
- 1 tablespoon sugar
- Salt to the taste

DIRECTIONS:
Put the water in your Slow cooker, add rice, mixed veggies, green chili, grated ginger, garlic, cinnamon stick, whole cloves, butter, cumin seeds, bay leaves, cardamoms, black peppercorns, salt and sugar, stir, cover and cook on Low for 5 hours. Discard cinnamon, divide between plates and serve as a side dish.

NUTRITION:
calories 300, fat 4, fiber 3, carbs 40, protein 13

Thyme Mushrooms and Corn

Preparation time: 10 minutes
Cooking time: 4 hours
Servings: 2

INGREDIENTS:
- 4 garlic cloves, minced
- 1 tablespoon olive oil
- 1 pound white mushroom caps, halved
- 1 cup corn
- 1 cup canned tomatoes, crushed
- ¼ teaspoon thyme, dried
- ½ cup veggie stock
- A pinch of salt and black pepper
- 2 tablespoons parsley, chopped

DIRECTIONS:
Grease your slow cooker with the oil, and mix the garlic with the mushrooms, corn and the other ingredients inside. Toss, put the lid on and cook on Low for 4 hours. Divide between plates and serve as a side dish.

NUTRITION:
calories 122, fat 6, fiber 1, carbs 8, protein 5

Farro

Preparation time: 10 minutes
Cooking time: 5 hours
Servings: 6

INGREDIENTS:
- 1 tablespoon apple cider vinegar
- 1 cup whole grain farro
- 1 teaspoon lemon juice
- Salt to the taste
- 3 cups water
- 1 tablespoon olive oil
- ½ cup cherries, dried and chopped
- ¼ cup green onions, chopped
- 10 mint leaves, chopped
- 2 cups cherries, pitted and halved

DIRECTIONS:
Put the water in your Slow cooker, add farro, stir, cover, cook on Low for 5 hours, drain and transfer to a bowl. Add salt, oil, lemon juice, vinegar, dried cherries, fresh cherries, green onions and mint, toss, divide between plates and serve as a side dish.

NUTRITION:
calories 162, fat 3, fiber 6, carbs 12, protein 4

Veggie Medley

Preparation time: 10 minutes
Cooking time: 3 hours
Servings: 2

INGREDIENTS:
- 1 zucchini, cubed
- 1 eggplant, cubed
- ½ cup baby carrots, peeled
- ½ cup baby kale
- 1 cup cherry tomatoes, halved
- 1 teaspoon sweet paprika
- 1 tablespoon olive oil
- 1 cup tomato sauce
- 1 teaspoon Italian seasoning
- A pinch of salt and black pepper
- 1 cup yellow squash, peeled and cut into wedges
- 1 teaspoon garlic powder
- 1 tablespoon cilantro, chopped
- A pinch of salt and black pepper

DIRECTIONS:
Grease your Crockpot with the oil, and mix the zucchini with the eggplant, carrots and the other ingredients inside. Toss, put the lid on and cook on Low for 3 hours. Divide the mix between plates and serve as a side dish.

NUTRITION:
calories 100, fat 2, fiber 4, carbs 8, protein 5

Mexican Rice

Preparation time: 10 minutes
Cooking time: 4 hours
Servings: 8

INGREDIENTS:
- 1 cup long grain rice
- 1 and ¼ cups veggie stock
- ½ cup cilantro, chopped
- ½ avocado, pitted, peeled and chopped
- Salt and black pepper to the taste
- ¼ cup green hot sauce

DIRECTIONS:
Put the rice in your Slow cooker, add stock, stir, cover, cook on Low for 4 hours, fluff with a fork and transfer to a bowl. In your food processor, mix avocado with hot sauce and cilantro, blend well, pour over rice, toss well, add salt and pepper, divide between plates and serve as a side dish.

NUTRITION:
calories 100, fat 3, fiber 6, carbs 18, protein 4

Paprika Green Beans and Zucchinis

Preparation time: 10 minutes
Cooking time: 3 hours
Servings: 2

INGREDIENTS:
- 1 pound green beans, trimmed and halved
- 1 cup zucchinis, cubed
- 1 cup tomato sauce

1 teaspoon smoked paprika
½ teaspoon cumin, ground
Salt and black pepper
to the taste
½ teaspoon garlic powder
¼ tablespoon chives, chopped

DIRECTIONS:
In your slow cooker, mix the green beans with the zucchinis, tomato sauce and the other ingredients, toss, put the lid on and cook on Low for 3 hours. Divide the mix between plates and serve as a side dish.

NUTRITION:
calories 114, fat 5, fiber 6, carbs 8, protein 9

Goat Cheese Rice

Preparation time: 10 minutes
Cooking time: 4 hours
Servings: 6

INGREDIENTS:
2 garlic cloves, minced
2 tablespoons olive oil
¾ cup yellow onion, chopped
1 and ½ cups Arborio rice
½ cup white wine
12 ounces spinach, chopped
3 and ½ cups hot veggie stock
Salt and black pepper to the taste
4 ounces goat cheese, soft and crumbled
2 tablespoons lemon juice
1/3 cup pecans, toasted and chopped

DIRECTIONS:
In your Slow cooker, mix oil with garlic, onion, rice, wine, salt, pepper and stock, stir, cover and cook on Low for 4 hours. Add spinach, toss and leave aside for a few minutes Add lemon juice and goat cheese, stir, divide between plates and serve with pecans on top as a side dish.

NUTRITION:
calories 300, fat 12, fiber 4, carbs 20, protein 15

Tarragon Sweet Potatoes

Preparation time: 10 minutes
Cooking time: 3 hours
Servings: 4

INGREDIENTS:
1 pound sweet potatoes, peeled and cut into wedges
1 cup veggie stock
½ teaspoon chili powder
½ teaspoon cumin, ground
Salt and black pepper to the taste
1 tablespoon olive oil
1 tablespoon tarragon, dried
2 tablespoons balsamic vinegar

DIRECTIONS:
In your slow cooker, mix the sweet potatoes with the stock, chili powder and the other ingredients, toss, put the lid on and cook on High for 3 hours. Divide the mix between plates and serve as a side dish.

NUTRITION:
calories 80, fat 4, fiber 4, carbs 8, protein 4

Rice and Artichokes

Preparation time: 10 minutes
Cooking time: 4 hours
Servings: 4

INGREDIENTS:
1 tablespoon olive oil
5 ounces Arborio rice
2 garlic cloves, minced
1 and ¼ cups chicken stock
1 tablespoon white wine
6 ounces graham crackers, crumbled
1 and ¼ cups water
15 ounces canned artichoke hearts, chopped
16 ounces cream cheese
1 tablespoon parmesan, grated
1 and ½ tablespoons thyme, chopped
Salt and black pepper to the taste

DIRECTIONS:
In your Slow cooker, mix oil with rice, garlic, stock, wine, water, artichokes and crackers, stir, cover and cook on Low for 4 hours. Add cream cheese, salt, pepper, parmesan and thyme, toss, divide between plates and serve as a side dish.

NUTRITION:
calories 230, fat 3, fiber 5, carbs 30, protein 4

Mustard Brussels Sprouts

Preparation time: 10 minutes
Cooking time: 3 hours
Servings: 2

INGREDIENTS:
1 pound Brussels sprouts, trimmed and halved
1 tablespoon olive oil
1 tablespoon mustard
1 tablespoon balsamic vinegar
Salt and black pepper to the taste
¼ cup veggie stock
A pinch of red pepper, crushed
2 tablespoons chives, chopped

DIRECTIONS:
In your slow cooker, mix the Brussels sprouts with the oil, mustard and the other ingredients, toss, put the lid on and cook on High for 3 hours. Divide the mix between plates and serve as a side dish.

NUTRITION:
calories 256, fat 12, fiber 6, carbs 8, protein 15

Green Beans and Mushrooms

Preparation time: 10 minutes

Cooking time: 3 hours

Servings: 4

INGREDIENTS:
- 1 pound fresh green beans, trimmed
- 1 small yellow onion, chopped
- 6 ounces bacon, chopped
- 1 garlic clove, minced
- 1 cup chicken stock
- 8 ounces mushrooms, sliced
- Salt and black pepper to the taste
- A splash of balsamic vinegar

DIRECTIONS:
In your Slow cooker, mix beans with onion, bacon, garlic, stock, mushrooms, salt, pepper and vinegar, stir, cover and cook on Low for 3 hours. Divide between plates and serve as a side dish.

NUTRITION:
calories 162, fat 4, fiber 5, carbs 8, protein 4

Parmesan Spinach Mix

Preparation time: 10 minutes

Cooking time: 2 hours

Servings: 2

INGREDIENTS:
- 2 garlic cloves, minced
- 1 pound baby spinach
- ¼ cup veggie stock
- A drizzle of olive oil
- Salt and black pepper to the taste
- 4 tablespoons heavy cream
- 2 tablespoons parmesan cheese, grated

DIRECTIONS:
Grease your Crockpot with the oil, and mix the spinach with the garlic and the other ingredients inside. Toss, put the lid on and cook on Low for 2 hours. Divide the mix between plates and serve as a side dish.

NUTRITION:
calories 133, fat 10, fiber 4, carbs 4, protein 2

Black Beans Mix

Preparation time: 10 minutes

Cooking time: 7 hours

Servings: 8

INGREDIENTS:
- 1 cup black beans, soaked overnight, drained and rinsed
- 1 cup water
- Salt and black pepper to the taste
- 1 spring onion, chopped
- 2 garlic cloves, minced
- ½ teaspoon cumin seeds

DIRECTIONS:
In your Slow cooker, mix beans with water, salt, pepper, onion, garlic and cumin seeds, stir, cover and cook on Low for 7 hours. Divide everything between plates and serve as a side dish.

NUTRITION:
calories 300, fat 4, fiber 6, carbs 20, protein 15

Minty Peas and Tomatoes

Preparation time: 10 minutes

Cooking time: 3 hours

Servings: 2

INGREDIENTS:
- 1 pound okra, sliced
- ½ pound tomatoes, cut into wedges
- 1 tablespoon olive oil
- ½ cup veggie stock
- ½ teaspoon chili powder
- Salt and black pepper to the taste
- 1 tablespoon mint, chopped
- 3 green onions, chopped
- 1 tablespoon chives, chopped

DIRECTIONS:
Grease your slow cooker with the oil, and mix the okra with the tomatoes and the other ingredients inside. Put the lid on, cook on Low for 3 hours, divide between plates and serve as a side dish.

NUTRITION:
calories 70, fat 1, fiber 1, carbs 4, protein 6

Rice and Beans

Preparation time: 20 minutes

Cooking time: 5 hours

Servings: 6

INGREDIENTS:
- 1 pound red kidney beans, soaked
- overnight and drained
- Salt to the taste

1 teaspoon olive oil
1 pound smoked sausage, roughly chopped
1 yellow onion, chopped
1 celery stalk, chopped
4 garlic cloves, chopped
1 green bell pepper, chopped
1 teaspoon thyme, dried
2 bay leaves
5 cups water
Long grain rice, already cooked
2 green onions, minced
2 tablespoons parsley, minced
Hot sauce for serving

DIRECTIONS:
In your Slow cooker, mix red beans with salt, oil, sausage, onion, celery, garlic, bell pepper, thyme, bay leaves and water, cover and cook on Low for 5 hours. Divide the rice between plates, add beans, sausage and veggies on top, sprinkle green onions and parsley and serve as a side dish with hot sauce drizzled all over.

NUTRITION:
calories 200, fat 5, fiber 6, carbs 20, protein 5

Savoy Cabbage Mix
Preparation time: 10 minutes

Cooking time: 2 hours

Servings: 2

INGREDIENTS:
1 pound Savoy cabbage, shredded
1 red onion, sliced
1 tablespoon olive oil
½ cup veggie stock
A pinch of salt and black pepper
1 carrot, grated
½ cup tomatoes, cubed
½ teaspoon sweet paprika
½ inch ginger, grated

DIRECTIONS:
In your slow cooker, mix the cabbage with the onion, oil and the other ingredients, toss, put the lid on and cook on High for 2 hours. Divide the mix between plates and serve as a side dish.

NUTRITION:
calories 100, fat 3, fiber 4, carbs 5, protein 2

Slow Cooker Snack Recipes

Tamale Dip
Preparation time: 10 minutes

Cooking time: 2 hours

Servings: 8

INGREDIENTS:
1 jalapeno, chopped
8 ounces cream cheese, cubed
¾ cup cheddar cheese, shredded
½ cup Monterey jack cheese, shredded
2 garlic cloves, minced
15 ounces enchilada sauce
1 cup canned corn, drained
1 cup rotisserie chicken, shredded
1 tablespoon chili powder
Salt and black pepper to the taste
1 tablespoon cilantro, chopped

DIRECTIONS:
In your Slow cooker, mix jalapeno with cream cheese, cheddar cheese, Monterey cheese, garlic, enchilada sauce, corn, chicken, chili powder, salt and pepper, stir, cover and cook on Low for 2 hours. Add cilantro, stir, divide into bowls and serve as a snack.

NUTRITION:
calories 200, fat 4, fiber 7, carbs 20, protein 4

Spinach Spread
Preparation time: 10 minutes

Cooking time: 2 hours

Servings: 2

INGREDIENTS:
4 ounces baby spinach
2 tablespoons mayonnaise
2 ounces heavy cream
½ teaspoon turmeric powder
A pinch of salt and black pepper
1 ounce Swiss cheese, shredded

DIRECTIONS:
In your slow cooker, mix the spinach with the cream, mayo and the other ingredients, toss, put the lid on and cook on Low for 2 hours. Divide into bowls and serve as a party spread.

NUTRITION:
calories 132, fat 4, fiber 3, carbs 10, protein 4

BBQ Chicken Dip
Preparation time: 10 minutes

Cooking time: 1 hour and 30 minutes

Servings: 10

INGREDIENTS:
- 1 and ½ cups bbq sauce
- 1 small red onion, chopped
- 24 ounces cream cheese, cubed
- 2 cups rotisserie chicken, shredded
- 3 bacon slices, cooked and crumbled
- 1 plum tomato, chopped
- ½ cup cheddar cheese, shredded
- 1 tablespoon green onions, chopped

DIRECTIONS:
In your Slow cooker, mix bbq sauce with onion, cream cheese, rotisserie chicken, bacon, tomato, cheddar and green onions, stir, cover and cook on Low for 1 hour and 30 minutes. Divide into bowls and serve.

NUTRITION:
calories 251, fat 4, fiber 6, carbs 10, protein 4

Artichoke Dip
Preparation time: 10 minutes
Cooking time: 2 hours
Servings: 2

INGREDIENTS:
- 2 ounces canned artichoke hearts, drained and chopped
- 2 ounces heavy cream
- 2 tablespoons mayonnaise
- ¼ cup mozzarella, shredded
- 2 green onions, chopped
- ½ teaspoon garam masala
- Cooking spray

DIRECTIONS:
Grease your slow cooker with the cooking spray, and mix the artichokes with the cream, mayo and the other ingredients inside. Stir, cover, cook on Low for 2 hours, divide into bowls and serve as a party dip.

NUTRITION:
calories 100, fat 3, fiber 2, carbs 7, protein 3

Mexican Dip
Preparation time: 10 minutes
Cooking time: 1 hour and 30 minutes
Servings: 10

INGREDIENTS:
- 24 ounces cream cheese, cubed
- 2 cups rotisserie chicken breast, shredded
- 3 ounces canned green chilies, chopped
- 1 and ½ cups Monterey jack cheese, shredded
- 1 and ½ cups salsa Verde
- 1 tablespoon green onions, chopped

DIRECTIONS:
In your Slow cooker, mix cream cheese with chicken, chilies, cheese, salsa Verde and green onions, stir, cover and cook on Low for 1 hour and 30 minutes. Divide into bowls and serve.

NUTRITION:
calories 222, fat 4, fiber 5, carbs 15, protein 4

Crab Dip
Preparation time: 10 minutes
Cooking time: 1 hour
Servings: 2

INGREDIENTS:
- 2 ounces crabmeat
- 1 tablespoon lime zest, grated
- ½ tablespoon lime juice
- 2 tablespoons mayonnaise
- 2 green onions, chopped
- 2 ounces cream cheese, cubed
- Cooking spray

DIRECTIONS:
Grease your slow cooker with the cooking spray, and mix the crabmeat with the lime zest, juice and the other ingredients inside. Put the lid on, cook on Low for 1 hour, divide into bowls and serve as a party dip.

NUTRITION:
calories 100, fat 3, fiber 2, carbs 9, protein 4

Tex Mex Dip
Preparation time: 10 minutes
Cooking time: 1 hour
Servings: 6

INGREDIENTS:
- 15 ounces canned chili con carne
- 1 cup Mexican cheese, shredded
- 1 yellow onion, chopped
- 8 ounces cream cheese, cubed
- ½ cup beer
- A pinch of salt
- 12 ounces macaroni, cooked
- 1 tablespoons cilantro, chopped

DIRECTIONS:
In your Slow cooker, mix chili con carne with cheese, onion, cream cheese, beer and salt, stir, cover and cook on High for 1 hour. Add macaroni and cilantro, stir, divide into bowls and serve.

NUTRITION:
calories 200, fat 4, fiber 6, carbs 17, protein 5

Lemon Shrimp Dip

Preparation time: 10 minutes
Cooking time: 2 hours
Servings: 2

INGREDIENTS:
3 ounces cream cheese, soft
½ cup heavy cream
1 pound shrimp, peeled, deveined and chopped
½ tablespoon balsamic vinegar
2 tablespoons mayonnaise
½ tablespoon lemon juice
A pinch of salt and black pepper
2 ounces mozzarella, shredded
1 tablespoon parsley, chopped

DIRECTIONS:
In your slow cooker, mix the cream cheese with the shrimp, heavy cream and the other ingredients, whisk, put the lid on and cook on Low for 2 hours. Divide into bowls and serve as a dip.

NUTRITION:
calories 342, fat 4, fiber 3, carbs 7, protein 10

Artichoke Dip

Preparation time: 10 minutes
Cooking time: 2 hours
Servings: 6

INGREDIENTS:
10 ounces spinach
30 ounces canned artichoke hearts
5 ounces boursin
1 and ½ cup cheddar cheese, shredded
½ cup parmesan, grated
2 garlic cloves, minced
1 teaspoon red pepper flakes, crushed
A pinch of salt

DIRECTIONS:
In your Slow cooker mix spinach with artichokes, boursin, cheddar, parmesan, garlic, pepper flakes and salt, stir, cover and cook on High for 1 hour. Stir the dip, cover and cook on Low for 1 more hour. Divide into bowls and serve.

NUTRITION:
calories 251, fat 6, fiber 8, carbs 16, protein 5

Squash Salsa

Preparation time: 10 minutes
Cooking time: 3 hours
Servings: 2

INGREDIENTS:
1 cup butternut squash, peeled and cubed
1 cup cherry tomatoes, cubed
1 cup avocado, peeled, pitted and cubed
½ tablespoon balsamic vinegar
½ tablespoon lemon juice
1 tablespoon lemon zest, grated
¼ cup veggie stock
1 tablespoon chives, chopped
A pinch of rosemary, dried
A pinch of sage, dried
A pinch of salt and black pepper

DIRECTIONS:
In your slow cooker, mix the squash with the tomatoes, avocado and the other ingredients, toss, put the lid on and cook on Low for 3 hours. Divide into bowls and serve as a snack.

NUTRITION:
calories 182, fat 5, fiber 7, carbs 12, protein 5

Taco Dip

Preparation time: 10 minutes
Cooking time: 2 hours and 30 minutes
Servings: 7

INGREDIENTS:
1 rotisserie chicken, shredded
2 cups pepper jack, cheese, grated
15 ounces canned enchilada sauce
1 jalapeno, sliced
8 ounces cream cheese, soft
1 tablespoon taco seasoning

DIRECTIONS:
In your Slow cooker, mix chicken with pepper jack, enchilada sauce, jalapeno, cream and taco seasoning, stir, cover and cook on High for 1 hour. Stir the dip, cover and cook on Low for 1 hour and 30 minutes more. Divide into bowls and serve as a snack.

NUTRITION:
calories 251, fat 5, fiber 8, carbs 17, protein 5

Beans Spread

Preparation time: 10 minutes
Cooking time: 6 hours
Servings: 2

INGREDIENTS:
1 cup canned black beans, drained
2 tablespoons tahini paste
½ teaspoon balsamic vinegar
¼ cup veggie stock
½ tablespoon olive oil

DIRECTIONS:
In your slow cooker, mix the beans with the tahini

paste and the other ingredients, toss, put the lid on and cook on Low for 6 hours. Transfer to your food processor, blend well, divide into bowls and serve.

NUTRITION:
calories 221, fat 6, fiber 5, carbs 19, protein 3

Lasagna Dip

Preparation time: 10 minutes
Cooking time: 1 hour
Servings: 10

INGREDIENTS:
8 ounces cream cheese
¾ cup parmesan, grated
1 and ½ cups ricotta
½ teaspoon red pepper flakes, crushed
2 garlic cloves, minced
3 cups marinara sauce
1 and ½ cups mozzarella, shredded
1 and ½ teaspoon oregano, chopped

DIRECTIONS:
In your Slow cooker, mix cream cheese with parmesan, ricotta, pepper flakes, garlic, marinara, mozzarella and oregano, stir, cover and cook on High for 1 hour. Stir, divide into bowls and serve as a dip.

NUTRITION:
calories 231, fat 4, fiber 7, carbs 21, protein 5

Rice Snack Bowls

Preparation time: 10 minutes
Cooking time: 6 hours
Servings: 2

INGREDIENTS:
½ cup wild rice
1 red onion, sliced
½ cup brown rice
2 cups veggie stock
½ cup baby spinach
½ cup cherry tomatoes, halved
2 tablespoons pine nuts, toasted
1 tablespoon raisins
1 tablespoon chives, chopped
1 tablespoon dill, chopped
½ tablespoon olive oil
A pinch of salt and black pepper

DIRECTIONS:
In your slow cooker, mix the rice with the onion, stock and the other ingredients, toss, put the lid on and cook on Low for 6 hours. Divide in to bowls and serve as a snack.

NUTRITION:
calories 301, fat 6, fiber 6, carbs 12, protein 3

Beer and Cheese Dip

Preparation time: 10 minutes
Cooking time: 1 hour
Servings: 10

INGREDIENTS:
12 ounces cream cheese
6 ounces beer
4 cups cheddar cheese, shredded
1 tablespoon chives, chopped

DIRECTIONS:
In your Slow cooker, mix cream cheese with beer and cheddar, stir, cover and cook on Low for 1 hour. Stir your dip, add chives, divide into bowls and serve.

NUTRITION:
calories 212, fat 4, fiber 7, carbs 16, protein 5

Cauliflower Spread

Preparation time: 10 minutes
Cooking time: 7 hours
Servings: 2

INGREDIENTS:
1 cup cauliflower florets
1 tablespoon mayonnaise
½ cup heavy cream
1 tablespoon lemon juice
½ teaspoon garlic powder
¼ teaspoon smoked paprika
¼ teaspoon mustard powder
A pinch of salt and black pepper

DIRECTIONS:
In your slow cooker, combine the cauliflower with the cream, mayonnaise and the other ingredients, toss, put the lid on and cook on Low for 7 hours. Transfer to a blender, pulse well, into bowls and serve as a spread.

NUTRITION:
calories 152, fat 13.8, fiber 1.5, carbs 6.2, protein 2

Queso Dip

Preparation time: 10 minutes
Cooking time: 1 hour
Servings: 10

INGREDIENTS:
16 ounces Velveeta
1 cup whole milk
½ cup cotija
2 jalapenos, chopped
2 teaspoons sweet paprika
2 garlic cloves, minced
A pinch of cayenne

pepper
1 tablespoon cilantro, chopped

DIRECTIONS:
In your Slow cooker, mix Velveeta with milk, cotija, jalapenos, paprika, garlic and cayenne, stir, cover and cook on High for 1 hour. Stir the dip, add cilantro, divide into bowls and serve as a dip.

NUTRITION:
calories 233, fat 4, fiber 7, carbs 10, protein 4

Mushroom Dip
Preparation time: 10 minutes
Cooking time: 5 hours
Servings: 2

INGREDIENTS:
- 4 ounces white mushrooms, chopped
- 1 eggplant, cubed
- ½ cup heavy cream
- ½ tablespoon tahini paste
- 2 garlic cloves, minced
- A pinch of salt and black pepper
- 1 tablespoon balsamic vinegar
- ½ tablespoon basil, chopped
- ½ tablespoon oregano, chopped

DIRECTIONS:
In your slow cooker, mix the mushrooms with the eggplant, cream and the other ingredients, toss, put the lid on and cook on High for 5 hours. Divide the mushroom mix into bowls and serve as a dip.

NUTRITION:
calories 261, fat 7, fiber 6, carbs 10, protein 6

Crab Dip
Preparation time: 10 minutes
Cooking time: 2 hours
Servings: 6

INGREDIENTS:
- 12 ounces cream cheese
- ½ cup parmesan, grated
- ½ cup mayonnaise
- ½ cup green onions, chopped
- 2 garlic cloves, minced
- Juice of 1 lemon
- 1 and ½ tablespoon Worcestershire sauce
- 1 and ½ teaspoons old bay seasoning
- 12 ounces crabmeat

DIRECTIONS:
In your Slow cooker, mix cream cheese with parmesan, mayo, green onions, garlic, lemon juice, Worcestershire sauce, old bay seasoning and crabmeat, stir, cover and cook on Low for 2 hours. Divide into bowls and serve as a dip.

NUTRITION:
calories 200, fat 4, fiber 6, carbs 12, protein 3

Chickpeas Spread
Preparation time: 10 minutes
Cooking time: 8 hours
Servings: 2

INGREDIENTS:
- ½ cup chickpeas, dried
- 1 tablespoons olive oil
- 1 tablespoon lemon juice
- 1 cup veggie stock
- 1 tablespoon tahini
- A pinch of salt and black pepper
- 1 garlic clove, minced
- ½ tablespoon chives, chopped

DIRECTIONS:
In your slow cooker, combine the chickpeas with the stock, salt, pepper and the garlic, stir, put the lid on and cook on Low for 8 hours. Drain chickpeas, transfer them to a blender, add the rest of the ingredients, pulse well, divide into bowls and serve as a party spread.

NUTRITION:
calories 211, fat 6, fiber 7, carbs 8, protein 4

Corn Dip
Preparation time: 10 minutes
Cooking time: 3 hours
Servings: 12

INGREDIENTS:
- 9 cups corn, rice and wheat cereal
- 1 cup cheerios
- 2 cups pretzels
- 1 cup peanuts
- 6 tablespoons hot, melted butter
- 1 tablespoon salt
- ¼ cup Worcestershire sauce
- 1 teaspoon garlic powder

DIRECTIONS:
In your Slow cooker, mix cereal with cheerios, pretzels, peanuts, butter, salt Worcestershire sauce and garlic powder, toss well, cover and cook on Low for 3 hours. Divide into bowls and serve as a snack.

NUTRITION:
calories 182, fat 4, fiber 5, carbs 8, protein 8

Spinach Dip
Preparation time: 10 minutes
Cooking time: 1 hour
Servings: 2

INGREDIENTS:

2 tablespoons heavy cream	2 garlic cloves, minced
½ cup Greek yogurt	Salt and black pepper to the taste
½ pound baby spinach	

DIRECTIONS:
In your slow cooker, mix the spinach with the cream and the other ingredients, toss, put the lid on and cook on High for 1 hour. Blend using an immersion blender, divide into bowls and serve as a party dip.

NUTRITION:
calories 221, fat 5, fiber 7, carbs 12, protein 5

Candied Pecans
Preparation time: 10 minutes
Cooking time: 3 hours
Servings: 4

INGREDIENTS:

1 cup white sugar	4 cups pecans
1 and ½ tablespoons cinnamon powder	2 teaspoons vanilla extract
½ cup brown sugar	¼ cup water
1 egg white, whisked	

DIRECTIONS:
In a bowl, mix white sugar with cinnamon, brown sugar and vanilla and stir. Dip pecans in egg white, then in sugar mix and put them in your Slow cooker, also add the water, cover and cook on Low for 3 hours. Divide into bowls and serve as a snack.

NUTRITION:
calories 152, fat 4, fiber 7, carbs 16, protein 6

Dill Potato Salad
Preparation time: 10 minutes
Cooking time: 8 hours
Servings: 2

INGREDIENTS:

1 red onion, sliced	1 tablespoons mustard
1 pound gold potatoes, peeled and roughly cubed	A pinch of salt and black pepper
2 tablespoons balsamic vinegar	1 tablespoon dill, chopped
½ cup heavy cream	½ cup celery, chopped

DIRECTIONS:
In your slow cooker, mix the potatoes with the cream, mustard and the other ingredients, toss, put the lid on and cook on Low for 8 hours. Divide salad into bowls, and serve as an appetizer.

NUTRITION:
calories 251, fat 6, fiber 7, carbs 8, protein 7

Chicken Bites
Preparation time: 10 minutes
Cooking time: 7 hours
Servings: 4

INGREDIENTS:

1 pound chicken thighs, boneless and skinless	paprika
1 tablespoon ginger, grated	1 and ½ cups chicken stock
1 yellow onion, sliced	2 tablespoons lemon juice
1 tablespoon garlic, minced	½ cup green olives, pitted and roughly chopped
2 teaspoons cumin, ground	Salt to the taste
1 teaspoon cinnamon powder	3 tablespoons olive oil
2 tablespoons sweet	5 pita breads, cut in quarters and heated in the oven

DIRECTIONS:
Heat up a pan with the olive oil over medium-high heat, add onions, garlic, ginger, salt and pepper, stir and cook for 2 minutes. Add cumin and cinnamon, stir well and take off heat. Put chicken pieces in your Slow cooker, add onions mix, lemon juice, olives and stock, stir, cover and cook on Low for 7 hours. Shred meat, stir the whole mixture again, divide it on pita chips and serve as a snack.

NUTRITION:
calories 265, fat 7, fiber 6, carbs 14, protein 6

Stuffed Peppers Platter
Preparation time: 10 minutes
Cooking time: 4 hours
Servings: 2

INGREDIENTS:

1 red onion, chopped	cooked
1 teaspoons olive oil	½ cup corn
½ teaspoon sweet paprika	A pinch of salt and black pepper
½ tablespoon chili powder	2 colored bell peppers, tops and insides scooped out
1 garlic clove, minced	
1 cup white rice,	½ cup tomato sauce

DIRECTIONS:
In a bowl, mix the onion with the oil, paprika and the other ingredients except the peppers and tomato sauce, stir well and stuff the peppers the with this mix. Put the peppers in the slow cooker, add the sauce, put the lid on and cook on Low for 4 hours. Transfer the peppers on a platter and serve as an appetizer.

NUTRITION:
calories 253, fat 5, fiber 4, carbs 12, protein 3

Peanut Snack
Preparation time: 10 minutes
Cooking time: 1 hour and 30 minutes
Servings: 4

INGREDIENTS:
1 cup peanuts
1 cup chocolate peanut butter
12 ounces dark chocolate chips
12 ounces white chocolate chips

DIRECTIONS:
In your Slow cooker, mix peanuts with peanut butter, dark and white chocolate chips, cover and cook on Low for 1 hour and 30 minutes. Divide this mix into small muffin cups, leave aside to cool down and serve as a snack.

NUTRITION:
calories 200, fat 4, fiber 6, carbs 10, protein 5

Corn Dip
Preparation time: 10 minutes
Cooking time: 2 hours
Servings: 2

INGREDIENTS:
1 cup corn
1 tablespoon chives, chopped
½ cup heavy cream
2 ounces cream cheese, cubed
¼ teaspoon chili powder

DIRECTIONS:
In your slow cooker, mix the corn with the chives and the other ingredients, whisk, put the lid on and cook on Low for 2 hours. Divide into bowls and serve as a dip.

NUTRITION:
calories 272, fat 5, fiber 10, carbs 12, protein 4

Apple Dip
Preparation time: 10 minutes
Cooking time: 1 hour and 30 minutes
Servings: 8

INGREDIENTS:
5 apples, peeled and chopped
½ teaspoon cinnamon powder
12 ounces jarred caramel sauce
A pinch of nutmeg, ground

DIRECTIONS:
In your Slow cooker, mix apples with cinnamon, caramel sauce and nutmeg, stir, cover and cook on High for 1 hour and 30 minutes. Divide into bowls and serve.

NUTRITION:
calories 200, fat 3, fiber 6, carbs 10, protein 5

Tomato and Mushroom Salsa
Preparation time: 10 minutes
Cooking time: 4 hours
Servings: 2

INGREDIENTS:
1 cup cherry tomatoes, halved
1 cup mushrooms, sliced
1 small yellow onion, chopped
1 garlic clove, minced
12 ounces tomato sauce
¼ cup cream cheese, cubed
1 tablespoon chives, chopped
Salt and black pepper to the taste

DIRECTIONS:
In your slow cooker, mix the tomatoes with the mushrooms and the other ingredients, toss, put the lid on and cook on Low for 4 hours. Divide into bowls and serve as a party salsa

NUTRITION:
calories 285, fat 4, fiber 7, carbs 12, protein 4

Beef and Chipotle Dip
Preparation time: 10 minutes
Cooking time: 2 hours
Servings: 10

INGREDIENTS:
8 ounces cream cheese, soft
2 tablespoons yellow onion, chopped
2 tablespoons mayonnaise
2 ounces hot pepper Monterey Jack cheese, shredded
¼ teaspoon garlic powder
2 chipotle chilies in adobo sauce, chopped
2 ounces dried beef, chopped
¼ cup pecans, chopped

DIRECTIONS:
In your Slow cooker, mix cream cheese with onion, mayo, Monterey Jack cheese, garlic powder,

chilies and dried beef, stir, cover and cook on Low for 2 hours. Add pecans, stir, divide into bowls and serve.

NUTRITION:
calories 130, fat 11, fiber 1, carbs 3, protein 4

Salsa Beans Dip

Preparation time: 10 minutes
Cooking time: 1 hour
Servings: 2

INGREDIENTS:
¼ cup salsa
1 cup canned red kidney beans, drained and rinsed
½ cup mozzarella, shredded
1 tablespoon green onions, chopped

DIRECTIONS:
In your slow cooker, mix the salsa with the beans and the other ingredients, toss, put the lid on cook on High for 1 hour. Divide into bowls and serve as a party dip

NUTRITION:
calories 302, fat 5, fiber 10, carbs 16, protein 6

Sugary Chicken Wings

Preparation time: 2 hours
Cooking time: 6 hours
Servings: 24

INGREDIENTS:
1 teaspoon garlic powder
½ cup brown sugar
¾ cup white sugar
1 teaspoon ginger powder
1 cup soy sauce
¼ cup pineapple juice
¾ cup water
¼ cup olive oil
24 chicken wings

DIRECTIONS:
In a bowl, mix chicken wings with garlic powder, brown sugar, white sugar, ginger powder, soy sauce, pineapple juice, water and oil, whisk well and leave aside for 2 hours in the fridge. Transfer chicken wings to your Slow cooker, add 1 cup of the marinade, cover and cook on Low for 6 hours. Serve chicken wings warm.

NUTRITION:
calories 140, fat 7, fiber 1, carbs 12, protein 6

Pineapple and Tofu Salsa

Preparation time: 10 minutes
Cooking time: 6 hours
Servings: 2

INGREDIENTS:
½ cup firm tofu, cubed
1 cup pineapple, peeled and cubed
1 cup cherry tomatoes, halved
½ tablespoons sesame oil
1 tablespoon soy sauce
½ cup pineapple juice
½ tablespoon ginger, grated
1 garlic clove, minced

DIRECTIONS:
In your slow cooker, mix the tofu with the pineapple and the other ingredients, toss, put the lid on and cook on Low for 6 hours. Divide into bowls and serve as an appetizer.

NUTRITION:
calories 201, fat 5, fiber 7, carbs 15, protein 4

Bean Dip

Preparation time: 10 minutes
Cooking time: 3 hours
Servings: 56

INGREDIENTS:
16 ounces Mexican cheese
5 ounces canned green chilies
16 ounces canned refried beans
2 pounds tortilla chips
Cooking spray

DIRECTIONS:
Grease your Slow cooker with cooking spray, line it, add Mexican cheese, green chilies and refried beans, stir, cover and cook on Low for 3 hours. Divide into bowls and serve with tortilla chips on the side.

NUTRITION:
calories 120, fat 2, fiber 1, carbs 14, protein 3

Chickpeas Salsa

Preparation time: 10 minutes
Cooking time: 6 hours
Servings: 2

INGREDIENTS:
1 cup canned chickpeas, drained
1 cup veggie stock
½ cup black olives, pitted and halved
1 small yellow onion, chopped
¼ tablespoon ginger, grated
4 garlic cloves, minced
¼ tablespoons coriander, ground
¼ tablespoons red chili powder
¼ tablespoons garam masala
1 tablespoon lemon juice

DIRECTIONS:
In your slow cooker, mix the chickpeas with the

stock, olives and the other ingredients, toss, put the lid on and cook on Low for 6 hours. Divide into bowls and serve as an appetizer.

NUTRITION:
calories 355, fat 5, fiber 14, carbs 16, protein 11

Buffalo Meatballs

Preparation time: 10 minutes
Cooking time: 3 hours and 10 minutes
Servings: 36

INGREDIENTS:
1 cup breadcrumbs
2 pounds chicken, ground
2 eggs
¾ cup buffalo wings sauce
½ cup yellow onion, chopped
3 garlic cloves, minced
Salt and black pepper to the taste
2 tablespoons olive oil
¼ cup butter, melted
1 cup blue cheese dressing

DIRECTIONS:
In a bowl, mix chicken with breadcrumbs, eggs, onion, garlic, salt and pepper, stir and shape small meatballs out of this mix. Heat up a pan with the oil over medium-high heat, add meatballs, brown them for a few minutes on each side and transfer them to your Slow cooker. Add melted butter and buffalo wings sauce, cover and cook on Low for 3 hours. Arrange meatballs on a platter and serve them with the blue cheese dressing on the side.

NUTRITION:
calories 100, fat 7, fiber 1, carbs 4, protein 4

Creamy Mushroom Spread

Preparation time: 10 minutes
Cooking time: 4 hours
Servings: 2

INGREDIENTS:
1 pound mushrooms, sliced
3 garlic cloves, minced
1 cup heavy cream
2 teaspoons smoked paprika
Salt and black pepper to the taste
2 tablespoons parsley, chopped

DIRECTIONS:
In your slow cooker, mix the mushrooms with the garlic and the other ingredients, whisk, put the lid on and cook on Low for 4 hours. Whisk, divide into bowls and serve as a party spread.

NUTRITION:
calories 300, fat 6, fiber 12, carbs 16, protein 6

Glazed Sausages

Preparation time: 10 minutes
Cooking time: 4 hours
Servings: 24

INGREDIENTS:
10 ounces jarred red pepper jelly
1/3 cup bbq sauce
½ cup brown sugar
16 ounces pineapple chunks and juice
24 ounces cocktail-size sausages
1 tablespoons cornstarch
2 tablespoons water
Cooking spray

DIRECTIONS:
Grease your Slow cooker with cooking spray, add pepper jelly, bbq sauce, brown sugar, pineapple and sausages, stir, cover and cook on Low for 3 hours. Add cornstarch mixed with the water, whisk everything and cook on High for 1 more hour. Arrange sausages on a platter and serve them as a snack.

NUTRITION:
calories 170, fat 10, fiber 1, carbs 17, protein 4

Bulgur and Beans Salsa

Preparation time: 10 minutes
Cooking time: 8 hours
Servings: 2

INGREDIENTS:
1 cup veggie stock
½ cup bulgur
1 small yellow onion, chopped
1 red bell pepper, chopped
1 garlic clove, minced
5 ounces canned
kidney beans, drained
½ cup salsa
1 tablespoon chili powder
¼ teaspoon oregano, dried
Salt and black pepper to the taste

DIRECTIONS:
In your slow cooker, mix the bulgur with the stock and the other ingredients, toss, put the lid on and cook on Low for 8 hours. Divide into bowls and serve cold as an appetizer.

NUTRITION:
calories 351, fat 4, fiber 6, carbs 12, protein 4

Cheesy Mix

Preparation time: 10 minutes
Cooking time: 2 hours
Servings: 24

INGREDIENTS:
- 2 cups small pretzels
- 2 cups wheat cereal
- 3 cups rice cereal
- 3 cups corn cereal
- 2 cups small cheese crackers
- 1/3 cup parmesan, grated
- 1/3 cup bacon flavor chips
- 1/2 cup melted butter
- 1/3 cup canola oil
- 1 ounce ranch dressing

DIRECTIONS:
In your Slow cooker, mix pretzels with wheat cereal, rice cereal, corn cereal, crackers, chips and parmesan, cover and cook on High for 2 hours stirring every 20 minutes. In a bowl, mix butter with oil and ranch dressing and whisk well. Divide the mix from the slow cooker into bowls and serve them with the ranch dressing on the side.

NUTRITION:
calories 182, fat 2, fiber 6, carbs 12, protein 4

Beets Salad
Preparation time: 10 minutes
Cooking time: 6 hours
Servings: 2

INGREDIENTS:
- 2 cups beets, cubed
- 1/4 cup carrots, grated
- 2 ounces tempeh, rinsed and cubed
- 1 cup cherry tomatoes, halved
- 1/4 cup veggie stock
- 3 ounces canned black beans, drained
- Salt and black pepper to the taste
- 1/2 teaspoon nutmeg, ground
- 1/2 teaspoon sweet paprika
- 1/2 cup parsley, chopped

DIRECTIONS:
In your slow cooker, mix the beets with the carrots, tempeh and the other ingredients, toss, put the lid on and cook on Low for 6 hours. Divide into bowls and serve cold as an appetizer.

NUTRITION:
calories 300, fat 6, fiber 6, carbs 16, protein 6

Cheeseburger Meatballs
Preparation time: 10 minutes
Cooking time: 3 hours
Servings: 12

INGREDIENTS:
- 2 bacon slices, chopped
- 1 pound beef, ground
- 1/4 cup milk
- 1/2 cup yellow onion, chopped
- 1/2 cup breadcrumbs
- 1 egg, whisked
- 1 tablespoon honey
- Salt and black pepper to the taste
- 3 ounces cheddar cheese, cubed
- 18 ounces bbq sauce
- 24 dill pickle slices

DIRECTIONS:
In a bowl, mix beef with bacon, milk, onion, breadcrumbs, egg, honey, salt and pepper, stir well and shape medium meatballs out of this mix. Place a cheddar cube in each meatball, seal them well, put them in your Slow cooker, add bbq sauce, cover and cook on Low for 3 hours. Thread dill pickles on cocktail picks and serve them with your cheeseburger meatballs.

NUTRITION:
calories 200, fat 8, fiber 1, carbs 24, protein 10

Lentils Salsa
Preparation time: 10 minutes
Cooking time: 3 hours
Servings: 2

INGREDIENTS:
- 1 cup canned lentils, drained
- 1 cup mild salsa
- 3 ounces tomato paste
- 2 tablespoons balsamic vinegar
- 1 small sweet onion, chopped
- 1 garlic clove, minced
- 1/2 tablespoon sugar
- A pinch of red pepper flakes
- A pinch of salt and black pepper
- 1 tablespoon chives, chopped

DIRECTIONS:
In your slow cooker, mix the lentils with the salsa and the other ingredients, toss, put the lid on and cook on High for 3 hours. Divide into bowls and serve as a party salsa.

NUTRITION:
calories 260, fat 3, fiber 4, carbs 6, protein 7

Caramel Corn
Preparation time: 10 minutes
Cooking time: 2 hours
Servings: 13

INGREDIENTS:
- 1/2 cup butter
- 1 teaspoon vanilla extract
- 1/4 cup corn syrup
- 1 cup brown sugar
- 1 teaspoon baking soda
- 12 cups plain popcorn
- 1 cup mixed nuts
- Cooking spray

DIRECTIONS:
Grease your Slow cooker with cooking spray, add butter, vanilla, corn syrup, brown sugar and baking soda, cover and cook on High for 1 hour, stirring after 30 minutes. Add popcorn, toss, cover and cook on Low for 1 hour more. Add nuts, toss, divide into bowls and serve as a snack.

NUTRITION:
calories 250, fat 14, fiber 1, carbs 20, protein 2

Tacos
Preparation time: 10 minutes
Cooking time: 4 hours
Servings: 2

INGREDIENTS:
- 13 ounces canned pinto beans, drained
- ¼ cup chili sauce
- 2 ounces chipotle pepper in adobo sauce, chopped
- ½ tablespoon cocoa powder
- ¼ teaspoon cinnamon powder
- 4 taco shells

DIRECTIONS:
In your slow cooker, mix the beans with the chili sauce and the other ingredients except the taco shells, toss, put the lid on and cook on Low for 4 hours. Divide the mix into the taco shells and serve them as an appetizer.

NUTRITION:
calories 352, fat 3, fiber 6, carbs 12, protein 10

Bourbon Sausage Bites
Preparation time: 10 minutes
Cooking time: 3 hours and 5 minutes
Servings: 12

INGREDIENTS:
- 1/3 cup bourbon
- 1 pound smoked sausage, sliced
- 12 ounces chili sauce
- ¼ cup brown sugar
- 2 tablespoons yellow onion, grated

DIRECTIONS:
Heat up a pan over medium-high heat, add sausage slices, brown them for 2 minutes on each side, drain them on paper towels and transfer to your Slow cooker. Add chili sauce, sugar, onion and bourbon, toss to coat, cover and cook on Low for 3 hours. Divide into bowls and serve as a snack.

NUTRITION:
calories 190, fat 11, fiber 1, carbs 12, protein 5

Almond Bowls
Preparation time: 10 minutes
Cooking time: 4 hours
Servings: 2

INGREDIENTS:
- 1 tablespoon cinnamon powder
- 1 cup sugar
- 2 cups almonds
- ½ cup water
- ½ teaspoons vanilla extract

DIRECTIONS:
In your slow cooker, mix the almonds with the cinnamon and the other ingredients, toss, put the lid on and cook on Low for 4 hours. Divide into bowls and serve as a snack.

NUTRITION:
calories 260, fat 3, fiber 4, carbs 12, protein 8

Curried Meatballs
Preparation time: 10 minutes
Cooking time: 4 hours
Servings: 40

INGREDIENTS:
- 12 ounces pineapple preserves
- 8 ounces pineapple tidbits in juice
- 8 ounces Dijon mustard
- ½ cup brown sugar
- 1 teaspoon curry powder
- 2 and ½ pounds frozen meatballs

DIRECTIONS:
In your Slow cooker, mix pineapple preserves with pineapple tidbits, mustard, sugar and curry powder and whisk well. Add meatballs, toss, cover and cook on High for 4 hours. Serve them hot.

NUTRITION:
calories 120, fat 5, fiber 1, carbs 13, protein 6

Eggplant Salsa
Preparation time: 10 minutes
Cooking time: 7 hours
Servings: 2

INGREDIENTS:
- 2 cups eggplant, chopped
- 1 teaspoon capers, drained
- 1 cup black olives, pitted and halved
- ½ cup mild salsa
- 2 garlic cloves, minced
- ½ tablespoon basil, chopped
- 1 teaspoon balsamic vinegar
- A pinch of salt and black pepper

DIRECTIONS:
In your slow cooker, mix the eggplant with the capers and the other ingredients, toss, put the lid on and cook on Low for 7 hours. Divide into bowls and serve as an appetizer.

NUTRITION:
calories 170, fat 3, fiber 5, carbs 10, protein 5

Pizza Dip

Preparation time: 10 minutes
Cooking time: 4 hours
Servings: 14

INGREDIENTS:
14 ounces pizza sauce
1 cup turkey pepperoni, chopped
½ red bell pepper, chopped
8 green onions, chopped
2 ounces black olives, pitted and sliced
4 ounces mozzarella cheese, shredded
8 ounces cream cheese, cubed

DIRECTIONS:
In your Slow cooker, mix pizza sauce with turkey pepperoni, bell pepper, green onions and black olives, stir, cover and cook on Low for 4 hours. Add mozzarella and cream cheese, stir, divide into bowls and serve as a snack.

NUTRITION:
calories 135, fat 12, fiber 1, carbs 3, protein 5

Almond Spread

Preparation time: 10 minutes
Cooking time: 8 hours
Servings: 2

INGREDIENTS:
¼ cup almonds
1 cup heavy cream
½ teaspoon nutritional yeast flakes
A pinch of salt and black pepper

DIRECTIONS:
In your slow cooker, mix the almonds with the cream and the other ingredients, toss, put the lid on and cook on Low for 8 hours. Transfer to a blender, pulse well, divide into bowls and serve.

NUTRITION:
calories 270, fat 4, fiber 4, carbs 8, protein 10

Sauerkraut Dip

Preparation time: 10 minutes
Cooking time: 2 hours
Servings: 12

INGREDIENTS:
15 ounces canned sauerkraut, drained
8 ounces sour cream
4 ounces cream cheese
4 ounces corned beef, chopped
8 ounces Swiss cheese, shredded

DIRECTIONS:
In your Slow cooker, mix sauerkraut with sour cream, cream cheese, beef and Swiss cheese, stir, cover and cook on Low for 2 hours. Divide into bowls and serve.

NUTRITION:
calories 166, fat 14, fiber 1, carbs 4, protein 7

Onion Dip

Preparation time: 10 minutes
Cooking time: 8 hours
Servings: 2

INGREDIENTS:
2 cups yellow onions, chopped
A pinch of salt and black pepper
1 tablespoon olive oil
½ cup heavy cream
2 tablespoons mayonnaise

DIRECTIONS:
In your slow cooker, mix the onions with the cream and the other ingredients, whisk, put the lid on and cook on Low for 8 hours. Divide into bowls and serve as a party dip.

NUTRITION:
calories 240, fat 4, fiber 4, carbs 9, protein 7

Spicy Dip

Preparation time: 10 minutes
Cooking time: 3 hours
Servings: 10

INGREDIENTS:
1 pound spicy sausage, chopped
8 ounces cream cheese, soft
8 ounces sour cream
20 ounces canned tomatoes and green chilies, chopped

DIRECTIONS:
In your Slow cooker, mix sausage with cream cheese, sour cream and tomatoes and chilies, stir, cover and cook on Low for 3 hours. Divide into bowls and serve as a snack.

NUTRITION:
calories 300, fat 12, fiber 7, carbs 30, protein 34

Nuts Bowls

Preparation time: 10 minutes
Cooking time: 2 hours
Servings: 2

INGREDIENTS:
- 2 tablespoons almonds, toasted
- 2 tablespoons pecans, halved and toasted
- 2 tablespoons hazelnuts, toasted and peeled
- 2 tablespoons sugar
- ½ cup coconut cream
- 2 tablespoons butter, melted
- A pinch of cinnamon powder
- A pinch of cayenne pepper

DIRECTIONS:
In your slow cooker, mix the nuts with the sugar and the other ingredients, toss, put the lid on, cook on Low for 2 hours, divide into bowls and serve as a snack.

NUTRITION:
calories 125, fat 3, fiber 2, carbs 5, protein 5

Salsa Corn Dip

Preparation time: 10 minutes
Cooking time: 2 hours and 30 minutes
Servings: 12

INGREDIENTS:
- 2 teaspoons cumin, ground
- 16 ounces salsa Verde
- 12 ounces corn
- 1 yellow onion, chopped
- 4 garlic cloves, minced
- 8 ounces cream cheese, soft
- 1 cup Monterey jack cheese, shredded
- 1-pint cherry tomatoes, quartered
- ½ cup cilantro, chopped
- Cooking spray

DIRECTIONS:
Grease your Slow cooker with cooking spray and mix salsa with cumin, corn, onion, garlic, cream cheese, Monterey Jack cheese, cherry tomatoes and cilantro. Stir, cover and cook on High for 2 hours and 30 minutes. Divide into bowls and serve as a snack.

NUTRITION:
calories 220, fat 4, fiber 7, carbs 12, protein 5

Eggplant Salad

Preparation time: 10 minutes
Cooking time: 8 hours
Servings: 2

INGREDIENTS:
- 2 eggplants, cubed
- 2 scallions, chopped
- 1 red bell pepper, chopped
- ½ teaspoon coriander, ground
- ½ cup mild salsa
- 1 teaspoon cumin, ground
- A pinch of salt and black pepper
- 1 tablespoon lemon juice

DIRECTIONS:
In your slow cooker, combine the eggplants with the scallions, pepper and the other ingredients, toss, put the lid on, cook on Low for 8 hours, divide into bowls and serve cold as an appetizer salad.

NUTRITION:
calories 203, fat 2, fiber 3, carbs 7, protein 8

Cheesy Corn Dip

Preparation time: 10 minutes
Cooking time: 4 hours
Servings: 12

INGREDIENTS:
- 3 cups corn
- 8 ounces cream cheese, soft
- 1 and ½ cup cheddar cheese, shredded
- ½ cup salsa Verde
- 2 ounces black olives, pitted and sliced
- 1 teaspoon chives, chopped
- Cooking spray

DIRECTIONS:
Grease your Slow cooker with the cooking spray, add corn, cream cheese, cheddar, salsa Verde, olives and chives, stir, cover and cook on Low for 4 hours. Divide into bowls and serve as a snack.

NUTRITION:
calories 223, fat 4, fiber 7, carbs 17, protein 5

Lentils Dip

Preparation time: 10 minutes
Cooking time: 6 hours
Servings: 2

INGREDIENTS:
- 2 carrots, peeled and grated
- 2 garlic cloves, minced
- A pinch of cayenne pepper
- 2 tablespoons tahini paste
- ¼ cup lemon juice
- 1 cup canned lentils, drained and rinsed
- A pinch of sea salt and black pepper
- ½ tablespoon rosemary, chopped

DIRECTIONS:
In your slow cooker, mix the lentils with the carrots, garlic and the other ingredients, toss, put the lid on and cook on Low for 6 hours. Transfer to a blender, pulse well, divide into bowls and serve.

NUTRITION:
calories 200, fat 2, fiber 5, carbs 8, protein 6

White Bean Spread
Preparation time: 10 minutes
Cooking time: 7 hours
Servings: 4

INGREDIENTS:
½ cup white beans, dried
2 tablespoons cashews, chopped
1 teaspoon apple cider vinegar
1 cup veggie stock
1 tablespoon water

DIRECTIONS:
In your Slow cooker, mix beans with cashews and stock, stir, cover and cook on Low for 6 hours. Drain, transfer to your food processor, add vinegar and water, pulse well, divide into bowls and serve as a spread.

NUTRITION:
calories 221, fat 6, fiber 5, carbs 19, protein 3

Turkey Meatballs
Preparation time: 10 minutes
Cooking time: 7 hours
Servings: 2

INGREDIENTS:
1 pound turkey breast, skinless, boneless and ground
1 egg, whisked
6 ounces canned tomato puree
2 tablespoons parsley, chopped
1 tablespoon oregano, chopped
1 garlic clove, minced
1 small yellow onion, chopped
Salt and black pepper to the taste

DIRECTIONS:
In a bowl, mix the meat with the egg, parsley and the other ingredients except the tomato puree, stir well and shape medium meatballs out of it. Put the meatballs in the slow cooker, add the tomato puree, put the lid on and cook on Low for 7 hours Arrange the meatballs on a platter and serve as an appetizer.

NUTRITION:
calories 170, fat 5, fiber 3, carbs 10, protein 7

Lentils Rolls
Preparation time: 10 minutes
Cooking time: 8 hours
Servings: 4

INGREDIENTS:
1 cup brown lentils, cooked
1 green cabbage head, leaves separated
½ cup onion, chopped
1 cup brown rice, already cooked
2 ounces white mushrooms, chopped
¼ cup pine nuts, toasted
¼ cup raisins
2 garlic cloves, minced
2 tablespoons dill, chopped
1 tablespoon olive oil
25 ounces marinara sauce
A pinch of salt and black pepper
¼ cup water

DIRECTIONS:
In a bowl, mix lentils with onion, rice, mushrooms, pine nuts, raisins, garlic, dill, salt and pepper and whisk well. Arrange cabbage leaves on a working surface, divide lentils mix and wrap them well. Add marinara sauce and water to your slow cooker and stir. Add cabbage rolls, cover and cook on Low for 8 hours. Arrange cabbage rolls on a platter and serve.

NUTRITION:
calories 281, fat 6, fiber 6, carbs 12, protein 3

Stuffed Mushrooms
Preparation time: 10 minutes
Cooking time: 3 hours
Servings: 2

INGREDIENTS:
¼ pound chorizo, chopped
4 Portobello mushroom caps
1 red onion, chopped
Salt and black pepper to the taste
¼ teaspoon garlic powder
¼ cup tomato sauce

DIRECTIONS:
In a bowl, mix the chorizo with the onion, garlic powder, salt and pepper, stir and stuff the mushroom caps with this mix. Put the mushroom caps in the slow cooker, add the tomato sauce, put the lid on and cook on High for 3 hours. Arrange the stuffed mushrooms on a platter and serve.

NUTRITION:
calories 170, fat 2, fiber 3, carbs 8, protein 3

Eggplant Salsa
Preparation time: 10 minutes
Cooking time: 7 hours
Servings: 4

INGREDIENTS:

1 and ½ cups tomatoes, chopped
3 cups eggplant, cubed
2 teaspoons capers
6 ounces green olives, pitted and sliced
4 garlic cloves, minced
2 teaspoons balsamic vinegar
1 tablespoon basil, chopped
Salt and black pepper to the taste

DIRECTIONS:
In your Slow cooker, mix tomatoes with eggplant cubes, capers, green olives, garlic, vinegar, basil, salt and pepper, toss, cover and cook on Low for 7 hours. Divide salsa into bowls and serve.

NUTRITION:
calories 200, fat 6, fiber 5, carbs 9, protein 2

Paprika Cod Sticks

Preparation time: 10 minutes
Cooking time: 2 hours
Servings: 2

INGREDIENTS:

1 eggs whisked
½ pound cod fillets, cut into medium strips
½ cup almond flour
½ teaspoon cumin, ground
½ teaspoon coriander, ground
½ teaspoon turmeric powder
A pinch of salt and black pepper
¼ teaspoon sweet paprika
Cooking spray

DIRECTIONS:
In a bowl, mix the flour with cumin, coriander and the other ingredients except the fish, eggs and cooking spray. Put the egg in another bowl and whisk it. Dip the fish sticks in the egg and then dredge them in the flour mix. Grease the slow cooker with cooking spray, add fish sticks, put the lid on, cook on High for 2 hours, arrange on a platter and serve.

NUTRITION:
calories 200, fat 2, fiber 4, carbs 13, protein 12

Veggie Spread

Preparation time: 10 minutes
Cooking time: 7 hours
Servings: 4

INGREDIENTS:

1 cup carrots, sliced
1 and ½ cups cauliflower florets
1/3 cup cashews
½ cup turnips, chopped
2 and ½ cups water
1 cup almond milk
1 teaspoon garlic powder
Salt and black pepper to the taste
¼ teaspoon smoked paprika
¼ teaspoon mustard powder
A pinch of salt

DIRECTIONS:
In your slow cooker, mix carrots with cauliflower, cashews, turnips and water, stir, cover and cook on Low for 7 hours. Drain, transfer to a blender, add almond milk, garlic powder, paprika, mustard powder, salt and pepper, blend well, divide into bowls and serve as a snack.

NUTRITION:
calories 291, fat 7, fiber 4, carbs 14, protein 3

Macadamia Nuts Snack

Preparation time: 10 minutes
Cooking time: 2 hours
Servings: 2

INGREDIENTS:

½ pound macadamia nuts
1 tablespoon avocado oil
¼ cup water
½ tablespoon chili powder
½ teaspoon oregano, dried
½ teaspoon onion powder

DIRECTIONS:
In your slow cooker, mix the macadamia nuts with the oil and the other ingredients, toss, put the lid on, cook on Low for 2 hours, divide into bowls and serve as a snack.

NUTRITION:
calories 108, fat 3, fiber 2, carbs 9, protein 2

Peas Dip

Preparation time: 10 minutes
Cooking time: 5 hours
Servings: 4

INGREDIENTS:

1 and ½ cups black-eyed peas
3 cups water
1 teaspoon Cajun seasoning
½ cup pecans, toasted
½ teaspoon garlic powder
½ teaspoon jalapeno powder
Salt and black pepper to the taste
¼ teaspoon liquid smoke
½ teaspoon Tabasco sauce

DIRECTIONS:
In your slow cooker, mix black-eyed pea with Cajun seasoning, salt, pepper and water, stir,

cover and cook on High for 5 hours. Drain, transfer to a blender, add pecans, garlic powder, jalapeno powder, Tabasco sauce, liquid smoke, more salt and pepper, pulse well and serve.

NUTRITION:
calories 221, fat 4, fiber 7, carbs 16, protein 4

Salmon Bites
Preparation time: 10 minutes
Cooking time: 2 hours
Servings: 2

INGREDIENTS:
1 pound salmon fillets, boneless
¼ cup chili sauce
A pinch of salt and black pepper
½ teaspoon turmeric powder
2 tablespoons grape jelly

DIRECTIONS:
In your slow cooker, mix the salmon with the chili sauce and the other ingredients, toss gently, put the lid on and cook on High for 2 hours. Serve as an appetizer.

NUTRITION:
calories 200, fat 6, fiber 3, carbs 15, protein 12

Hummus
Preparation time: 10 minutes
Cooking time: 8 hours
Servings: 10

INGREDIENTS:
1 cup chickpeas, dried
2 tablespoons olive oil
3 cups water
A pinch of salt and
black pepper
1 garlic clove, minced
1 tablespoon lemon juice

DIRECTIONS:
In your slow cooker, mix chickpeas with water, salt and pepper, stir, cover and cook on Low for 8 hours. Drain chickpeas, transfer to a blender, add oil, more salt and pepper, garlic and lemon juice, blend well, divide into bowls and serve.

NUTRITION:
calories 211, fat 6, fiber 7, carbs 8, protein 4

Spinach and Walnuts Dip
Preparation time: 10 minutes
Cooking time: 2 hours
Servings: 2

INGREDIENTS:
½ cup heavy cream
½ cup walnuts, chopped
1 cup baby spinach
1 garlic clove, chopped
1 tablespoon mayonnaise
Salt and black pepper to the taste

DIRECTIONS:
In your slow cooker, mix the spinach with the walnuts and the other ingredients, toss, put the lid on and cook on High for 2 hours. Blend using an immersion blender, divide into bowls and serve as a party dip.

NUTRITION:
calories 260, fat 4, fiber 2, carbs 12, protein 5

Cashew Dip
Preparation time: 10 minutes
Cooking time: 3 hours
Servings: 10

INGREDIENTS:
1 cup water
1 cup cashews
10 ounces hummus
¼ teaspoon garlic powder
¼ teaspoon onion powder
A pinch of salt and black pepper
¼ teaspoon mustard powder
1 teaspoon apple cider vinegar

DIRECTIONS:
In your slow cooker, mix water with cashews, salt and pepper, stir, cover and cook on High for 3 hours. Transfer to your blender, add hummus, garlic powder, onion powder, mustard powder and vinegar, pulse well, divide into bowls and serve.

NUTRITION:
calories 192, fat 7, fiber 7, carbs 12, protein 4

Curry Pork Meatballs
Preparation time: 10 minutes
Cooking time: 4 hours
Servings: 2

INGREDIENTS:
½ pound pork stew meat, ground
1 red onion, chopped
1 egg, whisked
Salt and black pepper to the taste
1 tablespoon cilantro, chopped
5 ounces coconut milk
¼ tablespoon green curry paste

DIRECTIONS:
In a bowl, mix the meat with the onion and the other ingredients except the coconut milk, stir well and shape medium meatballs out of this mix. Put the meatballs in your slow cooker, add the coconut milk, put the lid on and cook on High for 4 hours. Arrange the meatballs on a platter and serve them as an appetizer

NUTRITION:
calories 225, fat 6, fiber 2, carbs 8, protein 4

Potato Salsa
Preparation time: 10 minutes

Cooking time: 8 hours

Servings: 6

INGREDIENTS:
1 sweet onion, chopped
¼ cup white vinegar
2 tablespoons mustard
Salt and black pepper to the taste
1 and ½ pounds gold potatoes, cut into medium cubes
¼ cup dill, chopped
1 cup celery, chopped
Cooking spray

DIRECTIONS:
Spray your Slow cooker with cooking spray, add onion, vinegar, mustard, salt and pepper and whisk well. Add celery and potatoes, toss them well, cover and cook on Low for 8 hours. Divide salad into small bowls, sprinkle dill on top and serve.

NUTRITION:
calories 251, fat 6, fiber 7, carbs 12, protein 7

Calamari Rings Bowls
Preparation time: 10 minutes

Cooking time: 6 hours

Servings: 2

INGREDIENTS:
½ pound calamari rings
1 tablespoon balsamic vinegar
½ tablespoon soy sauce
1 tablespoon sugar
1 cup veggie stock
½ teaspoon turmeric powder
½ teaspoon sweet paprika
½ cup chicken stock

DIRECTIONS:
In your slow cooker, mix the calamari rings with the vinegar, soy sauce and the other ingredients, toss, put the lid on and cook on High for 6 hours. Divide into bowls and serve right away as an appetizer.

NUTRITION:
calories 230, fat 2, fiber 4, carbs 7, protein 5

Black Bean Salsa Salad
Preparation time: 10 minutes

Cooking time: 4 hours

Servings: 6

INGREDIENTS:
1 tablespoon soy sauce
½ teaspoon cumin, ground
1 cup canned black beans
1 cup salsa
6 cups romaine lettuce leaves
½ cup avocado, peeled, pitted and mashed

DIRECTIONS:
In your slow cooker, mix black beans with salsa, cumin and soy sauce, stir, cover and cook on Low for 4 hours. In a salad bowl, mix lettuce leaves with black beans mix and mashed avocado, toss and serve.

NUTRITION:
calories 221, fat 4, fiber 7, carbs 12, protein 3

Shrimp Salad
Preparation time: 10 minutes

Cooking time: 2 hours

Servings: 2

INGREDIENTS:
½ pound shrimp, peeled and deveined
1 green bell pepper, chopped
½ cup kalamata olives, pitted and halved
4 spring onions, chopped
1 red bell pepper, chopped
½ cup mild salsa
1 tablespoon olive oil
1 garlic clove, minced
¼ teaspoon oregano, dried
¼ teaspoon basil, dried
Salt and black pepper to the taste
A pinch of red pepper, crushed
1 tablespoon parsley, chopped

DIRECTIONS:
In your slow cooker, mix the shrimp with the peppers and the other ingredients, toss, put the lid on and cook on High for 2 hours. Divide into bowls and serve as an appetizer.

NUTRITION:
calories 240, fat 2, fiber 5, carbs 7, protein 2

Mushroom Dip
Preparation time: 10 minutes

Cooking time: 4 hours

Servings: 6

INGREDIENTS:
2 cups green bell peppers, chopped
1 cup yellow onion, chopped
3 garlic cloves, minced
1 pound mushrooms, chopped
28 ounces tomato sauce
½ cup goat cheese, crumbled
Salt and black pepper to the taste

DIRECTIONS:
In your Slow cooker, mix bell peppers with onion, garlic, mushrooms, tomato sauce, cheese, salt and pepper, stir, cover and cook on Low for 4 hours. Divide into bowls and serve.

NUTRITION:
calories 255, fat 4, fiber 7, carbs 9, protein 3

Chicken Salad
Preparation time: 10 minutes
Cooking time: 6 hours
Servings: 2

INGREDIENTS:
2 chicken breasts, skinless, boneless and cubed
½ cup mild salsa
½ tablespoon olive oil
1 red onion, chopped
½ cup mushrooms, sliced
½ cup kalamata olives, pitted and halved
½ cup cherry tomatoes, halved
1 chili pepper, chopped
2 ounces baby spinach
1 teaspoon oregano, chopped
½ tablespoon lemon juice
½ cup veggie stock
A pinch of salt and black pepper

DIRECTIONS:
In your slow cooker, mix the chicken with the salsa, oil and the other ingredients except the spinach, toss, put the lid on and cook on High for 5 hours. Add the spinach, cook on High for 1 more hour, divide into bowls and serve as an appetizer.

NUTRITION:
calories 245, fat 4, fiber 3, carbs 10, protein 6

Beef Meatballs
Preparation time: 10 minutes
Cooking time: 8 hours
Servings: 8

INGREDIENTS:
1 and ½ pounds beef, ground
1 egg, whisked
16 ounces canned tomatoes, crushed
14 ounces canned tomato puree
¼ cup parsley, chopped
2 garlic cloves, minced
1 yellow onion, chopped
Salt and black pepper to the taste

DIRECTIONS:
In a bowl, mix beef with egg, parsley, garlic, black pepper and onion, stir well and shape 16 meatballs. Place them in your slow cooker, add tomato puree and crushed tomatoes on top, cover and cook on Low for 8 hours. Arrange them on a platter and serve.

NUTRITION:
calories 160, fat 5, fiber 3, carbs 10, protein 7

Apple and Carrot Dip
Preparation time: 10 minutes
Cooking time: 6 hours
Servings: 2

INGREDIENTS:
2 cups apples, peeled, cored and chopped
1 cup carrots, peeled and grated
¼ teaspoon cloves, ground
¼ teaspoon ginger powder
1 tablespoon lemon juice
½ tablespoon lemon zest, grated
½ cup coconut cream
¼ teaspoon nutmeg, ground

DIRECTIONS:
In your slow cooker, mix the apples with the carrots, cloves and the other ingredients, toss, put the lid on and cook on Low for 6 hours. Bend using an immersion blender, divide into bowls and serve.

NUTRITION:
calories 212, fat 4, fiber 6, carbs 12, protein 3

Jalapeno Poppers
Preparation time: 10 minutes
Cooking time: 3 hours
Servings: 4

INGREDIENTS:
½ pound chorizo, chopped
10 jalapenos, tops cut off and deseeded
1 small white onion, chopped
½ pound beef, ground
¼ teaspoon garlic powder
1 tablespoon maple syrup
1 tablespoon mustard
1/3 cup water

DIRECTIONS:
In a bowl, mix beef with chorizo, garlic powder and onion and stir. Stuff your jalapenos with

the mix, place them in your Slow cooker, add the water, cover and cook on High for 3 hours. Transfer jalapeno poppers to a lined baking sheet. In a bowl, mix maple syrup with mustard, whisk well, brush poppers with this mix, arrange on a platter and serve.

NUTRITION:
calories 214, fat 2, fiber 3, carbs 8, protein 3

Sweet Potato Dip

Preparation time: 10 minutes
Cooking time: 4 hours
Servings: 2

INGREDIENTS:
- 2 sweet potatoes, peeled and cubed
- ½ cup coconut cream
- ½ teaspoon turmeric powder
- ½ teaspoon garam masala
- 2 garlic cloves, minced
- ½ cup veggie stock
- 1 cup basil leaves
- 2 tablespoons olive oil
- 1 tablespoon lemon juice
- A pinch of salt and black pepper

DIRECTIONS:
In your slow cooker, mix the sweet potatoes with the cream, turmeric and the other ingredients, toss, put the lid on and cook on High for 4 hours. Blend using an immersion blender, divide into bowls and serve as a party dip.

NUTRITION:
calories 253, fat 5, fiber 6, carbs 13, protein 4

Pecans Snack

Preparation time: 10 minutes
Cooking time: 2 hours and 15 minutes
Servings: 5

INGREDIENTS:
- 1 pound pecans, halved
- 2 tablespoons olive oil
- 1 teaspoon basil, dried
- 1 tablespoon chili powder
- 1 teaspoon oregano, dried
- ¼ teaspoon garlic powder
- 1 teaspoon thyme, dried
- ½ teaspoon onion powder
- A pinch of cayenne pepper

DIRECTIONS:
In your slow cooker, mix pecans with oil, basil, chili powder, oregano, garlic powder, onion powder, thyme and cayenne and toss to coat. Cover, cook on High for 15 minutes and on Low for 2 hours. Divide into bowls and serve as a snack.

NUTRITION:
calories 78, fat 3, fiber 2, carbs 9, protein 2

Spinach, Walnuts and Calamari Salad

Preparation time: 10 minutes
Cooking time: 4 hours and 30 minutes
Servings: 2

INGREDIENTS:
- 2 cups baby spinach
- ½ cup walnuts, chopped
- ½ cup mild salsa
- 1 cup calamari rings
- ½ cup kalamata olives, pitted and halved
- ½ teaspoons thyme, chopped
- 2 garlic cloves, minced
- 1 cup tomatoes, cubed
- A pinch of salt and black pepper
- ¼ cup veggie stock

DIRECTIONS:
In your slow cooker, mix the salsa with the calamari rings and the other ingredients except the spinach, toss, put the lid on and cook on High for 4 hours. Add the spinach, toss, put the lid on, cook on High for 30 minutes more, divide into bowls and serve.

NUTRITION:
calories 160, fat 1, fiber 4, carbs 18, protein 4

Apple Jelly Sausage Snack

Preparation time: 10 minutes
Cooking time: 2 hours
Servings: 15

INGREDIENTS:
- 2 pounds sausages, sliced
- 18 ounces apple jelly
- 9 ounces Dijon mustard

DIRECTIONS:
Place sausage slices in your Slow cooker, add apple jelly and mustard, toss to coat well, cover and cook on Low for 2 hours. Divide into bowls and serve as a snack.

NUTRITION:
calories 200, fat 3, fiber 1, carbs 9, protein 10

Chicken Meatballs

Preparation time: 10 minutes
Cooking time: 7 hours
Servings: 2

INGREDIENTS:
- A pinch of red pepper flakes, crushed
- ½ pound chicken breast, skinless,

boneless, ground
1 egg, whisked
½ cup salsa Verde
1 teaspoon oregano, dried
½ teaspoon chili powder
½ teaspoon rosemary, dried
1 tablespoon parsley, chopped
A pinch of salt and black pepper

DIRECTIONS:
In a bowl, mix the chicken with the egg and the other ingredients except the salsa, stir well and shape medium meatballs out of this mix. Put the meatballs in the slow cooker, add the salsa Verde, toss gently, put the lid on and cook on Low for 7 hours. Arrange the meatballs on a platter and serve.

NUTRITION:
calories 201, fat 4, fiber 5, carbs 8, protein 2

Eggplant Dip

Preparation time: 10 minutes

Cooking time: 4 hours and 10 minutes

Servings: 4

INGREDIENTS:
1 eggplant
1 zucchini, chopped
2 tablespoons olive oil
2 tablespoons balsamic vinegar
1 tablespoon parsley, chopped
1 yellow onion, chopped
1 celery stick, chopped
1 tomato, chopped
2 tablespoons tomato paste
1 and ½ teaspoons garlic, minced
A pinch of sea salt
Black pepper to the taste

DIRECTIONS:
Brush eggplant with the oil, place on preheated grill and cook over medium-high heat for 5 minutes on each side. Leave aside to cool down, chop it and put in your Slow cooker. Also add, zucchini, vinegar, onion, celery, tomato, parsley, tomato paste, garlic, salt and pepper and stir everything. Cover and cook on High for 4 hours. Stir your spread again very well, divide into bowls and serve.

NUTRITION:
calories 110, fat 1, fiber 2, carbs 7, protein 5

Cinnamon Pecans Snack

Preparation time: 10 minutes

Cooking time: 3 hours

Servings: 2

INGREDIENTS:
½ tablespoon cinnamon powder
¼ cup water
½ tablespoon avocado oil
½ teaspoon chili powder
2 cups pecans

DIRECTIONS:
In your slow cooker, mix the pecans with the cinnamon and the other ingredients, toss, put the lid on and cook on Low for 3 hours. Divide the pecans into bowls and serve as a snack.

NUTRITION:
calories 172, fat 3, fiber 5, carbs 8, protein 2

Lemon Peel Snack

Preparation time: 20 minutes

Cooking time: 4 hours

Servings: 80 pieces

INGREDIENTS:
5 big lemons, sliced halves, pulp removed and peel cut into strips
2 and ¼ cups white sugar
5 cups water

DIRECTIONS:
Put strips in your instant slow cooker, add water and sugar, stir cover and cook on Low for 4 hours. Drain lemon peel and keep in jars until serving.

NUTRITION:
calories 7, fat 1, fiber 1, carbs 2, protein 1

Cajun Almonds and Shrimp Bowls

Preparation time: 10 minutes

Cooking time: 2 hours

Servings: 2

INGREDIENTS:
1 cup almonds
1 pound shrimp, peeled and deveined
½ cup kalamata olives, pitted and halved
½ cup black olives, pitted and halved
½ cup mild salsa
½ tablespoon Cajun seasoning

DIRECTIONS:
In your slow cooker, mix the shrimp with the almonds, olives and the other ingredients, toss, put the lid on and cook on High for 2 hours. Divide between small plates and serve as an appetizer.

NUTRITION:
calories 100, fat 2, fiber 3, carbs 7, protein 3

Fava Bean Dip

Preparation time: 10 minutes

Cooking time: 5 hours

Servings: 6

INGREDIENTS:
1 pound fava bean, rinsed
1 cup yellow onion, chopped
4 and ½ cups water
1 bay leaf
¼ cup olive oil
1 garlic clove, minced
2 tablespoons lemon juice
Salt to the taste

DIRECTIONS:
Put fava beans in your Slow cooker, add 4 cups water, salt and bay leaf, cover and cook on Low for 3 hours. Drain beans, discard bay leaf, return beans to the slow cooker, add ½ cup water, garlic and onion, stir, cover and cook on Low for 2 more hours. Transfer beans mix to your food processor, add olive oil and lemon juice and blend well. Divide into bowls and serve cold.

NUTRITION:
calories 300, fat 3, fiber 1, carbs 20, protein 6

Broccoli Dip

Preparation time: 10 minutes

Cooking time: 2 hours

Servings: 2

INGREDIENTS:
1 green chili pepper, minced
2 tablespoons heavy cream
1 cup broccoli florets
1 tablespoon mayonnaise
2 tablespoons cream cheese, cubed
A pinch of salt and black pepper
1 tablespoon chives, chopped

DIRECTIONS:
In your slow cooker, mix the broccoli with the chili pepper, mayo and the other ingredients, toss, put the lid on and cook on Low for 2 hours. Blend using an immersion blender, divide into bowls and serve as a party dip.

NUTRITION:
calories 202, fat 3, fiber 3, carbs 7, protein 6

Tamales

Preparation time: 10 minutes

Cooking time: 8 hours and 30 minutes

Servings: 24

INGREDIENTS:
8 ounces dried corn husks, soaked for 1 day and drained
4 cups water
3 pounds pork shoulder, boneless and chopped
1 yellow onion, chopped
2 garlic cloves, crushed
1 tablespoon chipotle chili powder
2 tablespoons chili powder
Salt and black pepper to the taste
1 teaspoon cumin, ground
4 cups masa harina
¼ cup corn oil
¼ cup shortening
1 teaspoon baking powder

DIRECTIONS:
In your Slow cooker, mix 2 cups water with salt, pepper, onion, garlic, chipotle powder, chili powder, cumin and pork, stir, cover the slow cooker and cook on Low for 7 hours. Transfer meat to a cutting board, shred it with 2 forks, add to a bowl, mix with 1 tablespoon of cooking liquid, more salt and pepper, stir and leave aside. In another bowl, mix masa harina with salt, pepper, baking powder, shortening and oil and stir using a mixer. Add cooking liquid from the instant slow cooker and blend again well. Unfold corn husks, place them on a work surface, add ¼ cup masa mix near the top of the husk, press into a square and leaves 2 inches at the bottom. Add 1 tablespoon pork mix in the center of the masa, wrap the husk around the dough, place all of them in your Slow cooker, add the rest of the water, cover and cook on High for 1 hour and 30 minutes. Arrange tamales on a platter and serve.

NUTRITION:
calories 162, fat 4, fiber 3, carbs 10, protein 5

Walnuts Bowls

Preparation time: 10 minutes

Cooking time: 2 hours

Servings: 2

INGREDIENTS:
Cooking spray
1 cup walnuts, chopped
2 tablespoons balsamic vinegar
1 tablespoon smoked paprika
½ tablespoon lemon zest, grated
½ tablespoons olive oil
1 teaspoon rosemary, dried

DIRECTIONS:
Grease your slow cooker with the cooking spray, add walnuts and the other ingredients inside, toss, put the lid on and cook on Low for 2 hours. Divide into bowls and serve them as a snack.

NUTRITION:
calories 100, fat 2, fiber 2, carbs 3, protein 2

Tostadas

Preparation time: 10 minutes

Cooking time: 4 hours

Servings: 4

INGREDIENTS:
4 pounds pork shoulder, boneless and cubed
Salt and black pepper to the taste

2 cups coca cola	Corn tortillas, toasted
1/3 cup brown sugar	for a few minutes in
½ cup hot sauce	the oven
2 teaspoons chili powder	Mexican cheese, shredded for serving
2 tablespoons tomato paste	4 shredded lettuce leaves, for serving
¼ teaspoon cumin, ground	Salsa
1 cup enchilada sauce	Guacamole for serving

DIRECTIONS:
In your Slow cooker, mix 1 cup coke with hot sauce, salsa, sugar, tomato paste, chili powder, cumin and pork, stir, cover and cook on Low for 4 hours. Drain juice from the slow cooker, transfer meat to a cutting board, shred it, return it to slow cooker, add the rest of the coke and enchilada sauce and stir. Place tortillas on a working surface, divide pork mix, lettuce leaves, Mexican cheese and guacamole and serve as a snack.

NUTRITION:
calories 162, fat 3, fiber 6, carbs 12, protein 5

Cauliflower Bites

Preparation time: 10 minutes
Cooking time: 4 hours
Servings: 2

INGREDIENTS:

2 cups cauliflower florets	2 tablespoons tomato sauce
1 tablespoon Italian seasoning	1 teaspoon sweet paprika
1 tablespoon sweet paprika	1 tablespoon olive oil
	¼ cup veggie stock

DIRECTIONS:
In your slow cooker, mix the cauliflower florets with the Italian seasoning and the other ingredients, toss, put the lid on and cook on Low for 4 hours. Divide into bowls and serve as a snack.

NUTRITION:
calories 251, fat 4, fiber 6, carbs 7, protein 3

Mussels Salad

Preparation time: 10 minutes
Cooking time: 1 hour
Servings: 4

INGREDIENTS:

2 pounds mussels, cleaned and scrubbed	1 pound baby spinach
1 radicchio, cut into thin strips	½ cup dry white wine
	1 garlic clove, crushed
	½ cup water
1 white onion, chopped	A drizzle of olive oil

DIRECTIONS:
Divide baby spinach and radicchio in salad bowls and leave aside for now. In your Slow cooker, mix mussels with onion, wine, garlic, water and oil, toss, cover and cook on High for 1 hour. Divide mussels on top of spinach and radicchio, add cooking liquid all over and serve.

NUTRITION:
calories 59, fat 4, fiber 1, carbs 1, protein 1

Beef Dip

Preparation time: 10 minutes
Cooking time: 4 hours
Servings: 2

INGREDIENTS:

1 pound beef meat, ground	1 tablespoon sriracha sauce
1 carrot, peeled and grated	3 tablespoons beef stock
2 spring onions, chopped	1 teaspoon hot sauce
	3 ounces heavy cream

DIRECTIONS:
In your slow cooker, mix the beef meat with the stock, hot sauce and the other ingredients, whisk, put the lid on and cook on Low for 4 hours. Divide the mix into bowls and serve as a party dip.

NUTRITION:
calories 301, fat 3, fiber 6, carbs 11, protein 5

Italian Mussels Salad

Preparation time: 10 minutes
Cooking time: 1 hour
Servings: 4

INGREDIENTS:

28 ounces canned tomatoes, crushed	2 pounds mussels, cleaned and scrubbed
½ cup white onion, chopped	2 tablespoons red pepper flakes
2 jalapeno peppers, chopped	2 garlic cloves, minced
¼ cup dry white wine	Salt to the taste
¼ cup extra virgin olive oil	½ cup basil, chopped
¼ cup balsamic vinegar	Lemon wedges for serving

DIRECTIONS:
In your Slow cooker, mix tomatoes with onion,

jalapenos, wine, oil, vinegar, garlic, pepper flakes, salt, basil and mussels, cover and cook on High for 1 hour. Discard unopened mussels, divide everything into bowls and serve with lemon wedges.

NUTRITION:
calories 100, fat 1, fiber 1, carbs 7, protein 2

Zucchini Spread

Preparation time: 10 minutes
Cooking time: 6 hours
Servings: 2

INGREDIENTS:
1 tablespoon walnuts, chopped
2 zucchinis, grated
1 cup heavy cream
1 teaspoon balsamic vinegar
1 tablespoon tahini paste
1 tablespoon chives, chopped

DIRECTIONS:
In your slow cooker, combine the zucchinis with the cream, walnuts and the other ingredients, whisk, put the lid on and cook on Low for 6 hours. Blend using an immersion blender, divide into bowls and serve as a party spread.

NUTRITION:
calories 221, fat 6, fiber 5, carbs 9, protein 3

Spicy Mussels

Preparation time: 10 minutes
Cooking time: 1 hour
Servings: 4

INGREDIENTS:
2 pounds mussels, scrubbed and debearded
2 tablespoons olive oil
1 yellow onion, chopped
½ teaspoon red pepper flakes
14 ounces tomatoes, chopped
2 teaspoons garlic, minced
½ cup chicken stock
2 teaspoons oregano, dried

DIRECTIONS:
In your Slow cooker, mix oil with onions, pepper flakes, garlic, stock, oregano, tomatoes and mussels, stir, cover and cook on High for 1 hour Divide between bowls and serve.

NUTRITION:
calories 83, fat 2, fiber 2, carbs 8, protein 3

Beef Dip

Preparation time: 10 minutes
Cooking time: 7 hours and 10 minutes
Servings: 2

INGREDIENTS:
½ pounds beef, minced
3 spring onions, minced
1 tablespoon olive oil
1 cup mild salsa
2 ounces white mushrooms, chopped
¼ cup pine nuts, toasted
2 garlic cloves, minced
1 tablespoon hives, chopped
½ teaspoon coriander, ground
½ teaspoon rosemary, dried
A pinch of salt and black pepper

DIRECTIONS:
Heat up a pan with the oil over medium heat, add the spring onions, mushrooms, garlic and the meat, stir, brown for 10 minutes and transfer to your slow cooker. Add the rest of the ingredients, toss, put the lid on and cook on Low for 7 hours. Divide the dip into bowls and serve.

NUTRITION:
calories 361, fat 6, fiber 6, carbs 12, protein 3

Cheeseburger Dip

Preparation time: 10 minutes
Cooking time: 3 hours
Servings: 10

INGREDIENTS:
1 pound beef, ground
1 teaspoon garlic powder
Salt and black pepper to the taste
2 tablespoons Worcestershire sauce
8 bacon strips, chopped
3 garlic cloves, minced
1 yellow onion, chopped
12 ounces cream cheese, soft
1 cup sour cream
2 tablespoons ketchup
2 tablespoons mustard
10 ounces canned tomatoes and chilies, chopped
1 and ½ cup cheddar cheese, shredded
1 cup mozzarella, shredded

DIRECTIONS:
In your Slow cooker, mix beef with garlic, salt, pepper, Worcestershire sauce, bacon, garlic, onion, cream cheese, sour cream, ketchup, mustard, tomatoes and chilies, cheddar and mozzarella, stir, cover and cook on Low for 3 hours. Divide into bowls and serve.

NUTRITION:
calories 251, fat 5, fiber 8, carbs 16, protein 4

Eggplant Salsa

Preparation time: 10 minutes
Cooking time: 4 hours
Servings: 2

INGREDIENTS:
- 1 cup cherry tomatoes, cubed
- 2 cups eggplant, cubed
- 1 tablespoon capers, drained
- 1 tablespoon black olives, pitted and sliced
- 1 tablespoon lemon juice
- 1 tablespoon olive oil
- ¼ cup mild salsa
- 2 teaspoons balsamic vinegar
- 1 tablespoon basil, chopped
- 1 tablespoon chives, chopped
- Salt and black pepper to the taste

DIRECTIONS:
In your slow cooker, mix the eggplant with the cherry tomatoes, capers, olives and the other ingredients, toss, put the lid on and cook on High for 4 hours. Divide salsa into small bowls and serve.

NUTRITION:
calories 200, fat 6, fiber 5, carbs 9, protein 2

Onion Dip

Preparation time: 10 minutes
Cooking time: 1 hour
Servings: 6

INGREDIENTS:
- 8 ounces cream cheese, soft
- ¾ cup sour cream
- 1 cup cheddar cheese, shredded
- 10 bacon slices, cooked and chopped
- 2 yellow onions, chopped

DIRECTIONS:
In your Slow cooker, mix cream cheese with sour cream, cheddar cheese, bacon and onion, stir, cover and cook on High for 1 hour. Divide into bowls and serve.

NUTRITION:
calories 222, fat 4, fiber 5, carbs 17, protein 4

Carrots Spread

Preparation time: 10 minutes
Cooking time: 7 hours
Servings: 4

INGREDIENTS:
- 2 cups carrots, peeled and grated
- ½ cup heavy cream
- 1 teaspoon turmeric powder
- 1 teaspoon sweet paprika
- 1 cup coconut milk
- 1 teaspoon garlic powder
- ¼ teaspoon mustard powder
- A pinch of salt and black pepper

DIRECTIONS:
In your slow cooker, mix the carrots with the cream, turmeric and the other ingredients, whisk, put the lid on and cook on Low for 7 hours. Divide the mix into bowls and serve as a party spread.

NUTRITION:
calories 291, fat 7, fiber 4, carbs 14, protein 3

Caramel Dip

Preparation time: 10 minutes
Cooking time: 2 hours
Servings: 4

INGREDIENTS:
- 1 cup butter
- 12 ounces condensed milk
- 2 cups brown sugar
- 1 cup corn syrup

DIRECTIONS:
In your Slow cooker, mix butter with condensed milk, sugar and corn syrup, cover and cook on High for 2 hours stirring often. Divide into bowls and serve.

NUTRITION:
calories 172, fat 2, fiber 6, carbs 12, protein 4

Cauliflower Dip

Preparation time: 10 minutes
Cooking time: 5 hours
Servings: 2

INGREDIENTS:
- 1 cup cauliflower florets
- ½ cup heavy cream
- 1 tablespoon tahini paste
- ½ cup white mushrooms, chopped
- 2 garlic cloves, minced
- 2 tablespoons lemon juice
- 1 tablespoon basil, chopped
- 1 teaspoon rosemary, dried
- A pinch of salt and black pepper

DIRECTIONS:
In your slow cooker, mix the cauliflower with the cream, tahini paste and the other ingredients, toss, put the lid on and cook on Low for 5 hours. Transfer to a blender, pulse well, divide into bowls and serve as a party dip.

NUTRITION:
calories 301, fat 7, fiber 6, carbs 10, protein 6

Chicken Cordon Bleu Dip

Preparation time: 10 minutes
Cooking time: 1 hour and 30 minutes
Servings: 6

INGREDIENTS:
16 ounces cream cheese
2 chicken breasts, baked and shredded
1 cup cheddar cheese, shredded
1 cup Swiss cheese, shredded
3 garlic cloves, minced
6 ounces ham, chopped
2 tablespoons green onions
Salt and black pepper to the taste

DIRECTIONS:
In your Slow cooker, mix cream cheese with chicken, cheddar cheese, Swiss cheese, garlic, ham, green onions, salt and pepper, stir, cover and cook on Low for 1 hour and 30 minutes. Divide into bowls and serve as a snack.

NUTRITION:
calories 243, fat 5, fiber 8, carbs 15, protein 3

Lentils Hummus

Preparation time: 10 minutes
Cooking time: 4 hours
Servings: 2

INGREDIENTS:
1 cup chicken stock
1 cup canned lentils, drained
2 tablespoons tahini paste
¼ teaspoon onion powder
¼ cup heavy cream
A pinch of salt and black pepper
¼ teaspoon turmeric powder
1 teaspoon lemon juice

DIRECTIONS:
In your slow cooker, mix the lentils with the stock, onion powder, salt and pepper, toss, put the lid on and cook on High for 4 hours. Drain the lentils, transfer to your blender, add the rest of the ingredients, pulse well, divide into bowls and serve.

NUTRITION:
calories 192, fat 7, fiber 7, carbs 12, protein 4

Fajita Dip

Preparation time: 10 minutes
Cooking time: 4 hours
Servings: 6

INGREDIENTS:
3 chicken breasts, skinless and boneless
8 ounces root beer
3 red bell peppers, chopped
1 yellow onion, chopped
8 ounces cream cheese
8 ounces pepper jack cheese, shredded
16 ounces sour cream
2 fajita seasoning mix packets
1 tablespoons olive oil
Salt and black pepper to the taste

DIRECTIONS:
In your Slow cooker, mix chicken with root beer, bell peppers, onion, cream cheese, pepper jack cheese, sour cream, fajita seasoning, oil, salt and pepper, stir, cover and cook on High for 4 hours. Shred meat using 2 forks, divide into bowls and serve.

NUTRITION:
calories 261, fat 4, fiber 6, carbs 17, protein 5

Spinach Dip

Preparation time: 10 minutes
Cooking time: 1 hour
Servings: 2

INGREDIENTS:
1 cup coconut cream
10 ounces spinach, torn
2 spring onions, chopped
1 teaspoon rosemary, dried
½ teaspoon garam masala
1 garlic clove, minced
A pinch of salt and black pepper

DIRECTIONS:
In your slow cooker, mix the spinach with the cream, spring onions and the other ingredients, toss, put the lid on and cook on High for 1 hour. Blend using an immersion blender, divide into bowls and serve as a party dip.

NUTRITION:
calories 241, fat 5, fiber 7, carbs 12, protein 5

Simple Salsa

Preparation time: 10 minutes
Cooking time: 5 hours
Servings: 6

INGREDIENTS:
7 cups tomatoes, chopped
1 green bell pepper, chopped
1 red bell pepper, chopped
2 yellow onions, chopped
4 jalapenos, chopped
¼ cup apple cider

vinegar
1 teaspoon coriander, ground
1 tablespoon cilantro, chopped
3 tablespoons basil, chopped
Salt and black pepper to the taste

DIRECTIONS:
In your Slow cooker, mix tomatoes with green and red peppers, onions, jalapenos, vinegar, coriander, salt and pepper, stir, cover and cook on Low for 5 hours. Add basil and cilantro, stir, divide into bowls and serve.

NUTRITION:
calories 172, fat 3, fiber 5, carbs 8, protein 4

Peppers Salsa

Preparation time: 10 minutes
Cooking time: 5 hours and 5 minutes
Servings: 2

INGREDIENTS:
1 yellow onion, chopped
2 spring onions, chopped
2 teaspoons olive oil
1 teaspoon turmeric powder
1 red bell pepper, roughly cubed
1 green bell pepper, roughly cubed
1 orange bell pepper, roughly cubed
1 cup cherry tomatoes, halved
1 tablespoon chili powder
3 garlic cloves, minced
½ cup mild salsa
1 teaspoon oregano, dried
A pinch of salt and black pepper

DIRECTIONS:
Heat up a pan with the oil over medium-high heat, add the spring onions, onion and garlic, sauté for 5 minutes and transfer to the slow cooker. Add the rest of the ingredients, toss, put the lid on and cook on Low for 5 hours. Divide the mix into bowls and serve as a snack.

NUTRITION:
calories 221, fat 5, fiber 4, carbs 9, protein 3

Salsa Snack

Preparation time: 10 minutes
Cooking time: 3 hours
Servings: 6

INGREDIENTS:
10 roma tomatoes, chopped
2 jalapenos, chopped
1 sweet onion, chopped
28 ounces canned plum tomatoes
3 garlic cloves, minced
1 bunch cilantro, chopped
Salt and black pepper to the taste

DIRECTIONS:
In your Slow cooker, mix roma tomatoes with jalapenos, onion, plum tomatoes and garlic, stir, cover and cook on High for 3 hours. Add salt, pepper and cilantro, stir, divide into bowls and serve cold.

NUTRITION:
calories 162, fat 4, fiber 6, carbs 12, protein 3

Artichoke Dip

Preparation time: 10 minutes
Cooking time: 4 hours
Servings: 2

INGREDIENTS:
1 cup canned artichoke hearts, drained and chopped
1 cup baby spinach
1 cup heavy cream
2 spring onions, chopped
½ teaspoon sweet paprika
½ teaspoon turmeric powder
2 garlic cloves, minced
1/3 cup mayonnaise
1 tablespoon lemon juice
A pinch of salt and black pepper

DIRECTIONS:
In your slow cooker, mix the artichoke hearts with the spinach, cream and the other ingredients, toss, put the lid on and cook on Low for 4 hours. Divide into bowls and serve as a party dip.

NUTRITION:
calories 305, fat 14, fiber 4, carbs 9, protein 13

Onion Dip

Preparation time: 10 minutes
Cooking time: 4 hours
Servings: 6

INGREDIENTS:
7 cups tomatoes, chopped
1 yellow onion, chopped
1 red onion, chopped
3 jalapenos, chopped
1 red bell pepper, chopped
1 green bell pepper, chopped
¼ cup apple cider vinegar
1 tablespoon cilantro, chopped
1 tablespoon sage, chopped
3 tablespoons basil, chopped
Salt to the taste

DIRECTIONS:
In your Slow cooker, mix tomatoes with onion, jalapenos, red bell pepper, green bell pepper, vinegar, sage, cilantro and basil, stir, cover and cook on Low for 4 hours. Transfer to your food processor, add salt, pulse well, divide into bowls and serve.

NUTRITION:
calories 162, fat 7, fiber 4, carbs 7, protein 3

Mushroom Salsa

Preparation time: 10 minutes
Cooking time: 5 hours
Servings: 4

INGREDIENTS:

2 cups white mushrooms, sliced	dried
1 cup cherry tomatoes halved	½ teaspoon oregano, dried
1 cup spring onions, chopped	½ cup black olives, pitted and sliced
½ teaspoon chili powder	3 garlic cloves, minced
½ teaspoon rosemary,	1 cup mild salsa
	Salt and black pepper to the taste

DIRECTIONS:
In your slow cooker, mix the mushrooms with the cherry tomatoes and the other ingredients, toss, put the lid on and cook on Low for 5 hours. Divide into bowls and serve as a snack.

NUTRITION:
calories 205, fat 4, fiber 7, carbs 9, protein 3

Slow Cooker Poultry Recipes

Rotisserie Chicken

Preparation time: 10 minutes
Cooking time: 3 hours
Servings: 4

INGREDIENTS:

Cooking spray	powder
1 tablespoons smoked paprika	1 teaspoon thyme, chopped
2 tablespoons brown sugar	1 whole chicken
1 tablespoon chili	Salt and black pepper to the taste

DIRECTIONS:
In a bowl, mix smoked paprika with sugar, chili powder, thyme, salt and pepper, stir and rub the chicken with this mix. Grease the Slow cooker with cooking spray, line it with tin foil, add chicken, cover and cook on High for 3 hours and 30 minutes. Serve right away.

NUTRITION:
calories 324, fat 4, fiber 7, carbs 16, protein 3

Garlic Chicken and Green Beans

Preparation time: 10 minutes
Cooking time: 6 hours and 10 minutes.
Servings: 2

INGREDIENTS:

1 pound chicken thighs, boneless, skinless and cubed	1 red onion, chopped
	2 tablespoons olive oil
1 teaspoon sweet paprika	4 garlic cloves, minced
	1 cup chicken stock
½ teaspoon garam masala	1 tablespoon chives, chopped
1 cup green beans, trimmed and halved	A pinch of salt and black pepper

DIRECTIONS:
Heat up a pan with the oil over medium-high heat, add the chicken, onion and garlic, cook for 10 minutes and transfer to the slow cooker. Add the rest of the ingredients, toss, put the lid on and cook on Low for 6 hours. Divide everything into bowls and serve.

NUTRITION:
calories 263, fat 12, fiber 3, carbs 6, protein 14

Chicken and Dumplings

Preparation time: 10 minutes
Cooking time: 4 hours
Servings: 4

INGREDIENTS:
1 yellow onion, chopped
1 and ½ pounds chicken breast, skinless and boneless
Salt and black pepper to the taste
1 teaspoon oregano, dried
2 cups cream of chicken soup
2 cups chicken stock
4 thyme springs, chopped
1 bay leaf
2 celery stalks, chopped
2 carrots, chopped
1 cup peas
3 garlic cloves, minced
½ cup parmesan, grated
1 biscuit dough tube, cut into small pieces
1 tablespoon parsley, chopped

DIRECTIONS:
In your Slow cooker, mix onion with chicken, oregano, salt, pepper, cream of chicken soup, chicken stock, bay leaf and thyme, stir, cover and cook on High for 3 hours. Discard bay leaf, add celery, carrots, peas, garlic and biscuit pieces, stir, cover and cook on High for 1 hour. Add parmesan and parsley, divide into bowls and serve.

NUTRITION:
calories 311, fat 4, fiber 7, carbs 12, protein 5

Oregano Turkey and Tomatoes
Preparation time: 10 minutes
Cooking time: 7 hours
Servings: 4

INGREDIENTS:
1 pound turkey breast, skinless, boneless and sliced
1 tablespoon oregano, chopped
1 cup chicken stock
1 cup cherry tomatoes, halved
1 teaspoon turmeric powder
2 tablespoons olive oil
1 cup scallions, chopped
1 teaspoon chili powder
A pinch of salt and black pepper
½ cup tomato sauce

DIRECTIONS:
In your slow cooker, mix the turkey with the oregano, stock and the other ingredients, toss, put the lid on and cook on Low for 7 hours. Divide the mix between plates and serve.

NUTRITION:
calories 162, fat 8, fiber 2, carbs 5, protein 9

Balsamic Chicken
Preparation time: 10 minutes
Cooking time: 5 hours
Servings: 4

INGREDIENTS:
2 cups Brussels sprouts, halved
4 chicken breasts, skinless and boneless
2 cups red potatoes, halved
¼ cup balsamic vinegar
¼ cup honey
1/3 cup chicken stock
2 tablespoons Dijon mustard
½ teaspoon rosemary, dried
1 teaspoon thyme, dried
½ teaspoon oregano, dried
½ teaspoon red pepper flakes, crushed
2 garlic cloves, minced
Salt and black pepper to the taste
1 tablespoon parsley, chopped

DIRECTIONS:
In your Slow cooker, mix Brussels sprouts with chicken, potatoes, vinegar, honey, stock, mustard, rosemary, thyme, oregano, pepper flakes, garlic, salt and pepper, stir, cover and cook on Low for 5 hours. Add parsley, stir, divide between plates and serve.

NUTRITION:
calories 244, fat 4, fiber 6, carbs 12, protein 3

Mustard Chicken Mix
Preparation time: 10 minutes
Cooking time: 6 hours
Servings: 4

INGREDIENTS:
1 tablespoon olive oil
1 pound chicken breast, skinless, boneless and roughly cubed
2 tablespoons mustard
¾ cup chicken stock
1 teaspoon sweet paprika
1 teaspoon rosemary, dried
1 tablespoon lemon juice
A pinch of salt and black pepper
1 tablespoon chives, chopped

DIRECTIONS:
In your slow cooker, mix the chicken with the oil, mustard and the other ingredients, toss, put the lid on and cook on Low for 6 hours. Divide the mix into bowls and serve.

NUTRITION:
calories 200, fat 9, fiber 2, carbs 5, protein 10

Buffalo Chicken
Preparation time: 10 minutes
Cooking time: 4 hours
Servings: 12

INGREDIENTS:
2 pounds chicken breasts, skinless and

boneless
Salt and black pepper to the taste
2 garlic cloves, minced
1 cup cayenne sauce
½ cup chicken stock
½ packet ranch seasoning mix
1 tablespoon brown sugar

DIRECTIONS:
In your Slow cooker, mix chicken with salt, pepper, garlic, cayenne sauce, stock, seasoning and sugar, toss, cover and cook on High for 4 hours. Divide between plates and serve.

NUTRITION:
calories 273, fat 6, fiber 7, carbs 17, protein 2

Lemon Turkey and Spinach
Preparation time: 10 minutes
Cooking time: 7 hours
Servings: 4

INGREDIENTS:
1 pound turkey breasts, skinless, boneless and roughly cubed
1 cup baby spinach
Juice of ½ lemon
2 spring onions, chopped
½ teaspoon chili powder
1 cup chicken stock
1 tablespoon oregano, chopped
A pinch of salt and black pepper
1 teaspoon garam masala

DIRECTIONS:
In your slow cooker, mix the turkey with the lemon juice, spring onions and the other ingredients except the baby spinach, toss, put the lid on and cook on Low for 6 hours and 30 minutes. Add the spinach, cook everything on Low for 30 minutes more, divide between plates and serve.

NUTRITION:
calories 258, fat 4.5, fiber 3, carbs 13.4, protein 40.1

Alfredo Chicken
Preparation time: 10 minutes
Cooking time: 2 hours and 30 minutes
Servings: 4

INGREDIENTS:
1 pound chicken breasts, skinless and boneless
4 tablespoons soft butter
1 cup chicken stock
2 cups heavy cream
Salt and black pepper to the taste
½ teaspoon Italian seasoning
½ teaspoon garlic powder
1/3 cup parmesan, grated
½ pound rigatoni

DIRECTIONS:
In your Slow cooker, mix chicken with butter, stock, cream, salt, pepper, garlic powder and Italian seasoning, stir, cover and cook on High for 2 hours. Shred meat, return to slow cooker, also add rigatoni and parmesan, cover and cook on High for 30 minutes more. Divide between plates and serve.

NUTRITION:
calories 300, fat 7, fiber 7, carbs 17, protein 12

Paprika Chicken and Artichokes
Preparation time: 10 minutes
Cooking time: 7 hours and 10 minutes
Servings: 2

INGREDIENTS:
1 pound chicken breast, skinless, boneless and cut into strips
1 cup canned artichoke hearts, drained and halved
3 scallions, chopped
2 garlic cloves, minced
1 tablespoon olive oil
1 tablespoon sweet paprika
1 cup chicken stock
½ cup parsley, chopped

DIRECTIONS:
Heat up a pan with the oil over medium-high heat, add the scallions, garlic and the chicken, brown for 10 minutes and transfer to the slow cooker. Add the rest of the ingredients, toss, put the lid on and cook on Low for 7 hours. Divide everything between plates and serve.

NUTRITION:
calories 350, fat 13.6, fiber 2.4, carbs 5.9, protein 50

Slow Cooked Chicken
Preparation time: 10 minutes
Cooking time: 8 hours
Servings: 8

INGREDIENTS:
1 big chicken
1 garlic head, peeled
1 yellow onion, chopped
1 lemon, sliced
1 tablespoons sweet paprika
A pinch of sea salt
Black pepper to the taste
1 teaspoon thyme, dried
2 carrots, chopped

DIRECTIONS:
Stuff your chicken with half of the garlic and with half of the lemon slices and rub with salt, pepper, thyme and paprika both outside and inside. Put

the carrots on the bottom of your Slow cooker, add the rest of the garlic, onion and lemon slices, place the bird on top, cover and cook on Low for 8 hours. Transfer chicken to a platter, carve and serve with a side salad.

NUTRITION:
calories 200, fat 4, fiber 3, carbs 8, protein 16

Chives Chicken Wings

Preparation time: 10 minutes
Cooking time: 6 hours
Servings: 2

INGREDIENTS:
- 1 cup chicken stock
- 1 pound chicken wings
- ½ cup chives, chopped
- ½ teaspoon chili powder
- ½ teaspoon coriander, ground
- ½ teaspoon cumin, ground
- 1 teaspoon oregano, dried
- A pinch of salt and black pepper

DIRECTIONS:
In your slow cooker, mix the chicken with the stock, chives and the other ingredients, toss, put the lid on and cook on Low for 6 hours. Divide the mix between plates and serve with a side salad.

NUTRITION:
calories 220, fat 8, fiber 2, carbs 5, protein 11

Parsley Turkey Breast

Preparation time: 10 minutes
Cooking time: 8 hours
Servings: 4

INGREDIENTS:
- 3 pounds turkey breast, bone in
- 1 cup black figs
- 3 sweet potatoes, cut into wedges
- ½ cup dried cherries, pitted
- 2 white onions, cut into wedges
- ½ cup dried cranberries
- 1/3 cup water
- 1 teaspoon onion powder
- 1 teaspoon garlic powder
- 1 teaspoon parsley flakes
- 1 teaspoon thyme, dried
- 1 teaspoon sage, dried
- 1 teaspoon paprika, dried
- A pinch of sea salt
- Black pepper to the taste

DIRECTIONS:
Put the turkey breast in your Slow cooker, add sweet potatoes, figs, cherries, onions, cranberries, water, parsley, garlic and onion powder, thyme, sage, paprika, salt and pepper, toss, cover and cook on Low for 8 hours. Discard bone from turkey breast, slice meat, divide between plates and serve with the veggies, figs, cherries and berries on the side.

NUTRITION:
calories 320, fat 5, fiber 4, carbs 12, protein 15

Lime Chicken Mix

Preparation time: 10 minutes
Cooking time: 7 hours
Servings: 2

INGREDIENTS:
- 1 pound chicken thighs, boneless and skinless
- 1 tablespoon olive oil
- Juice of 1 lime
- Zest of 1 lime, grated
- ½ cup tomato sauce
- 2 spring onions, chopped
- Salt and black pepper to the taste
- 1 tablespoon oregano, chopped

DIRECTIONS:
In your slow cooker, mix the chicken with the oil, lime juice and the other ingredients, toss, put the lid on and cook on Low for 7 hours. Divide the mix between plates and serve.

NUTRITION:
calories 192, fat 12, fiber 3, carbs 5, protein 12

Chicken Breasts

Preparation time: 10 minutes
Cooking time: 6 hours
Servings: 4

INGREDIENTS:
- 2 red bell peppers, chopped
- 2 pounds chicken breasts, skinless and boneless
- 4 garlic cloves, minced
- 1 yellow onion, chopped
- 2 teaspoons paprika
- 1 cup low sodium chicken stock
- 2 teaspoons cinnamon powder
- ¼ teaspoon nutmeg, ground

DIRECTIONS:
In a bowl, mix bell peppers with chicken breasts, garlic, onion, paprika, cinnamon and nutmeg, toss to coat, transfer everything to your Slow cooker, add stock, cover and cook on Low for 6 hours. Divide chicken and veggies between plates and serve.

NUTRITION:
calories 250, fat 3, fiber 5, carbs 12, protein 10

Chicken and Olives

Preparation time: 10 minutes

Cooking time: 5 hours

Servings: 2

INGREDIENTS:
1 pound chicken breasts, skinless, boneless and sliced
1 cup black olives, pitted and halved
½ cup chicken stock
½ cup tomato sauce
1 tablespoon lime juice
1 tablespoon lime zest, grated
1 teaspoon chili powder
2 spring onions, chopped
1 tablespoon chives, chopped

DIRECTIONS:
In your slow cooker, mix the chicken with the olives, stock and the other ingredients except the chives, toss, put the lid on and cook on High for 5 hours. Divide the mix into bowls, sprinkle the chives on top and serve.

NUTRITION:
calories 200, fat 7, fiber 1, carbs 5, protein 12

Turkey Breast and Cranberries

Preparation time: 10 minutes

Cooking time: 6 hours

Servings: 6

INGREDIENTS:
6 pound turkey breast, skin and bone in
4 cups cranberries, rinsed
3 apples, peeled, cored and sliced
½ cup balsamic vinegar
½ cup maple syrup
A pinch of sea salt
Black pepper to the taste

DIRECTIONS:
Put the turkey breast in your Slow cooker, add cranberries, apple slices, a pinch of salt, black pepper, vinegar and maple syrup, toss a bit, cover and cook on Low for 6 hours. Slice turkey breast and divide between plates, mash cranberries and apples a bit, add them on top of the meat and serve right away.

NUTRITION:
calories 360, fat 4, fiber 3, carbs 9, protein 20

Turkey, Tomato and Fennel Mix

Preparation time: 10 minutes

Cooking time: 7 hours and 10 minutes

Servings: 2

INGREDIENTS:
1 pound turkey breast, skinless, boneless and cut into strips
1 fennel bulb, sliced
1 cup cherry tomatoes, halved
¼ cup chicken stock
½ cup tomato sauce
½ teaspoon hot paprika
½ teaspoon cumin, ground
½ teaspoon fennel seeds, crushed
1 tablespoon olive oil
1 red onion, chopped
A pinch of salt and black pepper
1 tablespoon cilantro, chopped

DIRECTIONS:
Heat up a pan with the oil over medium-high heat, add the meat, onion and fennel seeds, stir, brown for 10 minutes and transfer to the slow cooker. Add the rest of the ingredients, toss, put the lid on, cook on Low for 7 hours, divide between plates and serve.

NUTRITION:
calories 231, fat 7, fiber 2, carbs 6, protein 12

Thyme Chicken

Preparation time: 10 minutes

Cooking time: 6 hours

Servings: 6

INGREDIENTS:
1 whole chicken
5 thyme springs, chopped
2 celery stalks, chopped
3 garlic cloves, minced
2 carrots, chopped
1 yellow onion, chopped
A pinch of white pepper
Juice of 1 lemon

DIRECTIONS:
Put half of the thyme, garlic, celery, onion and carrots in your Slow cooker, add the chicken on top and season with a pinch of white pepper. Add the rest of the thyme, onion, garlic, celery and carrots on top, drizzle the lemon juice, cover and cook on Low for 6 hours. Divide chicken between plates and serve.

NUTRITION:
calories 230, fat 4, fiber 2, carbs 16, protein 6

Chicken with Tomatoes and Eggplant Mix

Preparation time: 10 minutes

Cooking time: 5 hours and 10 minutes.

Servings: 2

INGREDIENTS:
1 pound chicken breast, skinless, boneless and cubed
2 small eggplants, cubed
1 red onion, sliced

1 tablespoon olive oil
½ teaspoon cumin, ground
½ teaspoon sweet paprika
½ teaspoon red pepper flakes, crushed
½ cup canned tomatoes, crushed
1 cup chicken stock
1 teaspoon coriander, ground
A pinch of salt and black pepper
1 tablespoon oregano, chopped

DIRECTIONS:
Heat up a pan with the oil over medium-high heat, add the chicken, onion and pepper flakes, stir, brown for 10 minutes and transfer to your slow cooker. Add the rest of the ingredients, toss, put the lid on and cook on High for 5 hours. Divide everything between plates and serve.

NUTRITION:
calories 252, fat 12, fiber 4, carbs 7, protein 13

Mediterranean Chicken

Preparation time: 10 minutes
Cooking time: 4 hours
Servings: 4

INGREDIENTS:
1 and ½ pounds chicken breast, skinless and boneless
Juice of 2 lemons
1 rosemary spring, chopped
¼ cup olive oil
3 garlic cloves, minced
A pinch of salt and black pepper
1 cucumber, chopped
1 cup kalamata olives, pitted and sliced
¼ cup red onions, chopped
2 tablespoons red vinegar

DIRECTIONS:
In your Slow cooker, mix chicken with lemon juice, rosemary, oil, garlic, salt and pepper, stir, cover and cook on High for 4 hours. Transfer chicken to a cutting board, shred with 2 forks, transfer to a bowl, add cucumber, olives, onion and vinegar, toss, divide between plates and serve.

NUTRITION:
calories 240, fat 3, fiber 3, carbs 12, protein 3

Chicken and Onions Mix

Preparation time: 10 minutes
Cooking time: 7 hours
Servings: 2

INGREDIENTS:
1 pound chicken breasts, skinless, boneless and cubed
2 red onions, sliced
½ cup chicken stock
½ cup tomato passata
2 teaspoons olive oil
A pinch of salt and black pepper
1 teaspoon black peppercorns, crushed
2 garlic cloves, minced
1 tablespoon chives, chopped

DIRECTIONS:
Grease the slow cooker with the oil and mix the chicken with the onions, stock and the other ingredients inside. Put the lid on, cook on Low for 7 hours, divide between plates and serve.

NUTRITION:
calories 221, fat 14, fiber 3, carbs 7, protein 14

Chicken Chowder

Preparation time: 10 minutes
Cooking time: 6 hours
Servings: 4

INGREDIENTS:
3 chicken breasts, skinless and boneless and cubed
4 cups chicken stock
1 sweet potato, cubed
8 ounces canned green chilies, chopped
1 yellow onion, chopped
15 ounces coconut cream
1 teaspoon garlic powder
4 bacon strips, cooked and crumbled
A pinch of salt and black pepper
1 tablespoon parsley, chopped

DIRECTIONS:
In your Slow cooker, mix chicken with stock, sweet potato, green chilies, onion, garlic powder, salt and pepper, stir, cover and cook on Low for 5 hours and 40 minutes. Add coconut cream and parsley, stir, cover and cook on Low for 20 minutes more. Ladle chowder into bowls, sprinkle bacon on top and serve.

NUTRITION:
calories 232, fat 3, fiber 7, carbs 14, protein 7

Pesto Chicken Mix

Preparation time: 10 minutes
Cooking time: 6 hours and 10 minutes
Servings: 2

INGREDIENTS:
1 pound chicken breast, skinless, boneless and cut into strips
1 tablespoon basil pesto
1 tablespoon olive oil
4 scallions, chopped
½ cup kalamata olives, pitted and halved
1 cup chicken stock

1 tablespoon cilantro, chopped
A pinch of salt and black pepper

DIRECTIONS:
Heat up a pan with the oil over medium-high heat, add the scallions and the meat, brown for 10 minutes, transfer to the slow cooker and mix with the remaining ingredients. Toss, put the lid on, cook on Low for 6 hours, divide the mix between plates and serve.

NUTRITION:
calories 263, fat 14, fiber 1, carbs 8, protein 12

Chicken Thighs Delight
Preparation time: 10 minutes
Cooking time: 6 hours
Servings: 6

INGREDIENTS:
2 pounds chicken thighs, boneless and skinless
1 yellow onion, chopped
3 carrots, chopped
1/3 cup prunes, dried and halved
3 garlic cloves, minced
½ cup green olives, pitted
2 teaspoon sweet paprika
1 teaspoon cinnamon, ground
2 teaspoons cumin, ground
2 teaspoons ginger, grated
1 cup chicken stock
A pinch of salt and black pepper
1 tablespoon cilantro, chopped

DIRECTIONS:
In your Slow cooker, mix chicken with onion, carrots, prunes, garlic, olives, paprika, cinnamon, cumin, ginger, stock, salt and pepper, stir, cover and cook on Low for 6 hours. Divide between plates, sprinkle cilantro on top and serve.

NUTRITION:
calories 384, fat 12, fiber 4, carbs 20, protein 34

Ginger Turkey Mix
Preparation time: 10 minutes
Cooking time: 6 hours
Servings: 2

INGREDIENTS:
1 pound turkey breast, skinless, boneless and roughly cubed
1 tablespoon ginger, grated
2 teaspoons olive oil
1 cup tomato passata
½ cup chicken stock
A pinch of salt and black pepper
1 teaspoon chili powder
2 garlic cloves, minced
1 tablespoon cilantro, chopped

DIRECTIONS:
Grease the slow cooker with the oil and mix the turkey with the ginger and the other ingredients inside. Put the lid on, cook on High for 6 hours, divide between plates and serve.

NUTRITION:
calories 263, fat 12, fiber 3, carbs 6, protein 14

Chicken with Peach and Orange Sauce
Preparation time: 10 minutes
Cooking time: 6 hours
Servings: 8

INGREDIENTS:
6 chicken breasts, skinless and boneless
12 ounces orange juice
2 tablespoons lemon juice
15 ounces canned peaches and their juice
1 teaspoon soy sauce

DIRECTIONS:
In your slow cooker, mix chicken with orange juice, lemon juice, peaches and soy sauce, toss, cover and cook on Low for 6 hours. Divide chicken breasts on plates, drizzle peach and orange sauce all over and serve.

NUTRITION:
calories 251, fat 4, fiber 6, carbs 18, protein 14

Turkey and Plums Mix
Preparation time: 10 minutes
Cooking time: 7 hours
Servings: 2

INGREDIENTS:
1 pound turkey breast, skinless, boneless and sliced
1 cup plums, pitted and halved
½ cup chicken stock
½ teaspoon chili powder
½ teaspoon turmeric powder
½ teaspoon cumin, ground
1 tablespoon rosemary, chopped
A pinch of salt and black pepper

DIRECTIONS:
In your slow cooker, mix the turkey with the plums, stock and the other ingredients, toss, put the lid on and cook on Low for 7 hours. Divide the mix between plates and serve right away.

NUTRITION:
calories 253, fat 13, fiber 2, carbs 7, protein 16

Flavored Chicken Thighs

Preparation time: 10 minutes

Cooking time: 4 hours

Servings: 4

INGREDIENTS:
- 2 pounds chicken thighs
- Salt and black pepper to the taste
- ¾ cup sweet Bbq sauce
- A pinch of cayenne pepper
- 1 cup apple juice
- 1 teaspoon red pepper, crushed
- 2 teaspoons paprika
- ½ teaspoon basil, dried

DIRECTIONS:
In your Slow cooker, mix chicken with salt, pepper, bbq sauce, cayenne, apple juice, red pepper, paprika and basil, stir, cover and cook on High for 4 hours. Divide everything between plates and serve.

NUTRITION:
calories 200, fat 3, fiber 6, carbs 10, protein 17

Creamy Turkey Mix

Preparation time: 10 minutes

Cooking time: 7 hours

Servings: 2

INGREDIENTS:
- 1 pound turkey breast, skinless, boneless and cubed
- 1 teaspoon turmeric powder
- ½ teaspoon garam masala
- ½ cup heavy cream
- 1 red onion, chopped
- ½ cup chicken stock
- 4 garlic cloves, minced
- ¼ cup chives, chopped
- A pinch of salt and black pepper
- 1 tablespoon chives, chopped

DIRECTIONS:
In your slow cooker, mix the turkey with turmeric, garam masala and the other ingredients except the cream, toss, put the lid on and cook on Low for 6 hours. Add the cream, toss, put the lid on again, cook on Low for 1 more hour, divide everything between plates and serve.

NUTRITION:
calories 234, fat 14, fiber 4, carbs 7, protein 15

Turkey Gumbo

Preparation time: 10 minutes

Cooking time: 7 hours

Servings: 4

INGREDIENTS:
- 1 pound turkey wings
- Salt and black pepper to the taste
- 5 ounces water
- 1 yellow onion, chopped
- 1 yellow bell pepper, chopped
- 3 garlic cloves, chopped
- 2 tablespoons chili powder
- 1 and ½ teaspoons cumin, ground
- A pinch of cayenne pepper
- 2 cups veggies stock

DIRECTIONS:
In your Slow cooker, mix turkey with salt, pepper, onion, bell pepper, garlic, chili powder, cumin, cayenne and stock, stir, cover and cook on Low for 7 hours. Divide everything between plates and serve.

NUTRITION:
calories 232, fat 4, fiber 7, carbs 17, protein 20

Chicken and Apples Mix

Preparation time: 10 minutes

Cooking time: 7 hours

Servings: 2

INGREDIENTS:
- 1 pound chicken breast, skinless, boneless and sliced
- 1 cup apples, cored and cubed
- 1 teaspoon olive oil
- 1 red onion, sliced
- 1 tablespoon oregano, chopped
- ½ teaspoon turmeric powder
- ½ teaspoon chili powder
- 1 cup chicken stock
- A pinch of salt and black pepper
- 1 tablespoon chives, chopped

DIRECTIONS:
Grease the slow cooker with the oil, and mix the chicken with the apples, onion and the other ingredients inside. Toss, put the lid on, cook on Low for 7 hours, divide the mix between plates and serve.

NUTRITION:
calories 263, fat 13, fiber 2, carbs 7, protein 15

Chinese Duck

Preparation time: 10 minutes

Cooking time: 8 hours

Servings: 6

INGREDIENTS:
- 1 duck, chopped in medium pieces
- 1 celery stalk, chopped
- 2 carrots, chopped

2 cups chicken stock
Salt and black pepper to the taste
1 tablespoon ginger, grated

DIRECTIONS:
In your Slow cooker, mix duck with celery, carrots, stock, salt, pepper and ginger, stir, cover and cook on Low for 8 hours. Divide duck, ginger sauce between plates, and serve.

NUTRITION:
calories 200, fat 3, fiber 6, carbs 19, protein 17

Chicken and Endives

Preparation time: 5 minutes
Cooking time: 7 hours
Servings: 2

INGREDIENTS:
1 pound chicken breasts, skinless, boneless and sliced
4 scallions, chopped
2 endives, shredded
½ cup tomatoes, cubed
1 cup chicken stock
1 tablespoon oregano, chopped
A pinch of salt and black pepper

DIRECTIONS:
In your slow cooker, combine the chicken slices with the scallions and the other ingredients except the endives and the oregano, toss, put the lid on and cook on Low for 6 hours. Add the remaining ingredients, cook on Low for 1 more hour, divide everything between plates and serve.

NUTRITION:
calories 200, fat 13, fiber 2, carbs 5, protein 16

Turkey Wings and Veggies

Preparation time: 10 minutes
Cooking time: 8 hours
Servings: 4

INGREDIENTS:
4 turkey wings
1 yellow onion, chopped
1 carrot, chopped
3 garlic cloves, minced
1 celery stalk, chopped
1 cup chicken stock
Salt and black pepper to the taste
2 tablespoons olive oil
A pinch of rosemary, dried
2 bay leaves
A pinch of sage, dried
A pinch of thyme, dried

DIRECTIONS:
In your Slow cooker, mix turkey with onion, carrot, garlic, celery, stock, salt, pepper, oil, rosemary, sage, thyme and bay leaves, toss, cover and cook on Low for 8 hours. Divide between plates and serve hot.

NUTRITION:
calories 223, fat 5, fiber 7, carbs 18, protein 14

Basil Chicken Wings

Preparation time: 5 minutes
Cooking time: 5 hours
Servings: 2

INGREDIENTS:
1 pound chicken wings, halved
1 tablespoon olive oil
1 tablespoon honey
1 cup chicken stock
A pinch of salt and black pepper
1 tablespoon basil, chopped
½ teaspoon cumin, ground

DIRECTIONS:
In your slow cooker, mix the chicken wings with the oil, honey and the other ingredients, toss, put the lid on and cook on High for 5 hours. Divide the mix between plates and serve with a side salad.

NUTRITION:
calories 200, fat 12, fiber 2, carbs 6, protein 15

Turkey Wings and Sauce

Preparation time: 10 minutes
Cooking time: 8 hours
Servings: 4

INGREDIENTS:
4 turkey wings
2 tablespoons butter, melted
2 tablespoons olive oil
1 and ½ cups cranberries, dried
Salt and black pepper to the taste
1 yellow onion, roughly chopped
1 cup walnuts
1 cup orange juice
1 bunch thyme, chopped

DIRECTIONS:
In your slow cooker mix butter with oil, turkey wings, cranberries, salt, pepper, onion, walnuts, orange juice and thyme, stir a bit, cover and cook on Low for 8 hours. Divide turkey and orange sauce between plates and serve.

NUTRITION:
calories 300, fat 12, fiber 4, carbs 17, protein 1

Chicken and Broccoli

Preparation time: 10 minutes
Cooking time: 5 hours
Servings: 2

INGREDIENTS:
1 pound chicken breast, skinless, boneless and sliced
1 cup broccoli florets
½ cup tomato sauce
½ cup chicken stock
1 tablespoon avocado oil
1 yellow onion, sliced
3 garlic cloves, minced
A pinch of salt and black pepper
1 tablespoon cilantro, chopped

DIRECTIONS:
In your slow cooker, mix the chicken with the broccoli, tomato sauce and the other ingredients, toss, put the lid on and cook on High for 5 hours. Divide the mix between plates and serve hot.

NUTRITION:
calories 253, fat 14, fiber 2, carbs 7, protein 16

Chicken and Sauce

Preparation time: 10 minutes
Cooking time: 4 hours
Servings: 8

INGREDIENTS:
1 whole chicken, cut into medium pieces
1 tablespoon olive oil
1 and ½ tablespoons lemon juice
1 cup chicken stock
1 tablespoon cilantro, chopped
1 teaspoon cinnamon powder
Salt and black pepper to the taste
1 tablespoon sweet paprika
1 teaspoon onion powder

DIRECTIONS:
In your Slow cooker, mix chicken with oil, lemon juice, stock, cilantro, cinnamon, salt, pepper, paprika and onion powder, stir, cover and cook on High for 4 hours. Divide chicken between plates and serve with cooking sauce drizzled on top.

NUTRITION:
calories 261, fat 4, fiber 6, carbs 12, protein 22

Rosemary Chicken

Preparation time: 10 minutes
Cooking time: 7 hours
Servings: 2

INGREDIENTS:
1 pound chicken thighs, boneless, skinless and sliced
1 tablespoon avocado oil
1 teaspoon cumin, ground
1 tablespoon rosemary, chopped
1 cup chicken stock
A pinch of salt and black pepper
1 tablespoon chives, chopped

DIRECTIONS:
In your slow cooker, mix the chicken with the oil, cumin and the other ingredients, toss, put the lid on and cook on Low for 7 hours. Divide the mix between plates and serve.

NUTRITION:
calories 273, fat 13, fiber 3, carbs 7, protein 17

Chicken Wings and Mint Sauce

Preparation time: 20 minutes
Cooking time: 4 hours
Servings: 6

INGREDIENTS:
18 chicken wings, cut into halves
1 tablespoon turmeric
1 tablespoon cumin, ground
1 tablespoon ginger, grated
1 tablespoon coriander, ground
1 tablespoon paprika
A pinch of cayenne pepper
Salt and black pepper to the taste
2 tablespoons olive oil
For the sauce:
Juice of ½ lime
1 cup mint leaves
1 small ginger piece, chopped
¾ cup cilantro
1 tablespoon olive oil
1 tablespoon water
Salt and black pepper to the taste
1 Serrano pepper

DIRECTIONS:
In a bowl, mix 1 tablespoon ginger with cumin, coriander, paprika, turmeric, salt, pepper, cayenne and 2 tablespoons oil and stir well. Add chicken wings pieces to this mix, toss to coat well and keep in the fridge for 20 minutes. Add marinated wings to your Slow cooker, cook on High for 4 hours and transfer to a bowl. In your blender, mix mint with cilantro, 1 small ginger pieces, juice of ½ lime, tablespoon olive oil, salt, pepper, water and Serrano pepper and blend very well. Serve your chicken wings with this sauce on the side.

NUTRITION:
calories 230, fat 5, fiber 1, carbs 12, protein 9

Chicken Curry

Preparation time: 10 minutes
Cooking time: 7 hours
Servings: 2

INGREDIENTS:
1 pound chicken breast, skinless, boneless and cubed
1 tablespoon yellow
curry paste
1 yellow onion, chopped
1 tablespoon olive oil

1 teaspoon basil, dried
1 teaspoon black peppercorns, crushed
1 cup chicken stock
¼ cup coconut cream
1 tablespoon lime juice
1 tablespoon cilantro, chopped

DIRECTIONS:

In your slow cooker, mix the chicken with the curry paste, onion and the other ingredients, toss, put the lid on and cook on Low for 7 hours. Divide everything into bowls and serve hot.

NUTRITION:

calories 276, fat 15, fiber 3, carbs 7, protein 16

Lemony Chicken

Preparation time: 10 minutes
Cooking time: 4 hours
Servings: 6

INGREDIENTS:

1 whole chicken, cut into medium pieces
Salt and black pepper to the taste
Zest of 2 lemons
Juice of 2 lemons
Lemon rinds from 2 lemons

DIRECTIONS:

Put chicken pieces in your Slow cooker, season with salt and pepper to the taste, drizzle lemon juice, add lemon zest and lemon rinds, cover and cook on High for 4 hours. Discard lemon rinds, divide chicken between plates, drizzle sauce from the slow cooker over it and serve.

NUTRITION:

calories 334, fat 24, fiber 2, carbs 4.5, protein 27

Balsamic Turkey

Preparation time: 10 minutes
Cooking time: 5 hours
Servings: 2

INGREDIENTS:

1 pound turkey breast, skinless, boneless and cubed
1 tablespoon lemon juice
4 scallions, chopped
1 tablespoon balsamic vinegar
2 tablespoons avocado oil
A pinch of salt and black pepper
1 tablespoon chives, chopped
½ cup chicken stock

DIRECTIONS:

In your slow cooker, mix the turkey with the lemon juice, scallions and the other ingredients, toss, put the lid on and cook on High for 5 hours. Divide the mix between plates and serve right away.

NUTRITION:

calories 252, fat 15, fiber 2, carbs 6, protein 15

Chicken and Paprika Sauce

Preparation time: 10 minutes
Cooking time: 4 hours
Servings: 5

INGREDIENTS:

1 tablespoon coconut oil
3 and ½ pounds chicken breasts
1 cup chicken stock
1 and ¼ cups yellow onion, chopped
1 tablespoon lime juice
¼ cup coconut milk
2 teaspoons sweet paprika
1 teaspoon red pepper flakes
2 tablespoons green onions, chopped
Salt and black pepper to the taste

DIRECTIONS:

Heat up a pan with the oil over medium-high heat, add chicken, cook for 2 minutes on each side and transfer to your Slow cooker. Add stock, onion, lime juice, coconut milk, sweet paprika, pepper flakes, salt, pepper and green onions, toss, cover and cook on High for 4 hours. Divide everything between plates and serve.

NUTRITION:

calories 250, fat 4, fiber 3, carbs 12, protein 6

Turkey and Scallions Mix

Preparation time: 10 minutes
Cooking time: 7 hours
Servings: 2

INGREDIENTS:

1 pound turkey breasts, skinless, boneless and cubed
1 tablespoon avocado oil
½ cup tomato sauce
½ cup chicken stock
½ teaspoon sweet paprika
4 scallions, chopped
1 tablespoons lemon zest, grated
1 tablespoon lemon juice
A pinch of salt and black pepper
1 tablespoon chives, chopped

DIRECTIONS:

In your slow cooker, mix the turkey with the oil, tomato sauce and the other ingredients, toss, put the lid on and cook on Low for 7 hours. Divide everything between plates and serve.

NUTRITION:

calories 234, fat 12, fiber 3, carbs 5, protein 7

Chicken Thighs and Mushrooms

Preparation time: 10 minutes
Cooking time: 4 hours
Servings: 4

INGREDIENTS:
4 chicken thighs
2 cups mushrooms, sliced
¼ cup butter, melted
Salt and black pepper to the taste
½ teaspoon onion powder
½ teaspoon garlic powder
½ cup water
1 teaspoon Dijon mustard
1 tablespoon tarragon, chopped

DIRECTIONS:
In your Slow cooker, mix chicken with butter, mushrooms, salt, pepper, onion powder, garlic powder, water, mustard and tarragon, toss, cover and cook on High for 4 hours. Divide between plates and serve.

NUTRITION:
calories 453, fat 32, fiber 6, carbs 15, protein 36

Parsley Chicken Mix

Preparation time: 10 minutes
Cooking time: 5 hours
Servings: 2

INGREDIENTS:
1 pound chicken breast, skinless, boneless and sliced
½ cup parsley, chopped
2 tablespoons olive oil
1 tablespoon pine nuts
1 tablespoon lemon juice
½ cup chicken stock
¼ cup black olives, pitted and halved
1 teaspoon hot paprika
A pinch of salt and black pepper

DIRECTIONS:
In a blender, mix the parsley with the oil, pine nuts and lemon juice and pulse well. In your slow cooker, mix the chicken with the parsley mix and the remaining ingredients, toss, put the lid on and cook on High for 5 hours. Divide everything between plates and serve.

NUTRITION:
calories 263, fat 14, fiber 3, carbs 7, protein 16

Creamy Duck Breast

Preparation time: 10 minutes
Cooking time: 4 hours
Servings: 1

INGREDIENTS:
1 medium duck breast, skin scored
1 tablespoon sugar
1 tablespoon heavy cream
2 tablespoons butter, melted
½ teaspoon orange extract
Salt and black pepper to the taste
1 cup baby spinach
¼ teaspoon sage, dried

DIRECTIONS:
In your Slow cooker, mix butter with duck breast, cream, sugar, orange extract, salt, pepper and sage, stir, cover and cook on High for 4 hours. Add spinach, toss, leave aside for a few minutes, transfer to a plate and serve.

NUTRITION:
calories 567, fat 56, fiber 1, carbs 22, protein 35

Turkey Chili

Preparation time: 10 minutes
Cooking time: 5 hours
Servings: 2

INGREDIENTS:
1 pound turkey breast, skinless, boneless and cubed
1 red chili, minced
1 teaspoon chili powder
1 red onion, chopped
1 tablespoon avocado oil
½ cup tomato passata
½ cup chicken stock
A pinch of salt and black pepper
1 tablespoon cilantro, chopped

DIRECTIONS:
In your slow cooker, mix the turkey with the chili, chili powder and the other ingredients, toss, put the lid on and cook on High for 5 hours. Divide the mix into bowls and serve.

NUTRITION:
calories 263, fat 12, fiber 2, carbs 7, protein 18

Duck Breast and Veggies

Preparation time: 10 minutes
Cooking time: 4 hours
Servings: 2

INGREDIENTS:
2 duck breasts, skin on and thinly sliced
2 zucchinis, sliced
1 tablespoon olive oil
1 spring onion stack, chopped
1 radish, chopped
2 green bell peppers, chopped
Salt and black pepper to the taste

DIRECTIONS:

In your Slow cooker, mix duck with oil, salt and pepper and toss. Add zucchinis, onion, radish and bell peppers, cover and cook on High for 4 hours. Divide everything between plates and serve.

NUTRITION:

calories 450, fat 23, fiber 3, carbs 14, protein 50

Masala Turkey

Preparation time: 10 minutes

Cooking time: 5 hours

Servings: 2

INGREDIENTS:

1 pound turkey breasts, skinless, boneless and cubed
A pinch of salt and black pepper
2 scallions, chopped
1 teaspoon garam masala
1 cup coconut cream
1 cup chicken stock
1 tablespoon basil, chopped
1 tablespoon lime juice

DIRECTIONS:

In your slow cooker, mix the turkey with the scallions, garam masala and the other ingredients, toss, put the lid on and cook on High for 5 hours. Divide the mix into bowls and serve.

NUTRITION:

calories 201, fat 7, fiber 3, carbs 6, protein 8

Turkey Soup

Preparation time: 10 minutes

Cooking time: 3 hours

Servings: 4

INGREDIENTS:

3 celery stalks, chopped
1 yellow onion, chopped
1 tablespoon olive oil
6 cups turkey stock
Salt and black pepper to the taste
¼ cup parsley, chopped
3 cups baked spaghetti squash, chopped
3 cups turkey, cooked and shredded

DIRECTIONS:

In your Slow cooker, mix oil with celery, onion, stock, salt, pepper, squash, turkey and parsley, stir, cover, cook on High for 3 hours, ladle into bowls and serve.

NUTRITION:

calories 250, fat 4, fiber 1, carbs 13, protein 10

Chicken and Beans

Preparation time: 10 minutes

Cooking time: 7 hours

Servings: 2

INGREDIENTS:

1 cup canned black beans, drained and rinsed
½ cup canned kidney beans, drained and rinsed
1 pound chicken breast, skinless, boneless and cubed
1 red onion, chopped
2 garlic cloves, minced
1 tablespoon olive oil
½ teaspoon sweet paprika
1 tablespoon chili powder
1 cup tomato sauce
A pinch of salt and black pepper
1 tablespoon parsley, chopped

DIRECTIONS:

In your slow cooker, mix the chicken with the beans, onion and the other ingredients, toss, put the lid on and cook on Low for 7 hours. Divide the mix into bowls and serve hot.

NUTRITION:

calories 263, fat 12, fiber 3, carbs 7, protein 15

Slow Cooked Turkey Delight

Preparation time: 10 minutes

Cooking time: 4 hours

Servings: 8

INGREDIENTS:

4 cups zucchinis, cut with a spiralizer
1 egg, whisked
3 cups cabbage, shredded
3 cups turkey meat, cooked and shredded
½ cup turkey stock
½ cup cream cheese
1 teaspoon poultry seasoning
2 cup cheddar cheese, grated
½ cup parmesan cheese, grated
Salt and black pepper to the taste
¼ teaspoon garlic powder

DIRECTIONS:

In your Slow cooker, mix the egg, stock, cream, parmesan, cheddar cheese, salt, pepper, poultry seasoning and garlic powder and stir. Add turkey meat, cabbage and zucchini noodles, cover and cook on High for 4 hours. Divide between plates and serve.

NUTRITION:

calories 240, fat 15, fiber 1, carbs 13, protein 25

Turkey and Corn

Preparation time: 10 minutes
Cooking time: 7 hours
Servings: 2

INGREDIENTS:
- 1 red onion
- 1 cup corn
- 1 pound turkey breasts, skinless, boneless and cubed
- 1 cup heavy cream
- 2 tablespoons olive oil
- 1 tablespoon cumin, ground
- ½ cup chicken stock
- ½ teaspoon rosemary, dried
- A pinch of salt and black pepper
- 1 tablespoon cilantro, chopped

DIRECTIONS:
In your slow cooker, mix the turkey with the corn, onion and the other ingredients, toss, put the lid on and cook on Low for 7 hours. Divide everything into bowls and serve.

NUTRITION:
calories 214, fat 14, fiber 2, carbs 6, protein 15

Turkey Curry

Preparation time: 10 minutes
Cooking time: 4 hours
Servings: 4

INGREDIENTS:
- 18 ounces turkey meat, minced
- 3 ounces spinach
- 20 ounces canned tomatoes, chopped
- 2 tablespoons coconut oil
- 2 tablespoons coconut cream
- 2 garlic cloves, minced
- 2 yellow onions, sliced
- 1 tablespoon coriander, ground
- 2 tablespoons ginger, grated
- 1 tablespoons turmeric powder
- 1 tablespoon cumin, ground
- Salt and black pepper to the taste
- 2 tablespoons chili powder

DIRECTIONS:
In your Slow cooker, mix turkey with spinach, tomatoes, oil, cream, garlic, onion, coriander, ginger, turmeric, cumin, chili, salt and pepper, stir, cover and cook on High for 4 hours. Divide into bowls and serve.

NUTRITION:
calories 240, fat 4, fiber 3, carbs 13, protein 12

Coriander Turkey Mix

Preparation time: 10 minutes
Cooking time: 6 hours
Servings: 2

INGREDIENTS:
- 1 pound turkey breasts, skinless, boneless and cubed
- 1 tablespoon olive oil
- 3 scallions, chopped
- 1 cup chicken stock
- 1 teaspoon sweet paprika
- 1 tablespoon coriander, chopped

DIRECTIONS:
In your slow cooker, mix the turkey with the oil, scallions and the other ingredients, toss, put the lid on and cook Low for 6 hours. Divide the mix into bowls and serve.

NUTRITION:
calories 311, fat 11.2, fiber 2.1, carbs 12.2, protein 39.6

Chicken and Mustard Sauce

Preparation time: 10 minutes
Cooking time: 4 hours
Servings: 3

INGREDIENTS:
- 8 bacon strips, cooked and chopped
- 1/3 cup Dijon mustard
- Salt and black pepper to the taste
- 1 cup yellow onion, chopped
- 1 tablespoon olive oil
- 1 and ½ cups chicken stock
- 3 chicken breasts, skinless and boneless
- ¼ teaspoon sweet paprika

DIRECTIONS:
In a bowl, mix paprika with mustard, salt and pepper and stir well. Spread this on chicken breasts and massage. Heat up a pan with the oil over medium-high heat, add chicken breasts, cook for 2 minutes on each side and transfer to your Slow cooker. Add stock, bacon and onion, stir, cover and cook on High for 4 hours. Divide chicken between plates, drizzle mustard sauce all over and serve.

NUTRITION:
calories 223, fat 8, fiber 1, carbs 13, protein 26

Turkey with Olives and Corn

Preparation time: 10 minutes
Cooking time: 4 hours
Servings: 2

INGREDIENTS:
- 1 pound turkey breast, skinless, boneless and cubed
- 1 tablespoon olive oil
- ½ cup kalamata olives, pitted and halved
- 1 cup corn
- 1 red onion, sliced
- 1 cup tomato passata
- 1 tablespoon parsley, chopped

DIRECTIONS:
In your slow cooker, mix the turkey with the olives, corn and the other ingredients, toss, put the lid on and cook on High for 4 hours. Divide everything between plates and serve.

NUTRITION:
calories 423, fat 15.3, fiber 5.6, carbs 31.4, protein 42.2

Chicken Casserole

Preparation time: 10 minutes

Cooking time: 4 hours

Servings: 8

INGREDIENTS:

1 and ½ pounds chicken breast, skinless and boneless and cubed	powder
	1 and ½ teaspoons parsley, dried
Salt and black pepper to the taste	½ teaspoon basil, dried
	4 tablespoons olive oil
1 egg	4 cups spaghetti squash, already cooked
1 cup flour	
¼ cup parmesan, grated	6 ounces mozzarella, shredded
½ teaspoon garlic	1 and ½ cups marinara sauce

DIRECTIONS:
In a bowl, mix flour with parmesan, salt, pepper, garlic powder and 1 teaspoon parsley and stir. In another bowl, whisk the egg with a pinch of salt and pepper. Dip chicken in egg and then in flour mix. Heat up a pan with 3 tablespoons oil over medium-high heat, add chicken, cook until they are golden on both sides and transfer to your Slow cooker. In a bowl, mix spaghetti squash with salt, pepper, dried basil, 1 tablespoon oil and the rest of the parsley and stir. Spread this over chicken, add marinara sauce, top with mozzarella, cover and cook on High for 4 hours. Leave casserole aside to cool down a bit, divide between plates and serve.

NUTRITION:
calories 300, fat 6, fiber 3, carbs 15, protein 28

Dill Turkey and Peas

Preparation time: 10 minutes

Cooking time: 5 hours

Servings: 2

INGREDIENTS:

1 pound turkey breast, skinless, boneless and sliced	1 cup green peas
	½ cup tomato sauce
	½ cup scallions, chopped
A pinch of salt and black pepper	1 teaspoon garam masala
1 cup chicken stock	1 tablespoon dill, chopped

DIRECTIONS:
In your slow cooker, mix the turkey with the peas, tomato sauce and the other ingredients, toss, put the lid on and cook on High for 5 hours. Divide the mix into bowls and serve right away.

NUTRITION:
calories 326, fat 4.6, fiber 6.6, carbs 26.7, protein 44.6

Chicken and Broccoli Casserole

Preparation time: 10 minutes

Cooking time: 4 hours

Servings: 4

INGREDIENTS:

3 cups cheddar cheese, grated	1 cup mayonnaise
	1 tablespoon olive oil
10 ounces broccoli florets	1/3 cup chicken stock
3 chicken breasts, skinless, boneless, cooked and cubed	Salt and black pepper to the taste
	Juice of 1 lemon

DIRECTIONS:
Grease your Slow cooker with the oil and arrange chicken pieces on the bottom. Spread broccoli florets and then half of the cheese. In a bowl, mix mayo with stock, salt, pepper and lemon juice. Pour this over chicken, sprinkle the rest of the cheese, cover and cook on High for 4 hours. Serve hot.

NUTRITION:
calories 320, fat 5, fiber 4, carbs 16, protein 25

Turkey with Rice

Preparation time: 10 minutes

Cooking time: 7 hours

Servings: 2

INGREDIENTS:

1 pound turkey breasts, skinless, boneless and cubed	chopped
	2 tablespoons green onions, chopped
1 cup wild rice	½ teaspoon coriander, ground
2 cups chicken stock	
1 tablespoon cilantro, chopped	½ teaspoon rosemary, dried
1 tablespoon oregano,	½ teaspoon turmeric

powder
A pinch of salt and black pepper

DIRECTIONS:
In your slow cooker, mix the turkey with the rice, stock and the other ingredients, toss, put the lid on and cook on Low for 7 hours. Divide everything between plates and serve.

NUTRITION:
calories 232, fat 12, fiber 2, carbs 6, protein 15

Red Chicken Soup

Preparation time: 10 minutes

Cooking time: 3 hours

Servings: 4

INGREDIENTS:
3 tablespoons butter, melted
4 ounces cream cheese
2 cups chicken meat, cooked and shredded
1/3 cup red sauce
4 cups chicken stock
Salt and black pepper to the taste
½ cup sour cream
¼ cup celery, chopped

DIRECTIONS:
In your blender, mix stock with red sauce, cream cheese, butter, salt, pepper and sour cream, pulse well and transfer to your Slow cooker. Add celery and chicken, stir, cover and cook on High for 3 hours. Divide into bowls and serve.

NUTRITION:
calories 400, fat 23, fiber 5, carbs 15, protein 30

Italian Turkey

Preparation time: 10 minutes

Cooking time: 6 hours

Servings: 2

INGREDIENTS:
1 pound turkey breasts, skinless, boneless and roughly cubed
1 tablespoon olive oil
½ cup black olives, pitted and halved
½ cup pearl onions, peeled
1 cup chicken stock
1 tablespoon Italian seasoning
A pinch of salt and black pepper

DIRECTIONS:
In your slow cooker, mix the turkey with the olives, onions and the other ingredients, toss, put the lid on and coo on Low for 6 hours. Divide the mix between plates and serve.

NUTRITION:
calories 263, fat 14, fiber 4, carbs 6, protein 18

Citrus Chicken

Preparation time: 10 minutes

Cooking time: 4 hours

Servings: 4

INGREDIENTS:
2 pounds chicken thighs, skinless, boneless and cut into pieces
Salt and black pepper to the taste
3 tablespoons olive oil
¼ cup flour
For the sauce:
2 tablespoons fish sauce
1 and ½ teaspoons orange extract
1 tablespoon ginger, grated
¼ cup orange juice
2 teaspoons sugar
1 tablespoon orange zest
¼ teaspoon sesame seeds
2 tablespoons scallions, chopped
½ teaspoon coriander, ground
1 cup water
¼ teaspoon red pepper flakes
2 tablespoons soy sauce

DIRECTIONS:
In a bowl, mix flour and salt and pepper, stir, add chicken pieces and toss to coat well. Heat up a pan with the oil over medium heat, add chicken, cook until they are golden on both sides and transfer to your Slow cooker. In your blender, mix orange juice with ginger, fish sauce, soy sauce, stevia, orange extract, water and coriander and blend well. Pour this over the chicken, sesame seeds, orange zest, scallions and pepper flakes, stir, cover and cook on High for 4 hours. Divide between plates and serve.

NUTRITION:
calories 423, fat 20, fiber 5, carbs 12, protein 45

Duck and Mushrooms

Preparation time: 10 minutes

Cooking time: 6 hours

Servings: 2

INGREDIENTS:
1 pound duck leg, skinless, boneless and sliced
1 cup chicken stock
1 cup white mushrooms, sliced
½ teaspoon rosemary, dried
½ teaspoon cumin, ground
½ cup heavy cream
1 tablespoon olive oil
¼ cup chives, chopped

DIRECTIONS:
In your slow cooker, mix the duck with the stock, mushrooms and the other ingredients, toss, put the lid on and cook on Low for 6 hours. Divide everything between plates and serve.

NUTRITION:
calories 262, fat 16, fiber 2, carbs 8, protein 16

Chicken and Creamy Mushroom Sauce

Preparation time: 10 minutes
Cooking time: 4 hours
Servings: 4

INGREDIENTS:
8 chicken thighs
Salt and black pepper to the taste
1 yellow onion, chopped
1 tablespoon olive oil
4 bacon strips, cooked and chopped
4 garlic cloves, minced
10 ounces cremini mushrooms, halved
2 cups white chardonnay wine
1 cup whipping cream
A handful parsley, chopped

DIRECTIONS:
Heat up a pan with the oil over medium heat, add chicken pieces, season them with salt and pepper, cook until they brown and also transfer to your Slow cooker. Add onions, garlic, bacon, mushrooms, wine, parsley and cream, stir, cover and cook on High for 4 hours. Divide between plates and serve.

NUTRITION:
calories 340, fat 10, fiber 7, carbs 14, protein 24

Turkey and Tomato Sauce

Preparation time: 10 minutes
Cooking time: 7 hours
Servings: 2

INGREDIENTS:
1 cup tomato sauce
½ cup chicken stock
½ tablespoon rosemary, chopped
1 pound turkey breast, skinless, boneless and roughly cubed
1 teaspoon rosemary, dried
1 tablespoon cilantro, chopped
A pinch of salt and black pepper

DIRECTIONS:
In your slow cooker, mix the turkey with the sauce, stock and the other ingredients, toss, put the lid on and cook on Low for 7 hours. Divide everything between plates and serve.

NUTRITION:
calories 283, fat 16, fiber 2, carbs 6, protein 17

Slow Cooker Chicken Breasts

Preparation time: 10 minutes
Cooking time: 4 hours
Servings: 4

INGREDIENTS:
6 chicken breasts, skinless and boneless
Salt and black pepper to the taste
¼ cup jalapenos, chopped
5 bacon slices, chopped
8 ounces cream cheese
¼ cup yellow onion, chopped
½ cup mayonnaise
½ cup parmesan, grated
1 cup cheddar cheese, grated

DIRECTIONS:
Arrange chicken breasts in your Slow cooker, add salt, pepper, jalapenos, bacon, cream cheese, onion, mayo, parmesan and cheddar, cover and cook on High for 4 hours. Divide between plates and serve.

NUTRITION:
calories 340, fat 12, fiber 2, carbs 15, protein 20

Tomato Chicken and Chickpeas

Preparation time: 10 minutes
Cooking time: 7 hours
Servings: 2

INGREDIENTS:
1 tablespoon olive oil
1 red onion, chopped
1 cup canned chickpeas, drained
1 pound chicken breast, skinless, boneless and cubed
½ cup tomato sauce
½ cup cherry tomatoes, halved
½ teaspoon rosemary, dried
½ teaspoon turmeric powder
1 cup chicken stock
A pinch of salt and black pepper
1 tablespoon chives, chopped

DIRECTIONS:
Grease the slow cooker with the oil and mix the chicken with the onion, chickpeas and the other ingredients inside the pot. Put the lid on, cook on Low for 7 hours, divide between plates and serve.

NUTRITION:
calories 291, fat 17, fiber 3, carbs 7, protein 16

Chicken and Sour Cream

Preparation time: 10 minutes
Cooking time: 4 hours
Servings: 4

INGREDIENTS:
4 chicken thighs
Salt and black pepper to the taste
1 teaspoon onion powder
¼ cup sour cream
2 tablespoons sweet paprika

DIRECTIONS:
In a bowl, mix paprika with salt, pepper and onion powder and stir. Season chicken pieces with this paprika mix, place them in your Slow cooker, add sour cream, toss, cover and cook on High for 4 hours. Divide everything between plates and serve.

NUTRITION:
calories 384, fat 31, fiber 2, carbs 11, protein 33

Turkey with Leeks and Radishes

Preparation time: 10 minutes

Cooking time: 6 hours

Servings: 2

INGREDIENTS:
1 pound turkey breast, skinless, boneless and cubed
1 leek, sliced
1 cup radishes, sliced
1 red onion, chopped
1 tablespoon olive oil
A pinch of salt and black pepper
1 cup chicken stock
½ teaspoon sweet paprika
½ teaspoon coriander, ground
1 tablespoon cilantro, chopped

DIRECTIONS:
In your slow cooker, combine the turkey with the leek, radishes, onion and the other ingredients, toss, put the lid on and cook on High for 6 hours. Divide everything between plates and serve.

NUTRITION:
calories 226, fat 9, fiber 1, carbs 6, protein 12

Chicken Stroganoff

Preparation time: 10 minutes

Cooking time: 4 hours

Servings: 4

INGREDIENTS:
2 garlic cloves, minced
8 ounces mushrooms, roughly chopped
¼ teaspoon celery seeds, ground
1 cup chicken stock
1 cup coconut milk
1 yellow onion, chopped
1 pound chicken breasts, cut into medium pieces
1 and ½ teaspoons thyme, dried
2 tablespoons parsley, chopped
Salt and black pepper to the tasted
Already cooked pasta for serving

DIRECTIONS:
Put chicken in your Slow cooker, add salt, pepper, onion, garlic, mushrooms, coconut milk, celery seeds, stock, half of the parsley and thyme, stir, cover and cook on High for 4 hours. Add the rest of the parsley and pasta, toss, divide between plates and serve.

NUTRITION:
calories 364, fat 22, fiber 2, carbs 14, protein 24

Coconut Turkey

Preparation time: 10 minutes

Cooking time: 5 hours

Servings: 2

INGREDIENTS:
1 yellow onion, chopped
1 tablespoon olive oil
1 cup coconut cream
½ teaspoon curry powder
1 pound turkey breast, skinless, boneless and cubed
1 teaspoon turmeric powder
½ cup chicken stock
1 tablespoon parsley, chopped
A pinch of salt and black pepper

DIRECTIONS:
In your slow cooker, mix the turkey with the onion, oil and the other ingredients except the cream and the parsley, stir, put the lid on and cook on High for 4 hours and 30 minutes. Add the remaining ingredients, toss, put the lid on again, cook on High for 30 minutes more, divide the mix between plates and serve.

NUTRITION:
calories 283, fat 11, fiber 2, carbs 8, protein 15

Pepperoni Chicken

Preparation time: 10 minutes

Cooking time: 6 hours

Servings: 6

INGREDIENTS:
14 ounces pizza sauce
1 tablespoon olive oil
4 medium chicken breasts, skinless and boneless
Salt and black pepper to the taste
1 teaspoon oregano, dried
6 ounces mozzarella, sliced
1 teaspoon garlic powder
2 ounces pepperoni, sliced

DIRECTIONS:
Put the chicken in your Slow cooker, add pizza sauce, oil, salt, pepper, garlic powder, pepperoni and mozzarella, cover and cook on Low for 6 hours. Toss everything, divide between plates and serve.

NUTRITION:
calories 320, fat 10, fiber 6, carbs 14, protein 27

Hot Chicken and Zucchinis
Preparation time: 10 minutes
Cooking time: 6 hours
Servings: 2

INGREDIENTS:
- 1 pound chicken breasts, skinless, boneless and cubed
- 1 zucchini, cubed
- 2 garlic cloves, minced
- 1 red chili, minced
- ½ teaspoon hot paprika
- 1 red onion, chopped
- 2 tablespoons olive oil
- A pinch of salt and black pepper
- 1 cup chicken stock
- 1 tablespoon chives, chopped

DIRECTIONS:
In your slow cooker, mix the chicken with the zucchini, garlic, chili pepper and the other ingredients, toss, put the lid on and cook on Low for 6 hours. Divide everything between plates and serve.

NUTRITION:
calories 221, fat 12, fiber 2, carbs 5, protein 17

Creamy Spinach and Artichoke Chicken
Preparation time: 10 minutes
Cooking time: 4 hours
Servings: 4

INGREDIENTS:
- 4 ounces cream cheese
- 4 chicken breasts, boneless and skinless
- 10 ounces canned artichoke hearts, chopped
- 10 ounces spinach
- ½ cup parmesan, grated
- 1 tablespoon dried onion
- 1 tablespoon garlic, dried
- Salt and black pepper to the taste
- 4 ounces mozzarella, shredded

DIRECTIONS:
Place chicken breasts in your Slow cooker season with salt and pepper, add artichokes, cream cheese, spinach, onion, garlic, spinach and top with mozzarella. Cover slow cooker, cook on High for 4 hours, toss, divide everything between plates and serve.

NUTRITION:
calories 450, fat 23, fiber 1, carbs 14, protein 39

Turkey with Radishes
Preparation time: 10 minutes
Cooking time: 7 hours
Servings: 2

INGREDIENTS:
- 1 tablespoon olive oil
- 2 scallions, minced
- 1 pound turkey breast, skinless, boneless and cubed
- 2 garlic cloves, minced
- 1 cup radishes, sliced
- ½ cup tomato passata
- ½ cup chicken stock
- 1 teaspoon sweet paprika
- A pinch of salt and black pepper
- ½ teaspoon coriander, ground
- 1 tablespoon parsley, chopped

DIRECTIONS:
In your slow cooker, mix the turkey with the oil, scallions and the other ingredients, toss, put the lid on and cook on Low for 7 hours. Divide the mix between plates and serve.

NUTRITION:
calories 227, fat 12, fiber 3, carbs 7, protein 18

Chicken Meatloaf
Preparation time: 10 minutes
Cooking time: 4 hours and 20 minutes
Servings: 8

INGREDIENTS:
- 1 cup marinara sauce
- 2 pound chicken meat, ground
- 2 tablespoons parsley, chopped
- 4 garlic cloves, minced
- 2 teaspoons onion powder
- 2 teaspoons Italian seasoning
- Salt and black pepper to the taste
- Cooking spray
- For the filling:
- ½ cup ricotta cheese
- 1 cup parmesan, grated
- 1 cup mozzarella, shredded
- 2 teaspoons chives, chopped
- 2 tablespoons parsley, chopped
- 1 garlic clove, minced

DIRECTIONS:
In a bowl, mix chicken with half of the marinara sauce, salt, pepper, Italian seasoning, 4 garlic cloves, onion powder and 2 tablespoons parsley

and stir well. In another bowl, mix ricotta with half of the parmesan, half of the mozzarella, chives, 1 garlic clove, salt, pepper and 2 tablespoons parsley and stir well. Grease your Slow cooker with cooking spray, add half of the chicken mix into the slow cooker and spread evenly. Add cheese filling, spread, top with the rest of the meat, spread again, cover and cook on High for 4 hours. Spread the rest of the marinara sauce, the rest of the parmesan and the mozzarella over the meatloaf, cover slow cooker and cook on High for 20 minutes more. Leave meatloaf to cool down, slice, divide between plates and serve.

NUTRITION:
calories 273, fat 14, fiber 1, carbs 14, protein 28

Chives Duck

Preparation time: 10 minutes
Cooking time: 20 minutes
Servings: 4

INGREDIENTS:
1 pound duck breasts, boneless, skinless and sliced
1 tablespoon olive oil
1 red bell pepper, cut into strips
1 yellow onion, chopped
1 cup chicken stock
½ cup heavy cream
A pinch of salt and black pepper
1 tablespoon chives, chopped

DIRECTIONS:
Set the instant pot on Sauté mode, add the oil, heat it up, add the onion and the bell pepper and sauté for 5 minutes. Add the duck and the rest of the ingredients except the chives, put the lid on and cook on High for 15 minutes. Release the pressure naturally for 10 minutes, divide everything between plates, sprinkle the chives on top and serve.

NUTRITION:
calories 293, fat 15, fiber 4, carbs 6, protein 14

Chicken and Green Onion Sauce

Preparation time: 10 minutes
Cooking time: 4 hours
Servings: 4

INGREDIENTS:
2 tablespoons butter, melted
4 green onions, chopped
4 chicken breast halves, skinless and boneless
Salt and black pepper to the taste
8 ounces sour cream

DIRECTIONS:
In your Slow cooker, mix chicken with melted butter, green onion, salt, pepper and sour cream, cover and cook on High for 4 hours. Divide chicken between plates, drizzle green onions sauce all over and serve.

NUTRITION:
calories 200, fat 7, fiber 2, carbs 11, protein 20

Cilantro Chicken and Eggplant Mix

Preparation time: 10 minutes
Cooking time: 7 hours
Servings: 2

INGREDIENTS:
1 pound chicken breasts, skinless, boneless and sliced
2 eggplants, roughly cubed
½ cup chicken stock
½ cup tomato sauce
3 scallions, chopped
A pinch of salt and black pepper
1 teaspoon chili powder
1 tablespoon cilantro, chopped

DIRECTIONS:
In your slow cooker, mix the chicken with the eggplant, stock and the other ingredients, toss, put the lid on, cook on Low for 7 hours, divide the mix between plates and serve.

NUTRITION:
calories 223, fat 9, fiber 2, carbs 4, protein 11

Mushrooms Stuffed with Chicken

Preparation time: 10 minutes
Cooking time: 3 hours
Servings: 6

INGREDIENTS:
16 ounces button mushroom caps
4 ounces cream cheese
¼ cup carrot, chopped
1 teaspoon ranch seasoning mix
4 tablespoons hot sauce
¾ cup blue cheese, crumbled
¼ cup red onion, chopped
½ cup chicken meat, ground
Salt and black pepper to the taste
Cooking spray

DIRECTIONS:
In a bowl, mix cream cheese with blue cheese, hot sauce, ranch seasoning, salt, pepper, chicken, carrot and red onion, stir and stuff mushrooms with this mix. Grease your Slow cooker with cooking spray, add stuffed mushrooms, cover and cook on High for 3 hours. Divide mushrooms between plates and serve.

NUTRITION:
calories 240, fat 4, fiber 1, carbs 12, protein 7

Chicken with Brussels Sprouts

Preparation time: 10 minutes

Cooking time: 7 hours

Servings: 2

INGREDIENTS:

1 pound chicken breasts, skinless, boneless and roughly cubed
1 tablespoon olive oil
1 cup Brussels sprouts, halved
½ teaspoon garam masala
1 cup chicken stock
1 tablespoon olive oil
1 red onion, sliced
1 tablespoon cilantro, chopped

DIRECTIONS:

In your slow cooker, mix the chicken with the sprouts, oil and the other ingredients, toss, put the lid on and cook on Low for 7 hours. Divide the mix between plates and serve right away.

NUTRITION:

calories 210, fat 11, fiber 2, carbs 7, protein 14

Thai Peanut Chicken

Preparation time: 10 minutes

Cooking time: 4 hours

Servings: 8

INGREDIENTS:

2 and ½ pounds chicken thighs and drumsticks
1 tablespoon soy sauce
1 tablespoon apple cider vinegar
A pinch of red pepper flakes
Salt and black pepper to the taste
½ teaspoon ginger, ground
1/3 cup peanut butter
1 garlic clove, minced
½ cup warm water

DIRECTIONS:

In your blender mix peanut butter with water, soy sauce, salt, pepper, pepper flakes, ginger, garlic and vinegar and blend well. Pat dry chicken pieces, arrange them in your Slow cooker, cover and cook on High for 4 hours. Divide between plates and serve.

NUTRITION:

calories 375, fat 12, fiber 1, carbs 10, protein 42

Chicken and Mango Mix

Preparation time: 10 minutes

Cooking time: 5 hours

Servings: 2

INGREDIENTS:

1 pound chicken breast, skinless, boneless and sliced
1 cup mango, peeled and cubed
4 scallions, chopped
1 tablespoon avocado oil
½ teaspoon chili powder
½ teaspoon rosemary, dried
1 cup chicken stock
1 tablespoon sweet paprika
A pinch of salt and black pepper
1 tablespoon chives, chopped

DIRECTIONS:

In your slow cooker, mix the chicken with the mango, scallions, chili powder and the other ingredients, toss, put the lid on and cook on Low for 5 hours. Divide the mix between plates and serve.

NUTRITION:

calories 263, fat 8, fiber 2, carbs 7, protein 12

Flavored Chicken Drumsticks

Preparation time: 10 minutes

Cooking time: 4 hours

Servings: 4

INGREDIENTS:

1 bunch lemongrass, bottom removed and trimmed
1-inch piece ginger root, chopped
4 garlic cloves, minced
2 tablespoons fish sauce
3 tablespoons soy sauce
1 teaspoon Chinese five spice
10 chicken drumsticks
1 cup coconut milk
Salt and black pepper to the taste
1 teaspoon butter, melted
¼ cup cilantro, chopped
1 yellow onion, chopped
1 tablespoon lime juice

DIRECTIONS:

In your food processor, mix lemongrass with ginger, garlic, soy sauce, fish sauce, five spice and coconut milk and pulse well. In your Slow cooker, mix chicken with butter, onion, salt, pepper, lime juice and lemongrass mix, cover and cook on High for 4 hours. Toss chicken, divide everything between plates and serve with cilantro sprinkled on top.

NUTRITION:

calories 400, fat 12, fiber 3, carbs 6, protein 20

Turkey and Avocado

Preparation time: 10 minutes

Cooking time: 6 hours

Servings: 2

INGREDIENTS:
1 pound turkey breasts, skinless, boneless and cubed
1 cup avocado, peeled, pitted and cubed
1 cup tomatoes, cubed
1 tablespoon chives, chopped
½ teaspoon chili powder
4 garlic cloves, minced
¼ cup chicken stock

DIRECTIONS:
In slow cooker, mix the turkey with the tomatoes, chives and the other ingredients except the avocado, toss, put the lid on and cook on Low for 5 hours and 30 minutes. Add the avocado, toss, cook on Low for 30 minutes more, divide everything between plates and serve.

NUTRITION:
calories 220, fat 8, fiber 2, carbs 7, protein 15

Chicken Thighs and Romano Cheese Mix
Preparation time: 10 minutes
Cooking time: 4 hours
Servings: 4

INGREDIENTS:
6 chicken things, boneless and skinless and cut into medium chunks
Salt and black pepper to the taste
½ cup white flour
2 tablespoons olive oil
10 ounces tomato sauce
1 teaspoon white wine vinegar
4 ounces mushrooms, sliced
1 tablespoon sugar
1 tablespoon oregano, dried
1 teaspoon garlic, minced
1 teaspoon basil, dried
1 yellow onion, chopped
1 cup Romano cheese, grated

DIRECTIONS:
Grease your Slow cooker with the oil, add chicken pieces, onion, garlic, salt, pepper and flour and toss. Add tomato sauce, vinegar, mushrooms, sugar, oregano, basil and cheese, cover and cook on High for 4 hours. Divide between plates and serve.

NUTRITION:
calories 430, fat 12, fiber 6, carbs 25, protein 60

Chicken and Peppers
Preparation time: 10 minutes
Cooking time: 6 hours
Servings: 2

INGREDIENTS:
1 pound chicken breasts, skinless, boneless and cubed
¼ cup tomato sauce
2 red bell peppers, cut into strips
1 teaspoon olive oil
½ teaspoon rosemary, dried
½ teaspoon coriander, ground
1 teaspoon Italian seasoning
A pinch of cayenne pepper
1 cup chicken stock

DIRECTIONS:
In your slow cooker, mix the chicken with the peppers, tomato sauce and the other ingredients, toss, put the lid on and cook on Low for 6 hours. divide everything between plates and serve.

NUTRITION:
calories 282, fat 12, fiber 2, carbs 6, protein 18

Slow Cooker Chicken Thighs
Preparation time: 10 minutes
Cooking time: 4 hours
Servings: 6

INGREDIENTS:
5 pounds chicken thighs
Salt and black pepper to the taste
½ cup white vinegar
1 teaspoon black peppercorns
4 garlic cloves, minced
3 bay leaves
½ cup soy sauce

DIRECTIONS:
In your Slow cooker mix chicken, vinegar, soy sauce, salt, pepper, garlic, peppercorns and bay leaves, stir, cover and cook on High for 4 hours. Discard bay leaves, stir, divide chicken mix between plates and serve.

NUTRITION:
calories 430, fat 12, fiber 3, carbs 10, protein 36

Chicken and Cabbage Mix
Preparation time: 5 minutes
Cooking time: 7 hours
Servings: 2

INGREDIENTS:
1 pound chicken breasts, skinless, boneless and halved
2 cups red cabbage, shredded
1 cup chicken stock
½ teaspoon rosemary, dried
½ teaspoon sweet paprika
2 teaspoons cumin, ground
A pinch of salt and black pepper
¼ cup cilantro, chopped

DIRECTIONS:
In slow cooker, mix the chicken with the cabbage, stock and the other ingredients, toss, put the lid on and cook on Low for 7 hours. Divide everything between plates and serve.

NUTRITION:
calories 285, fat 16, fiber 4, carbs 8, protein 18

Chicken and Tomatillos

Preparation time: 10 minutes

Cooking time: 4 hours

Servings: 6

INGREDIENTS:
- 1 pound chicken thighs, skinless and boneless
- 2 tablespoons olive oil
- 1 yellow onion, chopped
- 1 garlic clove, minced
- 4 ounces canned green chilies, chopped
- A handful cilantro, chopped
- Salt and black pepper to the taste
- 15 ounces canned tomatillos, chopped
- 5 ounces canned garbanzo beans, drained
- 15 ounces rice, cooked
- 5 ounces tomatoes, chopped
- 15 ounces cheddar cheese, grated
- 4 ounces black olives, pitted and chopped

DIRECTIONS:
In your Slow cooker, mix oil with onions, garlic, chicken, chilies, salt, pepper, cilantro and tomatillos, stir, cover the slow cooker and cook on High for 3 hours Take chicken out of the slow cooker, shred, return to slow cooker, add rice, beans, cheese, tomatoes and olives, cover and cook on High for 1 more hour. Divide between plates and serve.

NUTRITION:
calories 300, fat 11, fiber 3, carbs 14, protein 30

Lime Turkey and Chard

Preparation time: 10 minutes

Cooking time: 6 hours

Servings: 2

INGREDIENTS:
- 1 pound turkey breasts, skinless, boneless and cubed
- 2 teaspoons olive oil
- 1 cup red chard, torn
- ½ teaspoon sweet paprika
- 1 cup chicken stock
- A pinch of salt and black pepper
- 2 tablespoons lime juice
- 1 tablespoon lime zest, grated
- 1 tablespoon tomato paste

DIRECTIONS:
In your slow cooker, mix the turkey with the oil, paprika and the other ingredients, toss, put the lid on and cook on Low for 6 hours. Divide everything into bowls and serve.

NUTRITION:
calories 292, fat 17, fiber 2, carbs 7, protein 16

Duck and Potatoes

Preparation time: 10 minutes

Cooking time: 6 hours

Servings: 4

INGREDIENTS:
- 1 duck, cut into small chunks
- Salt and black pepper to the taste
- 1 potato, cut into cubes
- 1-inch ginger root, sliced
- 4 garlic cloves, minced
- 4 tablespoons sugar
- 4 tablespoons soy sauce
- 2 green onions, chopped
- 4 tablespoons sherry wine
- ¼ cup water

DIRECTIONS:
In your Slow cooker mix duck pieces with garlic, ginger, green onions, soy sauce, sugar, wine, a pinch of salt, black pepper, potatoes and water, stir, cover and cook on Low for 6 hours. Divide between plates and serve right away,

NUTRITION:
calories 245, fat 12, fiber 1, carbs 6, protein 16

BBQ Turkey mix

Preparation time: 10 minutes

Cooking time: 6 hours

Servings: 2

INGREDIENTS:
- 1 pound turkey breast, skinless, boneless and sliced
- 1 teaspoon sweet paprika
- ½ teaspoon red pepper flakes, crushed
- ½ teaspoon turmeric powder
- 1 cup bbq sauce
- A pinch of salt and black pepper
- ¼ cup cilantro, chopped
- 1 cup chicken stock

DIRECTIONS:
In slow cooker, mix the turkey with the paprika, pepper flakes and the other ingredients, toss, put the lid on and cook on Low for 6 hours. Divide everything between plates and serve.

NUTRITION:
calories 224, fat 11, fiber 2, carbs 9, protein 11

Chicken Salad
Preparation time: 55 minutes
Cooking time: 3 hours
Servings: 2

INGREDIENTS:
1 chicken breast, skinless and boneless
1 cup chicken stock
2 cups water
Salt and black pepper to the taste
1 tablespoon mustard
3 garlic cloves, minced
1 tablespoon balsamic vinegar
1 tablespoon honey
3 tablespoons olive oil
Mixed salad greens
A handful cherry tomatoes, halved

DIRECTIONS:
In a bowl, mix water with salt to the taste, add chicken, stir, cover and keep in the fridge for 45 minutes. Drain chicken, add to your Slow cooker, add stock, salt and pepper, cover and cook on High for 3 hours. Transfer chicken breast to a cutting board and cut into thin strips. In a bowl, mix garlic with salt and pepper to the taste, mustard, honey, vinegar and olive oil and whisk very well. In a salad bowl, mix chicken strips with salad greens and tomatoes. Drizzle the vinaigrette on top and serve.

NUTRITION:
calories 200, fat 4, fiber 6, carbs 15, protein 12

Chicken and Asparagus
Preparation time: 10 minutes
Cooking time: 5 hours
Servings: 2

INGREDIENTS:
1 pound chicken breast, skinless, boneless and cubed
1 cup asparagus, sliced
1 tablespoon olive oil
2 scallions, chopped
A pinch of salt and black pepper
1 teaspoon garam masala
1 cup chicken stock
1 cup tomatoes, cubed
1 tablespoon parsley, chopped

DIRECTIONS:
In your slow cooker, mix the chicken with the asparagus, oil and the other ingredients except the asparagus, toss, put the lid on and cook on High for 4 hours. Add the asparagus, toss, cook on High for 1 more hour, divide everything between plates and serve.

NUTRITION:
calories 229, fat 9, fiber 4, carbs 7, protein 16

Sweet and Hot Chicken Wings
Preparation time: 10 minutes
Cooking time: 4 hours
Servings: 6

INGREDIENTS:
12 chicken wings, cut into 24 pieces
1 pound celery, cut into thin matchsticks
¼ cup honey
4 tablespoons hot sauce
Salt to the taste
¼ cup tomato puree
1 cup yogurt
1 tablespoon parsley, chopped

DIRECTIONS:
In your Slow cooker, mix chicken with celery, honey, hot sauce, salt, tomato puree and parsley, stir, cover and cook on High for 3 hours and 30 minutes. Add yogurt, toss, cover, cook on High for 30 minutes more, divide between plates and serve

NUTRITION:
calories 300, fat 4, fiber 4, carbs 14, protein 22

Lemon Turkey and Potatoes
Preparation time: 10 minutes
Cooking time: 7 hours
Servings: 2

INGREDIENTS:
1 pound turkey breast, skinless, boneless and cubed
2 teaspoons olive oil
1 tablespoon lemon juice
2 gold potatoes, peeled and cubed
1 red onion, chopped
½ cup tomato sauce
¼ cup chicken stock
1 tablespoon chives, chopped
A pinch of salt and black pepper

DIRECTIONS:
In your slow cooker, mix the turkey with the oil, lemon juice, potatoes and the other ingredients, toss, put the lid on and cook on Low for 7 hours. Divide everything between plates and serve.

NUTRITION:
calories 263, fat 12, fiber 3, carbs 6, protein 14

Duck Chili
Preparation time: 10 minutes
Cooking time: 7
Servings: 4

INGREDIENTS:
1 pound northern beans, soaked and rinsed
1 yellow onion, cut into half
1 garlic heat, top trimmed off
Salt and black pepper to the taste
2 cloves
1 bay leaf
6 cups water
For the duck:
1 pound duck, ground
1 tablespoon vegetable oil
1 yellow onion, minced
2 carrots, chopped
Salt and black pepper to the taste
4 ounces canned green chilies and their juice
1 teaspoon brown sugar
15 ounces canned tomatoes and their juices, chopped
A handful cilantro, chopped

DIRECTIONS:
Put the beans in your Slow cooker, add the whole onion, garlic head, cloves, bay leaf, the water and salt to the taste, stir, cover, cook on High for 4 hours, drain them and put them in a bowl. Clean the slow cooker, add oil, carrots, chopped onion, season with salt and pepper, duck, chilies, tomatoes and sugar, stir, cover and cook on High for 3 hours more. Divide on duck and beans mix plates and serve with cilantro sprinkled on top.

NUTRITION:
calories 283, fat 15, fiber 2, carbs 16, protein 22

Turkey and Okra

Preparation time: 10 minutes
Cooking time: 5 hours
Servings: 2

INGREDIENTS:
1 pound turkey breasts, skinless, boneless and cubed
1 cup okra, halved
1 tablespoon lime zest, grated
½ cup chicken stock
1 tablespoon lime juice
1 teaspoon olive oil
½ teaspoon sweet paprika
½ teaspoon coriander, ground
½ teaspoon oregano, dried
1 teaspoon chili powder
A pinch of salt and black pepper
1 tablespoon cilantro, chopped

DIRECTIONS:
In your slow cooker, mix the turkey with the okra, lime zest, juice and the other ingredients, toss, put the lid on and cook on High for 5 hours. Divide everything between plates and serve.

NUTRITION:
calories 162, fat 8, fiber 2, carbs 5, protein 9

Coca Cola Chicken

Preparation time: 10 minutes
Cooking time: 4 hours
Servings: 4

INGREDIENTS:
1 yellow onion, minced
4 chicken drumsticks
1 tablespoon balsamic vinegar
1 chili pepper, chopped
15 ounces coca cola
Salt and black pepper to the taste
2 tablespoons olive oil

DIRECTIONS:
Heat up a pan with the oil over medium-high heat, add chicken pieces, stir and brown them on all sides and then transfer them to your Slow cooker. Add vinegar, chili, coca cola, salt and pepper, cover and cook on High for 4 hours. Divide chicken mix between plates and serve.

NUTRITION:
calories 372, fat 14, fiber 3, carbs 20, protein 15

Mustard Duck Mix

Preparation time: 10 minutes
Cooking time: 5 hours
Servings: 2

INGREDIENTS:
2 teaspoons olive oil
1 red onion, sliced
1 pound duck leg, skinless, boneless and cut into strips
1 tablespoon mustard
1 tablespoon lemon juice
¾ cup chicken stock
1 teaspoon sweet paprika
A pinch of salt and black pepper
1 tablespoon coriander, chopped

DIRECTIONS:
In your slow cooker, mix the duck with the oil, onion, mustard and the other ingredients, toss, put the lid on and cook on High for 5 hours. Divide the mix between plates and serve with a side salad.

NUTRITION:
calories 200, fat 9, fiber 2, carbs 5, protein 10

Cuban Chicken

Preparation time: 10 minutes
Cooking time: 4 hours
Servings: 4

INGREDIENTS:
4 gold potatoes, cut into medium chunks
1 yellow onion, thinly sliced

4 big tomatoes, cut into medium chunks
1 chicken, cut into 8 pieces
Salt and black pepper to the taste
2 bay leaves
Salt and black pepper to the taste

DIRECTIONS:
In your instant slow cooker, mix potatoes with onion, chicken, tomato, bay leaves, salt and pepper, stir well, cover and cook on High for 4 hours. Add more salt and pepper, discard bay leaves, divide chicken mix between plates and serve.

NUTRITION:
calories 263, fat 2, fiber 1, carbs 27, protein 14

Orange Chicken Mix
Preparation time: 10 minutes
Cooking time: 6 hours
Servings: 2

INGREDIENTS:
1 pound chicken breast, skinless, boneless and cubed
1 cup oranges, peeled and cut into segments
2 teaspoons olive oil
1 teaspoon turmeric powder
1 teaspoon balsamic vinegar
4 scallions, minced
1 cup orange juice
1 tablespoon mint, chopped
A pinch of salt and black pepper

DIRECTIONS:
In your slow cooker, mix the chicken with the oranges, scallions and the other ingredients, toss, put the lid on and cook on Low for 6 hours. Divide the mix between plates and serve.

NUTRITION:
calories 200, fat 7, fiber 2, carbs 6, protein 11

Chicken and Lentils
Preparation time: 10 minutes
Cooking time: 4 hours
Servings: 4

INGREDIENTS:
8 ounces bacon, cooked and chopped
2 tablespoons olive oil
1 cup yellow onion, chopped
8 ounces lentils, dried
2 carrots, chopped
12 parsley springs, chopped
Salt and black pepper to the taste
2 bay leaves
2 and ½ pounds chicken pieces
1 quart chicken stock
2 teaspoons sherry vinegar

DIRECTIONS:
Grease your Slow cooker with the oil, add bacon, onions, lentils, carrots, chicken pieces, parsley, bay leaves, stock, salt and pepper to the taste, stir, cover and cook at High for 4 hours Transfer chicken to a cutting board, discard skin and bones, shred meat and return to the slow cooker, add vinegar, stir, divide between plates and serve.

NUTRITION:
calories 321, fat 3, fiber 12, carbs 29, protein 16

Turkey and Carrots
Preparation time: 10 minutes
Cooking time: 7 hours
Servings: 2

INGREDIENTS:
1 pound turkey breasts, skinless, boneless and cubed
1 cup carrots, peeled and sliced
2 tablespoons avocado oil
1 tablespoon balsamic vinegar
2 scallions, chopped
1 teaspoon turmeric powder
1 cup chicken stock
½ cup chives, chopped

DIRECTIONS:
In your slow cooker, mix the turkey with the carrots, oil, vinegar and the other ingredients, toss, put the lid on and cook on Low for 7 hours. Divide the mix between plates and serve right away.

NUTRITION:
calories 210, fat 8, fiber 2, carbs 6, protein 11

Chicken and Chickpeas
Preparation time: 10 minutes
Cooking time: 4 hours
Servings: 4

INGREDIENTS:
1 yellow onion, chopped
2 tablespoons butter
4 garlic cloves, minced
1 tablespoon ginger, grated
1 and ½ teaspoon paprika
1 tablespoon cumin, ground
1 and ½ teaspoons coriander, ground
1 teaspoon turmeric, ground
Salt and black pepper to the taste
A pinch of cayenne pepper
15 ounces canned tomatoes, crushed
¼ cup lemon juice
1 pound spinach, chopped
3 pounds chicken drumsticks and thighs
½ cup cilantro, chopped
½ cup chicken stock
15 ounces canned chickpeas, drained
½ cup heavy cream

DIRECTIONS:
Grease your Slow cooker with the butter, add onion, garlic, ginger, paprika, cumin, coriander, turmeric, salt, pepper, cayenne, tomatoes, lemon juice, spinach, chicken, stock, chickpeas and heavy cream, cover and cook on High for 4 hours. Add cilantro, stir everything, divide between plates and serve.

NUTRITION:
calories 300, fat 4, fiber 6, carbs 30, protein 17

Rosemary Chicken Thighs
Preparation time: 10 minutes
Cooking time: 7 hours
Servings: 2

INGREDIENTS:
1 pound chicken thighs, boneless
1 teaspoon rosemary, dried
½ teaspoon sweet paprika
½ teaspoon garam masala
1 tablespoon olive oil
½ cup chicken stock
A pinch of salt and black pepper
1 tablespoon cilantro, chopped

DIRECTIONS:
In your slow cooker, mix the chicken with the rosemary, paprika and the other ingredients, toss, put the lid on and cook on Low for 7 hours. Divide the chicken between plates and serve with a side salad.

NUTRITION:
calories 220, fat 8, fiber 2, carbs 5, protein 11

Chicken and Sauce
Preparation time: 10 minutes
Cooking time: 5 hours
Servings: 4

INGREDIENTS:
1 chicken, cut into medium pieces
Salt and black pepper to the taste
1 tablespoon olive oil
½ teaspoon sweet paprika
¼ cup white wine
½ teaspoon marjoram, dried
¼ cup chicken stock
2 tablespoons white vinegar
¼ cup apricot preserves
1 and ½ teaspoon ginger, grated
2 tablespoons honey

DIRECTIONS:
In your Slow cooker, mix chicken with salt, pepper, oil, paprika, wine, marjoram, stock, vinegar, apricots preserves, ginger and honey, stir, cover and cook on Low for 5 hours. Divide between plates and serve.

NUTRITION:
calories 230, fat 3, fiber 5, carbs 12, protein 22

Turkey and Kidney Beans
Preparation time: 10 minutes
Cooking time: 6 hours
Servings: 2

INGREDIENTS:
1 pound turkey breasts, skinless, boneless and cut into strips
2 cups canned red kidney beans, drained and rinsed
¼ cup chicken stock
1 cup tomato passata
1 tablespoon avocado oil
Salt and black pepper to the taste
½ teaspoon chili powder
1 tablespoon tarragon, chopped

DIRECTIONS:
In your slow cooker, mix the turkey with the beans, stock and the other ingredients, toss, put the lid on and cook on Low for 6 hours. Divide the mix between plates and serve.

NUTRITION:
calories 192, fat 12, fiber 3, carbs 5, protein 12

Goose Mix
Preparation time: 10 minutes
Cooking time: 5 hours
Servings: 5

INGREDIENTS:
1 goose breast, fat trimmed off and cut into pieces
1 goose leg, skinless
1 goose thigh, skinless
Salt and black pepper to the taste
3 and ½ cups water
2 teaspoons garlic, minced
1 yellow onion, chopped
12 ounces canned mushroom cream

DIRECTIONS:
In your Slow cooker mix goose breast, leg and thigh with onion, salt, pepper, water, garlic, and mushroom cream, stir, cover and cook on Low for 5 hours. Divide into bowls and serve

NUTRITION:
calories 272, fat 4, fiber 7, carbs 16, protein 22

Coriander and Turmeric Chicken
Preparation time: 10 minutes
Cooking time: 6 hours
Servings: 2

INGREDIENTS:
1 pound chicken breasts, skinless, boneless and cubed
1 tablespoon coriander, chopped
½ teaspoon turmeric powder
2 scallions, minced
1 tablespoon olive oil
1 tablespoon lime zest, grated
1 cup lime juice
1 tablespoon chives, chopped
¼ cup tomato sauce

DIRECTIONS:
In your slow cooker, mix the chicken with the coriander, turmeric, scallions and the other ingredients, toss, put the lid on and cook on Low for 6 hours. Divide the mix between plates and serve right away.

NUTRITION:
calories 200, fat 7, fiber 1, carbs 5, protein 12

Goose and Sauce
Preparation time: 10 minutes
Cooking time: 5 hours
Servings: 4

INGREDIENTS:
1 goose breast half, skinless, boneless and cut into thin slices
¼ cup olive oil
1 sweet onion, chopped
2 teaspoons garlic, chopped
Salt and black pepper to the taste
¼ cup sweet chili sauce

DIRECTIONS:
In your Slow cooker, mix goose with oil, onion, garlic, salt, pepper and chili sauce, stir, cover and cook on Low for 5 hours. Divide between plates and serve.

NUTRITION:
calories 192, fat 4, fiber 8, carbs 12, protein 22

Garlic Turkey
Preparation time: 10 minutes
Cooking time: 6 hours
Servings: 2

INGREDIENTS:
1 pound turkey breast, skinless, boneless and cubed
1 tablespoon avocado oil
½ cup chicken stock
2 tablespoons tomato paste
2 tablespoons garlic, minced
½ teaspoon chili powder
½ teaspoon oregano, dried
A pinch of salt and black pepper
1 tablespoon parsley, chopped

DIRECTIONS:
In your slow cooker, mix the turkey with the oil, stock, tomato paste and the other ingredients, toss, put the lid on and cook on Low for 6 hours. Divide the mix between plates and serve with a side salad.

NUTRITION:
calories 231, fat 7, fiber 2, carbs 6, protein 12

Chicken Liver Stew
Preparation time: 5 minutes
Cooking time: 2 hours
Servings: 8

INGREDIENTS:
1 teaspoon olive oil
¾ pound chicken livers
1 yellow onion, chopped
¼ cup tomato sauce
1 bay leaf
1 tablespoons capers
1 tablespoon butter
A pinch of salt and black pepper

DIRECTIONS:
In your Slow cooker, mix oil with chicken livers, onion, tomato sauce, bay leaf, capers, butter, salt and pepper, stir, cover and cook on High for 1 hour and 30 minutes. Divide between plates and serve

NUTRITION:
calories 152, fat 4, fiber 2, carbs 5, protein 7

Cumin Chicken Mix
Preparation time: 10 minutes
Cooking time: 6 hours
Servings: 2

INGREDIENTS:
1 pound chicken breast, skinless, boneless and cubed
2 teaspoons olive oil
½ cup tomato sauce
¼ cup chicken stock
½ teaspoon garam masala
½ teaspoon chili powder
½ teaspoon cumin, ground
1 yellow onion, chopped
½ teaspoon sweet paprika
A pinch of salt and black pepper
1 tablespoon chives, chopped

DIRECTIONS:
In your slow cooker, mix the chicken with the oil, tomato sauce, stock and the other ingredients, toss, put the lid on and cook on Low for 6 hours. Divide everything between plates and serve right away.

NUTRITION:
calories 252, fat 12, fiber 4, carbs 7, protein 13

Slow cooker Meat Recipes

Beef Roast

Preparation time: 10 minutes
Cooking time: 8 hours
Servings: 8

INGREDIENTS:

2 and ½ pounds beef chuck roast
2 cups carrots, chopped
1 tablespoon olive oil
2 cup yellow onion, chopped
1 cup celery, chopped
¾ cup dill pickle, chopped
½ cup dry red wine
1/3 cup German mustard
A pinch of salt and black pepper
¼ teaspoon cloves, ground
2 tablespoons flour
2 bay leaves
2 tablespoons beef stock

DIRECTIONS:

In your Slow cooker, mix beef with carrots, oil, onion, celery, pickle, wine, mustard, salt, pepper, cloves, flour, bay leaves and stock, toss well, cover and cook on Low for 8 hours. Slice roast, divide between plates, drizzle cooking juices all over and serve.

NUTRITION:

calories 256, fat 7, fiber 2, carbs 10, protein 31

Pork Chops and Mango Mix

Preparation time: 10 minutes
Cooking time: 6 hours
Servings: 2

INGREDIENTS:

1 pound pork chops
1 teaspoon sweet paprika
½ teaspoon chili powder
1 cup mango, peeled, and cubed
2 tablespoons ketchup
1 tablespoon balsamic vinegar
¼ cup beef stock
1 tablespoon cilantro, chopped

DIRECTIONS:

In your slow cooker, mix the pork chops with the paprika, chili powder, ketchup and the other ingredients, toss, put the lid on and cook on Low for 6 hours. Divide everything between plates and serve.

NUTRITION:

calories 345, fat 5, fiber 7, carbs 17, protein 14

Short Ribs

Preparation time: 10 minutes
Cooking time: 10 hours
Servings: 6

INGREDIENTS:

3 pounds beef short ribs
1 fennel bulb, cut into wedges
2 yellow onions, cut into wedges
1 cup carrot, sliced
14 ounces canned tomatoes, chopped
1 cup dry red wine
2 tablespoons tapioca, crushed
2 tablespoons tomato paste
1 teaspoon rosemary, dried
Salt and black pepper to the taste
4 garlic cloves, minced

DIRECTIONS:

In your Slow cooker, mix short ribs with fennel, onions, carrots, tomatoes, wine, tapioca, tomato paste, salt, pepper, rosemary and garlic, cover and cook on Low for 10 hours. Divide everything between plates and serve.

NUTRITION:

calories 432, fat 14, fiber 6, carbs 25, protein 42

Beef and Zucchinis Mix

Preparation time: 10 minutes
Cooking time: 8 hours
Servings: 2

INGREDIENTS:

1 pound beef stew meat, cut into strips
1 tablespoon olive oil
¼ cup beef stock
½ teaspoon sweet paprika
½ teaspoon chili powder
2 small zucchinis, cubed
1 tablespoon balsamic vinegar
1 tablespoon chives, chopped

DIRECTIONS:

In your slow cooker, mix the beef with the oil, stock and the other ingredients, toss, put the lid on and cook on Low for 8 hours. Divide the mix between plates and serve.

NUTRITION:

calories 400, fat 12, fiber 8, carbs 18, protein 20

Soy Pork Ribs

Preparation time: 12 hours
Cooking time: 6 hours
Servings: 4

INGREDIENTS:

4 cups vinegar
4 pounds pork ribs
2 tablespoons apple cider vinegar
2 cups water
3 tablespoons soy sauce
Salt and black pepper to the taste

A pinch of garlic powder
A pinch of Chinese 5 spice

DIRECTIONS:
Put your ribs in a big bowl, add white vinegar and water, toss, cover and keep in the fridge for 12 hours. Drain ribs, season with salt and black pepper to the taste, garlic powder and Chinese 5 spice, rub well, transfer them to your slow cooker and add apple cider vinegar and soy sauce as well. Toss to coat well, cover slow cooker and cook on High for 6 hours. Divide ribs between plates and serve.

NUTRITION:
calories 300, fat 6, fiber 3, carbs 15, protein 15

Pork and Olives Mix
Preparation time: 10 minutes
Cooking time: 8 hours
Servings: 2

INGREDIENTS:
1 pound pork roast, sliced
½ cup tomato passata
1 red onion, sliced
1 cup kalamata olives, pitted and halved
Juice of ½ lime
¼ cup beef stock
Salt and black pepper to the taste
1 tablespoon chives, hopped

DIRECTIONS:
In your slow cooker, mix the pork slices with the passata, onion, olives and the other ingredients, toss, put the lid on and cook on Low for 8 hours. Divide the mix between plates and serve.

NUTRITION:
calories 360, fat 4, fiber 3, carbs 17, protein 27

Beef Chuck Roast
Preparation time: 10 minutes
Cooking time: 8 hours and 30 minutes
Servings: 6

INGREDIENTS:
4 pounds beef chuck roast
1 cup veggie stock
1 tablespoon coconut oil
1 bay leaf
10 thyme springs
4 garlic cloves, minced
1 carrot, roughly
chopped
1 yellow onion, roughly chopped
2 celery ribs, roughly chopped
1 cauliflower head, florets separated
Salt and black pepper to the taste

DIRECTIONS:
Season beef with salt and some black pepper. Heat up a pan with the oil over medium-high heat, add beef roast, brown for 5 minutes on each side, transfer to your slow cooker, add thyme springs, stock, bay leaf, garlic, celery, onion and carrot, cover and cook on Low for 8 hours. Add cauliflower, cover slow cooker again, cook on High for 20 minutes more, divide everything between plates and serve.

NUTRITION:
calories 340, fat 5, fiber 3, carbs 14, protein 22

Pork and Soy Sauce Mix
Preparation time: 10 minutes
Cooking time: 8 hours
Servings: 2

INGREDIENTS:
1 pound pork loin roast, boneless and roughly cubed
1 tablespoon soy sauce
3 tablespoons honey
½ tablespoons oregano, dried
1 tablespoon garlic, minced
1 tablespoons olive oil
Salt and black pepper to the taste
½ cup beef stock
½ teaspoon sweet paprika

DIRECTIONS:
In your slow cooker, mix the pork loin with the honey, soy sauce and the other ingredients, toss, put the lid on and cook on Low for 8 hours. Divide everything between plates and serve.

NUTRITION:
calories 374, fat 6, fiber 8, carbs 29, protein 6

Mexican Pork Roast
Preparation time: 10 minutes
Cooking time: 8 hours
Servings: 6

INGREDIENTS:
1 yellow onion, chopped
2 tablespoons sweet paprika
15 ounces canned tomato, roasted and chopped
1 teaspoon cumin, ground
1 teaspoon coconut oil
Salt and black pepper to the taste
A pinch of nutmeg, ground
5 pounds pork roast
Juice of 1 lemon
¼ cup apple cider vinegar

DIRECTIONS:
Heat up a pan with the oil over medium-high heat,

add onions, brown them for a couple of minutes, transfer them to your slow cooker, add paprika, tomato, cumin, nutmeg, lemon juice, vinegar, salt, pepper and pork, toss coat and cook on Low for 8 hours. Slice roast, arrange on plates and serve with tomatoes and onions mix.

NUTRITION:
calories 350, fat 5, fiber 2, carbs 13, protein 24

Beef and Sauce

Preparation time: 10 minutes
Cooking time: 8 hours
Servings: 2

INGREDIENTS:
1 pound beef stew meat, cubed
1 teaspoon garam masala
½ teaspoon turmeric powder
Salt and black pepper to the taste
1 cup beef stock
1 teaspoon garlic, minced
½ cup sour cream
2 ounces cream cheese, soft
1 tablespoon chives, chopped

DIRECTIONS:
In your slow cooker, mix the beef with the turmeric, garam masala and the other ingredients, toss, put the lid on and cook on Low for 8 hours. Divide everything into bowls and serve.

NUTRITION:
calories 372, fat 6, fiber 9, carbs 18, protein 22

Pork Chops and Pineapple Mix

Preparation time: 10 minutes
Cooking time: 6 hours
Servings: 4

INGREDIENTS:
2 pounds pork chops
1/3 cup sugar
¼ cup ketchup
15 ounces pineapple, cubed
3 tablespoons apple cider vinegar
5 tablespoons soy sauce
2 teaspoons garlic, minced
3 tablespoons flour

DIRECTIONS:
In a bowl, mix ketchup with sugar, vinegar, soy sauce and tapioca, whisk well, add pork chops, toss well and transfer everything to your Slow cooker Add pineapple and garlic, toss again, cover, cook on Low for 6 hours, divide everything between plates and serve.

NUTRITION:
calories 345, fat 5, fiber 6, carbs 13, protein 14

Pork and Beans Mix

Preparation time: 10 minutes
Cooking time: 8 hours
Servings: 2

INGREDIENTS:
1 red bell pepper, chopped
1 pound pork stew meat, cubed
1 tablespoon olive oil
1 cup canned black beans, drained and rinsed
½ cup tomato sauce
1 yellow onion, chopped
1 teaspoon Italian seasoning
Salt and black pepper to the taste
1 tablespoon oregano, chopped

DIRECTIONS:
In your slow cooker, mix the pork with the bell pepper, oil and the other ingredients, toss, put the lid on and cook on Low for 8 hours. Divide the mix between plates and serve.

NUTRITION:
calories 385, fat 12, fiber 5, carbs 18, protein 40

Pork Tenderloin and Apples

Preparation time: 10 minutes
Cooking time: 8 hours
Servings: 4

INGREDIENTS:
A pinch of nutmeg, ground
2 pounds pork tenderloin
4 apples, cored and sliced
2 tablespoons maple syrup

DIRECTIONS:
Place apples in your Slow cooker, sprinkle nutmeg over them, add pork tenderloin, sprinkle some more nutmeg, drizzle the maple syrup, cover and cook on Low for 8 hours. Slice pork tenderloin, divide it between plates and serve with apple slices and cooking juices.

NUTRITION:
calories 400, fat 4, fiber 5, carbs 12, protein 20

Beef with Spinach

Preparation time: 10 minutes
Cooking time: 7 hours
Servings: 2

INGREDIENTS:
- 1 red onion, sliced
- 1 pound beef stew meat, cubed
- 1 cup tomato passata
- 1 cup baby spinach
- 1 teaspoon olive oil
- Salt and black pepper to the taste
- ½ cup bee stock
- 1 tablespoon basil, chopped

DIRECTIONS:
In your slow cooker, mix the beef with the onion, passata and the other ingredients except the spinach, toss, put the lid on and cook on Low for 6 hours and 30 minutes. Add the spinach, toss, put the lid on, cook on Low for 30 minutes more, divide into bowls and serve.

NUTRITION:
calories 400, fat 15, fiber 4, carbs 25, protein 14

Lamb Leg and Sweet Potatoes
Preparation time: 10 minutes
Cooking time: 8 hours
Servings: 4

INGREDIENTS:
- 2 tablespoons olive oil
- 1 lamb leg, bone in
- 1 garlic head, peeled and cloves separated
- 5 sweet potatoes, cubed
- 5 rosemary springs
- 2 cups chicken stock
- Salt and black pepper to the taste

DIRECTIONS:
Rub your lamb leg with the oil, salt and pepper. Place the potatoes and the garlic cloves on the bottom of your slow cooker, add lamb leg, rosemary springs and stock, cover and cook lamb on Low for 8 hours. Divide lamb and potatoes between plates and serve.

NUTRITION:
calories 350, fat 6, fiber 5, carbs 12, protein 22

Pork and Chilies Mix
Preparation time: 10 minutes
Cooking time: 7 hours
Servings: 2

INGREDIENTS:
- 1 pound pork stew meat, cubed
- 1 tablespoon olive oil
- ½ green bell pepper, chopped
- 1 red onion, sliced
- ½ red bell pepper, chopped
- 1 garlic clove, minced
- 2 ounces canned green chilies, chopped
- ½ cup tomato passata
- Salt and black pepper to the taste
- 1 tablespoon chili powder
- 1 tablespoon cilantro, chopped

DIRECTIONS:
In your slow cooker, mix the pork with the oil, bell pepper and the other ingredients, toss, put the lid on and cook on Low for 7 hours. Divide into bowls and serve right away.

NUTRITION:
calories 400, fat 14, fiber 5, carbs 29, protein 22

Lamb Shanks
Preparation time: 10 minutes
Cooking time: 8 hours and 10 minutes
Servings: 4

INGREDIENTS:
- 4 lamb shanks, trimmed
- 3 tablespoons olive oil
- 1 onion, chopped
- 2 carrots, chopped
- 15 ounces canned tomatoes, chopped
- 2 garlic cloves, minced
- 2 celery stalks, chopped
- 2 tablespoons tomato paste
- 2 cups veggie stock
- 1 tablespoon rosemary, dried
- 1 tablespoon thyme, dried
- 1 tablespoon oregano, dried
- Salt and black pepper to the taste

DIRECTIONS:
Heat up a pan with 2 tablespoons oil over medium-high heat, add lamb shanks, brown them for 5 minutes on each side and transfer to your Slow cooker. Add the rest of the oil, onion, carrots, tomatoes, garlic, celery, tomato paste, stock, rosemary, thyme, salt and pepper, stir, cover and cook on Low for 8 hours. Divide everything between plates and serve.

NUTRITION:
calories 350, fat 5, fiber 4, carbs 12, protein 20

Mustard Ribs
Preparation time: 10 minutes
Cooking time: 8 hours
Servings: 2

INGREDIENTS:
- 2 beef short ribs, cut into individual ribs
- Salt and black pepper to the taste
- ½ cup ketchup
- 1 tablespoon balsamic vinegar
- 1 tablespoon mustard
- 1 tablespoon chives, chopped

DIRECTIONS:
In your slow cooker, combine the ribs with the ketchup, salt, pepper and the other ingredients, toss, put the lid on and cook on Low for 8 hours. Divide between plates and serve with a side salad.

NUTRITION:
calories 284, fat 7, 4, carbs 18, protein 20

Flavored Pork Roast
Preparation time: 10 minutes
Cooking time: 4 hours
Servings: 6

INGREDIENTS:
1 pound sweet potatoes, chopped
3 and ½ pounds pork roast
8 medium carrots, chopped
Salt and black pepper to the taste
15 ounces canned tomatoes, chopped
1 yellow onion, chopped
Grated zest and juice of 1 lemon
4 garlic cloves, minced
3 bay leaves
Black pepper to the taste
½ cup kalamata olives, pitted

DIRECTIONS:
Put potatoes in your Slow cooker, add carrots, tomatoes, onions, lemon juice and zest, pork, bay leaves, salt, black pepper and garlic, stir, cover and cook on High for 4 hours. Transfer meat to a cutting board, slice it and divide between plates. Discard bay leaves, transfer veggies to a bowl, mash them, mix with olives, add next to the meat and serve right away!

NUTRITION:
calories 250, fat 4, fiber 3, carbs 6, protein 13

Beef and Corn Mix
Preparation time: 10 minutes
Cooking time: 8 hours
Servings: 2

INGREDIENTS:
2 teaspoons olive oil
3 scallions, chopped
1 pound beef stew meat, cubed
1 cup corn
½ cup heavy cream
½ cup beef stock
2 garlic cloves, minced
Salt and black pepper to the taste
1 tablespoon soy sauce
1 tablespoon parsley, chopped

DIRECTIONS:
In your slow cooker, combine the beef with the corn, oil, scallions and the other ingredients except the cream, toss, put the lid on and cook on Low for 7 hours. Add the cream, toss, cook on Low for 1 more hour, divide into bowls and serve.

NUTRITION:
calories 400, fat 10, fiber 4, carbs 15, protein 20

Beef and Onions
Preparation time: 10 minutes
Cooking time: 6 hours and 5 minutes
Servings: 6

INGREDIENTS:
3 pounds beef roast, trimmed and boneless
1 tablespoon Italian seasoning
Salt and black pepper to the taste
1 garlic clove, minced
1/3 cup sun-dried tomatoes, chopped
½ cup beef stock
½ cup kalamata olives pitted and halved
1 cup yellow onions chopped
1 tablespoon olive oil

DIRECTIONS:
Heat up a pan with the oil over medium-high heat, add beef, brown for 5 minutes, season with black pepper and Italian seasoning, transfer to your slow cooker, add tomatoes, onions and stock, cover and cook on Low for 6 hours. Transfer meat to a cutting board, slice, divide between plates, add onions and tomatoes on the side and serve with cooking juices on top.

NUTRITION:
calories 300, fat 5, fiber 5, carbs 12, protein 25

Cider Beef Mix
Preparation time: 10 minutes
Cooking time: 8 hours
Servings: 2

INGREDIENTS:
1 pound beef stew meat, cubed
1 tablespoon olive oil
Salt and black pepper to the taste
3 garlic cloves, minced
½ yellow onion, chopped
½ cup beef stock
1 tablespoon apple cider vinegar
1 tablespoon lime zest, grated

DIRECTIONS:
In your slow cooker, mix the beef with the oil, salt, pepper, garlic and the other ingredients, toss, put the lid on, and cook on Low for 8 hours. Divide everything between plates and serve.

NUTRITION:
calories 453, fat 10, fiber 12, carbs 20, protein 36

Lamb Shoulder
Preparation time: 10 minutes
Cooking time: 8 hours and 10 minutes
Servings: 6

INGREDIENTS:
3 pounds lamb shoulder, boneless
3 onions, roughly chopped
1 tablespoon olive oil
1 tablespoon oregano, chopped
6 garlic cloves, minced
1 tablespoon lemon zest, grated
Salt and black pepper to the taste
½ teaspoon allspice
1 and ½ cups veggie stock
14 ounces canned artichoke hearts, chopped
¼ cup tomato paste
2 tablespoons parsley, chopped

DIRECTIONS:
Heat up a pan with the oil over medium-high heat, add lamb, brown for 5 minutes on each side, transfer to your Slow cooker, add onion, lemon zest, garlic, a pinch of salt, pepper, oregano, allspice, stock and tomato paste, cover and cook on Low for 7 hours and 45 minutes. Add artichokes and parsley, stir gently, cover, cook on Low for 15 more minutes, divide into bowls and serve hot.

NUTRITION:
calories 370, fat 4, fiber 5, carbs 12, protein 16

Tarragon Pork Chops
Preparation time: 10 minutes

Cooking time: 6 hours

Servings: 2

INGREDIENTS:
½ pound pork chops
¼ tablespoons olive oil
2 garlic clove, minced
¼ teaspoon chili powder
½ cup beef stock
½ teaspoon coriander, ground
Salt and black pepper to the taste
¼ teaspoon mustard powder
1 tablespoon tarragon, chopped

DIRECTIONS:
Grease your slow cooker with the oil and mix the pork chops with the garlic, stock and the other ingredients inside. Toss, put the lid on, cook on Low for 6 hours, divide between plates and serve with a side salad.

NUTRITION:
calories 453, fat 16, fiber 8, carbs 7, protein 27

Chinese Pork Shoulder
Preparation time: 10 minutes

Cooking time: 7 hours

Servings: 4

INGREDIENTS:
2 and ½ pounds pork shoulder
4 cups chicken stock
½ cup soy sauce
¼ cup white vinegar
2 tablespoons chili sauce
Juice of 1 lime
1 tablespoon ginger, grated
1 tablespoon Chinese 5 spice
2 cups portabella mushrooms, sliced
Salt and black pepper to the taste
1 zucchini, sliced

DIRECTIONS:
In your Slow cooker, mix pork with stock, soy sauce, vinegar, chili sauce, lime juice, ginger, 5 spice, mushrooms, zucchini, salt and pepper, toss a bit, cover and cook on Low for 7 hours. Transfer pork shoulder to a cutting board, shred using 2 forks, return to Slow cooker, toss with the rest of the ingredients, divide between plates and serve.

NUTRITION:
calories 342, fat 6, fiber 8, carbs 27, protein 18

Honey Pork Chops
Preparation time: 10 minutes

Cooking time: 5 hours

Servings: 2

INGREDIENTS:
2 teaspoons avocado oil
1 pound pork chops, bone in
2 tablespoons mayonnaise
1 tablespoon ketchup
½ tablespoon honey
¼ cup beef stock
½ tablespoon lime juice

DIRECTIONS:
In your slow cooker, mix the pork chops with the oil, honey and the other ingredients, toss well, put the lid on, and cook on High for 5 hours. Divide pork chops between plates and serve.

NUTRITION:
calories 300, fat 8, fiber 10, carbs 16, protein 16

Roast and Pepperoncinis
Preparation time: 10 minutes

Cooking time: 8 hours

Servings: 4

INGREDIENTS:
5 pounds beef chuck roast
1 tablespoon soy sauce
10 pepperoncinis
1 cup beef stock
2 tablespoons butter, melted

DIRECTIONS:
In your Slow cooker, mix beef roast with soy sauce, pepperoncinis, stock and butter, toss well, cover and cook on Low for 8 hours. Transfer roast to a cutting board, shred using 2 forks, return to slow cooker, toss, divide between plates and serve.

NUTRITION:
calories 362, fat 4, fiber 8, carbs 17, protein 17

Turmeric Lamb
Preparation time: 10 minutes
Cooking time: 5 hours
Servings: 2

INGREDIENTS:
1 pound lamb chops
2 teaspoons avocado oil
1 teaspoon turmeric powder
½ teaspoon sweet paprika
1 cup beef stock
1 red onion, sliced
Salt and black pepper to the taste
1 tablespoon chives, chopped

DIRECTIONS:
In your slow cooker, mix the lamb chops with the oil, turmeric and the other ingredients, toss, put the lid on and cook on High for 5 hours. Divide everything between plates and serve.

NUTRITION:
calories 254, fat 12, fiber 2, carbs 6, protein 16

Balsamic Beef Cheeks
Preparation time: 10 minutes
Cooking time: 4 hours
Servings: 4

INGREDIENTS:
4 beef cheeks, halved
2 tablespoons olive oil
Salt and black pepper to the taste
1 white onion, chopped
4 garlic cloves, minced
2 cup beef stock
5 cardamom pods
1 tablespoon balsamic vinegar
3 bay leaves
7 cloves
2 vanilla beans, split
1 and ½ tablespoons tomato paste
1 carrot, sliced

DIRECTIONS:
In your Slow cooker, mix beef cheeks with the oil, salt, pepper, onion, garlic, stock, cardamom, vinegar, bay leaves, cloves, vanilla beans, tomato paste and carrot, toss, cover, cook on High for 4 hours, divide between plates and serve.

NUTRITION:
calories 321, fat 5, fiber 7, carbs 18, protein 12

Chili Lamb
Preparation time: 10 minutes
Cooking time: 4 hours
Servings: 2

INGREDIENTS:
1 pound lamb chops
2 teaspoons avocado oil
2 scallions, chopped
1 green chili pepper, minced
½ teaspoon turmeric powder
1 teaspoon chili powder
½ cup veggie stock
2 garlic cloves, minced
A pinch of salt and black pepper

DIRECTIONS:
In your slow cooker, mix the lamb chops with the oil, scallions and the other ingredients, toss, put the lid on and cook on High for 4 hours. Divide everything between plates and serve.

NUTRITION:
calories 243, fat 15, fiber 3, carbs 6, protein 20

Seasoned Beef
Preparation time: 10 minutes
Cooking time: 8 hours
Servings: 6

INGREDIENTS:
4 pounds beef roast
2 cups beef stock
2 sweet potatoes, cubed
6 carrots, sliced
7 celery stalks, chopped
1 yellow onion, chopped
1 tablespoon onion powder
1 tablespoon garlic powder
1 tablespoon sweet paprika
Salt and black pepper to the taste

DIRECTIONS:
In your Slow cooker, beef with stock, sweet potatoes, carrots, celery, onion, onion powder, garlic powder, paprika, salt and pepper, stir, cover, cook on Low for 8 hours, slice roast, divide between plates, drizzle sauce from the slow cooker all and serve with the veggies on the side.

NUTRITION:
calories 372, fat 6, fiber 12, carbs 19, protein 11

Beef and Red Onions Mix
Preparation time: 10 minutes
Cooking time: 7 hours
Servings: 2

INGREDIENTS:
1 pound beef stew meat, cubed
2 teaspoons olive oil
2 red onions, sliced
1 cup heavy cream
¼ cup beef stock
1 teaspoon chili powder
½ teaspoon rosemary, dried
1 tablespoon parsley, chopped
A pinch of salt and black pepper

DIRECTIONS:
In your slow cooker, mix the beef with the onions, oil and the other ingredients, toss, put the lid on and cook on low for 7 hours. Divide everything between plates and serve.

NUTRITION:
calories 263, fat 14, fiber 3, carbs 6, protein 16

Beef Soup

Preparation time: 10 minutes

Cooking time: 6 hours

Servings: 4

INGREDIENTS:
1 pound beef, ground
2 cups cauliflower, chopped
1 cup yellow onion, chopped
2 red bell peppers, chopped
15 ounces tomato sauce
15 ounces tomatoes, chopped
3 cups beef stock
½ teaspoon basil, dried
½ teaspoon oregano, dried
3 garlic cloves, minced
Salt and black pepper to the taste

DIRECTIONS:
In your Slow cooker, mix beef with cauliflower, onion, bell peppers, tomato sauce, tomatoes, stock, basil, oregano, garlic, salt and pepper, stir, cover, cook on Low for 6 hours, ladle into bowls and serve.

NUTRITION:
calories 214, fat 6, fiber 6, carbs 18, protein 7

Pork and Okra

Preparation time: 10 minutes

Cooking time: 6 hours

Servings: 2

INGREDIENTS:
1 pound pork stew meat, cubed
1 cup okra, sliced
2 teaspoons olive oil
1 red onion, chopped
¼ cup beef stock
½ teaspoon chili powder
½ teaspoon turmeric powder
1 cup tomato passata
A pinch of salt and black pepper

DIRECTIONS:
In your slow cooker, combine the pork with the okra, oil and the other ingredients, toss, put the lid on and cook on High for 6 hours. Divide the mix between plates and serve.

NUTRITION:
calories 264, fat 14, fiber 4, carbs 7, protein 15

Thai Cocoa Pork

Preparation time: 10 minutes

Cooking time: 7 hours

Servings: 4

INGREDIENTS:
2 tablespoons olive oil
2 pounds pork butt, boneless and cubed
Salt and black pepper to the taste
6 eggs, hard-boiled, peeled and sliced
1 tablespoon cilantro, chopped
1 tablespoon coriander seeds
1 tablespoon ginger, grated
1 tablespoon black peppercorns
2 tablespoons garlic, chopped
2 tablespoons five spice powder
1 and ½ cup soy sauce
2 tablespoons cocoa powder
1 yellow onion, chopped
8 cups water

DIRECTIONS:
In your Slow cooker, mix oil with pork, salt, pepper, cilantro, coriander, ginger, peppercorns, garlic, five spice, soy sauce, cocoa, onion and water, toss, cover and cook on Low for 7 hours. Divide stew into bowls, add egg slices on top and serve.

NUTRITION:
calories 400, fat 10, fiber 9, carbs 28, protein 22

Chives Lamb

Preparation time: 10 minutes

Cooking time: 4 hours

Servings: 2

INGREDIENTS:
1 pound lamb chops
½ cup chives, chopped
½ cup tomato passata
2 scallions, chopped
2 teaspoons olive oil
2 garlic cloves, minced
½ teaspoon sweet paprika
1 teaspoon cumin, ground
A pinch of salt and black pepper

DIRECTIONS:
In your slow cooer, mix the lamb chops with the chives, passata and the other ingredients, toss, put the lid on and cook on High for 4 hours, Divide the mix between plates and serve.

NUTRITION:
calories 263, fat 12, fiber 4, carbs 6, protein 16

Herbed and Cinnamon Beef
Preparation time: 10 minutes
Cooking time: 5 hours
Servings: 6

INGREDIENTS:
- 4 pounds beef brisket
- 2 oranges, sliced
- 2 garlic cloves, minced
- 2 yellow onions, thinly sliced
- 11 ounces celery, thinly sliced
- 1 tablespoon dill, dried
- 3 bay leaves
- 4 cinnamon sticks, cut into halves
- Salt and black pepper to the taste
- 17 ounces veggie stock

DIRECTIONS:
In your Slow cooker, mix beef with orange slices, garlic, onion, celery, dill, bay leaves, cinnamon, salt, pepper and stock, stir, cover and cook on High for 5 hours. Divide beef mix between plates and serve.

NUTRITION:
calories 300, fat 5, fiber 7, carbs 12, protein 4

Oregano Beef
Preparation time: 10 minutes
Cooking time: 4 hours
Servings: 2

INGREDIENTS:
- 1 pound beef stew meat, cubed
- 1 tablespoon olive oil
- 1 tablespoon balsamic vinegar
- ½ tablespoon lemon juice
- 1 tablespoon oregano, chopped
- ½ cup tomato sauce
- 1 red onion, chopped
- A pinch of salt and black pepper
- ½ teaspoon chili powder

DIRECTIONS:
In your slow cooker, mix the beef with the oil, vinegar, lemon juice and the other ingredients, toss, put the lid on and cook on High for 4 hours. Divide the mix between plates and serve right away.

NUTRITION:
calories 263, fat 14, fiber 4, carbs 6, protein 18

Beef Brisket and Turnips Mix
Preparation time: 10 minutes
Cooking time: 8 hours
Servings: 6

INGREDIENTS:
- 2 and ½ pounds beef brisket
- 4 cups veggie stock
- 2 bay leaves
- 3 garlic cloves, chopped
- 4 carrots, chopped
- 1 cabbage head cut into 6 wedges
- Salt and black pepper to the taste
- 3 turnips, cut into quarters

DIRECTIONS:
In your Slow cooker, mix beef with stock, bay leaves, garlic, carrots, cabbage, salt, pepper and turnips, stir, cover and cook on Low for 8 hours. Divide beef brisket and turnips mix between plates and serve.

NUTRITION:
calories 321, fat 15, fiber 4, carbs 18, protein 19

Pork and Green Beans
Preparation time: 10 minutes
Cooking time: 6 hours
Servings: 2

INGREDIENTS:
- 1 pound pork stew meat, cubed
- 1 tablespoon balsamic vinegar
- 1 cup green beans, trimmed and halved
- 1 tablespoon lime juice
- 1 tablespoon avocado oil
- ½ teaspoon rosemary, dried
- A pinch of salt and black pepper
- 1 cup beef stock
- 1 tablespoon chives, chopped

DIRECTIONS:
In your slow cooker, mix the pork stew meat with the green beans, vinegar and the other ingredients, toss, put the lid on and cook on Low for 6 hours. Divide the mix between plates and serve.

NUTRITION:
calories 264, fat 14, fiber 4, carbs 6, protein 17

Rich Lamb Shanks
Preparation time: 10 minutes
Cooking time: 7 hours
Servings: 4

INGREDIENTS:
4 lamb shanks
2 tablespoons olive oil
1 yellow onion, finely chopped
3 carrots, roughly chopped
2 garlic cloves, minced
2 tablespoons tomato paste
1 teaspoon oregano, dried
1 tomato, roughly chopped
4 ounces chicken stock
Salt and black pepper to the taste

DIRECTIONS:
In your Slow cooker, mix lamb with oil, onion, garlic, carrots, tomato paste, tomato, oregano, stock, salt and pepper, stir, cover and cook on Low for 7 hours. Divide into bowls and serve hot.

NUTRITION:
calories 400, fat 13, fiber 4, carbs 17, protein 24

Mint Lamb Chops

Preparation time: 10 minutes
Cooking time: 4 hours
Servings: 2

INGREDIENTS:
2 tablespoons olive oil
1 pound lamb chops
1 tablespoon mint, chopped
½ teaspoon garam masala
½ cup coconut cream
1 red onion, chopped
2 tablespoons garlic, minced
½ cup beef stock
A pinch of salt and black pepper

DIRECTIONS:
In your slow cooker, mix the lamb chops with the oil, mint and the other ingredients, toss, put the lid on and cook on High for 4 hours. Divide the mix between plates and serve warm.

NUTRITION:
calories 263, fat 14, fiber 3, carbs 7, protein 20

Lamb Leg and Mushrooms Mix

Preparation time: 10 minutes
Cooking time: 8 hours
Servings: 8

INGREDIENTS:
1 and ½ pounds lamb leg, bone-in
2 carrots, sliced
½ pounds mushrooms, sliced
4 tomatoes, chopped
1 small yellow onion, chopped
6 garlic cloves, minced
2 tablespoons tomato paste
1 teaspoon olive oil
Salt and black pepper to the taste
A handful parsley, chopped

DIRECTIONS:
In your Slow cooker, mix lamb with carrots, mushrooms, tomatoes, onion, garlic, tomato paste, oil, salt, pepper and parsley, toss, cover, cook on Low for 8 hours, divide between plates and serve.

NUTRITION:
calories 372, fat 12, fiber 7, carbs 18, protein 22

Beef and Artichokes

Preparation time: 10 minutes
Cooking time: 7 hours
Servings: 2

INGREDIENTS:
1 tablespoon avocado oil
1 pound beef stew meat, cubed
2 scallions, chopped
1 cup canned artichoke hearts, drained and quartered
½ teaspoon chili powder
A pinch of salt and black pepper
1 cup tomato passata
A pinch of salt and black pepper
¼ tablespoon dill, chopped

DIRECTIONS:
In your slow cooker, combine the beef with the artichokes and the other ingredients, toss, put the lid on and cook on Low for 7 hours. Divide the mix between plates and serve.

NUTRITION:
calories 263, fat 14, fiber 5, carbs 7, protein 15

Smoky Lamb

Preparation time: 10 minutes
Cooking time: 7 hours
Servings: 4

INGREDIENTS:
4 lamb chops
1 teaspoon liquid smoke
1 cup green onions, chopped
2 cups canned tomatoes, chopped
1 teaspoon smoked paprika
2 tablespoons garlic, minced
Salt and black pepper to the taste
3 cups beef stock

DIRECTIONS:
In your Slow cooker, mix lamb with liquid smoke, green onions, tomatoes, paprika, garlic, salt, pepper and stock, stir, cover and cook on Low for 7 hours. Divide everything between plates and serve.

NUTRITION:
calorie 364, fat 12, fiber 7, carbs 29, protein 28

Lamb and Potatoes
Preparation time: 10 minutes
Cooking time: 4 hours
Servings: 2

INGREDIENTS:
1 pound lamb stew meat, roughly cubed
2 sweet potatoes, peeled and cubed
½ cup beef stock
½ cup tomato sauce
½ teaspoon sweet paprika
½ teaspoon coriander, ground
1 tablespoon avocado oil
1 tablespoon balsamic vinegar
1 tablespoon cilantro, chopped
A pinch of salt and black pepper

DIRECTIONS:
In your slow cooker, mix the lamb with the potatoes, stock, sauce and the other ingredients, toss, put the lid on and cook on High for 4 hoursю. Divide everything between plates and serve.

NUTRITION:
calories 253, fat 14, fiber 3, carbs 7, protein 17

Sausage and Onion Jam
Preparation time: 15 minutes
Cooking time: 3 hours
Servings: 6

INGREDIENTS:
6 pork sausages
2 tablespoons olive oil
½ cup onion jam
3 ounces beef stock
3 ounces water
Salt and black pepper to the taste
1 tablespoon flour

DIRECTIONS:
In your slow cooker, mix sausages with oil, onion jam, stock, water, salt, pepper and flour, toss, cover, cook on High for 3 hours, divide everything between plates and serve.

NUTRITION:
calories 431, fat 15, fiber 4, carbs 29, protein 13

Lamb and Tomatoes Mix
Preparation time: 10 minutes
Cooking time: 4 hours
Servings: 2

INGREDIENTS:
1 teaspoon olive oil
1 pound lamb stew meat, cubed
1 cup cherry tomatoes, halved
1 tablespoon basil, chopped
½ teaspoon rosemary, dried
1 tablespoon oregano, chopped
1 cup beef stock
½ teaspoon sweet paprika
A pinch of salt and black pepper
1 tablespoon parsley, chopped

DIRECTIONS:
Grease the slow cooker with the oil and mix the lamb with the tomatoes, basil and the other ingredients inside. Toss, put the lid on, cook on High for 4 hours, divide the mix between plates and serve.

NUTRITION:
calories 276, fat 14, fiber 3, carbs 7, protein 20

French Lamb
Preparation time: 10 minutes
Cooking time: 8 hours
Servings: 4

INGREDIENTS:
4 lamb chops
1 cup onion, chopped
2 cups canned tomatoes, chopped
1 cup leek, chopped
2 tablespoons garlic, minced
1 teaspoon herbs de Provence
Salt and black pepper to the taste
3 cups water

DIRECTIONS:
In your Slow cooker mix, lamb chops with onion, tomatoes, leek, garlic, herbs de Provence, salt, pepper and water, stir, cover and cook on Low for 8 hours. Divide lamb and veggies between plates and serve.

NUTRITION:
calories 430, fat 12, fiber 8, carbs 20, protein 18

Pork and Eggplant Mix
Preparation time: 10 minutes
Cooking time: 7 hours
Servings: 2

INGREDIENTS:
1 pound pork stew meat, cubed
1 eggplant, cubed
2 scallions, chopped
2 garlic cloves, minced
½ cup beef stock
¼ cup tomato sauce
1 teaspoon sweet paprika
1 tablespoon chives, chopped

DIRECTIONS:
In your slow cooker, mix the pork stew meat with the scallions, eggplant and the other ingredients, toss, put the lid on and cook on Low for 7 hours. Divide the mix between plates and serve right away.

NUTRITION:
calories 287, fat 16, fiber 4, carbs 6, protein 20

Jamaican Pork

Preparation time: 10 minutes

Cooking time: 7 hours

Servings: 12

INGREDIENTS:
½ cup beef stock
1 tablespoon olive oil
¼ cup keto Jamaican spice mix
4 pounds pork shoulder

DIRECTIONS:
In your Slow cooker, mix pork with oil and Jamaican spice mix, rub well, add stock, cover and cook on Low for 7 hours. Slice roast and serve

NUTRITION:
calories 400, fat 6, fiber 7, carbs 10, protein 25

Lemon Lamb

Preparation time: 10 minutes

Cooking time: 7 hours

Servings: 2

INGREDIENTS:
1 pound lamb stew meat, cubed
1 red onion, sliced
½ cup tomato sauce
1 tablespoon balsamic vinegar
1 tablespoon lemon juice
1 tablespoon lemon zest, grated
1 teaspoon olive oil
3 garlic cloves, chopped
A pinch of salt and black pepper
1 tablespoon chives, chopped

DIRECTIONS:
In your slow cooker, mix the lamb with the onion, tomato sauce and the other ingredients, toss, put the lid on and cook on Low for 7 hours. Divide the mix between plates and serve right away.

NUTRITION:
calories 264, fat 8, fiber 3, carbs 6, protein 17

Pork Sirloin Salsa Mix

Preparation time: 10 minutes

Cooking time: 8 hours

Servings: 4

INGREDIENTS:
2 pounds pork sirloin roast, cut into thick slices
Salt and black pepper to the taste
2 teaspoons garlic powder
2 teaspoons cumin, ground
1 tablespoon olive oil
16 ounces green chili tomatillo salsa

DIRECTIONS:
In your Slow cooker, mix pork with cumin, salt, pepper and garlic powder and rub well. Add oil and salsa, toss, cover and cook on Low for 8 hours. Divide between plates and serve hot.

NUTRITION:
calories 400, fat 7, fiber 6, carbs 10, protein 25

Rosemary Lamb with Olives

Preparation time: 10 minutes

Cooking time: 4 hours

Servings: 2

INGREDIENTS:
1 pound lamb chops
1 tablespoon olive oil
3 garlic cloves, minced
1 tablespoon rosemary, chopped
1 cup kalamata olives, pitted and halved
3 scallions, chopped
1 teaspoon turmeric powder
1 cup beef stock
A pinch of salt and black pepper

DIRECTIONS:
In your slow cooker, mix the lamb chops with the oil, rosemary and the other ingredients, toss, put the lid on and cook on High for 4 hours. Divide the mix between plates and serve.

NUTRITION:
calories 275, fat 13, fiber 4, carbs 7, protein 20

Beef Meatloaf

Preparation time: 10 minutes

Cooking time: 4 hours

Servings: 4

INGREDIENTS:
2 pounds beef, ground
¼ cup parmesan, grated
¼ cup yellow onion, chopped
1 egg, whisked
Salt and black pepper to the taste
1 tablespoon garlic, minced
½ teaspoon thyme, dried
1 tablespoon olive oil
1 yellow onion, chopped
1 cup ketchup
½ cup beef stock

DIRECTIONS:
In a bowl mix beef, cheese, ¼ cup onion, egg, thyme, salt and pepper, stir and shape a meatloaf. Heat up a pan with the oil over medium-high heat, add onion, stock and ketchup, stir, bring to a simmer and transfer to your Slow cooker. Add meatloaf, cover and cook on High for 4 hours. Slice meatloaf, divide between plates and serve with the sauce drizzled all over.

NUTRITION:
calories 363, fat 6, fiber 3, carbs 12, protein 14

Nutmeg Lamb and Squash
Preparation time: 10 minutes

Cooking time: 6 hours

Servings: 2

INGREDIENTS:
- 1 pound lamb stew meat, roughly cubed
- 1 cup butternut squash, peeled and cubed
- ½ teaspoon nutmeg, ground
- ½ teaspoon chili powder
- ½ teaspoon coriander, ground
- 2 teaspoons olive oil
- 1 cup beef stock
- A pinch of salt and black pepper
- 1 tablespoon cilantro, chopped

DIRECTIONS:
In your slow cooker, mix the lamb with the squash, nutmeg and the other ingredients, toss, put the lid on and cook on Low for 6 hours. Divide the mix between plates and serve.

NUTRITION:
calories 263, fat 12, fiber 4, carbs 7, protein 12

Pork Loin and Cauliflower Rice
Preparation time: 10 minutes

Cooking time: 8 hours

Servings: 6

INGREDIENTS:
- 3 bacon slices, cooked and chopped
- 3 carrots, chopped
- 2 pounds pork loin roast
- 1 rhubarb stalk, chopped
- 2 bay leaves
- ¼ cup red wine vinegar
- 4 garlic cloves, minced
- Salt and black pepper to the taste
- ¼ cup olive oil
- 1 tablespoon garlic powder
- 1 tablespoon Italian seasoning
- 24 ounces cauliflower rice
- 1 teaspoon turmeric powder
- 1 cup beef stock

DIRECTIONS:
In your Slow cooker, mix bacon with carrots, pork, rhubarb, bay leaves, vinegar, salt, pepper, oil, garlic powder, Italian seasoning, stock and turmeric, toss, cover and cook on Low for 7 hours. Add cauliflower rice, cover, cook on Low for 1 more hour, divide between plates and serve.

NUTRITION:
calories 310, fat 6, fiber 3, carbs 14, protein 10

Lamb and Fennel Mix
Preparation time: 10 minutes

Cooking time: 4 hours

Servings: 2

INGREDIENTS:
- 1 pound lamb stew meat, roughly cubed
- 1 fennel bulb, sliced
- 1 tablespoon lemon juice
- 1 teaspoon avocado oil
- ½ teaspoon coriander, ground
- 1 cup tomato passata
- A pinch of salt and black pepper
- 1 tablespoon cilantro, chopped

DIRECTIONS:
In your slow cooker, combine the lamb with the fennel, lemon juice and the other ingredients, toss, put the lid on and cook on High for 4 hours. Divide the mix between plates and serve.

NUTRITION:
calories 263, fat 12, fiber 3, carbs 7, protein 10

Lamb and Spinach Salad
Preparation time: 10 minutes

Cooking time: 7 hours

Servings: 4

INGREDIENTS:
- 1 tablespoon olive oil
- 2 garlic cloves, minced
- 2 cups veggie stock
- 3 pounds leg of lamb, bone discarded
- Salt and black pepper to the taste
- 1 teaspoon cumin, ground
- ¼ teaspoon thyme, dried
- For the salad:
- 4 ounces feta cheese, crumbled
- ½ cup pecans, toasted
- 2 cups spinach
- 1 and ½ tablespoons lemon juice
- ¼ cup olive oil
- 1 cup mint, chopped

DIRECTIONS:
In your Slow cooker, mix 1 tablespoon oil with garlic, stock, lamb, salt, pepper, cumin and thyme, cover and cook on Low for 7 hours. Leave leg of

lamb aside to cool down, slice and divide between plates. In a bowl, mix spinach with mint, feta cheese, ¼ cup olive oil, lemon juice, pecans, salt and pepper, toss and divide next to lamb slices. Serve right away.

NUTRITION:
calories 234, fat 20, fiber 3, carbs 12, protein 32

Creamy Lamb
Preparation time: 10 minutes
Cooking time: 6 hours
Servings: 2

INGREDIENTS:
2 pounds lamb shoulder, cubed
1 cup heavy cream
1/3 cup beef stock
2 teaspoons avocado oil
1 teaspoon turmeric powder
1 red onion, sliced
A pinch of salt and black pepper
1 tablespoon cilantro, chopped

DIRECTIONS:
In your slow cooker, mix the lamb with the stock, oil and the other ingredients except the cream, toss, put the lid on and cook on Low for 5 hours. Add the cream, toss, cook on Low for 1 more hour, divide the mix into bowls and serve.

NUTRITION:
calories 233, fat 7, fiber 2, carbs 6, protein 12

Lamb Stew
Preparation time: 10 minutes
Cooking time: 7 hours
Servings: 4

INGREDIENTS:
1 yellow onion, chopped
2 pounds lamb meat, cubed
2 tablespoons butter, melted
3 carrots, chopped
2 cups beef stock
1 tomato, chopped
1 garlic clove, minced
Salt and black pepper to the taste
2 rosemary springs, chopped
1 teaspoon thyme, chopped

DIRECTIONS:
In your Slow cooker, mix butter with onion, lamb, carrots, tomato, garlic, thyme, rosemary, salt, pepper and stock, stir, cover and cook on Low for 7 hours. Divide into bowls and serve.

NUTRITION:
calories 260, fat 12, fiber 6, carbs 10, protein 36

Beef and Capers Sauce
Preparation time: 10 minutes
Cooking time: 7 hours
Servings: 2

INGREDIENTS:
1 pound beef stew meat, cubed
1 tablespoon capers, drained
1 cup heavy cream
½ cup beef stock
½ tablespoon mustard
3 scallions, chopped
2 teaspoons avocado oil
1 teaspoon cumin, ground
A pinch of salt and black pepper
1 tablespoon parsley, chopped

DIRECTIONS:
In your slow cooker, mix the beef with capers, stock and the other ingredients except the cream, toss, put the lid on and cook on Low for 6 hours. Add the cream, toss, cook on Low for 1 more hour, divide the mix between plates and serve.

NUTRITION:
calories 235, fat 12, fiber 5, carbs 7, protein 10

Sausages and Celeriac Mash
Preparation time: 15 minutes
Cooking time: 5 hours
Servings: 6

INGREDIENTS:
For the mash
2 celeriac, peeled and cut into cubes
Salt and black pepper to the taste
1 teaspoon mustard powder
1 tablespoon butter, melted
4 ounces warm coconut milk
6 ounces water
1 tablespoon cheddar cheese, grated
For the sausages:
6 pork sausages
2 tablespoons olive oil
½ cup onion jam
2 ounces veggie stock
3 ounces water
Salt and black pepper to the taste

DIRECTIONS:
Put celeriac cubes in your Slow cooker, add 6 ounces water, salt and pepper, stir, cover and cook on High for 2 hours. Add mustard powder, butter, milk and cheese, stir really well and leave aside for now. Clean the Slow cooker, add oil, sausages, onion jam, 3 ounces water, stock, salt and pepper, cover and cook on High for 3 hours. Divide sausages on plates, add mashed celeriac on the side and serve with some of the cooking juices from the slow cooker drizzled all over.

NUTRITION:
calories 421, fat 12, fiber 4, carbs 7, protein 15

Masala Beef and Sauce

Preparation time: 10 minutes

Cooking time: 7 hours

Servings: 2

INGREDIENTS:
1 pound beef stew meat, cubed
1 teaspoon garam masala
1 tablespoon olive oil
1 tablespoon lime zest, grated
1 tablespoon lime juice
½ teaspoon sweet paprika
½ teaspoon coriander, ground
1 cup beef stock
A pinch of salt and black pepper

DIRECTIONS:
In your slow cooker, mix the beef with the garam masala, oil and the other ingredients, toss, put the lid on and cook on Low for 7 hours. Divide the mix between plates and serve.

NUTRITION:
calories 211, fat 9, fiber 2, carbs 6, protein 12

Pork Belly and Applesauce

Preparation time: 10 minutes

Cooking time: 8 hours

Servings: 6

INGREDIENTS:
2 tablespoons sugar
1 tablespoon lemon juice
1 quart water
17 ounces apples, cored and cut into wedges
2 pounds pork belly, scored
Salt and black pepper to the taste
A drizzle of olive oil

DIRECTIONS:
In your blender, mix water with apples, lemon juice and sugar and pulse well Put the pork belly in your Slow cooker, add oil, salt, pepper and applesauce, toss, cover and cook on Low for 8 hours. Slice pork roast, divide between plates and serve with the applesauce on top.

NUTRITION:
calories 456, fat 34, fiber 4, carbs 10, protein 25

Lamb and Cabbage

Preparation time: 10 minutes

Cooking time: 5 hours

Servings: 2

INGREDIENTS:
2 pounds lamb stew meat, cubed
1 cup red cabbage, shredded
1 cup beef stock
1 teaspoon avocado oil
1 teaspoon sweet paprika
2 tablespoons tomato paste
A pinch of salt and black pepper
1 tablespoon cilantro, chopped

DIRECTIONS:
In your slow cooker, mix the lamb with the cabbage, stock and the other ingredients, toss, put the lid on and cook on High for 5 hours. Divide everything between plates and serve.

NUTRITION:
calories 254, fat 12, fiber 3, carbs 6, protein 16

Stuffed Pork

Preparation time: 2 hours

Cooking time: 8 hours

Servings: 4

INGREDIENTS:
Zest of 2 limes
Juice of 1 orange
Zest of 1 orange
Juice of 2 limes
4 teaspoons garlic, minced
¾ cup olive oil
1 cup cilantro, chopped
1 cup mint, chopped
1 teaspoon oregano, dried
Salt and black pepper to the taste
2 teaspoons cumin, ground
4 pork loin steaks
2 pickles, chopped
4 ham slices
6 Swiss cheese slices
2 tablespoons mustard

DIRECTIONS:
In your food processor, mix lime zest and juice with orange zest and juice, garlic, oil, cilantro, mint, oregano, cumin, salt and pepper and blend well. Season steaks with salt and pepper, place them in a bowl, add marinade you've made, toss to coat and leave aside for a couple of hours. Place steaks on a working surface, divide pickles, cheese, mustard and ham on them, roll, secure with toothpicks, put them in your Slow cooker, cover and cook on Low for 7 hours. Divide between plates and serve.

NUTRITION:
calories 270, fat 7, fiber 2, carbs 13, protein 20

Pork and Lentils

Preparation time: 10 minutes

Cooking time: 7 hours

Servings: 2

INGREDIENTS:
- 1 pound pork stew meat, cubed
- 1 cup canned lentils, drained and rinsed
- 1 tablespoon olive oil
- 1 yellow onion, chopped
- ¼ cup tomato sauce
- ¼ cup beef stock
- A pinch of salt and black pepper
- 1 tablespoon cilantro, chopped

DIRECTIONS:
In your slow cooker, mix the pork with the lentils, oil, onion and the other ingredients, toss, put the lid on and cook on Low for 7 hours. Divide the mix between plates and serve.

NUTRITION:
calories 232, fat 10, fiber 5, carbs 7, protein 11

Pork Rolls

Preparation time: 10 minutes

Cooking time: 8 hours

Servings: 6

INGREDIENTS:
- 6 prosciutto slices
- 2 tablespoons parsley, chopped
- 1 pound pork cutlets, thinly sliced and flattened
- 1/3 cup ricotta cheese
- 1 tablespoon coconut oil
- ¼ cup yellow onion, chopped
- 3 garlic cloves, minced
- 2 tablespoons parmesan, grated
- 15 ounces canned tomatoes, chopped
- 1/3 cup chicken stock
- Salt and black pepper to the taste
- ½ teaspoon Italian seasoning

DIRECTIONS:
Place prosciutto slices on top of each pork cutlet, then divide ricotta, parsley and parmesan, roll each pork piece and secure with a toothpick. In your Slow cooker, mix oil with onion, garlic, tomatoes, stock, Italian seasoning, salt, pepper and pork rolls, cover and cook on Low for 8 hours. Divide between plates and serve.

NUTRITION:
calories 280, fat 17, fiber 1, carbs 14, protein 34

Balsamic Lamb Mix

Preparation time: 10 minutes

Cooking time: 7 hours

Servings: 2

INGREDIENTS:
- 1 pound lamb stew meat, cubed
- 2 teaspoons avocado oil
- 1 tablespoon balsamic vinegar
- ½ teaspoon coriander, ground
- A pinch of salt and black pepper
- 1 cup beef stock

DIRECTIONS:
In your slow cooker, mix the lamb with the oil, vinegar and the other ingredients, toss, put the lid on and cook on Low for 7 hours. Divide the mix between plates and serve with a side salad.

NUTRITION:
calories 243, fat 11, fiber 4, carbs 6, protein 10

Tender Pork Chops

Preparation time: 10 minutes

Cooking time: 8 hours

Servings: 4

INGREDIENTS:
- 2 yellow onions, chopped
- 6 bacon slices, chopped
- ½ cup chicken stock
- Salt and black pepper to the taste
- 4 pork chops

DIRECTIONS:
In your Slow cooker, mix onions with bacon, stock, salt, pepper and pork chops, cover and cook on Low for 8 hours. Divide pork chops on plates, drizzle cooking juices all over and serve.

NUTRITION:
calories 325, fat 18, fiber 1, carbs 12, protein 36

Beef and Endives

Preparation time: 10 minutes

Cooking time: 7 hours

Servings: 2

INGREDIENTS:
- 1 pound beef stew meat, cubed
- 2 teaspoons avocado oil
- 2 endives, shredded
- ½ cup beef stock
- ½ teaspoon sweet paprika
- ¼ cup tomato passata
- 3 garlic cloves, minced
- A pinch of salt and black pepper
- 1 tablespoon chives, chopped

DIRECTIONS:
In your slow cooker, mix the meat with the oil, endives and the other ingredients, toss, put the lid on and cook on Low for 7 hours. Divide the mix between plates and serve.

NUTRITION:
calories 232, fat 12, fiber 4, carbs 6, protein 9

Worcestershire Pork Chops

Preparation time: 10 minutes
Cooking time: 7 hours and 12 minutes
Servings: 4

INGREDIENTS:
4 medium pork chops
1 teaspoon Dijon mustard
1 tablespoon Worcestershire sauce
1 teaspoon lemon juice
1 tablespoon water
Salt and black pepper to the taste
1 teaspoon lemon pepper
1 tablespoon olive
1 tablespoon chives, chopped

DIRECTIONS:
In a bowl, mix water with Worcestershire sauce, mustard and lemon juice and whisk well. Heat up a pan with the oil over medium heat, add pork chops, season with salt, pepper and lemon pepper, cook them for 6 minutes, flip and cook for 6 more minutes and transfer to your Slow cooker. Add Worcestershire sauce mix, toss, cover and cook on Low for 7 hours. Divide pork chops on plates, sprinkle chives on top and serve.

NUTRITION:
calories 132, fat 5, fiber 1, carbs 12, protein 18

Lamb and Lime Zucchinis

Preparation time: 10 minutes
Cooking time: 4 hours
Servings: 2

INGREDIENTS:
1 pound lamb stew meat, roughly cubed
2 small zucchinis, cubed
Juice of 1 lime
½ teaspoon rosemary, dried
2 tablespoons avocado oil
1 red onion, chopped
½ cup beef stock
1 tablespoon garlic, minced
A pinch of salt and black pepper
1 tablespoon cilantro, chopped

DIRECTIONS:
In your slow cooker, mix the lamb with the zucchinis, lime juice and the other ingredients, toss, put the lid on and cook on High for 4 hours. Divide the mix between plates and serve.

NUTRITION:
calories 274, fat 9, fiber 5, carbs 6, protein 12

Rosemary Pork

Preparation time: 10 minutes
Cooking time: 7 hours
Servings: 4

INGREDIENTS:
4 pork chops, bone in
1 cup chicken stock
Salt and black pepper to the taste
1 teaspoon rosemary, dried
3 garlic cloves, minced

DIRECTIONS:
Season pork chops with salt and pepper and place in your Slow cooker. Add rosemary, garlic and stock, cover and cook on Low for 7 hours. Divide pork between plates and drizzle cooking juices all over.

NUTRITION:
calories 165, fat 2, fiber 1, carbs 12, protein 26

Beef and Peas

Preparation time: 10 minutes
Cooking time: 5 hours
Servings: 2

INGREDIENTS:
1 pound beef stew meat, cubed
1 tablespoon olive oil
½ teaspoon coriander, ground
½ teaspoon sweet paprika
½ cup beef stock
½ cup tomato sauce
1 cup fresh peas
1 tablespoon lime juice
A pinch of salt and black pepper
1 tablespoon dill, chopped

DIRECTIONS:
In your slow cooker, mix the beef with the oil, coriander, peas and the other ingredients, toss, put the lid on and cook on High for 5 hours. Divide everything between plates and serve.

NUTRITION:
calories 232, fat 9, fiber 3, carbs 6, protein 10

Oregano Pork Chops

Preparation time: 10 minutes
Cooking time: 8 hours
Servings: 4

INGREDIENTS:
4 pork chops
1 tablespoon oregano, chopped
2 garlic cloves, minced
1 tablespoon olive oil
15 ounces canned tomatoes, chopped
1 tablespoon tomato paste
Salt and black pepper to the taste
¼ cup tomato juice

DIRECTIONS:
In your Slow cooker, mix pork with oregano,

garlic, oil, tomatoes, tomato paste, salt, pepper and tomato juice, cover and cook on Low for 8 hours. Divide everything between plates and serve.

NUTRITION:
calories 210, fat 10, fiber 2, carbs 15, protein 25

Maple Beef

Preparation time: 10 minutes
Cooking time: 7 hours
Servings: 2

INGREDIENTS:
1 pound beef roast, sliced
1 tablespoon maple syrup
2 tablespoons balsamic vinegar
2 teaspoons olive oil
½ teaspoon Italian seasoning
A pinch of salt and black pepper
1 tablespoon coriander, chopped
½ cup beef stock

DIRECTIONS:
In your slow cooker, mix the roast with the maple syrup, vinegar and the other ingredients, toss, put the lid on and cook on Low for 7 hours. Divide the mix between plates and serve.

NUTRITION:
calories 200, fat 11, fiber 3, carbs 6, protein 15

Spicy Pork

Preparation time: 4 hours and 10 minutes
Cooking time: 7 hours
Servings: 4

INGREDIENTS:
¼ cup lime juice
4 pork rib chops
1 tablespoon olive oil
2 garlic cloves, minced
1 tablespoon chili powder
1 teaspoon cinnamon, ground
2 teaspoons cumin, ground
Salt and black pepper to the taste
½ teaspoon hot pepper sauce
Sliced mango for serving

DIRECTIONS:
In a bowl, mix lime juice with oil, garlic, cumin, cinnamon, chili powder, salt, pepper and hot pepper sauce, whisk well, add pork chops, toss to coat and leave aside in the fridge for 4 hours. Transfer pork and marinade to your Slow cooker, cover and cook on Low for 7 hours. Divide between plates and serve with mango slices on the side.

NUTRITION:
calories 200, fat 8, fiber 1, carbs 12, protein 26

Rosemary Beef

Preparation time: 10 minutes
Cooking time: 7 hours
Servings: 2

INGREDIENTS:
1 pound beef roast, sliced
1 tablespoon rosemary, chopped
Juice of ½ lemon
1 tablespoon olive oil
½ cup tomato sauce
A pinch of salt and black pepper

DIRECTIONS:
In your slow cooker, mix the roast with the rosemary, lemon juice and the other ingredients, toss, put the lid on and cook on Low for 7 hours. Divide everything between plates and serve.

NUTRITION:
calories 210, fat 5, fiber 3, carbs 8, protein 12

Beef Meatballs Casserole

Preparation time: 10 minutes
Cooking time: 7 hours
Servings: 8

INGREDIENTS:
1/3 cup flour
2 eggs
1 pound beef sausage, chopped
1 pound beef, ground
Salt and black pepper to taste
1 tablespoons parsley, dried
¼ teaspoon red pepper flakes
¼ cup parmesan, grated
¼ teaspoon onion powder
½ teaspoon garlic powder
¼ teaspoon oregano, dried
1 cup ricotta cheese
2 cups marinara sauce
1 and ½ cups mozzarella cheese, shredded

DIRECTIONS:
In a bowl, mix sausage with beef, salt, pepper, almond flour, parsley, pepper flakes, onion powder, garlic powder, oregano, parmesan and eggs, stir well and shape meatballs out of this mix. Arrange meatballs in your Slow cooker, add half of the marinara sauce, ricotta cheese and top with the rest of the marinara. Add mozzarella at the end, cover and cook on Low for 7 hours. Divide between plates and serve.

NUTRITION:
calories 456, fat 35, fiber 3, carbs 12, protein 32

Parsley and Chili Lamb

Preparation time: 10 minutes
Cooking time: 4 hours
Servings: 2

INGREDIENTS:
- 1 pound lamb meat, roughly cubed
- 1 tablespoon avocado oil
- 2 red chilies, chopped
- ½ teaspoon chili powder
- 1 tablespoon parsley, chopped
- ½ cup tomato sauce
- ½ teaspoon oregano, dried
- Juice of 1 lime
- Salt and black pepper to the taste

DIRECTIONS:
In your slow cooker, mix the lamb with the oil, chilies and the other ingredients, toss, put the lid on and cook on High for 4 hours. Divide the mix between plates and serve right away.

NUTRITION:
calories 248, fat 11, fiber 3, carbs 6, protein 15

Beef Stuffed Squash

Preparation time: 10 minutes
Cooking time: 7 hours
Servings: 2

INGREDIENTS:
- 2 pounds spaghetti squash, halved
- 1 cup chicken stock
- Salt and black pepper to the taste
- 3 garlic cloves, minced
- 1 yellow onion, chopped
- 1 Portobello mushroom, sliced
- 28 ounces canned tomatoes, chopped
- 1 teaspoon oregano, dried
- ¼ teaspoon cayenne pepper
- ½ teaspoon thyme, dried
- 1 pound beef, ground
- 1 green bell pepper, chopped

DIRECTIONS:
Heat up a pan over medium-high heat, add meat, garlic, onion and mushroom, stir and cook until meat browns. Add salt, pepper, thyme, oregano, cayenne, tomatoes and green pepper, stir and cook for 10 minutes. Stuff squash halves with this beef mix, return to the slow cooker, cover and cook on High for 4 hours. Divide between 2 plates and serve.

NUTRITION:
calories 260, fat 7, fiber 2, carbs 14, protein 10

Cumin Pork Chops

Preparation time: 10 minutes
Cooking time: 5 hours
Servings: 2

INGREDIENTS:
- 1 pound pork chops
- 2 tablespoons olive oil
- 2 tablespoons balsamic vinegar
- ½ teaspoon cumin, ground
- ½ cup beef stock
- A pinch of salt and black pepper
- 1 tablespoon chives, chopped

DIRECTIONS:
In your slow cooker, mix the pork chops with the oil, vinegar and the other ingredients, toss, put the lid on and cook on High for 5 hours. Divide everything between plates and serve.

NUTRITION:
calories 233, fat 9, fiber 3, carbs 7, protein 14

Beef and Tzatziki

Preparation time: 10 minutes
Cooking time: 7 hours
Servings: 6

INGREDIENTS:
- ¼ cup milk
- 17 ounces beef, ground
- 1 yellow onion, grated
- 5 bread slices, torn
- 1 egg, whisked
- ¼ cup parsley, chopped
- Salt and black pepper to the taste
- 2 garlic cloves, minced
- ¼ cup mint, chopped
- 2 and ½ teaspoons oregano, dried
- ¼ cup olive oil
- 7 ounces cherry tomatoes, cut into halves
- 1 cucumber, thinly sliced
- 1 cup baby spinach
- 1 and ½ tablespoons lemon juice
- 7 ounces jarred tzatziki

DIRECTIONS:
Put torn bread in a bowl, add milk and leave aside for 3 minutes. Squeeze bread, chop, put into a bowl, add beef, egg, salt, pepper, oregano, mint, parsley, garlic and onion, stir well, shape balls from this mix and place them in your Slow cooker. Add tzatziki, cover and cook on Low for 7 hours. In a salad bowl, mix spinach with cucumber, tomatoes, oil, meatballs, salt, pepper and lemon juice, toss and serve.

NUTRITION:
calories 200, fat 4, fiber 1, carbs 12, protein 7

Paprika Lamb

Preparation time: 10 minutes

Cooking time: 4 hours

Servings: 2

INGREDIENTS:
1 pound lamb chops
1 tablespoon sweet paprika
½ cup beef stock
2 tablespoons avocado oil
2 scallions, chopped
A pinch of salt and black pepper

DIRECTIONS:
In your slow cooker, mix the lamb chops with the paprika, stock and the other ingredients, toss, put the lid on and cook on High for 4 hours. Divide the mix between plates and serve with a side salad.

NUTRITION:
calories 227, fat 14, fiber 4, carbs 6, protein 16

German Beef Soup

Preparation time: 10 minutes

Cooking time: 6 hours

Servings: 8

INGREDIENTS:
3 teaspoons olive oil
1 pound beef, ground
14 ounces beef stock
2 cups chicken stock
14 ounces canned tomatoes and juice
1 tablespoon sugar
14 ounces sauerkraut, chopped
1 tablespoon Worcestershire sauce
4 bay leaves
Salt and black pepper to the taste
3 tablespoons parsley, chopped
1 onion, chopped
1 teaspoon sage, dried
1 tablespoon garlic, minced
2 cups water

DIRECTIONS:
Heat up a pan with the oil over medium heat, add beef, stir, brown for 10 minutes and transfer to your Slow cooker. Add chicken and beef stock, sauerkraut, sugar, canned tomatoes, Worcestershire sauce, parsley, sage, bay leaves, onions, garlic, water, salt and pepper, stir, cover and cook on Low for 6 hours. Divide into bowls and serve.

NUTRITION:
calories 250, fat 5, fiber 1, carbs 12, protein 23

Beef with Peas and Corn

Preparation time: 10 minutes

Cooking time: 7 hours

Servings: 2

INGREDIENTS:
1 pound beef stew meat, cubed
½ cup corn
½ cup fresh peas
2 scallions, chopped
1 tablespoon lime juice
1 cup beef stock
2 tablespoons tomato paste
½ cup chives, chopped

DIRECTIONS:
In your slow cooker, mix the beef with the corn, peas and the other ingredients, toss, put the lid on and cook on Low for 7 hours. Divide the mix between plates and serve right away.

NUTRITION:
calories 236, fat 12, fiber 2, carbs 7, protein 15

Oregano Lamb

Preparation time: 10 minutes

Cooking time: 7 hours

Servings: 4

INGREDIENTS:
2 teaspoons paprika
2 garlic cloves, minced
2 teaspoons oregano, dried
2 tablespoons sumac
12 lamb cutlets
¼ cup olive oil
2 tablespoons water
2 teaspoons cumin, ground
4 carrots, sliced
¼ cup parsley, chopped
2 teaspoons harissa
1 tablespoon red wine vinegar
Salt and black pepper to the taste
2 tablespoons black olives, pitted and sliced
6 radishes, thinly sliced

DIRECTIONS:
In a bowl, mix cutlets with paprika, garlic, oregano, sumac, salt, pepper, half of the oil and the water and rub well. Put carrots in your Slow cooker and add olives and radishes. In another bowl, mix harissa with the rest of the oil, parsley, cumin, vinegar and a splash of water and stir well. Add this over carrots mix, season with salt and pepper and toss to coat. Add lamb cutlets, cover, cook on Low for 7 hours, divide everything between plates and serve.

NUTRITION:
calories 245, fat 32, fiber 6, carbs 12, protein 34

Lime Pork Chops

Preparation time: 10 minutes

Cooking time: 7 hours

Servings: 2

INGREDIENTS:
1 pound pork chops
1 tablespoon lime zest,

grated
Juice of 1 lime
½ teaspoon turmeric powder
1 cup beef stock
2 tablespoons olive oil
A pinch of salt and black pepper

DIRECTIONS:
In your slow cooker, mix the pork chops with the lime juice, zest and the other ingredients, toss, put the lid on and cook on Low for 7 hours. Divide the mix between plates and serve.

NUTRITION:
calories 273, fat 12, fiber 4, carbs 7, protein 17

Lamb Casserole

Preparation time: 10 minutes

Cooking time: 7 hours

Servings: 2

INGREDIENTS:
2 garlic cloves, minced
1 red onion, chopped
1 tablespoon olive oil
1 celery stick, chopped
10 ounces lamb fillet, cut into medium pieces
Salt and black pepper to the taste
1 and ¼ cups lamb stock
2 carrots, chopped
½ tablespoon rosemary, chopped
1 leek, chopped
1 tablespoon mint sauce
1 teaspoon sugar
1 tablespoon tomato puree
½ cauliflower, florets separated
½ celeriac, chopped
2 tablespoons butter

DIRECTIONS:
Heat up a slow cooker with the oil over medium heat, add garlic, onion and celery, stir and cook for 5 minutes. Add lamb pieces, stir, brown for 3 minutes and transfer everything to your Slow cooker. Add carrot, leek, rosemary, stock, tomato puree, mint sauce, sugar, cauliflower, celeriac, butter, salt and black pepper, cover and cook on Low for 7 hours. Divide lamb and all the veggies between plates and serve.

NUTRITION:
calories 324, fat 4, fiber 5, carbs 12, protein 20

Lamb with Capers

Preparation time: 10 minutes

Cooking time: 4 hours

Servings: 2

INGREDIENTS:
1 pound lamb chops
1 tablespoon capers
½ cup beef stock
¼ cup tomato passata
½ teaspoon sweet paprika
½ teaspoon chili powder
2 tablespoons olive oil
3 scallions, chopped
A pinch of salt and black pepper

DIRECTIONS:
In your slow cooker, mix the lamb chops with the capers, stock and the other ingredients, toss, put the lid on and cook on High for 4 hours. Divide the mix between plates and serve.

NUTRITION:
calories 244, fat 12, fiber 2, carbs 5, protein 16

Lavender and Orange Lamb

Preparation time: 2 hours

Cooking time: 7 hours

Servings: 4

INGREDIENTS:
2 tablespoons rosemary, chopped
1 and ½ pounds lamb chops
Salt and black pepper to the taste
1 tablespoon lavender, chopped
2 garlic cloves, minced
1 red orange, cut into halves
2 red oranges, peeled and cut into segments
2 small pieces of orange peel
1 teaspoon butter

DIRECTIONS:
In a bowl, mix lamb chops with salt, pepper, rosemary, lavender, garlic and orange peel, toss to coat and leave aside for a couple of hours in the fridge. Put the butter in your Slow cooker, add lamb chops, squeeze 1 orange over them, add the rest of the oranges over the lamb, cover slow cooker and cook on Low for 7 hours. Divide lamb and sauce all over and serve.

NUTRITION:
calories 250, fat 5, fiber 7, carbs 15, protein 20

Lamb and Zucchini Mix

Preparation time: 10 minutes

Cooking time: 4 hours

Servings: 2

INGREDIENTS:
1 pound lamb stew meat, ground
2 zucchinis, cubed
2 teaspoons olive oil
1 carrot, peeled and sliced
½ cup beef stock
2 tablespoons tomato paste
½ teaspoon cumin, ground
1 tablespoon chives, chopped
A pinch of salt and black pepper

DIRECTIONS:
In your slow cooker, mix the lamb with the zucchinis, oil, carrot and the other ingredients, toss, put the lid on and cook on High for 4 hours. Divide the mix into bowls and serve hot.

NUTRITION:
calories 254, fat 14, fiber 3, carbs 6, protein 17

Lamb and Orange Sauce

Preparation time: 10 minutes

Cooking time: 4 hours

Servings: 4

INGREDIENTS:
- 2 lamb shanks
- Salt and black pepper to the taste
- 1 garlic head, peeled
- 4 tablespoons olive oil
- Zest of ½ orange
- Juice of ½ orange
- ½ teaspoon oregano, dried

DIRECTIONS:
In your Slow cooker, mix lamb with salt, pepper and garlic, cover and cook on High for 4 hours. In a bowl, mix orange juice with orange zest, salt, pepper, olive oil and oregano and whisk very well. Shred lamb meat, discard bone, divide meat between plates. Drizzle the orange sauce all over and serve.

NUTRITION:
calories 260, fat 7, fiber 3, carbs 15, protein 12

Beef and Peppers

Preparation time: 10 minutes

Cooking time: 4 hours

Servings: 2

INGREDIENTS:
- 1 pound lamb stew meat, cubed
- 1 red bell pepper, cut into strips
- 1 green bell pepper, cut into strips
- 1 orange bell pepper, cut into strips
- 2 teaspoons olive oil
- A pinch of salt and black pepper
- 1 cup beef stock
- 1 tablespoon chives, chopped
- ½ teaspoon sweet paprika

DIRECTIONS:
In your slow cooker, mix the lamb with the peppers and the other ingredients, toss, put the lid on and cook on High for 4 hours. Divide the mix between plate sand serve.

NUTRITION:
calories 263, fat 14, fiber 3, carbs 6, protein 20

Lamb and Mint Pesto

Preparation time: 1 hour

Cooking time: 7 hours

Servings: 4

INGREDIENTS:
- 1 cup parsley
- 1 cup mint
- 1 small yellow onion, roughly chopped
- 1/3 cup pistachios
- 1 teaspoon lemon zest
- 5 tablespoons avocado oil
- Salt to the taste
- 2 pounds lamb riblets
- ½ onion, chopped
- 5 garlic cloves, minced
- Juice of 1 orange

DIRECTIONS:
In your food processor, mix parsley with mint, 1 small onion, pistachios, lemon zest, salt and avocado oil and blend very well. Rub lamb with this mix, place in a bowl, cover and leave in the fridge for 1 hour. Transfer lamb and pesto to your Slow cooker, add garlic and ½ onion, drizzle orange juice, cover, cook on Low for 7 hours. Divide everything between plates and serve.

NUTRITION:
calories 200, fat 4, fiber 1, carbs 15, protein 16

Cayenne Lamb Mix

Preparation time: 10 minutes

Cooking time: 4 hours

Servings: 2

INGREDIENTS:
- 1 pound lamb stew meat, cubed
- ½ cup tomato sauce
- ½ teaspoon cayenne pepper
- 1 red onion, sliced
- 2 teaspoons olive oil
- ½ teaspoon sweet paprika
- A pinch of salt and black pepper
- 1 tablespoon cilantro, chopped

DIRECTIONS:
In your slow cooker, mix the lamb with the tomato sauce, cayenne and the other ingredients, toss, put the lid on and cook on High for 4 hours.. Divide the mix between plates and serve.

NUTRITION:
calories 283, fat 13, fiber 4, carbs 6, protein 16

Lamb and Fennel Mix

Preparation time: 10 minutes

Cooking time: 7 hours

Servings: 4

INGREDIENTS:
12 ounces lamb racks
2 fennel bulbs, sliced
Salt and black pepper to the taste
2 tablespoons olive oil
4 figs, cut into halves
1/8 cup apple cider vinegar
1 tablespoon sugar

DIRECTIONS:
In a bowl, mix fennel with figs, vinegar, sugar and oil, toss to coat well and transfer to your Slow cooker. Add lamb, salt and pepper, cover and cook on Low for 7 hours. Divide between plates and serve.

NUTRITION:
calories 230, fat 3, fiber 3, carbs 5, protein 10

Cinnamon Lamb
Preparation time: 10 minutes
Cooking time: 6 hours
Servings: 2

INGREDIENTS:
1 pound lamb chops
1 teaspoon cinnamon powder
1 red onion, chopped
1 tablespoon avocado oil
1 tablespoon oregano, chopped
½ cup beef stock
1 tablespoon chives, chopped

DIRECTIONS:
In your slow cooker, mix the lamb chops with the cinnamon and the other ingredients, toss, put the lid on and cook on Low for 6 hours. Divide the chops between plates and serve with a side salad.

NUTRITION:
calories 253, fat 14, fiber 2, carbs 6, protein 18

Beef and Pancetta
Preparation time: 10 minutes
Cooking time: 4 hours and 10 minutes
Servings: 4

INGREDIENTS:
8 ounces pancetta, chopped
4 pounds beef, cubed
4 garlic cloves, minced
2 brown onions, chopped
2 tablespoons olive oil
4 tablespoons red vinegar
4 cups beef stock
2 tablespoons tomato paste
2 cinnamon sticks
3 lemon peel strips
A handful parsley, chopped
4 thyme springs
2 tablespoons butter
Salt and black pepper to the taste

DIRECTIONS:
Heat up a pan with the oil over medium-high heat, add pancetta, onion and garlic, stir, cook for 5 minutes, add beef, stir and brown for a few minutes Add vinegar, salt, pepper, stock, tomato paste, cinnamon, lemon peel, thyme and butter, stir, cook for 3 minutes more, transfer everything to your Slow cooker, cook on High for 4 hours, discard cinnamon, lemon peel and thyme, add parsley, stir, divide between plates and serve.

NUTRITION:
calories 250, fat 6, fiber 1, carbs 17, protein 33

Lamb and Kale
Preparation time: 10 minutes
Cooking time: 4 hours
Servings: 2

INGREDIENTS:
1 pound lamb shoulder, cubed
1 cup baby kale
1 tablespoon olive oil
1 yellow onion, chopped
½ teaspoon coriander, ground
½ teaspoon cumin, ground
½ teaspoon sweet paprika
A pinch of salt and black pepper
¼ cup beef stock
1 tablespoon chives, chopped

DIRECTIONS:
In your slow cooker, mix the lamb with the kale, oil, onion and the other ingredients, toss, put the lid on and cook on High for 4 hours. Divide everything between plates and serve.

NUTRITION:
calories 264, fat 14, fiber 3, carbs 6, protein 17

Veal Stew
Preparation time: 10 minutes
Cooking time: 8 hours
Servings: 12

INGREDIENTS:
2 tablespoons avocado oil
3 pounds veal, cubed
1 yellow onion, chopped
1 small garlic clove, minced
Salt and black pepper to the taste
1 cup water
1 and ½ cups marsala wine
10 ounces canned tomato paste
1 carrot, chopped
7 ounces mushrooms, chopped
3 egg yolks
½ cup heavy cream
2 teaspoons oregano, dried

DIRECTIONS:
Heat up a slow cooker with the oil over medium-high heat, add veal, stir, brown for a few minutes, transfer to your Slow cooker, add garlic, onion, wine, water, oregano, tomato paste, mushrooms, carrots, salt and pepper, stir, cover and cook on Low for 7 hours and 30 minutes In a bowl, mix cream with egg yolks and whisk well. Pour this over the meat, cover and cook on Low for 30 minutes more. Divide between plates and serve hot.

NUTRITION:
calories 254, fat 15, fiber 6, carbs 13, protein 23

Beef and Sprouts
Preparation time: 10 minutes
Cooking time: 7 hours
Servings: 2

INGREDIENTS:
1 teaspoon olive oil
1 pound beef stew meat, roughly cubed
1 cup Brussels sprouts, trimmed and halved
1 red onion, chopped
1 cup tomato passata
A pinch of salt and black pepper
1 tablespoon chives, chopped

DIRECTIONS:
In your slow cooker, mix the beef with the sprouts, oil and the other ingredients, toss, put the lid on and cook on Low for 7 hours. Divide the mix between plates and serve.

NUTRITION:
calories 273, fat 13, fiber 2, carbs 6, protein 15

Veal and Tomatoes
Preparation time: 10 minutes
Cooking time: 7 hours
Servings: 4

INGREDIENTS:
4 medium veal leg steaks
1 teaspoon avocado oil
2 garlic cloves, minced
1 red onion, chopped
Salt and black pepper to the taste
2 teaspoons sage, chopped
15 ounces canned tomatoes, chopped
2 tablespoons parsley, chopped
1 ounce bocconcini, sliced

DIRECTIONS:
Heat up a pan with the oil over medium-high heat, add veal, brown for 2 minutes on each side and transfer to your Slow cooker. Add onion, sage, garlic, tomatoes, parsley, bocconcini, salt and pepper, cover and cook on Low for 7 hours. Divide between plates and serve.

NUTRITION:
calories 276, fat 6, fiber 4, carbs 15, protein 36

Veal Piccata
Preparation time: 10 minutes
Cooking time: 7 hours
Servings: 2

INGREDIENTS:
2 tablespoons butter
¼ cup white wine
¼ cup chicken stock
1 and ½ tablespoons capers
1 garlic clove, minced
8 ounces veal cutlets
Salt and black pepper to the taste

DIRECTIONS:
Heat up a pan with half of the butter over medium-high heat, add veal cutlets, season with salt and pepper, cook for 1 minute on each side and transfer to your Slow cooker. Add garlic, wine, stock, capers and the rest of the butter, cover and cook on Low for 7 hours. Divide between plates and serve right away.

NUTRITION:
calories 204, fat 12, fiber 1, carbs 15, protein 29

Pork Chops and Spinach
Preparation time: 10 minutes
Cooking time: 4 hours
Servings: 2

INGREDIENTS:
1 pound pork chops
1 cup baby spinach
½ cup beef stock
¼ cup tomato passata
½ teaspoon sweet paprika
½ teaspoon coriander, ground
4 scallions, chopped
2 teaspoons olive oil
A pinch of salt and black pepper
1 tablespoon chives, chopped

DIRECTIONS:
In your slow cooker, mix the pork chops with the stock, passata and the other ingredients except the spinach, toss, put the lid on and cook on High for 3 hours and 30 minutes. Add the spinach, cook on High for 30 minutes more, divide the mix between plates and serve.

NUTRITION:
calories 274, fat 14, fiber 2, carbs 6, protein 16

Sausage Mix

Preparation time: 5 minutes
Cooking time: 4 hours
Servings: 4

INGREDIENTS:

1 cup yellow onion, chopped
1 and ½ pound Italian pork sausage, sliced
½ cup red bell pepper, chopped
Salt and black pepper to the taste
5 pounds kale, chopped
1 teaspoon garlic, minced
¼ cup red hot chili pepper, chopped
1 cup water

DIRECTIONS:
In your Slow cooker, mix onion with sausage, bell pepper, salt, pepper, garlic, chili pepper and water, cover and cook on High for 3 hours. Add kale, toss a bit, cover and cook on High for 1 more hour. Divide between plates and serve.

NUTRITION:
calories 250, fat 4, fiber 1, carbs 12, protein 20

Green Curry Lamb

Preparation time: 10 minutes
Cooking time: 6 hours
Servings: 2

INGREDIENTS:

1 pound lamb stew meat, cubed
2 garlic cloves, minced
1 tablespoon green curry paste
A pinch of salt and black pepper
1 cup beef stock
½ teaspoon rosemary, dried
1 tablespoon cilantro, chopped

DIRECTIONS:
In your slow cooker, mix the lamb with the garlic, curry paste and the other ingredients, toss, put the lid on and cook on Low for 6 hours. Divide the mix between plates and serve.

NUTRITION:
calories 264, fat 14, fiber 2, carbs 8, protein 12

Cheesy Sausage Casserole

Preparation time: 10 minutes
Cooking time: 4 hours
Servings: 4

INGREDIENTS:

2 tablespoons olive oil
2 pounds Italian pork sausage, chopped
1 onion, sliced
4 sun-dried tomatoes, thinly sliced
Salt and black pepper to the taste
½ pound Gouda cheese, grated
3 yellow chopped
3 orange bell pepper chopped
A pinch of red pepper flakes
1 tablespoon parsley, chopped

DIRECTIONS:
Heat up a pan with the oil over medium-high heat, add sausage slices, stir, cook for 3 minutes on each side and transfer to your Slow cooker. Add onion, tomatoes, salt, pepper, orange bell pepper, red bell pepper, pepper flakes and sprinkle Gouda cheese at the end. Cover slow cooker, cook on High for 4 hours, sprinkle parsley on top, divide between plates and serve.

NUTRITION:
calories 260, fat 5, fiber 3, carbs 16, protein 14

Oregano Lamb

Preparation time: 10 minutes
Cooking time: 6 hours
Servings: 2

INGREDIENTS:

1 pound lamb stew meat, roughly cubed
1 teaspoon hot paprika
1 tablespoon oregano, chopped
½ teaspoon turmeric
powder
4 scallions, chopped
A pinch of salt and black pepper
1 cup beef stock

DIRECTIONS:
In your slow cooker, mix the lamb with the paprika, oregano and the other ingredients, toss, put the lid on and cook on Low for 6 hours. Divide the mix between plates and serve with a side salad.

NUTRITION:
calories 200, fat 9, fiber 2, carbs 6, protein 12

Sausage Soup

Preparation time: 10 minutes
Cooking time: 6 hours
Servings: 6

INGREDIENTS:

1 tablespoon avocado oil
32 ounces pork sausage meat, ground
10 ounces canned tomatoes and jalapenos, chopped
10 ounces spinach
1 green bell pepper, chopped

...blespoon chili
...wder
...teaspoon garlic powder
1 teaspoon Italian seasoning

DIR...

Heat up a p... ne oil over medium heat, add sausage, stir, bro.. n for a couple of minutes on all sides and transfer to your Slow cooker. Add green bell pepper, canned tomatoes and jalapenos, stock, onion powder, salt, pepper, cumin, chili powder, garlic powder, Italian seasoning and stock, stir, cover and cook on Low for 5 hours and 30 minutes. Add spinach, cover, cook on Low for 30 minutes more, stir soup, ladle it into bowls and serve.

NUTRITION:
calories 524, fat 43, fiber 2, carbs 15, protein 26

Pesto Lamb Chops

Preparation time: 10 minutes
Cooking time: 6 hours
Servings: 2

INGREDIENTS:
1 pound lamb chops
2 tablespoons basil pesto
1 tablespoon sweet paprika
2 tablespoons olive oil
A pinch of salt and black pepper
½ cup beef stock

DIRECTIONS:
In your slow cooker, mix the lamb chops with the pesto, paprika and the other ingredients, toss, put the lid on and cook on Low for 6 hours. Divide the mix between plates and serve.

NUTRITION:
calories 234, fat 11, fiber 3, carbs 7, protein 15

Italian Sausage Soup

Preparation time: 10 minutes
Cooking time: 6 hours
Servings: 12

INGREDIENTS:
64 ounces chicken stock
1 teaspoon olive oil
1 cup heavy cream
10 ounces spinach
6 bacon slices, chopped
1 pound radishes, chopped
2 garlic cloves, minced
Salt and black pepper to the taste
A pinch of red pepper flakes, crushed
1 yellow onion, chopped
1 and ½ pounds hot pork sausage, chopped

DIRECTIONS:
Heat up a pan with the oil over medium-high heat, add sausage, onion and garlic, stir, brown for a few minutes and transfer to your Slow cooker. Add stock, spinach, radishes, bacon, cream, salt, pepper and red pepper flakes, stir, cover and cook on Low for 6 hours. Ladle soup into bowls and serve.

NUTRITION:
calories 291, fat 22, fiber 2, carbs 14, protein 17

Beef with Green Beans and Cilantro

Preparation time: 10 minutes
Cooking time: 7 hours
Servings: 2

INGREDIENTS:
1 pound beef stew meat, cubed
1 cup green beans, trimmed and halved
1 red onion, sliced
½ teaspoon chili powder
½ teaspoon rosemary, chopped
2 teaspoons olive oil
1 cup beef stock
1 tablespoon cilantro, chopped

DIRECTIONS:
In your slow cooker, mix the beef with the green beans, onion and the other ingredients, toss, put the lid on and cook on Low for 7 hours. Divide the mix between plates and serve right away.

NUTRITION:
calories 273, fat 14, fiber 2, carbs 6, protein 15

Beef Curry

Preparation time: 10 minutes
Cooking time: 8 hours
Servings: 4

INGREDIENTS:
2 pounds beef steak, cubed
2 tablespoons olive oil
3 potatoes, diced
1 tablespoon mustard
2 and ½ tablespoons curry powder
2 yellow onions, chopped
2 garlic cloves, minced
10 ounces canned coconut milk
2 tablespoons tomato sauce
Salt and black pepper to the taste

DIRECTIONS:
In your Slow cooker, mix oil with steak, potatoes,

mustard, curry powder, garlic, coconut milk, tomato sauce, salt and pepper, toss, cover and cook on Low for 8 hours. Stir curry one more time, divide into bowls and serve.

NUTRITION:
calories 432, fat 12, fiber 5, carbs 15, protein 26

Balsamic Lamb Chops

Preparation time: 10 minutes

Cooking time: 6 hours

Servings: 2

INGREDIENTS:
- 1 pound lamb chops
- 2 tablespoons balsamic vinegar
- 1 tablespoon chives, chopped
- 1 tablespoon olive oil
- 4 garlic cloves, minced
- ½ cup beef stock
- A pinch of salt and black pepper

DIRECTIONS:
In your slow cooker, mix the lamb chops with the vinegar and the other ingredients, toss, put the lid on and cook on Low for 6 hours. Divide everything between plates and serve.

NUTRITION:
calories 292, fat 12, fiber 3, carbs 7, protein 16

Flavored and Spicy Beef Mix

Preparation time: 10 minutes

Cooking time: 8 hours

Servings: 6

INGREDIENTS:
- 1 and ½ pounds beef, ground
- 1 sweet onion, chopped
- Salt and black pepper to the taste
- 16 ounces mixed beans, soaked overnight and drained
- 28 ounces canned tomatoes, chopped
- 17 ounces beef stock
- 12 ounces pale ale
- 6 garlic cloves, chopped
- 7 jalapeno peppers, diced
- 2 tablespoons vegetable oil
- 4 carrots, chopped
- 3 tablespoons chili powder
- 1 bay leaf
- 1 teaspoon chipotle powder

DIRECTIONS:
In your Slow cooker, mix oil with beef, onion, salt, pepper, beans, tomatoes, stock, garlic, jalapenos, carrots, chili powder, bay leaf, chipotle powder and pale ale, toss, cover and cook on Low for 8 hours. Divide into bowls and serve.

NUTRITION:
calories 300, fat 4, fiber 5, carbs 20, protein 16

Creamy Beef

Preparation time: 10 minutes

Cooking time: 6 hours

Servings: 2

INGREDIENTS:
- 1 pound beef stew meat, cubed
- 1 cup heavy cream
- 1 red onion, sliced
- ½ teaspoon turmeric powder
- 2 tablespoons olive oil
- 3 scallions, chopped
- 1 tablespoon chives, chopped
- A pinch of salt and black pepper

DIRECTIONS:
In your slow cooker, mix the beef with the cream, onion and the other ingredients, toss, put the lid on and cook on Low for 6 hours. Divide everything between plates and serve.

NUTRITION:
calories 277, fat 14, fiber 3, carbs 7, protein 17

Walnut and Coconut Beef

Preparation time: 10 minutes

Cooking time: 7 hours

Servings: 2

INGREDIENTS:
- 1 pound beef stew meat, cubed
- 2 tablespoons walnuts, chopped
- ½ cup coconut cream
- 2 scallions, chopped
- 1 cup beef stock
- ½ teaspoon Italian seasoning
- A pinch of salt and black pepper
- 1 tablespoon rosemary, chopped

DIRECTIONS:
In your slow cooker, mix the beef with the walnuts, scallions and the other ingredients except the cream, toss, put the lid on and cook on Low for 6 hours. Add the cream, toss, cook on Low for 1 more hour, divide everything between plates and serve.

NUTRITION:
calories 274, fat 12, fiber 4, carbs 7, protein 16

Slow Cooker Fish Recipes

Salmon and Green Onions Mix

Preparation time: 10 minutes
Cooking time: 2 hours
Servings: 4

INGREDIENTS:
- 1 green onions bunch, halved
- 10 tablespoons lemon juice
- 4 salmon fillets, boneless
- Salt and black pepper to the taste
- 2 tablespoons avocado oil

DIRECTIONS:
Grease your Slow cooker with the oil, add salmon, top with onion, lemon juice, salt and pepper, cover, cook on High for 2 hours, divide everything between plates and serve.

NUTRITION:
calories 260, fat 3, fiber 1, carbs 14, protein 14

Lime Shrimp

Preparation time: 10 minutes
Cooking time: 1 hour
Servings: 2

INGREDIENTS:
- 1 pound shrimp, peeled and deveined
- Juice of 1 lime
- 2 scallions, chopped
- ½ teaspoon turmeric powder
- ¼ cup chickens stock
- A pinch of salt and black pepper
- 1 tablespoon chives, chopped

DIRECTIONS:
In your slow cooker, mix the shrimp with the lime juice, scallions and the other ingredients, toss, put the lid on and cook on High for 1 hour. Divide the mix into bowls and serve.

NUTRITION:
calories 198, fat 7, fiber 2, carbs 6, protein 7

Seafood Chowder

Preparation time: 10 minutes
Cooking time: 8 hours and 30 minutes
Servings: 4

INGREDIENTS:
- 2 cups water
- ½ fennel bulb, chopped
- 2 sweet potatoes, cubed
- 1 yellow onion, chopped
- 2 bay leaves
- 1 tablespoon thyme, dried
- 1 celery rib, chopped
- Salt and black pepper to the taste
- 1 bottle clam juice
- 2 tablespoons tapioca powder
- 1 cup coconut milk
- 1 pounds salmon fillets, cubed
- 5 sea scallops, halved
- 24 shrimp, peeled and deveined
- ¼ cup parsley, chopped

DIRECTIONS:
In your Slow cooker, mix water with fennel, potatoes, onion, bay leaves, thyme, celery, clam juice, salt, pepper and tapioca, stir, cover and cook on Low for 8 hours. Add salmon, coconut milk, scallops, shrimp and parsley, cook on Low for 30 minutes more, ladle chowder into bowls and serve.

NUTRITION:
calories 354, fat 10, fiber 2, carbs 10, protein 12

Chili Salmon

Preparation time: 10 minutes
Cooking time: 3 hours
Servings: 2

INGREDIENTS:
- 1 tablespoon avocado oil
- 1 pound salmon fillets, boneless
- 1 red chili pepper, minced
- ½ teaspoon chili powder
- 2 scallions, chopped
- ½ cup chicken stock
- A pinch of salt and black pepper

DIRECTIONS:
In your slow cooker, mix the salmon with the chili pepper, the oil and the other ingredients, rub gently, put the lid on and cook on High for 3 hours. Divide the salmon between plates and serve with a side salad.

NUTRITION:
calories 221, fat 8, fiber 3, carbs 6, protein 7

Asian Salmon Mix

Preparation time: 10 minutes
Cooking time: 3 hours
Servings: 2

INGREDIENTS:
- 2 medium salmon fillets, boneless
- Salt and black pepper to the taste
- 2 tablespoons soy sauce
- 2 tablespoons maple syrup
- 16 ounces mixed broccoli and cauliflower florets
- 2 tablespoons lemon juice
- 1 teaspoon sesame seeds

DIRECTIONS:

Put the cauliflower and broccoli florets in your Slow cooker and top with salmon fillets.

In a bowl, mix maple syrup with soy sauce and lemon juice, whisk well, pour this over salmon fillets, season with salt, pepper, sprinkle sesame seeds on top and cook on Low for 3 hours. Divide everything between plates and serve.

NUTRITION:
calories 230, fat 4, fiber 2, carbs 12, protein 6

Rosemary Shrimp

Preparation time: 10 minutes

Cooking time: 1 hour

Servings: 2

INGREDIENTS:
- 1 pound shrimp, peeled and deveined
- 1 tablespoon avocado oil
- 1 tablespoon rosemary, chopped
- ½ teaspoon sweet paprika
- ½ teaspoon cumin, ground
- 3 garlic cloves, crushed
- 1 cup chicken stock
- A pinch of salt and black pepper

DIRECTIONS:
In your slow cooker, mix the shrimp with the oil, rosemary and the other ingredients, toss, put the lid on and cook on High for 1 hour. Divide the mix into bowls and serve.

NUTRITION:
calories 235, fat 8, fiber 4, carbs 7, protein 9

Shrimp Mix

Preparation time: 10 minutes

Cooking time: 1 hour and 30 minutes

Servings: 4

INGREDIENTS:
- 2 tablespoons olive oil
- 1 pound shrimp, peeled and deveined
- ¼ cup chicken stock
- 1 tablespoon garlic, minced
- 2 tablespoons parsley, chopped
- Juice of ½ lemon
- Salt and black pepper to the taste

DIRECTIONS:
Put the oil in your Slow cooker, add stock, garlic, parsley, lemon juice, salt and pepper and whisk really well. Add shrimp, stir, cover, cook on High for 1 hour and 30 minutes, divide into bowls and serve.

NUTRITION:
calories 240, fat 4, fiber 3, carbs 9, protein 3

Paprika Cod

Preparation time: 10 minutes

Cooking time: 3 hours

Servings: 2

INGREDIENTS:
- 1 tablespoon olive oil
- 1 pound cod fillets, boneless
- 1 teaspoon sweet paprika
- ¼ cup chicken stock
- ¼ cup white wine
- 2 scallions, chopped
- ½ teaspoon rosemary, dried
- A pinch of salt and black pepper

DIRECTIONS:
In your slow cooker, mix the cod with the paprika, oil and the other ingredients, toss gently, put the lid on and cook on High for 3 hours. Divide everything between plates and serve.

NUTRITION:
calories 211, fat 8, fiber 4, carbs 8, protein 8

Asian Steamed Fish

Preparation time: 10 minutes

Cooking time: 1 hour

Servings: 4

INGREDIENTS:
- 2 tablespoons sugar
- 4 salmon fillets, boneless
- 2 tablespoons soy sauce
- ¼ cup olive oil
- ¼ cup veggie stock
- 1 small ginger piece, grated
- 6 garlic cloves, minced
- 2 tablespoons Worcestershire sauce
- 1 bunch leeks, chopped
- 1 bunch cilantro, chopped

DIRECTIONS:
Put the oil in your slow cooker, add leeks and top with the fish. In a bowl, mix stock with ginger, sugar, garlic, cilantro and soy sauce, stir, add this over fish, cover and cook on High for 1 hour. Divide fish between plates and serve with the sauce drizzled on top.

NUTRITION:
calories 300, fat 8, fiber 2, carbs 12, protein 6

Spicy Tuna

Preparation time: 10 minutes

Cooking time: 2 hours

Servings: 2

INGREDIENTS:
- 1 pound tuna fillets, boneless and cubed
- ½ teaspoon red pepper flakes, crushed
- ¼ teaspoon cayenne pepper
- ½ cup chicken stock
- ½ teaspoon chili powder
- 1 tablespoon olive oil
- A pinch of salt and black pepper
- 1 tablespoon chives, chopped

DIRECTIONS:
In your slow cooker, mix the tuna with the pepper flakes, cayenne and the other ingredients, toss, put the lid on and cook on High for 2 hours. Divide the tuna mix between plates and serve.

NUTRITION:
calories 193, fat 7, fiber 3, carbs 6, protein 6

Poached Cod and Pineapple Mix

Preparation time: 10 minutes
Cooking time: 4 hours
Servings: 2

INGREDIENTS:
- 1 pound cod, boneless
- 6 garlic cloves, minced
- 1 small ginger pieces, chopped
- ½ tablespoon black peppercorns
- 1 cup pineapple juice
- 1 cup pineapple, chopped
- ¼ cup white vinegar
- 4 jalapeno peppers, chopped
- Salt and black pepper to the taste

DIRECTIONS:
Put the fish in your crock, season with salt and pepper. Add garlic, ginger, peppercorns, pineapple juice, pineapple chunks, vinegar and jalapenos. Stir gently, cover and cook on Low for 4 hours. Divide fish between plates, top with the pineapple mix and serve.

NUTRITION:
calories 240, fat 4, fiber 4, carbs 14, protein 10

Ginger Tuna

Preparation time: 5 minutes
Cooking time: 2 hours
Servings: 2

INGREDIENTS:
- 1 pound tuna fillets, boneless and roughly cubed
- 1 tablespoon ginger, grated
- 1 red onion, chopped
- 2 teaspoons olive oil
- Juice of 1 lime
- ¼ cup chicken stock
- 1 tablespoon chives, chopped
- A pinch of salt and black pepper

DIRECTIONS:
In your slow cooker, mix the tuna with the ginger, onion and the other ingredients, toss, put the lid on and cook on High for 2 hours. Divide the mix into bowls and serve.

NUTRITION:
calories 200, fat 11, fiber 4, carbs 5, protein 12

Chili Catfish

Preparation time: 10 minutes
Cooking time: 6 hours
Servings: 4

INGREDIENTS:
- 1 catfish, boneless and cut into 4 pieces
- 3 red chili peppers, chopped
- ½ cup sugar
- ¼ cup water
- 1 tablespoon soy sauce
- 1 shallot, minced
- A small ginger piece, grated
- 1 tablespoon coriander, chopped

DIRECTIONS:
Put catfish pieces in your Slow cooker. Heat up a pan with the coconut sugar over medium-high heat and stir until it caramelizes. Add soy sauce, shallot, ginger, water and chili pepper, stir, pour over the fish, add coriander, cover and cook on Low for 6 hours. Divide fish between plates and serve with the sauce from the slow cooker drizzled on top.

NUTRITION:
calories 200, fat 4, fiber 4, carbs 8, protein 10

Chives Shrimp

Preparation time: 10 minutes
Cooking time: 1 hour
Servings: 2

INGREDIENTS:
- 1 pound shrimp, peeled and deveined
- 1 tablespoon chives, chopped
- ½ teaspoon basil, dried
- 1 teaspoon turmeric powder
- 1 tablespoon olive oil
- ½ cup chicken stock

DIRECTIONS:
In your slow cooker, mix the shrimp with the basil, chives and the other ingredients, toss, put the lid on and cook on High for 1 hour. Divide the shrimp between plates and serve with a side salad.

NUTRITION:
calories 200, fat 12, fiber 3, carbs 7, protein 9

Tuna Loin Mix

Preparation time: 10 minutes
Cooking time: 4 hours and 10 minutes
Servings: 2

INGREDIENTS:
½ pound tuna loin, cubed
1 garlic clove, minced
4 jalapeno peppers, chopped
1 cup olive oil
3 red chili peppers, chopped
2 teaspoons black peppercorns, ground
Salt and black pepper to the taste

DIRECTIONS:
Put the oil in your Slow cooker, add chili peppers, jalapenos, peppercorns, salt, pepper and garlic, whisk, cover and cook on Low for 4 hours. Add tuna, stir again, cook on High for 10 minutes more, divide between plates and serve.

NUTRITION:
calories 200, fat 4, fiber 3, carbs 10, protein 4

Coriander Salmon Mix

Preparation time: 5 minutes
Cooking time: 3 hours
Servings: 2

INGREDIENTS:
1 pound salmon fillets, boneless and roughly cubed
1 tablespoon coriander, chopped
½ teaspoon chili powder
¼ cup chicken stock
3 scallions, chopped
Juice of 1 lime
2 teaspoons avocado oil
A pinch of salt and black pepper

DIRECTIONS:
In your slow cooker, mix the salmon with the coriander, chili powder and the other ingredients, toss gently, put the lid on and cook on High for 3 hours. Divide the mix between plates and serve.

NUTRITION:
calories 232, fat 10, fiber 4, carbs 6, protein 9

Creamy Sea Bass

Preparation time: 10 minutes
Cooking time: 1 hour and 30 minutes
Servings: 2

INGREDIENTS:
1 pound sea bass
2 scallion stalks, chopped
1 small ginger piece, grated
1 tablespoon soy sauce
2 cups coconut cream
4 bok choy stalks, chopped
3 jalapeno peppers, chopped
Salt and black pepper to the taste

DIRECTIONS:
Put the cream in your Slow cooker, add ginger, soy sauce, scallions, a pinch of salt, black pepper, jalapenos, stir, top with the fish and bok choy, cover and cook on High for 1 hour and 30 minutes. Divide the fish mix between plates and serve.

NUTRITION:
calories 270, fat 3, fiber 3, carbs 18, protein 17

Tuna and Green Beans

Preparation time: 10 minutes
Cooking time: 3 hours
Servings: 2

INGREDIENTS:
1 pound tuna fillets, boneless
1 cup green beans, trimmed and halved
½ cup chicken stock
½ teaspoon sweet paprika
½ teaspoon garam masala
3 scallions, minced
½ teaspoon ginger, ground
1 tablespoon olive oil
1 tablespoon chives, chopped
Salt and black pepper to the taste

DIRECTIONS:
In your slow cooker, mix the tuna with the green beans, stock and the other ingredients, toss gently, put the lid on and cook on High for 3 hours. Divide the mix between plates and serve.

NUTRITION:
calories 182, fat 7, fiber 3, carbs 6, protein 9

Flavored Cod Fillets

Preparation time: 10 minutes
Cooking time: 2 hours
Servings: 4

INGREDIENTS:
4 medium cod fillets, boneless
¼ teaspoon nutmeg, ground
1 teaspoon ginger, grated
Salt and black pepper to the taste
1 teaspoon onion powder
¼ teaspoon sweet paprika
1 teaspoon cayenne pepper
½ teaspoon cinnamon powder

DIRECTIONS:
In a bowl, mix cod fillets with nutmeg, ginger, salt, pepper, onion powder, paprika, cayenne black pepper and cinnamon, toss, transfer to your Slow cooker, cover and cook on Low for 2 hours. Divide between plates and serve with a side salad.

NUTRITION:
calories 200, fat 4, fiber 2, carbs 14, protein 4

Cod and Corn
Preparation time: 5 minutes
Cooking time: 2 hours
Servings: 2

INGREDIENTS:
1 pound cod fillets, boneless
1 tablespoon avocado oil
½ teaspoon chili powder
½ teaspoon coriander, ground
1 cup corn
½ tablespoon lime juice
1 tablespoon chives, chopped
¼ cup chicken stock
A pinch of salt and black pepper

DIRECTIONS:
In your slow cooker, mix the cod with the oil, corn and the other ingredients, toss, put the lid on and cook on High for 2 hours. Divide the mix between plates and serve.

NUTRITION:
calories 210, fat 8, fiber 3, carbs 6, protein 14

Shrimp and Baby Carrots Mix
Preparation time: 10 minutes
Cooking time: 4 hours and 30 minutes
Servings: 2

INGREDIENTS:
1 small yellow onion, chopped
15 baby carrots
2 garlic cloves, minced
1 small green bell pepper, chopped
8 ounces canned coconut milk
3 tablespoons tomato paste
½ teaspoon red pepper, crushed
¾ tablespoons curry powder
¾ tablespoon tapioca flour
1 pound shrimp, peeled and deveined

DIRECTIONS:
In your food processor, mix onion with garlic, bell pepper, tomato paste, coconut milk, red pepper and curry powder, blend well, add to your Slow cooker, also add baby carrots, stir, cover and cook on Low for 4 hours. Add tapioca and shrimp, stir, cover and cook on Low for 30 minutes more. Divide into bowls and serve.

NUTRITION:
calories 230, fat 4, fiber 3, carbs 14, protein 5

Turmeric Salmon
Preparation time: 5 minutes
Cooking time: 2 hours
Servings: 2

INGREDIENTS:
1 pound salmon fillets, boneless
1 red onion, chopped
½ teaspoon turmeric powder
½ teaspoon oregano, dried
½ cup chicken stock
1 teaspoon olive oil
Salt and black pepper to the taste
1 tablespoon chives, chopped

DIRECTIONS:
In your slow cooker, mix the salmon with the turmeric, onion and the other ingredients, toss gently, put the lid on and cook on High for 2 hours. Divide the mix between plates and serve.

NUTRITION:
calories 200, fat 12, fiber 3, carbs 6, protein 11

Dill Trout
Preparation time: 10 minutes
Cooking time: 2 hours
Servings: 4

INGREDIENTS:
2 lemons, sliced
¼ cup chicken stock
Salt and black pepper to the taste
2 tablespoons dill, chopped
12 ounces spinach
4 medium trout

DIRECTIONS:
Put the stock in your Slow cooker, add the fish inside, season with salt and pepper, top with lemon slices, dill and spinach, cover and cook on High for 2 hours. Divide fish, lemon and spinach between plates and drizzle some of the juice from the slow cooker all over.

NUTRITION:
calories 240, fat 5, fiber 4, carbs 9, protein 14

Sea Bass and Chickpeas
Preparation time: 5 minutes
Cooking time: 3 hours
Servings: 2

INGREDIENTS:
1 pound sea bass fillets,   boneless

½ cup chicken stock
½ cup canned chickpeas, drained and rinsed
2 tablespoons tomato paste
½ teaspoon rosemary, dried
½ teaspoon oregano, dried
2 scallions, minced
1 tablespoon olive oil
Salt and black pepper to the taste

DIRECTIONS:
In your slow cooker, mix the sea bass with the chickpeas, stock and the other ingredients, toss, put the lid on and cook on High for 3 hours. Divide everything between plates and serve.

NUTRITION:
calories 132, fat 9, fiber 2, carbs 5, protein 11

Fish Pie
Preparation time: 10 minutes
Cooking time: 2 hours and 30 minutes
Servings: 6

INGREDIENTS:
1 red onion, chopped
2 salmon fillets, skinless and cut into medium pieces
2 mackerel fillets, skinless and cut into medium pieces
3 haddock fillets and cut into medium pieces
2 bay leaves
¼ cup butter+ 2 tablespoons
1 cauliflower head, florets separated and riced
4 eggs, hard-boiled, peeled and sliced
4 cloves
1 cup whipping cream
½ cup water
A pinch of nutmeg, ground
1 cup cheddar cheese, shredded+ ½ cup
1 tablespoon parsley, chopped
Salt and black pepper to the taste
4 tablespoons chives, chopped

DIRECTIONS:
Put cream and ½ cup water in your Slow cooker, add salmon, mackerel and haddock, onion, cloves and bay leaves, cover and cook on High for 1 hour and 30 minutes Add nutmeg, eggs, 1 cup cheese, ¼ cup butter, cauliflower rice, the rest of the cheddar, chives, parsley, salt, pepper and the rest of the butter, cover and cook on High for 1 more hour. Slice pie, divide between plates and serve.

NUTRITION:
calories 300, fat 45, fiber 3, carbs 5, protein 26

Creamy Shrimp
Preparation time: 10 minutes
Cooking time: 1 hour
Servings: 2

INGREDIENTS:
1 pound shrimp, peeled and deveined
2 scallions, chopped
¼ cup chicken stock
2 tablespoons avocado oil
½ cup heavy cream 1 teaspoon garam masala
1 tablespoon ginger, grated
A pinch of salt and black pepper
1 tablespoon parsley, chopped

DIRECTIONS:
In your slow cooker, mix the shrimp with the scallions, stock and the other ingredients, toss, put the lid on and cook on High for 1 hour. Divide the mix into bowls and serve.

NUTRITION:
calories 200, fat 12, fiber 2, carbs 6, protein 11

Slow Cooked Haddock
Preparation time: 10 minutes
Cooking time: 2 hours
Servings: 4

INGREDIENTS:
1 pound haddock
3 teaspoons water
2 tablespoons lemon juice
Salt and black pepper to the taste
2 tablespoons mayonnaise
1 teaspoon dill, chopped
Cooking spray
½ teaspoon old bay seasoning

DIRECTIONS:
Spray your Slow cooker with the cooking spray, add lemon juice, water, fish, salt, pepper, mayo, dill and old bay seasoning, cover, cook on High for 2 hours. Divide between plates and serve.

NUTRITION:
calories 274, fat 12, fiber 1, carbs 6, protein 20

Parsley Cod
Preparation time: 5 minutes
Cooking time: 2 hours
Servings: 2

INGREDIENTS:
1 pound cod fillets, boneless
3 scallions, chopped
2 teaspoons olive oil
Juice of 1 lime
1 teaspoon coriander, ground
Salt and black pepper to the taste
1 tablespoon parsley, chopped

DIRECTIONS:
In your slow cooker, mix the cod with the scallions, the oil and the other ingredients, rub gently, put

the lid on and cook on High for 1 hour. Divide everything between plates and serve.

NUTRITION:
calories 200, fat 12, fiber 2, carbs 6, protein 9

Buttery Trout

Preparation time: 10 minutes
Cooking time: 2 hours
Servings: 4

INGREDIENTS:
4 trout fillets, boneless
Salt and black pepper to the taste
3 teaspoons lemon zest, grated
3 tablespoons chives, chopped
6 tablespoons butter, melted
2 tablespoons olive oil
2 teaspoons lemon juice

DIRECTIONS:
Put the butter in your Slow cooker, add trout fillets, season with salt, pepper, lemon zest, chives, oil and lemon juice, rub fish a bit, cover and cook on High for 2 hours. Divide fish between plates and serve with the butter sauce drizzled on top.

NUTRITION:
calories 320, fat 12, fiber 6, carbs 12, protein 24

Pesto Cod and Tomatoes

Preparation time: 10 minutes
Cooking time: 3 hours
Servings: 2

INGREDIENTS:
1 pound cod, boneless and roughly cubed
2 tablespoons basil pesto
1 tablespoon olive oil
1 cup cherry tomatoes, halved
1 tablespoon chives, chopped
½ cup veggie stock
A pinch of salt and black pepper

DIRECTIONS:
In your slow cooker, mix the cod with the pesto, oil and the other ingredients, toss, put the lid on and cook on High for 3 hours. Divide the mix between plates and serve.

NUTRITION:
calories 211, fat 13, fiber 2, carbs 7, protein 11

Easy Salmon and Kimchi Sauce

Preparation time: 10 minutes
Cooking time: 2 hours
Servings: 4

INGREDIENTS:
2 tablespoons butter, soft
1 and ¼ pound salmon fillet
2 ounces Kimchi, finely chopped
Salt and black pepper to the taste

DIRECTIONS:
In your food processor, mix butter with Kimchi, blend well, rub salmon with salt, pepper and Kimchi mix, place in your Slow cooker, cover and cook on High for 2 hours. Divide between plates and serve with a side salad.

NUTRITION:
calories 270, fat 12, fiber 5, carbs 13, protein 21

Orange Cod

Preparation time: 5 minutes
Cooking time: 3 hours
Servings: 2

INGREDIENTS:
1 pound cod fillets, boneless
Juice of 1 orange
1 tablespoon avocado oil
2 scallions, chopped
½ teaspoon turmeric powder
½ teaspoon sweet paprika
A pinch of salt and black pepper

DIRECTIONS:
In your slow cooker, mix the cod with the orange juice, oil and the other ingredients, toss, put the lid on and cook on High 3 hours. Divide the mix between plates and serve.

NUTRITION:
calories 200, fat 12, fiber 4, carbs 6, protein 8

Salmon Meatballs and Sauce

Preparation time: 10 minutes
Cooking time: 2 hours
Servings: 4

INGREDIENTS:
2 tablespoons butter
2 garlic cloves, minced
1/3 cup onion, chopped
1 pound wild salmon, boneless and minced
¼ cup chives, chopped
1 egg
2 tablespoons Dijon mustard
1 tablespoon flour
Salt and black pepper to the taste
For the sauce:
4 garlic cloves, minced
2 tablespoons butter, melted
2 tablespoons Dijon mustard
Juice and Zest of 1 lemon
2 cups coconut cream
2 tablespoons chives, chopped

DIRECTIONS:
Heat up a pan with 2 tablespoons butter over medium heat, add onion and 2 garlic cloves, stir, cook for 3 minutes and transfer to a bowl. In another bowl, mix onion and garlic with salmon, chives, flour, salt, pepper, 2 tablespoons mustard and egg and stir well. Shape meatballs from the salmon mix and put them in your Slow cooker. Add 2 tablespoons butter, 4 garlic cloves, coconut cream, 2 teaspoons mustard, lemon juice, lemon zest and chives, cover and cook on High for 2 hours. Divide meatballs on plates, drizzle the sauce all over and serve.

NUTRITION:
calories 271, fat 5, fiber 1, carbs 6, protein 23

Garlic Sea Bass
Preparation time: 5 minutes
Cooking time: 4 hours
Servings: 2

INGREDIENTS:
- 1 pound sea bass fillets, boneless
- 2 teaspoons avocado oil
- 3 garlic cloves, minced
- 1 green chili pepper, minced
- ½ teaspoon rosemary, dried
- ½ cup chicken stock
- A pinch of salt and black pepper
- 1 tablespoon cilantro, chopped

DIRECTIONS:
In your slow cooker, mix the sea bass with the oil, garlic and the other ingredients, toss gently, put the lid on and cook on Low for 4 hours. Divide the mix between plates and serve.

NUTRITION:
calories 232, fat 7, fiber 3, carbs 7, protein 9

Salmon and Caper Sauce
Preparation time: 10 minutes
Cooking time: 20 minutes
Servings: 3

INGREDIENTS:
- 3 salmon fillets, boneless
- Salt and black pepper to the taste
- 1 tablespoon olive oil
- 1 tablespoon Italian seasoning
- 2 tablespoons capers
- 3 tablespoons lemon juice
- 4 garlic cloves, minced
- 2 tablespoons butter

DIRECTIONS:
Put the butter in your Slow cooker, add salmon fillets, salt, pepper, oil, seasoning, capers, lemon juice and garlic, cover and cook on High for 2 hours. Divide fish and sauce between plates and serve.

NUTRITION:
calories 245, fat 12, fiber 1, carbs 13, protein 23

Tuna and Brussels Sprouts
Preparation time: 5 minutes
Cooking time: 3 hours
Servings: 2

INGREDIENTS:
- 1 pound tuna fillets, boneless
- ½ cup chicken stock
- 1 teaspoon sweet paprika
- ½ teaspoon chili powder
- 1 cup Brussels sprouts, trimmed and halved
- 1 red onion, chopped
- ½ teaspoon garlic powder
- A pinch of salt and black pepper
- 1 tablespoon cilantro, chopped

DIRECTIONS:
In your slow cooker, mix the tuna with the stock, sprouts and the other ingredients, put the lid on and cook on High for 3 hours. Divide the mix between plates and serve.

NUTRITION:
calories 232, fat 9, fiber 2, carbs 6, protein 8

Tabasco Halibut
Preparation time: 10 minutes
Cooking time: 2 hours
Servings: 4

INGREDIENTS:
- ½ cup parmesan, grated
- ¼ cup butter, melted
- ¼ cup mayonnaise
- 2 tablespoons green onions, chopped
- 6 garlic cloves, minced
- ½ teaspoon Tabasco sauce
- 4 halibut fillets, boneless
- Salt and black pepper to the taste
- Juice of ½ lemon

DIRECTIONS:
Season halibut with salt, pepper and some of the lemon juice, place in your Slow cooker, add butter, mayo, green onions, garlic, Tabasco sauce and lemon juice, toss a bit, cover and cook on High for 2 hours. Add parmesan, leave fish mix aside for a few more minutes, divide between plates and serve.

NUTRITION:
calories 240, fat 12, fiber 1, carbs 15, protein 23

Shrimp with Spinach

Preparation time: 10 minutes
Cooking time: 1 hour
Servings: 2

INGREDIENTS:
1 pound shrimp, peeled and deveined
1 cup baby spinach
¼ cup tomato passata
½ cup chicken stock
3 scallions, chopped
1 tablespoon olive oil
½ teaspoon sweet paprika
A pinch of salt and black pepper
1 tablespoon chives, chopped

DIRECTIONS:
In your slow cooker, mix the shrimp with the spinach, tomato passata and the other ingredients, toss, put the lid on and cook on High for 1 hour. Divide the mix between plates and serve.

NUTRITION:
calories 200, fat 13, fiber 3, carbs 6, protein 11

Creamy Salmon

Preparation time: 10 minutes
Cooking time: 2 hours
Servings: 4

INGREDIENTS:
4 salmon fillets, boneless
1 tablespoon olive oil
Salt and black pepper to the taste
1/3 cup parmesan, grated
1 and ½ teaspoon mustard
½ cup sour cream

DIRECTIONS:
Place salmon in your Slow cooker, season with salt and pepper, drizzle the oil and rub.

In a bowl, mix sour cream with parmesan, mustard, salt and pepper, stir well, spoon this over the salmon fillets, cover and cook on High for 2 hours. Divide between plates and serve.

NUTRITION:
calories 263, fat 6, fiber 1, carbs 14, protein 20

Shrimp and Avocado

Preparation time: 5 minutes
Cooking time: 1 hour
Servings: 2

INGREDIENTS:
1 pound shrimp, peeled and deveined
1 cup avocado, peeled, pitted and cubed
½ cup chicken stock
½ teaspoon sweet paprika
Juice of 1 lime
1 tablespoon olive oil
2 tablespoons chili pepper, minced
A pinch of salt and black pepper
1 tablespoon chives, chopped

DIRECTIONS:
In your slow cooker, mix the shrimp with the avocado, stock and the other ingredients, toss, put the lid on and cook on High for 1 hour. Divide the mix into bowls and serve.

NUTRITION:
calories 490, fat 25.4, fiber 5.8, carbs 11.9, protein 53.6

Chinese Cod

Preparation time: 10 minutes
Cooking time: 2 hours
Servings: 4

INGREDIENTS:
1 pound cod, cut into medium pieces
Salt and black pepper to the taste
2 green onions, chopped
3 garlic cloves, minced
3 tablespoons soy sauce
1 cup fish stock
1 tablespoons balsamic vinegar
1 tablespoon ginger, grated
½ teaspoon chili pepper, crushed

DIRECTIONS:
In your Slow cooker, mix fish with salt, pepper green onions, garlic, soy sauce, fish stock, vinegar, ginger and chili pepper, toss, cover and cook on High for 2 hours. Divide everything between plates and serve.

NUTRITION:
calories 204, fat 3, fiber 6, carbs 14, protein 24

Chives Mackerel

Preparation time: 10 minutes
Cooking time: 4 hours
Servings: 2

INGREDIENTS:
1 pound mackerel fillets, boneless
½ teaspoon cumin, ground
½ teaspoon coriander, ground
2 garlic cloves, minced
1 tablespoon avocado oil
1 tablespoon lime juice
½ cup chicken stock
A pinch of salt and black pepper
2 tablespoons chives, chopped

DIRECTIONS:
In your slow cooker, mix the mackerel with the cumin, coriander and the other ingredients, put the lid on and cook on Low for 4 hours. Divide the mix between plates and serve with a side salad.

NUTRITION:
calories 613, fat 41.6, fiber 0.5, carbs 2, protein 54.7

Fish Mix

Preparation time: 10 minutes
Cooking time: 2 hours and 30 minutes
Servings: 4

INGREDIENTS:
- 4 white fish fillets, skinless and boneless
- ½ teaspoon mustard seeds
- Salt and black pepper to the taste
- 2 green chilies, chopped
- 1 teaspoon ginger, grated
- 1 teaspoon curry powder
- ¼ teaspoon cumin, ground
- 2 tablespoons olive oil
- 1 small red onion, chopped
- 1-inch turmeric root, grated
- ¼ cup cilantro, chopped
- 1 and ½ cups coconut cream
- 3 garlic cloves, minced

DIRECTIONS:
Heat up a slow cooker with half of the oil over medium heat, add mustard seeds, ginger, onion, garlic, turmeric, chilies, curry powder and cumin, stir and cook for 3-4 minutes. Add the rest of the oil to your Slow cooker, add spice mix, fish, coconut milk, salt and pepper, cover and cook on High for 2 hours and 30 minutes. Divide into bowls and serve with the cilantro sprinkled on top.

NUTRITION:
calories 500, fat 34, fiber 7, carbs 13, protein 44

Dill Cod

Preparation time: 10 minutes
Cooking time: 3 hours
Servings: 2

INGREDIENTS:
- 1 tablespoon olive oil
- 1 pound cod fillets, boneless and cubed
- 1 tablespoon dill, chopped
- ½ teaspoon sweet paprika
- ½ teaspoon cumin, ground
- 2 garlic cloves, minced
- 1 teaspoon lemon juice
- 1 cup tomato passata
- A pinch of salt and black pepper

DIRECTIONS:
In your slow cooker, mix the cod with the oil, dill and the other ingredients, toss, put the lid on and cook on Low for 3 hours. Divide the mix between plates and serve.

NUTRITION:
calories 192, fat 9, fiber 2, carbs 8, protein 7

Italian Barramundi and Tomato Relish

Preparation time: 10 minutes
Cooking time: 2 hours
Servings: 4

INGREDIENTS:
- 2 barramundi fillets, skinless
- 2 teaspoon olive oil
- 2 teaspoons Italian seasoning
- ¼ cup green olives, pitted and chopped
- ¼ cup cherry tomatoes, chopped
- ¼ cup black olives, chopped
- 1 tablespoon lemon zest
- 2 tablespoons lemon zest
- Salt and black pepper to the taste
- 2 tablespoons parsley, chopped
- 1 tablespoon olive oil

DIRECTIONS:
Rub fish with salt, pepper, Italian seasoning and 2 teaspoons olive oil and put into your Slow cooker. In a bowl, mix tomatoes with all the olives, salt, pepper, lemon zest and lemon juice, parsley and 1 tablespoon olive oil, toss, add over fish, cover and cook on High for 2 hours. Divide fish between plates, top with tomato relish and serve.

NUTRITION:
calories 140, fat 4, fiber 2, carbs 11, protein 10

Shrimp and Mango Mix

Preparation time: 10 minutes
Cooking time: 1 hour
Servings: 2

INGREDIENTS:
- 1 pound shrimp, peeled and deveined
- ½ cup mango, peeled and cubed
- ½ cup cherry tomatoes, halved
- ½ cup shallots, chopped
- 1 tablespoon lime juice
- ½ teaspoon rosemary, dried
- 1 tablespoon olive oil
- ½ teaspoon chili powder
- ½ cup chicken stock
- A pinch of salt and black pepper
- 1 tablespoon chives, chopped

DIRECTIONS:
In your slow cooker, mix the shrimp with the mango, tomatoes and the other ingredients, toss, put the lid on and cook on High for 1 hour. Divide the mix into bowls and serve.

NUTRITION:
calories 210, fat 9, fiber 2, carbs 6, protein 7

Spicy Creole Shrimp

Preparation time: 10 minutes
Cooking time: 1 hour and 30 minutes
Servings: 2

INGREDIENTS:
½ pound big shrimp, peeled and deveined
2 teaspoons Worcestershire sauce
2 teaspoons olive oil
Juice of 1 lemon
Salt and black pepper to the taste
1 teaspoon Creole seasoning

DIRECTIONS:
In your Slow cooker, mix shrimp with Worcestershire sauce, oil, lemon juice, salt, pepper and Creole seasoning, toss, cover and cook on High for 1 hour and 30 minutes. Divide into bowls and serve.

NUTRITION:
calories 140, fat 3, fiber 1, carbs 6, protein 6

Balsamic Tuna

Preparation time: 5 minutes
Cooking time: 3 hours
Servings: 2

INGREDIENTS:
1 pound tuna fillets, boneless and roughly cubed
1 tablespoon balsamic vinegar
3 garlic cloves, minced
1 tablespoon avocado oil
¼ cup chicken stock
1 tablespoon hives, chopped
A pinch of salt and black pepper

DIRECTIONS:
In your slow cooker, mix the tuna with the garlic, vinegar and the other ingredients, toss, put the lid on and cook on Low for 3 hours. Divide the mix into bowls and serve.

NUTRITION:
calories 200, fat 10, fiber 2, carbs 5, protein 9

Sriracha Shrimp

Preparation time: 10 minutes
Cooking time: 1 hour and 30 minutes
Servings: 6

INGREDIENTS:
¼ cup yellow onion, chopped
2 tablespoons olive oil
1 garlic clove, minced
1 and ½ pounds shrimp, peeled and deveined
¼ cup red pepper, roasted and chopped
14 ounces canned tomatoes, chopped
¼ cup cilantro, chopped
2 tablespoons sriracha sauce
1 cup coconut milk
Salt and black pepper to the taste
2 tablespoons lime juice

DIRECTIONS:
Put the oil in your Slow cooker, add onion, garlic, shrimp, red pepper, tomatoes, cilantro, sriracha sauce, milk, salt, pepper and lime juice, toss, cover and cook on High for 1 hour and 30 minutes. Divide into bowls and serve.

NUTRITION:
calories 250, fat 12, fiber 3, carbs 5, protein 20

Lime Trout Mix

Preparation time: 10 minutes
Cooking time: 2 hours
Servings: 2

INGREDIENTS:
1 pound trout fillets, boneless
1 tablespoon olive oil
½ cup chicken stock
2 tablespoons lime zest, grated
2 tablespoons lemon juice
1 teaspoon garam masala
A pinch of salt and black pepper

DIRECTIONS:
In your slow cooker, mix the trout with the olive oil, lime juice and the other ingredients, toss, put the lid on and cook on High for 2 hours. Divide everything between plates and serve.

NUTRITION:
calories 200, fat 13, fiber 3, carbs 6, protein 11

Shrimp and Peas Soup

Preparation time: 10 minutes
Cooking time: 1 hour
Servings: 4

INGREDIENTS:
4 scallions, chopped
1 tablespoon olive oil
1 small ginger root, grated
8 cups chicken stock
¼ cup soy sauce
5 ounces canned bamboo shoots, sliced
Black pepper to the taste

¼ teaspoon fish sauce
1 pound shrimp, peeled and deveined
½ pound snow peas
1 tablespoon sesame oil
½ TABLESPOON CHILI OIL DIRECTIONS:

In your Slow cooker, mix olive oil with scallions, ginger, stock, soy sauce, bamboo, black pepper, fish sauce, shrimp, peas, sesame oil and chili oil, cover and cook on High for 1 hour. Stir soup, ladle into bowls and serve.

NUTRITION:
calories 240, fat 3, fiber 2, carbs 12, protein 14

Creamy Tuna and Scallions

Preparation time: 10 minutes

Cooking time: 2 hours

Servings: 2

INGREDIENTS:
1 pound tuna fillets, boneless and cubed
4 scallions, chopped
½ cup heavy cream
½ cup chicken stock
1 tablespoon olive oil
1 teaspoon turmeric powder
A pinch of salt and black pepper
1 tablespoon chives, chopped

DIRECTIONS:
In your slow cooker, mix the tuna with the scallions, cream and the other ingredients, toss, put the lid on and cook on High for 2 hours. Divide the mix into bowls and serve.

NUTRITION:
calories 198, fat 7, fiber 2, carbs 6, protein 7

Calamari and Sauce

Preparation time: 10 minutes

Cooking time: 2 hours and 20 minutes

Servings: 2

INGREDIENTS:
1 squid, cut into medium rings
A pinch of cayenne pepper
2 tablespoons flour
Salt and black pepper to the taste
¼ cup fish stock
1 tablespoons lemon juice
4 tablespoons mayo
1 teaspoon sriracha sauce

DIRECTIONS:
Season squid rings with salt, pepper and cayenne and put them in your Slow cooker. Add flour, stock, lemon juice and sriracha sauce, toss, cover and cook on High for 2 hour and 20 minutes. Add mayo, toss, divide between plates and serve.

NUTRITION:
calories 345, fat 32, fiber 3, carbs 12, protein 13

Cod and Mustard Sauce

Preparation time: 10 minutes

Cooking time: 3 hours

Servings: 2

INGREDIENTS:
1 tablespoon olive oil
1 pound cod fillets, boneless
2 tablespoons mustard
½ cup heavy cream
¼ cup chicken stock
2 garlic cloves, minced
A pinch of salt and black pepper
1 tablespoon chives, chopped

DIRECTIONS:
In your slow cooker, mix the cod with the oil, mustard and the other ingredients, toss gently, put the lid on and cook on Low for 3 hours. Divide the mix between plates and serve.

NUTRITION:
calories 221, fat 8, fiber 3, carbs 6, protein 7

Calamari and Shrimp

Preparation time: 10 minutes

Cooking time: 2 hours and 30 minutes

Servings: 2

INGREDIENTS:
8 ounces calamari, cut into medium rings
7 ounces shrimp, peeled and deveined
3 tablespoons flour
1 tablespoon olive oil
2 tablespoons avocado, chopped
1 teaspoon tomato paste
1 tablespoon mayonnaise
1 teaspoon Worcestershire sauce
1 teaspoon lemon juice
2 lemon slices
Salt and black pepper to the taste
½ teaspoon turmeric powder

DIRECTIONS:
In your Slow cooker, mix calamari with flour, oil, tomato paste, mayo, Worcestershire sauce, lemon juice, lemon slices, salt, pepper and turmeric, cover and cook on High for 2 hours. Add shrimp, cover and cook on High for 30 minutes more. Divide between plates and serve.

NUTRITION:
calories 368, fat 23, fiber 3, carbs 10, protein 34

Shrimp and Pineapple Bowls

Preparation time: 5 minutes

Cooking time: 1 hour

Servings: 2

INGREDIENTS:
1 pound shrimp, peeled and deveined
1 cup pineapple, peeled and cubed
1 teaspoon sweet paprika
1 tablespoon avocado oil
3 scallions, chopped
½ cup chicken stock
A pinch of salt and black pepper

DIRECTIONS:
In your slow cooker, mix the shrimp with the pineapple, paprika and the other ingredients, toss, put the lid on and cook on High for 1 hour. Divide the mix into bowls and serve.

NUTRITION:
calories 235, fat 8, fiber 4, carbs 7, protein 9

Clam Chowder
Preparation time: 10 minutes
Cooking time: 2 hours
Servings: 4

INGREDIENTS:
1 cup celery stalks, chopped
Salt and black pepper to the taste
1 teaspoon thyme, ground
2 cups chicken stock
14 ounces canned baby clams
2 cups whipping cream
1 cup onion, chopped
13 bacon slices, chopped

DIRECTIONS:
Heat up a pan over medium heat, add bacon slices, brown them and transfer to a bowl. Heat up the same pan over medium heat, add celery and onion, stir and cook for 5 minutes. Transfer everything to your Slow cooker, also add bacon, baby clams, salt, pepper, stock, thyme and whipping cream, stir and cook on High for 2 hours. Divide into bowls and serve.

NUTRITION:
calories 420, fat 22, fiber 0, carbs 5, protein 25

Lime Crab
Preparation time: 10 minutes
Cooking time: 2 hours
Servings: 2

INGREDIENTS:
1 tablespoon avocado oil
1 pound crab meat
¼ cup shallots, chopped
1 tablespoon lime juice
½ cup fish stock
1 teaspoon sweet paprika
1 tablespoon chives, chopped
A pinch of salt and black pepper

DIRECTIONS:
In your slow cooker, mix the crab with the oil, shallots and the other ingredients, toss, put the lid on and cook on High for 2 hours. Divide everything into bowls and serve.

NUTRITION:
calories 211, fat 8, fiber 4, carbs 8, protein 8

Shrimp Salad
Preparation time: 10 minutes
Cooking time: 1 hour
Servings: 4

INGREDIENTS:
2 tablespoons olive oil
1 pound shrimp, peeled and deveined
Salt and black pepper to the taste
2 tablespoons lime juice
3 endives, leaves separated
3 tablespoons parsley, chopped
2 teaspoons mint, chopped
1 tablespoon tarragon, chopped
1 tablespoon lemon juice
2 tablespoons mayonnaise
1 teaspoon lime zest
½ cup sour cream

DIRECTIONS:
In a bowl, mix shrimp with salt, pepper and the olive oil, toss to coat and spread into the Slow cooker, Add lime juice, endives, parsley, mint, tarragon, lemon juice, lemon zest, mayo and sour cream, toss, cover and cook on High for 1 hour. Divide into bowls and serve.

NUTRITION:
calories 200, fat 11, fiber 2, carbs 11, protein 13

Hot Salmon and Carrots
Preparation time: 10 minutes
Cooking time: 3 hours
Servings: 2

INGREDIENTS:
1 pound salmon fillets, boneless
1 cup baby carrots, peeled
½ teaspoon hot paprika
½ teaspoon chili powder
¼ cup chicken stock
2 scallions, chopped
1 tablespoon smoked paprika
A pinch of salt and black pepper
2 tablespoons chives, chopped

DIRECTIONS:
In your slow cooker, mix the salmon with the carrots, paprika and the other ingredients, toss, put the lid on and cook on Low for 3 hours. Divide the mix between plates and serve.

NUTRITION:
calories 193, fat 7, fiber 3, carbs 6, protein 6

Italian Clams
Preparation time: 10 minutes
Cooking time: 2 hours
Servings: 6

INGREDIENTS:
½ cup butter, melted
36 clams, scrubbed
1 teaspoon red pepper flakes, crushed
1 teaspoon parsley, chopped
5 garlic cloves, minced
1 tablespoon oregano, dried
2 cups white wine

DIRECTIONS:
In your Slow cooker, mix butter with clams, pepper flakes, parsley, garlic, oregano and wine, stir, cover and cook on High for 2 hours. Divide into bowls and serve.

NUTRITION:
calories 224, fat 15, fiber 2, carbs 7, protein 4

Shrimp and Eggplant
Preparation time: 5 minutes
Cooking time: 1 hour
Servings: 2

INGREDIENTS:
1 pound shrimp, peeled and deveined
2 teaspoons avocado oil
1 eggplant, cubed
2 tomatoes, cubed
Juice of 1 lime
½ cup chicken stock
4 garlic cloves, minced
1 tablespoon coriander, chopped
1 tablespoon chives, chopped
A pinch of salt and black pepper

DIRECTIONS:
In your slow cooker, mix the shrimp with the oil, eggplant, tomatoes and the other ingredients, toss, put the lid on and cook on High for 1 hour. Divide the mix into bowls and serve.

NUTRITION:
calories 200, fat 11, fiber 4, carbs 5, protein 12

Orange Salmon
Preparation time: 10 minutes
Cooking time: 2 hours
Servings: 2

INGREDIENTS:
2 lemons, sliced
1 pound wild salmon, skinless and cubed
¼ cup balsamic vinegar
¼ cup red orange juice
1 teaspoon olive oil
1/3 cup orange marmalade

DIRECTIONS:
Heat up a slow cooker over medium heat, add vinegar, orange juice and marmalade, stir well, bring to a simmer for 1 minute and transfer to your Slow cooker. Add salmon, lemon slices and oil, toss, cover and cook on High for 2 hours. Divide salmon plates and serve with a side salad.

NUTRITION:
calories 260, fat 3, fiber 2, carbs 16, protein 8

Sea Bass and Squash
Preparation time: 10 minutes
Cooking time: 3 hours
Servings: 2

INGREDIENTS:
1 pound sea bass, boneless and cubed
1 cup butternut squash, peeled and cubed
1 teaspoon olive oil
½ teaspoon turmeric powder
½ teaspoon Italian seasoning
1 cup chicken stock
1 tablespoon cilantro, chopped

DIRECTIONS:
In your slow cooker, mix the sea bass with the squash, oil, turmeric and the other ingredients, toss, the lid on and cook on Low for 3 hours. Divide everything between plates and serve.

NUTRITION:
calories 200, fat 12, fiber 3, carbs 7, protein 9

Tuna and Chimichurri
Preparation time: 10 minutes
Cooking time: 1 hour and 15 minutes
Servings: 4

INGREDIENTS:
½ cup cilantro, chopped
1/3 cup olive oil
1 small red onion, chopped
3 tablespoon balsamic vinegar
2 tablespoons parsley, chopped
2 tablespoons basil, chopped
1 jalapeno pepper, chopped
1 pound tuna steak, boneless, skinless and cubed
Salt and black pepper to the taste
1 teaspoon red pepper flakes

2 garlic cloves, minced
1 teaspoon thyme, chopped
A pinch of cayenne
pepper
2 avocados, pitted, peeled and sliced
6 ounces baby arugula

DIRECTIONS:
In a bowl, mix the oil with jalapeno, vinegar, onion, cilantro, basil, garlic, parsley, pepper flakes, thyme, cayenne, salt and pepper, whisk well, transfer to your Slow cooker, cover and cook on High for 1 hour. Add tuna, cover and cook on High for 15 minutes more. Divide arugula on plates, top with tuna slices, drizzle the chimichurri sauce and serve with avocado slices on the side.

NUTRITION:
calories 186, fat 3, fiber 1, carbs 4, protein 20

Coconut Mackerel

Preparation time: 5 minutes

Cooking time: 3 hours

Servings: 2

INGREDIENTS:
1 pound mackerel fillets, boneless, skinless and cubed
1 tablespoon avocado oil
1 cup coconut cream
½ teaspoon cumin, ground
2 scallions, chopped
A pinch of salt and black pepper
½ teaspoon garam masala
1 tablespoon cilantro, chopped

DIRECTIONS:
In your slow cooker, mix the mackerel with the oil, cream and the other ingredients, toss, put the lid on and cook on Low for 3 hours. Divide the mix into bowls and serve.

NUTRITION:
calories 232, fat 10, fiber 4, carbs 6, protein 9

Cider Clams

Preparation time: 10 minutes

Cooking time: 2 hours

Servings: 4

INGREDIENTS:
2 pounds clams, scrubbed
3 ounces pancetta
1 tablespoon olive oil
3 tablespoons butter, melted
2 garlic cloves, minced
1 bottle infused cider
Salt and black pepper to the taste
Juice of ½ lemon
1 small green apple, chopped
2 thyme springs, chopped

DIRECTIONS:
Heat up a pan with the oil over medium-high heat, add pancetta, brown for 3 minutes and transfer to your Slow cooker. Add butter, garlic, salt, pepper, shallot, cider, clams, thyme, lemon juice and apple, cover and cook on High for 2 hours. Divide everything into bowls and serve.

NUTRITION:
calories 270, fat 2, fiber 1, carbs 11, protein 20

Salmon and Peas

Preparation time: 10 minutes

Cooking time: 2 hours

Servings: 2

INGREDIENTS:
1 pound salmon fillets, boneless and cubed
1 tablespoon olive oil
1 cup sugar snap peas
1 tablespoon lemon juice
½ cup tomato passata
1 tablespoon chives, chopped
Salt and black pepper to the taste

DIRECTIONS:
In your slow cooker, mix the salmon with the peas, oil and the other ingredients, toss, put the lid on and cook on High for 2 hour. Divide the mix between plates and serve.

NUTRITION:
calories 182, fat 7, fiber 3, carbs 6, protein 9

Mustard Salmon

Preparation time: 10 minutes

Cooking time: 2 hours

Servings: 1

INGREDIENTS:
1 big salmon fillet
Salt and black pepper to the taste
2 tablespoons mustard
1 tablespoon olive oil
1 tablespoon maple extract

DIRECTIONS:
In a bowl, mix maple extract with mustard and whisk well. Season salmon with salt and pepper, brush with the mustard mix, put in your Slow cooker, cover and cook on High for 2 hours. Serve the salmon with a side salad.

NUTRITION:
calories 240, fat 7, fiber 1, carbs 15, protein 23

Chili Shrimp and Zucchinis

Preparation time: 10 minutes
Cooking time: 1 hour
Servings: 4

INGREDIENTS:
1 pound shrimp, peeled and deveined
1 zucchini, cubed
2 scallions, minced
1 cup tomato passata
2 green chilies, chopped
A pinch of salt and black pepper
1 tablespoon chives, chopped

DIRECTIONS:
In your slow cooker, mix the shrimp with the zucchini and the other ingredients, toss, put the lid on and cook on High for 1 hour. Divide the shrimp mix into bowls and serve.

NUTRITION:
calories 210, fat 8, fiber 3, carbs 6, protein 14

Salmon and Relish

Preparation time: 10 minutes
Cooking time: 2 hours
Servings: 2

INGREDIENTS:
2 medium salmon fillets, boneless
Salt and black pepper to the taste
1 shallot, chopped
1 tablespoon lemon juice
1 big lemon, peeled and cut into wedges
¼ cup olive oil+ 1 teaspoon
2 tablespoons parsley, finely chopped

DIRECTIONS:
Brush salmon fillets with the olive oil, sprinkle with salt and pepper, put in your Slow cooker, add shallot and lemon juice, cover and cook on High for 2 hours. Shed salmon and divide into 2 bowls. Add lemon segments to your Slow cooker, also add ¼ cup oil and parsley and whisk well. Divide this mix over salmon, toss and serve.

NUTRITION:
calories 200, fat 10, fiber 1, carbs 5, protein 20

Italian Shrimp

Preparation time: 5 minutes
Cooking time: 1 hour
Servings: 2

INGREDIENTS:
1 pound shrimp, peeled and deveined
1 tablespoon avocado oil
½ teaspoon sweet paprika
1 teaspoon Italian seasoning
Salt and black pepper to the taste
Juice of 1 lime
¼ cup chicken stock
1 tablespoon chives, chopped

DIRECTIONS:
In your slow cooker, mix the shrimp with the oil, seasoning and the other ingredients, toss, put the lid on and cook on High for 1 hour. Divide the mix into bowls and serve.

NUTRITION:
calories 200, fat 12, fiber 3, carbs 6, protein 11

Mussels Soup

Preparation time: 10 minutes
Cooking time: 2 hours
Servings: 6

INGREDIENTS:
2 pounds mussels
28 ounces canned tomatoes, crushed
28 ounces canned tomatoes, chopped
2 cup chicken stock
1 teaspoon red pepper flakes, crushed
3 garlic cloves, minced
1 handful parsley, chopped
1 yellow onion, chopped
Salt and black pepper to the taste
1 tablespoon olive oil

DIRECTIONS:
In your Slow cooker, mix mussels with canned and crushed tomatoes, stock, pepper flakes, garlic, parsley, onion, salt, pepper and oil, stir, cover and cook on High for 2 hours. Divide into bowls and serve.

NUTRITION:
calories 250, fat 3, fiber 3, carbs 8, protein 12

Basil Cod and Olives

Preparation time: 5 minutes
Cooking time: 3 hours
Servings: 2

INGREDIENTS:
1 pound cod fillets, boneless
1 cup black olives, pitted and halved
½ tablespoon tomato paste
1 tablespoon basil, chopped
¼ cup chicken stock
1 red onion, sliced
1 tablespoon lime juice
1 tablespoon chives, chopped
Salt and black pepper to the taste

DIRECTIONS:
In your slow cooker, mix the cod with the olives, basil and the other ingredients, toss, put the lid on and cook on Low for 3 hours. Divide everything between plates and serve.

NUTRITION:
calories 132, fat 9, fiber 2, carbs 5, protein 11

Fish and Olives Mix
Preparation time: 10 minutes
Cooking time: 2 hours
Servings: 4

INGREDIENTS:
- 4 white fish fillets, boneless
- 1 cup olives, pitted and chopped
- 1 pound cherry tomatoes, halved
- A pinch of thyme, dried
- 1 garlic clove, minced
- A drizzle of olive oil
- Salt and black pepper to the taste
- ¼ cup chicken stock

DIRECTIONS:
Put the stock in your Slow cooker, add fish, olives, tomatoes, thyme, garlic, oil, salt and pepper, cover and cook on High for 2 hours. Divide everything between plates and serve.

NUTRITION:
calories 200, fat 3, fiber 3, carbs 12, protein 20

Indian Fish
Preparation time: 10 minutes
Cooking time: 2 hours
Servings: 6

INGREDIENTS:
- 6 white fish fillets, cut into medium pieces
- 1 tomato, chopped
- 14 ounces coconut milk
- 2 yellow onions, sliced
- 2 red bell peppers, cut into strips
- 2 garlic cloves, minced
- 6 curry leaves
- 1 tablespoons coriander, ground
- 1 tablespoon ginger, finely grated
- ½ teaspoon turmeric, ground
- 2 teaspoons cumin, ground
- Salt and black pepper to the taste
- ½ teaspoon fenugreek, ground
- 1 teaspoon hot pepper flakes
- 2 tablespoons lemon juice

DIRECTIONS:
In your Slow cooker, mix fish with tomato, milk, onions, bell peppers, garlic cloves, curry leaves, coriander, turmeric, cumin, salt, pepper, fenugreek, pepper flakes and lemon juice, cover and cook on High for 2 hours. Toss fish, divide the whole mix between plates and serve.

Nutrition: calories 231, fat 4, fiber 6, carbs 16, protein 22

Tuna and Fennel
Preparation time: 10 minutes
Cooking time: 2 hours
Servings: 2

INGREDIENTS:
- 1 pound tuna fillets, boneless and cubed
- 1 fennel bulb, sliced
- ½ cup chicken stock
- ½ teaspoon sweet paprika
- ½ teaspoon chili powder
- 1 red onion, chopped
- A pinch of salt and black pepper
- 2 tablespoons cilantro, chopped

DIRECTIONS:
In your slow cooker, mix the tuna with the fennel, stock and the other ingredients, toss, put the lid on and cook on High for 2 hour. Divide the mix between plates and serve.

NUTRITION:
calories 200, fat 12, fiber 2, carbs 6, protein 11

Cod and Peas
Preparation time: 15 minutes
Cooking time: 2 hours
Servings: 4

INGREDIENTS:
- 16 ounces cod fillets
- 1 tablespoon parsley, chopped
- 10 ounces peas
- 9 ounces wine
- ½ teaspoon oregano, dried
- ½ teaspoon paprika
- 2 garlic cloves, chopped
- Salt and pepper to the taste

DIRECTIONS:
In your food processor mix garlic with parsley, oregano, paprika and wine, blend well and add to your Slow cooker. Add fish, peas, salt and pepper, cover and cook on High for 2 hours. Divide into bowls and serve.

NUTRITION:
calories 251, far 2, fiber 6, carbs 7, protein 22

Shrimp and Mushrooms
Preparation time: 10 minutes
Cooking time: 1 hour
Servings: 2

INGREDIENTS:
1 pound shrimp, peeled and deveined
1 cup white mushrooms, halved
1 tablespoon avocado oil
½ tablespoon tomato paste
4 scallions, minced
½ cup chicken stock
Juice of 1 lime
Salt and black pepper to the taste
1 tablespoon chives, minced

DIRECTIONS:
In your slow cooker, mix the shrimp with the mushrooms, oil and the other ingredients, toss, put the lid on and cook on High for 1 hour. Divide the mix into bowls and serve.

NUTRITION:
calories 200, fat 12, fiber 2, carbs 6, protein 9

Salmon and Rice
Preparation time: 5 minutes
Cooking time: 2 hours
Servings: 2

INGREDIENTS:
2 wild salmon fillets, boneless
Salt and black pepper to the taste
½ cup jasmine rice
1 cup chicken stock
¼ cup veggie stock
1 tablespoon butter
A pinch of saffron

DIRECTIONS:
In your Slow cooker mix stock with rice, stock, butter and saffron and stir. Add salmon, salt and pepper, cover and cook on High for 2 hours. Divide salmon on plates, add rice mix on the side and serve.

NUTRITION:
calories 312, fat 4, fiber 6, carbs 20, protein 22

Salmon and Berries
Preparation time: 10 minutes
Cooking time: 3 hours
Servings: 2

INGREDIENTS:
1 pound salmon fillets, boneless and roughly cubed
½ cup blackberries
Juice of 1 lime
1 tablespoon avocado oil
2 scallions, chopped
½ teaspoon Italian seasoning
½ cup fish stock
A pinch of salt and black pepper

DIRECTIONS:
In your slow cooker, mix the salmon with the berries, lime juice and the other ingredients, toss, put the lid on and cook on Low for 3 hours. Divide the mix between plates and serve.

NUTRITION:
calories 211, fat 13, fiber 2, carbs 7, protein 11

Milky Fish
Preparation time: 10 minutes
Cooking time: 2 hours
Servings: 6

INGREDIENTS:
17 ounces white fish, skinless, boneless and cut into medium chunks
1 yellow onion, chopped
13 ounces potatoes, peeled and cut into chunks
13 ounces milk
Salt and black pepper to the taste
14 ounces chicken stock
14 ounces water
14 ounces half and half

DIRECTIONS:
In your Slow cooker, mix fish with onion, potatoes, water, milk and stock, cover and cook on High for 2 hours. Add salt, pepper, half and half, stir, divide into bowls and serve.

NUTRITION:
calories 203, fat 4, fiber 5, carbs 20, protein 15

Cod and Artichokes
Preparation time: 5 minutes
Cooking time: 3 hours
Servings: 2

INGREDIENTS:
1 pound cod fillets, boneless and roughly cubed
1 cup canned artichoke hearts, drained and quartered
2 scallions, chopped
1 tablespoon olive oil
½ cup chicken stock
1 tablespoon lime juice
1 tablespoon cilantro, chopped
A pinch of salt and black pepper

DIRECTIONS:
In your slow cooker, mix the cod with the artichokes, scallions and the other ingredients, toss, put the lid on and cook on Low for 3 hours. Divide the mix between plates and serve.

NUTRITION:
calories 200, fat 12, fiber 4, carbs 6, protein 8

Salmon and Raspberry Vinaigrette

Preparation time: *2 hours*

Cooking time: *2 hours*

Servings: *6*

INGREDIENTS:
- 6 salmon steaks
- 2 tablespoons olive oil
- 4 leeks, sliced
- 2 garlic cloves, minced
- 2 tablespoons parsley, chopped
- 1 cup clam juice
- 2 tablespoons lemon juice
- Salt and white pepper to the taste
- 1 teaspoon sherry
- 1/3 cup dill, chopped
- For the raspberry vinegar:
- 2 pints red raspberries
- 1-pint cider vinegar

DIRECTIONS:
In a bowl, mix red raspberries with vinegar and salmon, toss, cover and keep in the fridge for 2 hours. In your Slow cooker, mix oil with parsley, leeks, garlic, clam juice, lemon juice, salt, pepper, sherry, dill and salmon, cover and cook on High for 2 hours. Divide everything between plates and serve.

NUTRITION:
calories 251, fat 6, fiber 7, carbs 16, protein 26

Salmon, Tomatoes and Green Beans

Preparation time: *5 minutes*

Cooking time: *2 hours*

Servings: *2*

INGREDIENTS:
- 1 pound salmon fillets, boneless and cubed
- 1 cup cherry tomatoes, halved
- 1 cup green beans, trimmed and halved
- 1 cup tomato passata
- 1/2 cup chicken stock
- A pinch of salt and black pepper
- 1 tablespoon parsley, chopped

DIRECTIONS:
In your slow cooker, mix the salmon with the tomatoes, green beans and the other ingredients, toss, put the lid on and cook on High for 2 hours. Divide the mix into bowls and serve.

NUTRITION:
calories 232, fat 7, fiber 3, carbs 7, protein 9

Fish Pudding

Preparation time: *10 minutes*

Cooking time: *2 hours*

Servings: *4*

INGREDIENTS:
- 1 pound cod fillets, cut into medium pieces
- 2 tablespoons parsley, chopped
- 4 ounces breadcrumbs
- 2 teaspoons lemon juice
- 2 eggs, whisked
- 2 ounces butter, melted
- 1/2 pint milk
- 1/2 pint shrimp sauce
- Salt and black pepper to the taste

DIRECTIONS:
In a bowl, mix fish with crumbs, lemon juice, parsley, salt and pepper and stir. Add butter to your Slow cooker, add milk and whisk well. Add egg and fish mix, stir, cover and cook on High for 2 hours. Divide between plates and serve with shrimp sauce on top.

NUTRITION:
calories 231, fat 3, fiber 5, carbs 10, protein 5

Shrimp and Rice Mix

Preparation time: *5 minutes*

Cooking time: *1 hour and 30 minutes*

Servings: *2*

INGREDIENTS:
- 1 pound shrimp, peeled and deveined
- 1 cup chicken stock
- 1/2 cup wild rice
- 1/2 cup carrots, peeled and cubed
- 1 green bell pepper, cubed
- 1/2 teaspoon turmeric powder
- 1/2 teaspoon coriander, ground
- 1 tablespoon olive oil
- 1 red onion, chopped
- A pinch of salt and black pepper
- 1 tablespoon cilantro, chopped

DIRECTIONS:
In your slow cooker, mix the stock with the rice, carrots and the other ingredients except the shrimp, toss, put the lid on and cook on High for 1 hour. Add the shrimp, toss, put the lid back on and cook on High for 30 minutes. Divide the mix between plates and serve.

NUTRITION:
calories 232, fat 9, fiber 2, carbs 6, protein 8

Jambalaya

Preparation time: *10 minutes*

Cooking time: *4 hours and 30 minutes*

Servings: *8*

INGREDIENTS:
- 1 pound chicken breast, chopped
- 1 pound shrimp,
- peeled and deveined
- 2 tablespoons extra virgin olive oil

1 pound sausage, chopped
2 cups onions, chopped
1 and ½ cups rice
2 tablespoons garlic, chopped
2 cups green, yellow and red bell peppers, chopped
3 and ½ cups chicken stock
1 tablespoon Creole seasoning
1 tablespoon Worcestershire sauce
1 cup tomatoes, crushed

DIRECTIONS:
Add the oil to your Slow cooker and spread. Add chicken, sausage, onion, rice, garlic, mixed bell peppers, stock, seasoning, tomatoes and Worcestershire sauce, cover and cook on High for 4 hours. Add shrimp, cover, cook on High for 30 minutes more, divide everything between plates and serve.

NUTRITION:
calories 251, fat 10, fiber 3, carbs 20, protein 25

Shrimp and Red Chard
Preparation time: 5 minutes
Cooking time: 1 hour
Servings: 2

INGREDIENTS:
1 pound shrimp, peeled and deveined
Juice of 1 lime
1 cup red chard, torn
½ cup tomato sauce
2 garlic cloves, minced
1 red onion, sliced
1 tablespoon olive oil
½ teaspoon sweet paprika
A pinch of salt and black pepper
1 tablespoon parsley, chopped

DIRECTIONS:
In your slow cooker, mix the shrimp with the lime juice, chard and the other ingredients, toss, put the lid on and cook on High for 1 hour. Divide the mix into bowls and serve.

NUTRITION:
calories 200, fat 13, fiber 3, carbs 6, protein 11

Mushroom Tuna Mix
Preparation time: 5 minutes
Cooking time: 2 hours
Servings: 4

INGREDIENTS:
14 ounces canned tuna, drained
16 ounces egg noodles
28 ounces cream of mushroom
1 cup peas, frozen
3 cups water
4 ounces cheddar cheese, grated
¼ cup breadcrumbs

DIRECTIONS:
Add pasta and water to your Slow cooker, also add tuna, peas and cream, stir, cover and cook on High for 1 hour. Add cheese, stir, spread breadcrumbs all over, cover, cook on High for 1 more hour, divide into bowls and serve.

NUTRITION:
calories 251, fat 6, fiber 1, carbs 20, protein 12

Chives Mussels
Preparation time: 5 minutes
Cooking time: 1 hour
Servings: 2

INGREDIENTS:
1 pound mussels, debearded
½ teaspoon coriander, ground
½ teaspoon rosemary, dried
1 tablespoon lime zest, grated
Juice of 1 lime
1 cup tomato passata
¼ cup chicken stock
A pinch of salt and black pepper
1 tablespoon chives, chopped

DIRECTIONS:
In your slow cooker, mix the mussels with the coriander, rosemary and the other ingredients, toss, put the lid on and cook on High for 1 hour. Divide the mix into bowls and serve.

NUTRITION:
calories 200, fat 12, fiber 2, carbs 6, protein 9

Chili Mackerel
Preparation time: 10 minutes
Cooking time: 2 hours
Servings: 4

INGREDIENTS:
18 ounces mackerel, cut into pieces
3 garlic cloves, minced
8 shallots, chopped
1 teaspoon dried shrimp powder
1 teaspoon turmeric powder
1 tablespoon chili paste
2 lemongrass sticks, cut into halves
1 small piece of ginger, chopped
6 stalks laska leaves
3 and ½ ounces water
5 tablespoons vegetable oil
1 tablespoon tamarind paste mixed with 3 ounces water
Salt to the taste
1 tablespoon sugar

DIRECTIONS:
In your blender, mix garlic with shallots, chili paste, turmeric powder and shrimp powder and

blend well. Add the oil to your Slow cooker, also add fish, spices paste, ginger, lemongrass, laska leaves, tamarind mix, water, salt and sugar, stir, cover, cook on High for 2 hours, divide between plates and serve.

NUTRITION:
calories 200, fat 3, fiber 1, carbs 20, protein 22

Calamari and Sauce

Preparation time: 10 minutes
Cooking time: 2 hours
Servings: 2

INGREDIENTS:
- 1 pound calamari rings
- 2 scallions, chopped
- 2 garlic cloves, minced
- ½ cup heavy cream
- ½ cup chicken stock
- 1 tablespoon lime juice
- ½ cup black olives, pitted and halved
- A pinch of salt and black pepper
- 2 tablespoons chives, chopped

DIRECTIONS:
In your slow cooker, mix the calamari with the scallions, garlic and the other ingredients except the cream, toss, put the lid on and cook on High for 1 hour. Add the cream, toss, cook on High for 1 more hour, divide into bowls and serve.

NUTRITION:
calories 200, fat 12, fiber 2, carbs 5, protein 6

Chinese Mackerel

Preparation time: 10 minutes
Cooking time: 2 hours
Servings: 4

INGREDIENTS:
- 2 pounds mackerel, cut into medium pieces
- 1 cup water
- 1 garlic clove, crushed
- 1 shallot, sliced
- 1-inch ginger piece, chopped
- 1/3 cup sake
- 1/3 cup mirin
- ¼ cup miso
- 1 sweet onion, thinly sliced
- 2 celery stalks, sliced
- 1 tablespoon rice vinegar
- 1 teaspoon Japanese hot mustard
- Salt to the taste
- 1 teaspoon sugar

DIRECTIONS:
In your Slow cooker, mix mirin, sake, ginger, garlic and shallot. Add miso, water and mackerel, stir, cover the slow cooker and cook on High for 2 hours. Put onion and celery in a bowl and cover with ice water. In another bowl, mix vinegar with salt, sugar and mustard and stir well. Divide mackerel on plates, drain onion and celery well, mix with mustard dressing, divide next to mackerel and serve.

NUTRITION:
calories 300, fat 12, fiber 1, carbs 14, protein 20

Salmon Salad

Preparation time: 5 minutes
Cooking time: 3 hours
Servings: 2

INGREDIENTS:
- 1 pound salmon fillets, boneless and cubed
- ¼ cup chicken stock
- 1 zucchini, cut with a spiralizer
- 1 carrot, sliced
- 1 eggplant, cubed
- ½ cup cherry tomatoes, halved
- 1 red onion, sliced
- ½ teaspoon turmeric powder
- ½ teaspoon chili powder
- ½ tablespoon rosemary, chopped
- A pinch of salt and black pepper
- 1 tablespoon chives, chopped

DIRECTIONS:
In your slow cooker, mix the salmon with the zucchini, stock, carrot and the other ingredients, toss, put the lid on and cook on High for 3 hours. Divide the mix into bowls and serve.

NUTRITION:
calories 424, fat 15.1, fiber 12.4, carbs 28.1, protein 49

Mackerel and Lemon

Preparation time: 10 minutes
Cooking time: 2 hours
Servings: 4

INGREDIENTS:
- 4 mackerels
- 3 ounces breadcrumbs
- Juice and rind of 1 lemon
- 1 tablespoon chives, finely chopped
- Salt and black pepper to the taste
- 1 egg, whisked
- 1 tablespoon butter
- 1 tablespoon vegetable oil
- 3 lemon wedges

DIRECTIONS:
In a bowl, mix breadcrumbs with lemon juice, lemon rind, salt, pepper, egg and chives, stir very well and coat mackerel with this mix. Add the oil and the butter to your Slow cooker and arrange mackerel inside. Cover, cook on High for 2 hours,

divide fish between plates and serve with lemon wedges on the side.

NUTRITION:
calories 200, fat 3, fiber 1, carbs 3, protein 12

Walnut Tuna Mix

Preparation time: 10 minutes
Cooking time: 3 hours
Servings: 2

INGREDIENTS:
- 1 pound tuna fillets, boneless
- ½ tablespoon walnuts, chopped
- ½ cup chicken stock
- ½ teaspoon chili powder
- ½ teaspoon sweet paprika
- 1 red onion, sliced
- 2 tablespoons parsley, chopped
- A pinch of salt and black pepper

DIRECTIONS:
In your slow cooker, mix the tuna with the walnuts, stock and the other ingredients, toss, put the lid on and cook on High for 3 hours. Divide everything between plates and serve.

NUTRITION:
calories 200, fat 10, fiber 2, carbs 5, protein 9

Mussels and Sausage Mix

Preparation time: 5 minutes
Cooking time: 2 hours
Servings: 4

INGREDIENTS:
- 2 pounds mussels, scrubbed and debearded
- 12 ounces amber beer
- 1 tablespoon olive oil
- 1 yellow onion, chopped
- 8 ounces spicy sausage
- 1 tablespoon paprika

DIRECTIONS:
Grease your Slow cooker with the oil, add onion, paprika, sausage, mussels and beer, cover and cook on High for 2 hours. Discard unopened mussels, divide the rest between bowls and serve.

NUTRITION:
calories 124, fat 3, fiber 1, carbs 7, protein 12

Almond Shrimp and Cabbage

Preparation time: 5 minutes
Cooking time: 1 hour
Servings: 2

INGREDIENTS:
- 1 pound shrimp, peeled and deveined
- 1 cup red cabbage, shredded
- 1 tablespoon almonds, chopped
- 1 cup cherry tomatoes, halved
- 1 tablespoon balsamic vinegar
- 2 tablespoons olive oil
- ½ cup tomato passata
- A pinch of salt and black pepper

DIRECTIONS:
In your slow cooker, mix the shrimp with the cabbage, almonds and the other ingredients, toss, put the lid on and cook on High for 1 hour. Divide everything into bowls and serve.

NUTRITION:
calories 200, fat 13, fiber 3, carbs 6, protein 11

Mussels, Clams and Chorizo Mix

Preparation time: 10 minutes
Cooking time: 2 hours
Servings: 4

INGREDIENTS:
- 15 small clams
- 30 mussels, scrubbed
- 2 chorizo links, sliced
- 1 pound baby red potatoes, peeled
- 1 yellow onion, chopped
- 10 ounces beer
- 2 tablespoons parsley, chopped
- 1 teaspoon olive oil
- Lemon wedges for serving

DIRECTIONS:
Grease your Slow cooker with the oil, add clams, mussels, chorizo, potatoes, onion, beer and parsley, cover and cook on High for 2 hours. Add parsley, stir, divide into bowls and serve with lemon wedges on the side.

NUTRITION:
calories 251, fat 4, fiber 7, carbs 10, protein 20

Indian Shrimp

Preparation time: 5 minutes
Cooking time: 1 hours
Servings: 2

INGREDIENTS:
- 4 scallions, chopped
- 1 tablespoon olive oil
- 1 pound shrimp, peeled and deveined
- ½ teaspoon garam masala
- ½ teaspoon coriander, ground
- ½ teaspoon turmeric powder
- 1 tablespoon lime juice
- ½ cup chicken stock
- ¼ cup lime leaves, torn

DIRECTIONS:
In your slow cooker, mix the shrimp with the oil, scallions, masala and the other ingredients, toss, put the lid on and cook on High for 1 hour. Divide the mix into bowls and serve.

NUTRITION:
calories 211, fat 12, fiber 3, carbs 6, protein 7

Crab Legs
Preparation time: 5 minutes
Cooking time: 1 hour and 30 minutes
Servings: 4

INGREDIENTS:
4 pounds king crab legs, broken in half
3 lemon wedges
¼ cup butter, melted
½ cup chicken stock

DIRECTIONS:
In your Slow cooker, mix stock with crab legs and butter, cover and cook on High for 1 hour and 30 minutes. Divide crab legs between bowls, drizzle melted butter all over and serve with lemon wedges on the side.

NUTRITION:
calories 100, fat 1, fiber 5, carbs 12, protein 3

Shrimp, Tomatoes and Kale
Preparation time: 5 minutes
Cooking time: 1 hour
Servings: 2

INGREDIENTS:
1 pound shrimp, peeled and deveined
½ cup cherry tomatoes, halved
1 cup baby kale
½ cup chicken stock
1 tablespoon olive oil
Salt and black pepper to the taste
Juice of 1 lime
½ teaspoon sweet paprika
1 tablespoon cilantro, chopped

DIRECTIONS:
In your slow cooker, mix the shrimp with the cherry tomatoes, kale and the other ingredients, toss, put the lid on and cook on High for 1 hour. Divide the mix into bowls and serve.

NUTRITION:
calories 200, fat 12, fiber 3, carbs 6, protein 11

Shrimp and Sausage Boil
Preparation time: 10 minutes
Cooking time: 2 hours and 30 minutes
Servings: 4

INGREDIENTS:
1 and ½ pounds shrimp, head removed
12 ounces Andouille sausage, already cooked and chopped
4 ears of corn, each cut into 3 pieces
1 tablespoon old bay seasoning
16 ounces beer
Salt and black pepper to the taste
1 teaspoon red pepper flakes, crushed
2 sweet onions, cut into wedges
1 pound potatoes, cut into medium chunks
8 garlic cloves, crushed
French baguettes for serving

DIRECTIONS:
In your Slow cooker mix beer with old bay seasoning, red pepper flakes, salt, black pepper, onions, garlic, potatoes, corn and sausage, cover and cook on High for 2 hours. Add shrimp, cover, cook on High for 30 minutes more, divide into bowls and serve with French baguettes on the side.

NUTRITION:
calories 261, fat 5, fiber 6, carbs 20, protein 16

Trout Bowls
Preparation time: 5 minutes
Cooking time: 3 hours
Servings: 2

INGREDIENTS:
1 pound trout fillets, boneless, skinless and cubed
1 cup kalamata olives, pitted and chopped
1 cup baby spinach
2 garlic cloves, minced
1 tablespoon olive oil
Juice of ½ lime
Salt and black pepper to the taste
1 tablespoon parsley, chopped

DIRECTIONS:
In your slow cooker, mix the trout with the olives, spinach and the other ingredients, toss, put the lid on and cook on Low for 3 hours. Divide everything into bowls and serve.

NUTRITION:
calories 132, fat 9, fiber 2, carbs 5, protein 11

Mushroom and Shrimp Curry
Preparation time: 10 minutes
Cooking time: 2 hours and 30 minutes
Servings: 4

INGREDIENTS:
1 pound shrimp, peeled and deveined
1 cup bouillon
4 lemon slices

Salt and black pepper to the taste
½ teaspoon curry powder
¼ cup mushrooms, sliced
¼ cup yellow onion, chopped
1 tablespoon olive oil
½ cup raisins
3 tablespoons flour
1 cup milk

DIRECTIONS:
In your Slow cooker, mix bouillon with lemon, salt, pepper, curry powder, mushrooms, onion, flour and milk, whisk well, cover and cook on High for 2 hours. Add shrimp and raisins, cover and cook on High for 30 minutes more. Divide curry into bowls and serve.

NUTRITION:
calories 300, fat 4, fiber 2, carbs 30, protein 17

Calamari Curry
Preparation time: 10 minutes
Cooking time: 3 hours
Servings: 2

INGREDIENTS:
1 pound calamari rings
½ tablespoon yellow curry paste
1 cup coconut milk
½ teaspoon turmeric powder
½ cup chicken stock
2 garlic cloves, minced
½ tablespoon coriander, chopped
A pinch of salt and black pepper
2 tablespoons lemon juice

DIRECTIONS:
In your slow cooker, mix the rings with the curry paste, coconut milk and the other ingredients, toss, put the lid on and cook on High for 3 hours. Divide the curry into bowls and serve.

NUTRITION:
calories 200, fat 12, fiber 2, carbs 6, protein 11

Dill Shrimp Mix
Preparation time: 10 minutes
Cooking time: 1 hours
Servings: 4

INGREDIENTS:
1 pound shrimp, peeled and deveined
2 tablespoons olive oil
1 tablespoon yellow onion, chopped
1 cup white wine
2 tablespoons cornstarch
¾ cup milk
1 tablespoon dill, chopped

DIRECTIONS:
In your Slow cooker, mix oil with onion, cornstarch, milk, wine, dill and shrimp, cover and cook on High for 1 hour. Divide everything into bowls and serve.

NUTRITION:
calories 300, fat 13, fiber 2, carbs 10, protein 10

Balsamic Trout
Preparation time: 10 minutes
Cooking time: 3 hours
Servings: 2

INGREDIENTS:
1 pound trout fillets, boneless
½ cup chicken stock
2 garlic cloves, minced
2 tablespoons balsamic vinegar
½ teaspoon cumin, ground
Salt and black pepper to the taste
1 tablespoon parsley, chopped
1 tablespoon olive oil

DIRECTIONS:
In your slow cooker, mix the trout with the stock, garlic and the other ingredients, toss gently, put the lid on and cook on High for 3 hours. Divide the mix between plates and serve.

NUTRITION:
calories 200, fat 12, fiber 2, carbs 6, protein 9

Japanese Shrimp
Preparation time: 10 minutes
Cooking time: 1 hour
Servings: 4

INGREDIENTS:
1 pounds shrimp, peeled and deveined
2 tablespoons soy sauce
½ pound pea pods
3 tablespoons vinegar
¾ cup pineapple juice
1 cup chicken stock
3 tablespoons sugar

DIRECTIONS:
Put shrimp and pea pods in your Slow cooker, add soy sauce, vinegar, pineapple juice, stock and sugar, stir, cover and cook on High for 1 hour, Divide between plates and serve.

NUTRITION:
calories 251, fat 4, fiber 1, carbs 12, protein 30

Oregano Shrimp Bowls
Preparation time: 10 minutes
Cooking time: 1 hour
Servings: 2

INGREDIENTS:

1 pound shrimp, peeled and deveined	¼ cup fish stock
½ cup cherry tomatoes, halved	½ teaspoon sweet paprika
½ cup baby spinach	2 garlic cloves, chopped
1 tablespoon lime juice	A pinch of salt and black pepper
1 tablespoon oregano, chopped	

DIRECTIONS:

In your slow cooker, mix the shrimp with the cherry tomatoes, spinach and the other ingredients, toss, put the lid on and cook on High for 1 hour. Divide everything between plates and serve.

NUTRITION:

calories 211, fat 13, fiber 2, carbs 7, protein 11

Octopus and Veggies Mix

Preparation time: 1 day

Cooking time: 3 hours

Servings: 4

INGREDIENTS:

- 1 octopus, already prepared
- 1 cup red wine
- 1 cup white wine
- 1 cup water
- 1 cup olive oil
- 2 teaspoons pepper sauce
- 1 tablespoon hot sauce
- 1 tablespoon paprika
- 1 tablespoon tomato sauce
- Salt and black pepper to the taste
- ½ bunch parsley, chopped
- 2 garlic cloves, minced
- 1 yellow onion, chopped
- 4 potatoes, cut into quarters.

DIRECTIONS:

Put octopus in a bowl, add white wine, red one, water, half of the oil, pepper sauce, hot sauce, paprika, tomato paste, salt, pepper and parsley, toss to coat, cover and keep in a cold place for 1 day. Add the rest of the oil to your Slow cooker and arrange onions and potatoes on the bottom. Add the octopus and the marinade, stir, cover, cook on High for 3 hours, divide everything between plates and serve.

NUTRITION:

calories 230, fat 4, fiber 1, carbs 7, protein 23

Salmon and Strawberries Mix

Preparation time: 10 minutes

Cooking time: 2 hours

Servings: 2

INGREDIENTS:

1 pound salmon fillets, boneless	1 teaspoon balsamic vinegar
1 cup strawberries, halved	1 tablespoon chives, chopped
½ cup orange juice	A pinch of salt and black pepper
Zest of 1 lemon, grated	
4 scallions, chopped	

DIRECTIONS:

In your slow cooker, mix the salmon with the strawberries, orange juice and the other ingredients, toss, put the lid on and cook on High for 2 hours. Divide everything into bowls and serve.

NUTRITION:

calories 200, fat 12, fiber 4, carbs 6, protein 8

Mediterranean Octopus

Preparation time: 1 hour and 10 minutes

Cooking time: 3 hours

Servings: 6

INGREDIENTS:

- 1 octopus, cleaned and prepared
- 2 rosemary springs
- 2 teaspoons oregano, dried
- ½ yellow onion, roughly chopped
- 4 thyme springs
- ½ lemon
- 1 teaspoon black peppercorns
- 3 tablespoons extra virgin olive oil
- For the marinade:
- ¼ cup extra virgin olive oil
- Juice of ½ lemon
- 4 garlic cloves, minced
- 2 thyme springs
- 1 rosemary spring
- Salt and black pepper to the taste

DIRECTIONS:

Put the octopus in your Slow cooker, add oregano, 2 rosemary springs, 4 thyme springs, onion, lemon, 3 tablespoons olive oil, peppercorns and salt, stir, cover and cook on High for 2 hours. Transfer octopus on a cutting board, cut tentacles, put them in a bowl, mix with ¼ cup olive oil, lemon juice, garlic, 1 rosemary springs, 2 thyme springs, salt and pepper, toss to coat and leave aside for 1 hour. Transfer octopus and the marinade to your Slow cooker again, cover and cook on High for 1 more hour. Divide octopus on plates, drizzle the marinade all over and serve.

NUTRITION:

calories 200, fat 4, fiber 3, carbs 10, protein 11

Shrimp, Salmon and Tomatoes Mix

Preparation time: 5 minutes

Cooking time: 1 hour and 30 minutes

Servings: 2

INGREDIENTS:
- 1 pound shrimp, peeled and deveined
- ½ pound salmon fillets, boneless and cubed
- 1 cup cherry tomatoes, halved
- ½ cup chicken stock
- ½ teaspoon chili powder
- ½ teaspoon rosemary, dried
- A pinch of salt and black pepper
- 1 tablespoon parsley, chopped
- 2 tablespoons tomato sauce
- 2 garlic cloves, minced

DIRECTIONS:
In your slow cooker, combine the shrimp with the salmon, tomatoes and the other ingredients, toss gently, put the lid on and cook on High for 1 hour and 30 minutes. Divide the mix into bowls and serve.

NUTRITION:
calories 232, fat 7, fiber 3, carbs 7, protein 9

Stuffed Squid

Preparation time: 10 minutes

Cooking time: 3 hours

Servings: 4

INGREDIENTS:
- 4 squid
- 1 cup sticky rice
- 14 ounces dashi stock
- 2 tablespoons sake
- 4 tablespoons soy sauce
- 1 tablespoon mirin
- 2 tablespoons sugar

DIRECTIONS:
Chop tentacles from 1 squid, mix with the rice, stuff each squid with this mix and seal ends with toothpicks. Place squid in your Slow cooker, add stock, soy sauce, sake, sugar and mirin, stir, cover and cook on High for 3 hours. Divide between plates and serve.

NUTRITION:
calories 230, fat 4, fiber 4, carbs 7, protein 11

Shrimp and Cauliflower Bowls

Preparation time: 5 minutes

Cooking time: 2 hours

Servings: 2

INGREDIENTS:
- 1 pound shrimp, peeled and deveined
- ½ cup chicken stock
- 1 cup cauliflower florets
- ½ teaspoon turmeric powder
- ½ teaspoon coriander, ground
- ½ cup tomato passata
- A pinch of salt and black pepper
- 1 tablespoon cilantro, chopped

DIRECTIONS:
In your slow cooker, mix the cauliflower with the stock, turmeric and the other ingredients except the shrimp, toss, put the lid on and cook on High for 1 hour. Add the shrimp, toss, cook on High for 1 more hour, divide into bowls and serve.

NUTRITION:
calories 232, fat 9, fiber 2, carbs 6, protein 8

Flavored Squid

Preparation time: 10 minutes

Cooking time: 3 hours

Servings: 4

INGREDIENTS:
- 17 ounces squids
- 1 and ½ tablespoons red chili powder
- Salt and black pepper to the taste
- ¼ teaspoon turmeric powder
- 2 cups water
- 5 pieces coconut, shredded
- 4 garlic cloves, minced
- ½ teaspoons cumin seeds
- 3 tablespoons olive oil
- ¼ teaspoon mustard seeds
- 1-inch ginger pieces, chopped

DIRECTIONS:
Put squids in your Slow cooker, add chili powder, turmeric, salt, pepper and water, stir, cover and cook on High for 2 hours. In your blender, mix coconut with ginger, oil, garlic and cumin and blend well. Add this over the squids, cover and cook on High for 1 more hour. Divide everything into bowls and serve.

NUTRITION:
calories 261, fat 3, fiber 8, carbs 19, protein 11

Cod and Broccoli

Preparation time: 10 minutes

Cooking time: 3 hours

Servings: 2

INGREDIENTS:
- 1 pound cod fillets, boneless
- 1 cup broccoli florets
- ½ cup veggie stock
- 2 tablespoons tomato paste
- 2 garlic cloves, minced
- 1 red onion, minced
- ½ teaspoon rosemary, dried
- A pinch of salt and black pepper
- 1 tablespoon chives, chopped

DIRECTIONS:
In your slow cooker, mix the cod with the broccoli, stock, tomato paste and the other ingredients, toss,

put the lid on and cook on Low for 3 hours. Divide the mix between plates and serve.

NUTRITION:
calories 200, fat 13, fiber 3, carbs 6, protein 11

Cinnamon Trout

Preparation time: 5 minutes
Cooking time: 3 hours
Servings: 2

INGREDIENTS:
1 pound trout fillets, boneless
1 tablespoon cinnamon powder
¼ cup chicken stock
2 tablespoons chili pepper, minced
A pinch of salt and black pepper
A pinch of cayenne pepper
1 tablespoon chives, chopped

DIRECTIONS:
In your slow cooker, mix the trout with the cinnamon, stock and the other ingredients, toss gently, put the lid on and cook on Low for 3 hours. Divide the mix between plates and serve with a side salad.

NUTRITION:
calories 200, fat 12, fiber 2, carbs 6, protein 9

Slow Cooker Dessert Recipes

Pudding Cake

Preparation time: 10 minutes
Cooking time: 2 hours and 30 minutes
Servings: 8

INGREDIENTS:
1 and ½ cup sugar
1 cup flour
¼ cup cocoa powder+ 2 tablespoons
½ cup chocolate almond milk
2 teaspoons baking powder
2 tablespoons vegetable oil
1 teaspoon vanilla extract
1 and ½ cups hot water
Cooking spray

DIRECTIONS:
In a bowl, mix flour with 2 tablespoons cocoa, baking powder, milk, oil and vanilla extract, whisk well and spread on the bottom of the Slow cooker, greased with cooking spray. In another bowl, mix sugar with the rest of the cocoa and the water, whisk well, spread over the batter in the Slow cooker, cover, cook your cake on High for 2 hours and 30 minutes. Leave the cake to cool down, slice and serve.

NUTRITION:
calories 250, fat 4, fiber 3, carbs 40, protein 4

Cinnamon Apples

Preparation time: 10 minutes
Cooking time: 2 hours
Servings: 2

INGREDIENTS:
2 tablespoons brown sugar
1 pound apples, cored and cut into wedges
1 tablespoon cinnamon powder
2 tablespoons walnuts, chopped
A pinch of nutmeg, ground
½ tablespoon lemon juice
¼ cup water
2 apples, cored and tops cut off

DIRECTIONS:
In your slow cooker, mix the apples with the sugar, cinnamon and the other ingredients, toss, put the lid on and cook on High for 2 hours. Divide the mix between plates and serve.

NUTRITION:
calories 189, fat 4, fiber 7, carbs 19, protein 2

Peanut Butter Cake

Preparation time: 10 minutes
Cooking time: 2 hours and 30 minutes
Servings: 8

INGREDIENTS:
- 1 cup sugar
- 1 cup flour
- 3 tablespoons cocoa powder+ ½ cup
- 1 and ½ teaspoons baking powder
- ½ cup milk
- 2 tablespoons vegetable oil
- 2 cups hot water
- 1 teaspoon vanilla extract
- ½ cup peanut butter
- Cooking spray

DIRECTIONS:
In a bowl, mix half of the sugar with 3 tablespoons cocoa, flour, baking powder, oil, vanilla and milk, stir well and pour into your Slow cooker greased with cooking spray. In another bowl, mix the rest of the sugar with the rest of the cocoa, peanut butter and hot water, stir well and pour over the batter in the slow cooker. Cover slow cooker, cook on High for 2 hours and 30 minutes, slice cake and serve.

NUTRITION:
calories 242, fat 4, fiber 7, carbs 8, protein 4

Vanilla Pears

Preparation time: 10 minutes
Cooking time: 2 hours
Servings: 2

INGREDIENTS:
- 2 tablespoons avocado oil
- 1 teaspoon vanilla extract
- 2 pears, cored and halved
- ½ tablespoon lime juice
- 1 tablespoon sugar

DIRECTIONS:
In your slow cooker combine the pears with the sugar, oil and the other ingredients, toss, put the lid on and cook on High for 2 hours. Divide between plates and serve.

NUTRITION:
calories 200, fat 4, fiber 6, carbs 16, protein 3

Blueberry Cake

Preparation time: 10 minutes
Cooking time: 1 hour
Servings: 6

INGREDIENTS:
- ½ cup flour
- ¼ teaspoon baking powder
- ¼ teaspoon sugar
- ¼ cup blueberries
- 1/3 cup milk
- 1 teaspoon olive oil
- 1 teaspoon flaxseed, ground
- ½ teaspoon lemon zest, grated
- ¼ teaspoon vanilla extract
- ¼ teaspoon lemon extract
- Cooking spray

DIRECTIONS:
In a bowl, mix flour with baking powder, sugar, blueberries, milk, oil, flaxseeds, lemon zest, vanilla extract and lemon extract and whisk well. Spray your slow cooker with cooking spray, line it with parchment paper, pour cake batter, cover slow cooker, cook on High for 1 hour, leave the cake to cool down, slice and serve.

NUTRITION:
calories 200, fat 4, fiber 4, carbs 10, protein 4

Avocado Cake

Preparation time: 10 minutes
Cooking time: 2 hours
Servings: 2

INGREDIENTS:
- ½ cup brown sugar
- 2 tablespoons coconut oil, melted
- 1 cup avocado, peeled and mashed
- ½ teaspoon vanilla extract
- 1 egg
- ½ teaspoon baking powder
- 1 cup almond flour
- ¼ cup almond milk
- Cooking spray

DIRECTIONS:
In a bowl, mix the sugar with the oil, avocado and the other ingredients except the cooking spray and whisk well. Grease your slow cooker with cooking spray, add the cake batter, spread, put the lid on and cook on High for 2 hours. Leave the cake to cool down, slice and serve.

NUTRITION:
calories 300, fat 4, fiber 4, carbs 27, protein 4

Peach Pie

Preparation time: 10 minutes
Cooking time: 4 hours
Servings: 4

INGREDIENTS:
- 4 cups peaches, peeled and sliced
- 1 cup sugar
- ½ teaspoon cinnamon powder
- 1 and ½ cups crackers, crushed
- ¼ teaspoon nutmeg, ground
- ½ cup milk
- 1 teaspoon vanilla extract
- Cooking spray

DIRECTIONS:
In a bowl, mix peaches with half of the sugar and cinnamon and stir. In another bowl, mix crackers with the rest of the sugar, nutmeg, milk and vanilla

extract and stir. Spray your Slow cooker with cooking spray, spread peaches on the bottom, add crackers mix, spread, cover and cook on Low for 4 hours. Divide cobbler between plates and serve.

NUTRITION:
calories 212, fat 4, fiber 4, carbs 7, protein 3

Coconut Cream
Preparation time: 10 minutes
Cooking time: 1 hour
Servings: 2

INGREDIENTS:
2 ounces coconut cream
1 cup coconut milk
½ teaspoon almond extract
2 tablespoons sugar

DIRECTIONS:
In your slow cooker, mix the cream with the milk and the other ingredients, whisk, put the lid on, cook on High for 1 hour, divide into bowls and serve cold.

NUTRITION:
calories 242, fat 12, fiber 6, carbs 9, protein 4

Sweet Strawberry Mix
Preparation time: 10 minutes
Cooking time: 3 hours
Servings: 10

INGREDIENTS:
2 tablespoons lemon juice
2 pounds strawberries
4 cups sugar
1 teaspoon cinnamon powder
1 teaspoon vanilla extract

DIRECTIONS:
In your Slow cooker, mix strawberries with sugar, lemon juice, cinnamon and vanilla, cover, cook on Low for 3 hours, divide into bowls and serve cold.

NUTRITION:
calories 100, fat 1, fiber 1, carbs 6, protein 2

Almond Rice Pudding
Preparation time: 10 minutes
Cooking time: 1 hour
Servings: 2

INGREDIENTS:
2 tablespoons almonds, chopped
1 cup white rice
2 cups almond milk
1 tablespoon sugar
1 tablespoons maple syrup
¼ teaspoon cinnamon powder
¼ teaspoon ginger, grated

DIRECTIONS:
In your slow cooker, mix the milk with the rice, sugar and the other ingredients, toss, put the lid on and cook on High for 1 hour. Divide the pudding into bowls and serve cold

NUTRITION:
calories 205, fat 2, fiber 7, carbs 11, protein 4

Sweet Plums
Preparation time: 10 minutes
Cooking time: 3 hours
Servings: 6

INGREDIENTS:
14 plums, halved
1 and ¼ cups sugar
1 teaspoon cinnamon powder
¼ cup water

DIRECTIONS:
Put the plums in your Slow cooker, add sugar, cinnamon and water, stir, cover, cook on Low for 3 hours, divide into bowls and serve cold

NUTRITION:
calories 150, fat 2, fiber 1, carbs 5, protein 3

Cherry Bowls
Preparation time: 10 minutes
Cooking time: 1 hour
Servings: 2

INGREDIENTS:
1 cup cherries, pitted
1 tablespoon sugar
½ cup red cherry juice
2 tablespoons maple syrup

DIRECTIONS:
In your slow cooker, mix the cherries with the sugar and the other ingredients, toss gently, put the lid on, cook on High for 1 hour, divide into bowls and serve.

NUTRITION:
calories 200, fat 1, fiber 4, carbs 5, protein 2

Bananas and Sweet Sauce
Preparation time: 10 minutes
Cooking time: 2 hours
Servings: 4

INGREDIENTS:
Juice of ½ lemon
3 tablespoons agave nectar
1 tablespoon vegetable oil
4 bananas, peeled and sliced
½ teaspoon cardamom seeds

DIRECTIONS:
Put the bananas in your Slow cooker, add agave nectar, lemon juice, oil and cardamom, cover, cook on Low for 2 hours, divide bananas between plates, drizzle agave sauce all over and serve.

NUTRITION:
calories 120, fat 1, fiber 2, carbs 8, protein 3

Berry Cream
Preparation time: 10 minutes
Cooking time: 2 hours
Servings: 2

INGREDIENTS:
2 tablespoons cashews, chopped
1 cup heavy cream
½ cup blueberries
½ cup maple syrup
½ tablespoon coconut oil, melted

DIRECTIONS:
In your slow cooker, mix the cream with the berries and the other ingredients, whisk, put the lid on and cook on Low for 2 hours. Divide the mix into bowls and serve cold.

NUTRITION:
calories 200, fat 3, fiber 5, carbs 12, protein 3

Orange Cake
Preparation time: 10 minutes
Cooking time: 5 hours
Servings: 4

INGREDIENTS:
Cooking spray
1 teaspoon baking powder
1 cup flour
1 cup sugar
½ teaspoon cinnamon powder
3 tablespoons vegetable oil
½ cup milk
½ cup pecans, chopped
¾ cup water
½ cup raisins
½ cup orange peel, grated
¾ cup orange juice

DIRECTIONS:
In a bowl, mix flour with half of the sugar, baking powder, cinnamon, 2 tablespoons oil, milk, pecans and raisins, stir and pour this into your Slow cooker greased with cooking spray. Heat up a small pan over medium heat, add water, orange juice, orange peel, the rest of the oil and the rest of the sugar, stir, bring to a boil, pour over the mix in the Slow cooker, cover and cook on Low for 5 hours. Divide into dessert bowls and serve cold.

NUTRITION:
calories 182, fat 3, fiber 1, carbs 4, protein 3

Maple Pudding
Preparation time: 10 minutes
Cooking time: 1 hour
Servings: 2

INGREDIENTS:
¼ cup cashew butter
1 tablespoon coconut oil, melted
½ cup white rice
1 cup almond milk
2 tablespoons lemon juice
½ teaspoon lemon zest, grated
1 tablespoon maple syrup

DIRECTIONS:
In your slow cooker, mix the rice with the milk, coconut oil and the other ingredients, whisk, put the lid on and cook on High for 1 hour. Divide into bowls and serve.

NUTRITION:
calories 202, fat 4, fiber 5, carbs 14, protein 1

Apples Stew
Preparation time: 10 minutes
Cooking time: 1 hour and 30 minutes
Servings: 5

INGREDIENTS:
5 apples, tops cut off and cored
1/3 cup sugar
¼ cup pecans, chopped
2 teaspoons lemon zest, grated
½ teaspoon cinnamon powder
1 tablespoon lemon juice
1 tablespoon vegetable oil
½ cup water

DIRECTIONS:
Arrange apples in your Slow cooker, add sugar, pecans, lemon zest, cinnamon, lemon juice, coconut oil and water, toss, cover and cook on High for 1 hour and 30 minutes. Divide apple stew between plates and serve.

NUTRITION:
calories 200, fat 1, fiber 2, carbs 6, protein 3

Chia and Orange Pudding

Preparation time: 10 minutes
Cooking time: 1 hour
Servings: 2

INGREDIENTS:
1 tablespoon chia seeds
½ cup almond milk
½ cup oranges, peeled and cut into segments
1 tablespoon sugar
½ teaspoon cinnamon powder
1 tablespoon coconut oil, melted
2 tablespoons pecans, chopped

DIRECTIONS:
In your slow cooker, mix the chia seeds with the almond milk, orange segments and the other ingredients, toss, put the lid on and cook on High for 1 hour. Divide the pudding into bowls and serve cold.

NUTRITION:
calories 252, fat 3, fiber 3, carbs 7, protein 3

Pears and Sauce

Preparation time: 10 minutes
Cooking time: 4 hours
Servings: 4

INGREDIENTS:
4 pears, peeled and cored
2 cups orange juice
¼ cup maple syrup
2 teaspoons cinnamon powder
1 tablespoon ginger, grated

DIRECTIONS:
In your Slow cooker, mix pears with orange juice, maple syrup, cinnamon and ginger, cover and cook on Low for 4 hours. Divide pears and sauce between plates and serve warm.

NUTRITION:
calories 210, fat 1, fiber 2, carbs 6, protein 4

Creamy Berries Mix

Preparation time: 10 minutes
Cooking time: 1 hour
Servings: 2

INGREDIENTS:
½ teaspoon nutmeg, ground
½ teaspoon vanilla extract
½ cup blackberries
½ cup blueberries
¼ cup whipping cream
1 tablespoon sugar
2 tablespoons walnuts, chopped

DIRECTIONS:
In your slow cooker, combine the berries with the cream and the other ingredients, toss gently, put the lid on, cook on High for 1 hour, divide into bowls, and serve.

NUTRITION:
calories 260, fat 3, fiber 2, carbs 14, protein 3

Vanilla Cookies

Preparation time: 10 minutes
Cooking time: 2 hours and 30 minutes
Servings: 12

INGREDIENTS:
2 eggs
¼ cup vegetable oil
1 cup sugar
½ teaspoon vanilla extract
1 teaspoon baking powder
1 and ½ cups almond meal
½ cup almonds, chopped

DIRECTIONS:
In a bowl, mix oil with sugar, vanilla extract and eggs and whisk. Add baking powder, almond meal and almonds and stir well. Line your slow cooker with parchment paper, spread cookie mix on the bottom of the slow cooker, cover and cook on Low for 2 hours and 30 minutes. Leave cookie sheet to cool down, cut into medium pieces and serve.

NUTRITION:
calories 220, fat 2, fiber 1, carbs 3, protein 6

Apple Compote

Preparation time: 10 minutes
Cooking time: 1 hour
Servings: 2

INGREDIENTS:
1 pound apples, cored and cut into wedges
½ cup water
1 tablespoon sugar
1 teaspoon vanilla extract
½ teaspoon almond extract

DIRECTIONS:
In your slow cooker, mix the apples with the water and the other ingredients, toss, put the lid on and cook on High for 1 hour. Divide into bowls and serve cold.

NUTRITION:
calories 203, fat 0, fiber 1, carbs 5, protein 4

Pumpkin Pie

Preparation time: 10 minutes
Cooking time: 2 hours and 20 minutes
Servings: 10

INGREDIENTS:
1 and ½ teaspoons baking powder
Cooking spray
1 cup pumpkin puree
2 cups flour
½ teaspoon baking soda
1 and ½ teaspoons cinnamon powder
¼ teaspoon ginger, grated
1 tablespoon vegetable oil
2 eggs
1 tablespoon vanilla extract
1/3 cup maple syrup
1 teaspoon lemon juice

DIRECTIONS:
In a bowl, flour with baking powder, baking soda, cinnamon, ginger, eggs, oil, vanilla, pumpkin puree, maple syrup and lemon juice, stir and pour in your slow cooker greased with cooking spray and lined. Cover slow cooker and cook on Low for 2 hours and 20 minutes. Leave the cake to cool down, slice and serve.

NUTRITION:
calories 182, fat 3, fiber 2, carbs 10, protein 3

Plums Stew

Preparation time: 10 minutes
Cooking time: 1 hour
Servings: 2

INGREDIENTS:
1 pound plums, pitted and halved
½ teaspoon nutmeg, ground
1 cup water
1 and ½ tablespoons sugar
1 tablespoon vanilla extract

DIRECTIONS:
In your slow cooker, mix the plums with the water and the other ingredients, toss gently, put the lid on and cook on High for 1 hour. Divide the mix into bowls and serve.

NUTRITION:
calories 200, fat 2, fiber 1, carbs 5, protein 4

Strawberries Marmalade

Preparation time: 10 minutes
Cooking time: 4 hours
Servings: 10

INGREDIENTS:
32 ounces strawberries, chopped
2 pounds sugar
Zest of 1 lemon, grated
4 ounces raisins
3 ounces water

DIRECTIONS:
In your slow cooker, mix strawberries with coconut sugar, lemon zest, raisins and water, stir, cover and cook on High for 4 hours. Divide into small jars and serve cold.

NUTRITION:
calories 140, fat 3, fiber 2, carbs 2, protein 1

Cinnamon Peach Mix

Preparation time: 10 minutes
Cooking time: 2 hours
Servings: 2

INGREDIENTS:
2 cups peaches, peeled and halved
3 tablespoons sugar
½ teaspoon cinnamon powder
½ cup heavy cream
1 teaspoon vanilla extract

DIRECTIONS:
In your slow cooker, mix the peaches with the sugar and the other ingredients, toss, put the lid on and cook on High for 2 hours. Divide the mix into bowls and serve.

NUTRITION:
calories 212, fat 4, fiber 4, carbs 7, protein 3

Rhubarb Marmalade

Preparation time: 10 minutes
Cooking time: 3 hours
Servings: 8

INGREDIENTS:
1/3 cup water
2 pounds rhubarb, chopped
2 pounds strawberries, chopped
1 cup sugar
1 tablespoon mint, chopped

DIRECTIONS:
In your Slow cooker, mix water with rhubarb, strawberries, sugar and mint, stir, cover and cook on High for 3 hours. Divide into cups and serve cold.

NUTRITION:
calories 100, fat 1, fiber 4, carbs 10, protein 2

Strawberry Cake

Preparation time: 10 minutes
Cooking time: 1 hour
Servings: 2

INGREDIENTS:
- ¼ cup coconut flour
- ¼ teaspoon baking soda
- 1 tablespoon sugar
- ¼ cup strawberries, chopped
- ½ cup coconut milk
- 1 teaspoon butter, melted
- ½ teaspoon lemon zest, grated
- ¼ teaspoon vanilla extract
- Cooking spray

DIRECTIONS:
In a bowl, mix the coconut flour with the baking soda, sugar and the other ingredients except the cooking spray and stir well. Grease your slow cooker with the cooking spray, line it with parchment paper, pour the cake batter inside, put the lid on and cook on High for 1 hour. Leave the cake to cool down, slice and serve.

NUTRITION:
calories 200, fat 4, fiber 4, carbs 10, protein 4

Sweet Potato Pudding
Preparation time: 10 minutes
Cooking time: 5 hours
Servings: 8

INGREDIENTS:
- 1 cup water
- 1 tablespoon lemon peel, grated
- ½ cup sugar
- 3 sweet potatoes peeled and sliced
- ¼ cup butter
- ¼ cup maple syrup
- 1 cup pecans, chopped

DIRECTIONS:
In your Slow cooker, mix water with lemon peel, sugar, potatoes, butter, maple syrup and pecans, stir, cover and cook on High for 5 hours. Divide sweet potato pudding into bowls and serve cold.

NUTRITION:
calories 200, fat 4, fiber 3, carbs 10, protein 4

Ginger Pears Mix
Preparation time: 10 minutes
Cooking time: 2 hours
Servings: 2

INGREDIENTS:
- 2 pears, peeled and cored
- 1 cup apple juice
- ½ tablespoon brown sugar
- 1 tablespoon ginger, grated

DIRECTIONS:
In your slow cooker, mix the pears with the apple juice and the other ingredients, toss, put the lid on and cook on Low for 2 hour. Divide the mix into bowls and serve warm.

NUTRITION:
calories 250, fat 1, fiber 2, carbs 12, protein 4

Cherry Jam
Preparation time: 10 minutes
Cooking time: 3 hours
Servings: 6

INGREDIENTS:
- 2 tablespoons lemon juice
- 3 tablespoons gelatin
- 4 cups cherries, pitted
- 2 cups sugar

DIRECTIONS:
In your Slow cooker, mix lemon juice with gelatin, cherries and coconut sugar, stir, cover and cook on High for 3 hours. Divide into cups and serve cold.

NUTRITION:
calories 211, fat 3, fiber 1, carbs 3, protein 3

Raisin Cookies
Preparation time: 10 minutes
Cooking time: 2 hours and 30 minutes
Servings: 2

INGREDIENTS:
- 1 tablespoon coconut oil, melted
- 2 eggs, whisked
- ¼ cup brown sugar
- ½ cup raisins
- ¼ cup almond milk
- ¼ teaspoon vanilla extract
- ¼ teaspoon baking powder
- 1 cup almond flour

DIRECTIONS:
In a bowl, mix the eggs with the raisins, almond milk and the other ingredients and whisk well. Line your slow cooker with parchment paper, spread the cookie mix on the bottom of the pot, put the lid on, cook on Low for 2 hours and 30 minutes, leave aside to cool down, cut with a cookie cutter and serve.

NUTRITION:
calories 220, fat 2, fiber 1, carbs 6, protein 6

Sweet Cookies
Preparation time: 10 minutes
Cooking time: 2 hours and 30 minutes
Servings: 10

INGREDIENTS:
1 egg white
¼ cup vegetable oil
1 cup sugar
½ teaspoon vanilla extract
1 teaspoon baking powder
1 and ½ cups almond meal
½ cup dark chocolate chips

DIRECTIONS:
In a bowl, mix coconut oil with sugar, vanilla extract and egg white and beat well using your mixer. Add baking powder and almond meal and stir well. Fold in chocolate chips and stir gently. Line your slow cooker with parchment paper and grease it. Transfer cookie mix to your Slow cooker, press it on the bottom, cover and cook on low for 2 hours and 30 minutes. Take cookie sheet out of the Slow cooker, cut in 10 bars and serve.

NUTRITION:
calories 220, fat 2, fiber 1, carbs 3, protein 6

Blueberries Jam
Preparation time: 10 minutes
Cooking time: 4 hours
Servings: 2

INGREDIENTS:
2 cups blueberries
½ cup water
¼ pound sugar
Zest of 1 lime

DIRECTIONS:
In your slow cooker, combine the berries with the water and the other ingredients, toss, put the lid on and cook on High for 4 hours. Divide into small jars and serve cold.

NUTRITION:
calories 250, fat 3, fiber 2, carbs 6, protein 1

Maple Pears
Preparation time: 10 minutes
Cooking time: 4 hours
Servings: 4

INGREDIENTS:
4 pears, peeled and tops cut off and cored
5 cardamom pods
2 cups orange juice
¼ cup maple syrup
1 cinnamon stick
1-inch ginger, grated

DIRECTIONS:
Put the pears in your Slow cooker, add cardamom, orange juice, maple syrup, cinnamon and ginger, cover and cook on Low for 4 hours. Divide pears between plates and serve them with the sauce on top.

NUTRITION:
calories 200, fat 4, fiber 2, carbs 3, protein 4

Orange Bowls
Preparation time: 10 minutes
Cooking time: 3 hours
Servings: 2

INGREDIENTS:
½ pound oranges, peeled and cut into segments
1 cup heavy cream
½ tablespoon almonds, chopped
1 tablespoon chia seeds
1 tablespoon sugar

DIRECTIONS:
In your slow cooker, mix the oranges with the cream and the other ingredients, toss, put the lid on and cook on Low for 3 hours. Divide into bowls and serve.

NUTRITION:
calories 170, fat 0, fiber 2, carbs 7, protein 4

Stuffed Apples
Preparation time: 10 minutes
Cooking time: 1 hour and 30 minutes
Servings: 5

INGREDIENTS:
5 apples, tops cut off and cored
5 figs
1/3 cup sugar
1 teaspoon dried ginger
¼ cup pecans, chopped
2 teaspoons lemon zest, grated
¼ teaspoon nutmeg, ground
½ teaspoon cinnamon powder
1 tablespoon lemon juice
1 tablespoon vegetable oil
½ cup water

DIRECTIONS:
In a bowl, mix figs with sugar, ginger, pecans, lemon zest, nutmeg, cinnamon, oil and lemon juice, whisk really well, stuff your apples with this mix and put them in your Slow cooker. Add the water, cover, cook on High for 1 hour and 30 minutes, divide between dessert plates and serve.

NUTRITION:
calories 200, fat 1, fiber 2, carbs 4, protein 7

Quinoa Pudding
Preparation time: 10 minutes
Cooking time: 2 hours
Servings: 2

INGREDIENTS:
1 cup quinoa
2 cups almond milk
½ cup sugar
½ tablespoon walnuts, chopped
½ tablespoon almonds, chopped

DIRECTIONS:
In your slow cooker, mix the quinoa with the milk and the other ingredients, toss, put the lid on and cook on High for 2 hours. Divide the pudding into cups and serve.

NUTRITION:
calories 213, fat 4, fiber 6, carbs 10, protein 4

Chocolate Cake

Preparation time: 10 minutes

Cooking time: 3 hours

Servings: 10

INGREDIENTS:
1 cup flour
3 egg whites, whisked
½ cup cocoa powder
½ cup sugar
1 and ½ teaspoons baking powder
3 eggs
4 tablespoons vegetable oil
¾ teaspoon vanilla extract
2/3 cup milk
1/3 cup dark chocolate chips

DIRECTIONS:
In a bowl, mix sugar with flour, egg whites, cocoa powder, baking powder, milk, oil, eggs, chocolate chips and vanilla extract and whisk really well. Pour this into your lined and greased Slow cooker and cook on Low for 2 hours. Leave the cake aside to cool down, slice and serve.

NUTRITION:
calories 200, fat 12, fiber 4, carbs 8, protein 6

Chia and Avocado Pudding

Preparation time: 10 minutes

Cooking time: 3 hours

Servings: 2

INGREDIENTS:
½ cup almond flour
1 tablespoon lime juice
2 tablespoons chia seeds
1 cup avocado, peeled, pitted and cubed
1 teaspoons baking powder
¼ teaspoon nutmeg, ground
¼ cup almond milk
2 tablespoons brown sugar
1 egg, whisked
2 tablespoons coconut oil, melted
Cooking spray

DIRECTIONS:
Grease your slow cooker with the cooking spray and mix the chia seeds with the flour, avocado and the other ingredients inside. Put the lid on, cook on High for 3 hours, leave the pudding to cool down, divide into bowls and serve

NUTRITION:
calories 220, fat 4, fiber 4, carbs 9, protein 6

Berry Cobbler

Preparation time: 10 minutes

Cooking time: 2 hours

Servings: 6

INGREDIENTS:
1 pound fresh blackberries
1 pound fresh blueberries
¾ cup water
¾ cup sugar+ 2 tablespoons
¾ cup flour
¼ cup tapioca flour
½ cup arrowroot powder
1 teaspoon baking powder
2 tablespoons palm sugar
1/3 cup milk
1 egg, whisked
1 teaspoon lemon zest, grated
3 tablespoons vegetable oil

DIRECTIONS:
Put blueberries, blackberries, ¾ cup sugar, water and tapioca in your Slow cooker, cover and cook on High for 1 hour. In a bowl, mix flour with arrowroot, the rest of the sugar and baking powder and stir well. In a second bowl, mix the egg with milk, oil and lemon zest. Combine egg mixture with flour mixture, stir well, drop tablespoons of this mix over the berries, cover and cook on High for 1 more hour. Leave cobbler to cool down, divide into dessert bowls and serve.

NUTRITION:
calories 240, fat 4, fiber 3, carbs 10, protein 6

Almond and Cherries Pudding

Preparation time: 10 minutes

Cooking time: 3 hours

Servings: 2

INGREDIENTS:
½ cup almonds, chopped
½ cup cherries, pitted and halved
½ cup heavy cream
½ cup almond milk
1 tablespoon butter, soft
1 egg
2 tablespoons sugar
½ cup almond flour
½ teaspoon baking powder
Cooking spray

DIRECTIONS:
Grease the slow cooker with the cooking spray and mix the almonds with the cherries, cream and the other ingredients inside. Put the lid on, cook on High for 3 hours, divide into bowls and serve.

NUTRITION:
calories 200, fat 4, fiber 2, carbs 8, protein 6

Apple Bread
Preparation time: 10 minutes
Cooking time: 2 hours and 20 minutes
Servings: 6

INGREDIENTS:
3 cups apples, cored and cubed
1 cup sugar
1 tablespoon vanilla extract
2 eggs
1 tablespoon apple pie spice
2 cups flour
1 tablespoon baking powder
1 tablespoon butter

DIRECTIONS:
In a bowl, mix apples with sugar, vanilla, eggs, apple spice, flour, baking powder and butter, whisk well, pour into your Slow cooker, cover and cook on High for 2 hours and 20 minutes. Leave the bread to cool down, slice and serve.

NUTRITION:
calories 236, fat 2, fiber 4, carbs 12, protein 4

Vanilla Peach Cream
Preparation time: 10 minutes
Cooking time: 3 hours
Servings: 2

INGREDIENTS:
¼ teaspoon cinnamon powder
1 cup peaches, pitted and chopped
¼ cup heavy cream
Cooking spray
1 tablespoon maple syrup
½ teaspoons vanilla extract
2 tablespoons sugar

DIRECTIONS:
In a blender, mix the peaches with the cinnamon and the other ingredients except the cooking spray and pulse well. Grease the slow cooker with the cooking spray, pour the cream mix inside, put the lid on and cook on Low for 3 hours. Divide the cream into bowls and serve cold.

NUTRITION:
calories 200, fat 3, fiber 4, carbs 10, protein 9

Banana Cake
Preparation time: 10 minutes
Cooking time: 2 hours
Servings: 6

INGREDIENTS:
¾ cup sugar
1/3 cup butter, soft
1 teaspoon vanilla
1 egg
3 bananas, mashed
1 teaspoon baking powder
1 and ½ cups flour
½ teaspoons baking soda
1/3 cup milk
Cooking spray

DIRECTIONS:
In a bowl, mix butter with sugar, vanilla extract, eggs, bananas, baking powder, flour, baking soda and milk and whisk. Grease your Slow cooker with the cooking spray, add the batter, spread, cover and cook on High for 2 hours. Leave the cake to cool down, slice and serve.

NUTRITION:
calories 300, fat 4, fiber 4, carbs 27, protein 4

Cinnamon Plums
Preparation time: 10 minutes
Cooking time: 2 hours
Servings: 2

INGREDIENTS:
½ pound plums, pitted and halved
2 tablespoons sugar
1 teaspoon cinnamon, ground
½ cup orange juice

DIRECTIONS:
In your slow cooker, mix the plums with the cinnamon and the other ingredients, toss, put the lid on and cook on Low for 2 hours. Divide into bowls and serve as a dessert.

NUTRITION:
calories 180, fat 2, fiber 1, carbs 8, protein 8

Chocolate Pudding
Preparation time: 10 minutes
Cooking time: 1 hour
Servings: 4

INGREDIENTS:
4 ounces heavy cream
4 ounces dark chocolate, cut into chunks
1 teaspoon sugar

DIRECTIONS:
In a bowl, mix the cream with chocolate and sugar,

whisk well, pour into your slow cooker, cover and cook on High for 1 hour. Divide into bowls and serve cold.

NUTRITION:
calories 232, fat 12, fiber 6, carbs 9, protein 4

Cardamom Apples

Preparation time: 10 minutes

Cooking time: 2 hours

Servings: 2

INGREDIENTS:
1 pound apples, cored and cut into wedges
½ cup almond milk
¼ teaspoon cardamom, ground
2 tablespoons brown sugar

DIRECTIONS:
In your slow cooker, mix the apples with the cardamom and the other ingredients, toss, put the lid on and cook on High for 2 hours. Divide the mix into bowls and serve cold.

NUTRITION:
calories 280, fat 2, fiber 1, carbs 10, protein 6

Cauliflower Pudding

Preparation time: 5 minutes

Cooking time: 2 hours

Servings: 6

INGREDIENTS:
1 tablespoon butter, melted
7 ounces cauliflower rice
4 ounces water
16 ounces milk
3 ounces sugar
1 egg
1 teaspoon cinnamon powder
1 teaspoon vanilla extract

DIRECTIONS:
In your Slow cooker, mix butter with cauliflower rice, water, milk, sugar, egg, cinnamon and vanilla extract, stir, cover and cook on High for 2 hours. Divide pudding into bowls and serve cold.

NUTRITION:
calories 202, fat 2, fiber 6, carbs 18, protein 4

Cherry and Rhubarb Mix

Preparation time: 10 minutes

Cooking time: 2 hours

Servings: 2

INGREDIENTS:
2 cups rhubarb, sliced
½ cup cherries, pitted
1 tablespoon butter, melted
¼ cup coconut cream
½ cup sugar

DIRECTIONS:
In your slow cooker, mix the rhubarb with the cherries and the other ingredients, toss, put the lid on and cook on High for 2 hours. Divide the mix into bowls and serve cold.

NUTRITION:
calories 200, fat 2, fiber 3, carbs 6, protein 1

Chia Pudding

Preparation time: 10 minutes

Cooking time: 1 hour

Servings: 4

INGREDIENTS:
1 cup milk
½ cup pumpkin puree
2 tablespoons maple syrup
½ cup coconut milk
¼ cup chia seeds
½ teaspoon cinnamon powder
¼ teaspoon ginger, grated

DIRECTIONS:
In your Slow cooker, mix milk with coconut milk, pumpkin puree, maple syrup, chia, cinnamon and ginger, stir, cover and cook on High for 1 hour. Divide pudding into bowls and serve.

NUTRITION:
calories 105, fat 2, fiber 7, carbs 11, protein 4

Peaches and Wine Sauce

Preparation time: 10 minutes

Cooking time: 2 hours

Servings: 2

INGREDIENTS:
3 tablespoons brown sugar
1 pound peaches, pitted and cut into wedges
½ cup red wine
½ teaspoon vanilla extract
1 teaspoon lemon zest, grated

DIRECTIONS:
In your slow cooker, mix the peaches with the sugar and the other ingredients, toss, put the lid on and cook on High for 2 hours. Divide into bowls and serve.

NUTRITION:
calories 200, fat 4, fiber 6, carbs 9, protein 4

Stewed Grapefruit

Preparation time: 10 minutes
Cooking time: 2 hours
Servings: 6

INGREDIENTS:
1 cup water
1 cup maple syrup
½ cup mint, chopped
64 ounces red grapefruit juice
2 grapefruits, peeled and chopped

DIRECTIONS:
In your Slow cooker, mix grapefruit with water, maple syrup, mint and grapefruit juice, stir, cover and cook on High for 2 hours. Divide into bowls and serve cold.

NUTRITION:
calories 170, fat 1, fiber, 2, carbs 5, protein 1

Apricot and Peaches Cream

Preparation time: 10 minutes
Cooking time: 2 hours
Servings: 2

INGREDIENTS:
1 cup apricots, pitted and chopped
1 cup peaches, pitted and chopped
1 cup heavy cream
3 tablespoons brown sugar
1 teaspoon vanilla extract

DIRECTIONS:
In a blender, mix the apricots with the peaches and the other ingredients, and pulse well. Put the cream in the slow cooker, put the lid on, cook on High for 2 hours, divide into bowls and serve.

NUTRITION:
calories 200, fat 4, fiber 5, carbs 10, protein 4

Cocoa Cherry Compote

Preparation time: 10 minutes
Cooking time: 2 hours
Servings: 6

INGREDIENTS:
½ cup dark cocoa powder
¾ cup red cherry juice
¼ cup maple syrup
1 pound cherries, pitted and halved
2 tablespoons sugar
2 cups water

DIRECTIONS:
In your Slow cooker, mix cocoa powder with cherry juice, maple syrup, cherries, water and sugar, stir, cover and cook on High for 2 hours. Divide into bowls and serve cold.

NUTRITION:
calories 197, fat 1, fiber 4, carbs 5, protein 2

Vanilla Grapes Mix

Preparation time: 10 minutes
Cooking time: 2 hours
Servings: 2

INGREDIENTS:
1 cup grapes, halved
½ teaspoon vanilla extract
1 cup oranges, peeled and cut into segments
¼ cup water
1 and ½ tablespoons sugar
1 teaspoon lemon juice

DIRECTIONS:
In your slow cooker, mix the grapes with the oranges, water and the other ingredients, toss, put the lid on and cook on Low for 2 hours. Divide into bowls and serve.

NUTRITION:
calories 100, fat 3, fiber 6, carbs 8, protein 3

Cashew Cake

Preparation time: 10 minutes
Cooking time: 2 hours
Servings: 6

INGREDIENTS:
For the crust:
½ cup dates, pitted
1 tablespoon water
½ teaspoon vanilla
½ cup almonds
For the cake:
2 and ½ cups cashews, soaked for 8 hours
1 cup blueberries
¾ cup maple syrup
1 tablespoon vegetable oil

DIRECTIONS:
In your blender, mix dates with water, vanilla and almonds, pulse well, transfer dough to a working surface, flatten and arrange on the bottom of your Slow cooker. In your blender, mix maple syrup with the oil, cashews and blueberries, blend well, spread over crust, cover and cook on High for 2 hours. Leave the cake to cool down, slice and serve.

NUTRITION:
calories 200, fat 3, fiber 5, carbs 12, protein 3

Pomegranate and Mango Bowls

Preparation time: 10 minutes
Cooking time: 3 hours
Servings: 2

INGREDIENTS:
2 cups pomegranate seeds
1 cup mango, peeled and cubed
½ cup heavy cream
1 tablespoon lemon juice
½ teaspoon vanilla extract
2 tablespoons white sugar

DIRECTIONS:
In your slow cooker, combine the mango with the pomegranate seeds and the other ingredients, toss, put the lid on and cook on Low for 3 hours. Divide into bowls and serve cold.

NUTRITION:
calories 162, fat 4, fiber 5, carbs 20, protein 6

Lemon Pudding

Preparation time: 10 minutes
Cooking time: 1 hour
Servings: 4

INGREDIENTS:
1/3 cup butter, soft
1 and ½ tablespoons vegetable oil
5 tablespoons lemon juice
½ teaspoon lemon zest, grated
1 tablespoons maple syrup

DIRECTIONS:
In a bowl, mix butter with oil, lemon juice, lemon zest and maple syrup and stir really well. Pour into your Slow cooker, cook on High for 1 hour, divide into bowls and serve.

NUTRITION:
calories 182, fat 4, fiber 0, carbs 6, protein 1

Mandarin Cream

Preparation time: 10 minutes
Cooking time: 2 hours
Servings: 2

INGREDIENTS:
1 tablespoon ginger, grated
3 tablespoons sugar
3 mandarins, peeled and chopped
2 tablespoons agave nectar
½ cup coconut cream

DIRECTIONS:
In your slow cooker, mix the ginger with the sugar, mandarins and the other ingredients, whisk, put the lid on and cook on High for 2 hours. Blend the cream using an immersion blender, divide into bowls and serve cold.

NUTRITION:
calories 100, fat 4, fiber 5, carbs 6, protein 7

Lemon Jam

Preparation time: 10 minutes
Cooking time: 2 hours
Servings: 8

INGREDIENTS:
2 pounds lemons, sliced
2 cups dates
1 cup water
1 tablespoon vinegar
2 tablespoons sugar

DIRECTIONS:
Put dates in your blender, add water, pulse really well, transfer to your Slow cooker, add lemon slices, sugar and vinegar, stir, cover and cook on Low for 2 hours Divide into small jars and serve cold.

NUTRITION:
calories 172, fat 2, fiber 1, carbs 2, protein 4

Cranberries Cream

Preparation time: 10 minutes
Cooking time: 1 hour
Servings: 2

INGREDIENTS:
3 cups cranberries
½ cup water
½ cup coconut cream
½ teaspoon vanilla extract
½ teaspoon almond extract
½ cup sugar

DIRECTIONS:
In your slow cooker, mix the cranberries with the water, cream and the other ingredients, whisk, put the lid on and cook on High for 1 hour. Transfer to a blender, pulse well, divide into bowls and serve cold.

NUTRITION:
calories 100, fat 3, fiber 6, carbs 7, protein 3

Chocolate Cream

Preparation time: 10 minutes
Cooking time: 2 hours
Servings: 4

INGREDIENTS:
1 cup chocolate chips
2 tablespoons butter
2/3 cup heavy cream
2 teaspoons brandy
2 tablespoons sugar
¼ teaspoon vanilla extract

DIRECTIONS:
In your Slow cooker, mix chocolate chips with butter, cream, brandy, sugar and vanilla extract, cover and cook on Low for 2 hours. Divide into bowls and serve warm.

NUTRITION:
calories 150, fat 5, fiber 4, carbs 6, protein 1

Buttery Pineapple

Preparation time: 10 minutes

Cooking time: 2 hours

Servings: 2

INGREDIENTS:
- 2 cups pineapple, peeled and roughly cubed
- 1 and ½ tablespoons butter
- ½ cup heavy cream
- 2 tablespoons brown sugar
- ½ teaspoon cinnamon powder
- ½ teaspoon ginger, grated

DIRECTIONS:
In your slow cooker, mix the pineapple with the butter, cream and the other ingredients, toss, put the lid on and cook on High for 2 hours. Divide into bowls and serve cold.

NUTRITION:
calories 152, fat 3, fiber 1, carbs 17, protein 3

Coconut and Macadamia Cream

Preparation time: 10 minutes

Cooking time: 1 hour and 30 minutes

Servings: 4

INGREDIENTS:
- 4 tablespoons vegetable oil
- 3 tablespoons macadamia nuts, chopped
- 2 tablespoons sugar
- 1 cup heavy cream
- 5 tablespoons coconut powder

DIRECTIONS:
Put the oil in your Slow cooker, add nuts, sugar, coconut powder and cream, stir, cover, cook on Low for 1 hour and 30 minutes. Stir well, divide into bowls and serve.

NUTRITION:
calories 154, fat 1, fiber 0, carbs 7, protein 2

Strawberry and Orange Mix

Preparation time: 10 minutes

Cooking time: 1 hour

Servings: 2

INGREDIENTS:
- 2 tablespoons sugar
- 1 cup orange segments
- 1 cup strawberries, halved
- A pinch of ginger powder
- ½ teaspoon vanilla extract
- ½ cup orange juice
- 1 tablespoon chia seeds

DIRECTIONS:
In your slow cooker, mix the oranges with the berries, ginger powder and the other ingredients, toss, put the lid on and cook on High for 1 hour. Divide into bowls and serve cold.

NUTRITION:
calories 100, fat 2, fiber 2, carbs 10, protein 2

Strawberry Pie

Preparation time: 10 minutes

Cooking time: 2 hours

Servings: 12

INGREDIENTS:
For the crust:
- 1 cup coconut, shredded
- 1 cup sunflower seeds
- ¼ cup butter
- Cooking spray

For the filling:
- 1 teaspoon gelatin
- 8 ounces cream cheese
- 4 ounces strawberries
- 2 tablespoons water
- ½ tablespoon lemon juice
- ¼ teaspoon stevia
- ½ cup heavy cream
- 8 ounces strawberries, chopped for serving
- 16 ounces heavy cream for serving

DIRECTIONS:
In your food processor, mix sunflower seeds with coconut and butter and stir well. Put this into your Slow cooker greased with cooking spray. Heat up a pan with the water over medium heat, add gelatin, stir until it dissolves, take off heat and leave aside to cool down. Add this to your food processor, mix with 4 ounces strawberries, cream cheese, lemon juice and stevia and blend well. Add ½ cup heavy cream, stir well and spread this over crust. Top with 8 ounces strawberries, cover and cook on High for 2 hours. Spread heavy cream all over, leave the cake to cool down and keep it in the fridge until you serve it.

NUTRITION:
calories 234, fat 23, fiber 2, carbs 6, protein 7

Maple Plums and Mango

Preparation time: 10 minutes

Cooking time: 1 hour

Servings: 2

INGREDIENTS:
2 teaspoons orange zest
1 tablespoon orange juice
1 cup plums, pitted and halved
1 cup mango, peeled and cubed
1 tablespoon maple syrup
3 tablespoons sugar

DIRECTIONS:
In your slow cooker, mix the plums with the mango and the other ingredients, toss, put the lid on and cook on High for 1 hour. Divide into bowls and serve cold

NUTRITION:
calories 123, fat 1, fiber 2, carbs 20, protein 3

Sweet Raspberry Mix
Preparation time: 10 minutes
Cooking time: 1 hour
Servings: 12

INGREDIENTS:
½ cup coconut butter
½ cup vegetable oil
½ cup raspberries, dried
¼ cup sugar
½ cup coconut, shredded

DIRECTIONS:
In your food processor, blend dried berries very well. In a bowl, mix oil, coconut and sugar and spread half of this mix on the bottom of your Slow cooker. Add raspberry powder, spread, top with the rest of the butter mix, spread, cover and cook on High for 1 hour. Cut into pieces and serve.

NUTRITION:
calories 234, fat 22, fiber 2, carbs 4, protein 2

Cantaloupe Cream
Preparation time: 5 minutes
Cooking time: 1 hour
Servings: 2

INGREDIENTS:
2 cups cantaloupe, peeled and cubed
2 tablespoons sugar
1 cup coconut cream
1 tablespoon butter
1 tablespoon lemon zest, grated
Juice of ½ lemon

DIRECTIONS:
In your slow cooker, mix the cantaloupe with the sugar, cream and the other ingredients, toss, put the lid on and cook on High for 1 hour. Blend using an immersion blender, divide into bowls and serve cold.

NUTRITION:
calories 100, fat 2, fiber 3, carbs 6, protein 1

Sweet Mascarpone Cream
Preparation time: 10 minutes
Cooking time: 1 hour
Servings: 12

INGREDIENTS:
8 ounces mascarpone cheese
¾ teaspoon vanilla extract
1 tablespoon sugar
1 cup whipping cream
½ pint blueberries
½ pint strawberries

DIRECTIONS:
In your Slow cooker, mix whipping cream with sugar, vanilla and mascarpone and blend well. Add blueberries and strawberries, cover cook on High for 1 hour, stir your cream, divide it into glasses and serve cold.

NUTRITION:
calories 143, fat 12, fiber 1, carbs 6, protein 2

Yogurt Cheesecake
Preparation time: 1 hour
Cooking time: 3 hours
Servings: 2

INGREDIENTS:
For the crust:
1 tablespoon coconut oil, melted
½ cup graham cookies, crumbled
For the filling:
3 ounces cream cheese, soft
1 cup Greek yogurt
½ tablespoon cornstarch
3 tablespoons sugar
1 egg, whisked
1 teaspoon almond extract
Cooking spray

DIRECTIONS:
In a bowl mix the cookie crumbs with butter and stir well. Grease your slow cooker with the cooking spray, line it with parchment paper and press the crumbs on the bottom. In a bowl, mix the cream cheese with the yogurt and the other ingredients, whisk well and spread over the crust. Put the lid on, cook on Low for 3 hours, cool down and keep in the fridge for 1 hour before serving.

NUTRITION:
calories 276, fat 12, fiber 3, carbs 20, protein 4

Lemon Cream
Preparation time: 10 minutes
Cooking time: 1 hour
Servings: 4

INGREDIENTS:
1 cup heavy cream
1 teaspoon lemon zest, grated
¼ cup lemon juice
8 ounces mascarpone cheese

DIRECTIONS:
In your Slow cooker, mix heavy cream with mascarpone, lemon zest and lemon juice, stir, cover and cook on Low for 1 hour. Divide into dessert glasses and keep in the fridge until you serve.

NUTRITION:
calories 165, fat 7, fiber 0, carbs 7, protein 4

Chocolate Mango Mix
Preparation time: 10 minutes
Cooking time: 1 hour
Servings: 2

INGREDIENTS:
1 cup crème fraiche
¼ cup dark chocolate, cut into chunks
1 cup mango, peeled and chopped
2 tablespoons sugar
½ teaspoon almond extract

DIRECTIONS:
In your slow cooker, mix the crème fraiche with the chocolate and the other ingredients, toss, put the lid on and cook on Low for 1 hour. Blend using an immersion blender, divide into bowls and serve.

NUTRITION:
calories 200, fat 12, fiber 4, carbs 7, protein 3

Coconut Vanilla Cream
Preparation time: 10 minutes
Cooking time: 1 hour
Servings: 4

INGREDIENTS:
14 ounces canned coconut milk
1 teaspoon vanilla extract
2 tablespoons sugar
4 ounces blueberries
2 tablespoons walnuts, chopped

DIRECTIONS:
In a bowl, mix coconut milk with sugar and vanilla extract and whisk using your mixer. In another bowl, mix berries with walnuts and stir. Pour half of the vanilla cream in your Slow cooker, add a layer of berries and walnuts, add the rest of the vanilla cream, cover and cook on Low for 1 hour. Spoon this into dessert cups and serve cold.

NUTRITION:
calories 160, fat 23, fiber 4, carbs 6, protein 7

Lemon Jam
Preparation time: 10 minutes
Cooking time: 3 hours
Servings: 2

INGREDIENTS:
½ cup lemon juice
1 orange, peeled and cut into segments
1 lemon, peeled and cut into segments
½ cup water
2 tablespoons lemon zest, grated
¼ cup sugar
A pinch of cinnamon powder
½ tablespoon cornstarch

DIRECTIONS:
In your slow cooker, mix the lemon juice with the sugar, water and the other ingredients, whisk, put the lid on and cook on Low for 3 hours. Divide into small jars and serve cold.

NUTRITION:
calories 70, fat 1, fiber 3, carbs 13, protein 1

Avocado Pudding
Preparation time: 2 hours
Cooking time: 1 hour
Servings: 3

INGREDIENTS:
½ cup vegetable oil
½ tablespoon sugar
1 tablespoon cocoa powder
For the pudding:
1 teaspoon peppermint oil
14 ounces coconut milk
1 avocado, pitted, peeled and chopped
1 tablespoon sugar

DIRECTIONS:
In a bowl, mix vegetable oil with cocoa powder and ½ tablespoon sugar, stir well, transfer to a lined container, keep in the fridge for 1 hour and chop into small pieces. In your blender, mix coconut milk with avocado, 1 tablespoon sugar and peppermint oil, pulse well, transfer to your Slow cooker, cook on Low for 1 hour and mix with the chocolate chips you made at the beginning. Divide pudding into bowls and keep in the fridge for 1 more hour before serving.

NUTRITION:
calories 140, fat 3, fiber 2, carbs 3, protein 4

Lemon Peach Mix
Preparation time: 10 minutes
Cooking time: 3 hours
Servings: 2

INGREDIENTS:
1 cup peaches, peeled and halved
2 tablespoons sugar
½ tablespoon lemon juice
½ cup heavy cream
1 tablespoon lemon zest, grated

DIRECTIONS:
In your slow cooker, mix the peaches with the sugar and the other ingredients, toss gently, put the lid on and cook on Low for 3 hours. Divide into cups and serve cold.

NUTRITION:
calories 50, fat 0, fiber 2, carbs 10, protein 0

Coconut Pudding
Preparation time: 10 minutes
Cooking time: 1 hour
Servings: 4

INGREDIENTS:
1 and 2/3 cups coconut milk
1 tablespoon gelatin
6 tablespoons sugar
3 egg yolks
½ teaspoon vanilla extract

DIRECTIONS:
In a bowl, mix gelatin with 1 tablespoon coconut milk and stir. Put the rest of the milk in your Slow cooker, add whisked egg yolks, gelatin, vanilla and sugar, stir everything, cover, cook on High for 1 hour, divide into bowls and serve cold.

NUTRITION:
calories 170, fat 2, fiber 0, carbs 6, protein 2

Rhubarb Stew
Preparation time: 10 minutes
Cooking time: 2 hours
Servings: 2

INGREDIENTS:
½ pound rhubarb, roughly sliced
2 tablespoons sugar
½ teaspoon vanilla extract
½ teaspoon lemon extract
1 tablespoon lemon juice
¼ cup water

DIRECTIONS:
In your slow cooker, mix the rhubarb with the sugar, vanilla and the other ingredients, toss, put the lid on and cook on Low for 2 hours. Divide the mix into bowls and serve cold.

NUTRITION:
calories 60, fat 1, fiber 0, carbs 10, protein 1

Cocoa Cake
Preparation time: 2 minutes
Cooking time: 2 hour
Servings: 3

INGREDIENTS:
10 tablespoons flour
3 tablespoon butter, melted
4 teaspoons sugar
1 tablespoon cocoa powder
4 eggs
¼ teaspoon vanilla extract
½ teaspoon baking powder

DIRECTIONS:
In a bowl, mix butter with sugar, cocoa powder, eggs, vanilla extract and baking powder and stir well. Add flour, stir the whole batter really well, pour into your Slow cooker, cover and cook on High for 2 hours. Slice cake, divide it between plates and serve.

NUTRITION:
calories 240, fat 34, fiber 7, carbs 10, protein 20

Strawberry and Blackberry Jam
Preparation time: 10 minutes
Cooking time: 3 hours
Servings: 2

INGREDIENTS:
½ pound strawberries, halved
1 cup blackberries
1 tablespoon lemon zest, grated
½ teaspoon almond extract
2 tablespoons lemon juice
1 cup sugar

DIRECTIONS:
In your slow cooker, combine the berries with the lemon zest and the other ingredients, toss, put the lid on and cook on Low for 3 hours. Stir the mix well, divide into bowls and serve cold.

NUTRITION:
calories 451, fat 0.8, fiber 6.3, carbs 112, protein 2

Dark Chocolate Cream
Preparation time: 1 minute
Cooking time: 1 hour
Servings: 6

INGREDIENTS:
½ cup heavy cream
4 ounces dark chocolate, unsweetened and chopped

DIRECTIONS:
In your Slow cooker, mix cream with chocolate, stir, cover, cook on High for 1 hour, divide into bowls and serve cold.

NUTRITION:
calories 78, fat 1, fiber 1, carbs 2, protein 1

Pear Cream

Preparation time: 10 minutes
Cooking time: 3 hours
Servings: 2

INGREDIENTS:

½ pound pears, peeled and chopped
½ cup heavy cream
½ cup honey
1 tablespoon lemon zest, grated
Juice of ½ lemon

DIRECTIONS:
In your slow cooker, mix the pears with the cream and the other ingredients, whisk, put the lid on and cook on Low for 3 hours. Blend using an immersion blender, divide into cups and serve cold.

NUTRITION:
calories 429, fat 11.3, fiber 3.9, carbs 88.6, protein 1.4

Mango Cream

Preparation time: 10 minutes
Cooking time: 1 hour
Servings: 4

INGREDIENTS:

1 mango, sliced
14 ounces coconut cream

DIRECTIONS:
In your Slow cooker, mix mango with the cream, cover and cook on High for 1 hour. Divide into bowls and serve right away.

NUTRITION:
calories 150, fat 12, fiber 2, carbs 6, protein 1

Rhubarb Jam

Preparation time: 10 minutes
Cooking time: 2 hours
Servings: 2

INGREDIENTS:

½ pound rhubarb, sliced
½ tablespoon cornstarch
¼ cup sugar
1 tablespoon lemon juice
1 cup water

DIRECTIONS:
In your slow cooker, mix the rhubarb with the sugar and the other ingredients, toss, put the lid on and cook on High for 2 hours. Whisk the jam, divide into bowls and serve cold.

NUTRITION:
calories 40, fat 0, fiber 1, carbs 10, protein 1

Lime Cheesecake

Preparation time: 10 minutes
Cooking time: 1 hour
Servings: 10

INGREDIENTS:

2 tablespoons butter, melted
2 teaspoons sugar
4 ounces almond meal
¼ cup coconut, shredded
Cooking spray

For the filling:
1 pound cream cheese
Zest of 1 lime
Juice from 1 lime
2 sachets lime jelly
2 cup hot water

DIRECTIONS:
In a bowl, mix coconut with almond meal, butter and sugar, stir well and press on the bottom of your Slow cooker greased with cooking spray. Put the water in a bowl, add jelly sachets and stir until they dissolve. Put cream cheese in a bowl, add jelly, lime juice and lime zest, blend well and spread over your crust. Cover the slow cooker, cook on High for 1 hour and then keep in the fridge until you serve it.

NUTRITION:
calories 300, fat 23, fiber 2, carbs 5, protein 7

Apricot Marmalade

Preparation time: 10 minutes
Cooking time: 3 hours
Servings: 2

INGREDIENTS:

1 cup apricots, chopped
½ cup water
1 teaspoon vanilla extract
2 tablespoons lemon juice
1 teaspoon fruit pectin
2 cups sugar

DIRECTIONS:
In your slow cooker, mix the apricots with the water, vanilla and the other ingredients, whisk,

put the lid on and cook on High for 3 hours. Stir the marmalade, divide into bowls and serve cold. Nutrition: calories 100, fat 1, fiber 2, carbs 20, protein 1

Caramel Cream

Preparation time: 10 minutes
Cooking time: 2 hours
Servings: 2

INGREDIENTS:
1 and ½ teaspoons caramel extract
1 cup water
2 ounces cream cheese
2 eggs
1 and ½ tablespoons sugar

For the caramel sauce:
2 tablespoons sugar
2 tablespoons butter, melted
¼ teaspoon caramel extract

DIRECTIONS:
In your blender, mix cream cheese with water, 1 and ½ tablespoons sugar, 1 and ½ teaspoons caramel extract and eggs and blend well. Pour this into your Slow cooker, cover and cook on High for 2 hours. Put the butter in a slow cooker, heat up over medium heat add ¼ teaspoon caramel extract and 2 tablespoons sugar, stir well and cook until everything melts. Pour this over caramel cream, leave everything to cool down and serve in dessert cups.

NUTRITION:
calories 254, fat 24, fiber 1, carbs 6, protein 8

Apple, Avocado and Mango Bowls

Preparation time: 10 minutes
Cooking time: 2 hours
Servings: 2

INGREDIENTS:
1 cup avocado, peeled, pitted and cubed
1 cup mango, peeled and cubed
1 apple, cored and cubed
2 tablespoons brown sugar
1 cup heavy cream
1 tablespoon lemon juice

DIRECTIONS:
In your slow cooker, combine the avocado with the mango and the other ingredients, toss gently, put the lid on and cook on Low for 2 hours. Divide the mix into bowls and serve.

NUTRITION:
calories 60, fat 1, fiber 2, carbs 20, protein 1

Ricotta Cream

Preparation time: 2 hours and 10 minutes
Cooking time: 1 hour
Servings: 10

INGREDIENTS:
½ cup hot coffee
2 cups ricotta cheese
2 and ½ teaspoons gelatin
1 teaspoon vanilla extract
1 teaspoon espresso powder
1 teaspoon sugar
1 cup whipping cream

DIRECTIONS:
In a bowl, mix coffee with gelatin, stir well and leave aside until coffee is cold. In your Slow cooker, mix espresso, sugar, vanilla extract and ricotta and stir. Add coffee mix and whipping cream, cover, cook on Low for 1 hour. Divide into dessert bowls and keep in the fridge for 2 hours before serving.

NUTRITION:
calories 200, fat 13, fiber 0, carbs 5, protein 7

Tomato Jam

Preparation time: 10 minutes
Cooking time: 3 hours
Servings: 2

INGREDIENTS:
½ pound tomatoes, chopped
1 green apple, grated
2 tablespoons red wine vinegar
4 tablespoons sugar

DIRECTIONS:
In your slow cooker, mix the tomatoes with the apple and the other ingredients, whisk, put the lid on and cook on Low for 3 hours. Whisk the jam well, blend a bit using an immersion blender, divide into bowls and serve cold.

NUTRITION:
calories 70, fat 1, fiber 1, carbs 18, protein 1

Green Tea Pudding

Preparation time: 10 minutes
Cooking time: 1 hour
Servings: 2

INGREDIENTS:
½ cup coconut milk
1 and ½ cup avocado, pitted and peeled
2 tablespoons green tea powder
2 teaspoons lime zest, grated
1 tablespoon sugar

DIRECTIONS:
In your Slow cooker, mix coconut milk with avocado, tea powder, lime zest and sugar, stir, cover and cook on Low for 1 hour. Divide into cups and serve cold.

NUTRITION:
calories 107, fat 5, fiber 3, carbs 6, protein 8

Cinnamon and Chocolate Peaches
Preparation time: 10 minutes
Cooking time: 2 hours
Servings: 2

INGREDIENTS:
4 peaches, stoned and halved
1 tablespoon cinnamon powder
1 tablespoon cocoa powder
2 tablespoons coconut oil, melted
2 tablespoons sugar
1 cup heavy cream

DIRECTIONS:
In your slow cooker, mix the peaches with the cinnamon, cocoa and the other ingredients, toss, put the lid on and cook on Low for 2 hours. Divide the mix into bowls and serve cold.

NUTRITION:
calories 40, fat 1, fiber 1, carbs 5, protein 0

Sweet Lemon Mix
Preparation time: 5 minutes
Cooking time: 1 hour
Servings: 4

INGREDIENTS:
2 cups heavy cream
Sugar to the taste
2 lemons, peeled and roughly chopped

DIRECTIONS:
In your Slow cooker, mix cream with sugar and lemons, stir, cover and cook on Low for 1 hour. Divide into glasses and serve very cold.

NUTRITION:
calories 177, fat 0, fiber 0, carbs 6, protein 1

Coconut Jam
Preparation time: 10 minutes
Cooking time: 3 hours
Servings: 2

INGREDIENTS:
½ cup coconut flesh, shredded
1 cup coconut cream
½ cup heavy cream
3 tablespoons sugar
1 tablespoon lemon juice

DIRECTIONS:
In your slow cooker, mix the coconut cream with the lemon juice and the other ingredients, whisk, put the lid on and cook on Low for 3 hours. Whisk well, divide into bowls and serve cold.

NUTRITION:
calories 50, fat 1, fiber 1, carbs 10, protein 2

Banana Bread
Preparation time: 10 minutes
Cooking time: 3 hours
Servings: 6

INGREDIENTS:
¾ cup sugar
1/3 cup butter, soft
1 teaspoon vanilla extract
1 egg
2 bananas, mashed
1 teaspoon baking powder
1 and ½ cups flour
½ teaspoons baking soda
1/3 cup milk
1 and ½ teaspoons cream of tartar
Cooking spray

DIRECTIONS:
In a bowl, combine milk with cream of tartar and stir well. Add sugar, butter, egg, vanilla and bananas and stir everything. In another bowl, mix flour with salt, baking powder and soda. Combine the 2 mixtures and stir them well. Grease your Slow cooker with cooking spray, add bread batter, cover, cook on High for 3 hours. Leave the bread to cool down, slice and serve it.

NUTRITION:
calories 300, fat 3, fiber 4, carbs 28, protein 5

Bread and Berries Pudding
Preparation time: 10 minutes
Cooking time: 3 hours
Servings: 2

INGREDIENTS:
2 cups white bread, cubed
1 cup blackberries
2 tablespoons butter, melted
2 tablespoons white sugar
1 cup almond milk
¼ cup heavy cream
2 eggs, whisked
1 tablespoon lemon zest, grated
¼ teaspoon vanilla extract

DIRECTIONS:
In your slow cooker, mix the bread with the berries, butter and the other ingredients, toss

gently, put the lid on and cook on Low for 3 hours. Divide pudding between dessert plates and serve.

NUTRITION:
calories 354, fat 12, fiber 4, carbs 29, protein 11

Candied Lemon
Preparation time: 20 minutes
Cooking time: 4 hours
Servings: 4

INGREDIENTS:
5 lemons, peeled and cut into medium segments
3 cups white sugar
3 cups water

DIRECTIONS:
In your Slow cooker, mix lemons with sugar and water, cover, cook on Low for 4 hours transfer them to bowls and serve cold.

NUTRITION:
calories 62, fat 3, fiber 5, carbs 3, protein 4

Tapioca and Chia Pudding
Preparation time: 10 minutes
Cooking time: 3 hours
Servings: 2

INGREDIENTS:
1 cup almond milk
¼ cup tapioca pearls
2 tablespoons chia seeds
2 eggs, whisked
½ teaspoon vanilla extract
3 tablespoons sugar
½ tablespoon lemon zest, grated

DIRECTIONS:
In your slow cooker, mix the tapioca pearls with the milk, eggs and the other ingredients, whisk, put the lid on and cook on Low for 3 hours. Divide the pudding into bowls and serve cold.

NUTRITION:
calories 180, fat 3, fiber 4, carbs 12, protein 4

Chocolate and Liquor Cream
Preparation time: 10 minutes
Cooking time: 2 hours
Servings: 4

INGREDIENTS:
3.5 ounces crème fraiche
3.5 ounces dark chocolate, cut into chunks
1 teaspoon liquor
1 teaspoon sugar

DIRECTIONS:
In your Slow cooker, mix crème fraiche with chocolate, liquor and sugar, stir, cover, cook on Low for 2 hours, divide into bowls and serve cold

NUTRITION:
calories 200, fat 12, fiber 4, carbs 6, protein 3

Dates and Rice Pudding
Preparation time: 10 minutes
Cooking time: 3 hours
Servings: 2

INGREDIENTS:
1 cup dates, chopped
½ cup white rice
1 cup almond milk
2 tablespoons brown sugar
1 teaspoon almond extract

DIRECTIONS:
In your slow cooker, mix the rice with the milk and the other ingredients, whisk, put the lid on and cook on Low for 3 hours. Divide the pudding into bowls and serve.

NUTRITION:
calories 152, fat 5, fiber 2, carb 6, protein 3

Butternut Squash Sweet Mix
Preparation time: 10 minutes
Cooking time: 3 hours
Serving: 8

INGREDIENTS:
2 pounds butternut squash, steamed, peeled and mashed
2 eggs
1 cup milk
¾ cup maple syrup
1 teaspoon cinnamon powder
½ teaspoon ginger powder
¼ teaspoon cloves, ground
1 tablespoon cornstarch
Whipped cream for serving

DIRECTIONS:
In a bowl, mix squash with maple syrup, milk, eggs, cinnamon, cornstarch, ginger, cloves and cloves and stir very well. Pour this into your Slow cooker, cover, cook on Low for 2 hours, divide into cups and serve with whipped cream on top.

NUTRITION:
calories 152, fat 3, fiber 4, carbs 16, protein 4

Almonds, Walnuts and Mango Bowls
Preparation time: 10 minutes
Cooking time: 2 hours
Servings: 2

INGREDIENTS:
1 cup walnuts, chopped
2 tablespoons almonds, chopped
1 cup mango, peeled and roughly cubed
1 cup heavy cream
½ teaspoon vanilla extract
1 teaspoon almond extract
1 tablespoon brown sugar

DIRECTIONS:
In your slow cooker, mix the nuts with the mango, cream and the other ingredients, toss, put the lid on and cook on High for 2 hours. Divide the mix into bowls and serve.

NUTRITION:
calories 220, fat 4, fiber 2, carbs 4, protein 6

Tapioca Pudding

Preparation time: 10 minutes
Cooking time: 1 hour
Servings: 6

INGREDIENTS:
1 and ¼ cups milk
1/3 cup tapioca pearls, rinsed
½ cup water
½ cup sugar
Zest of ½ lemon

DIRECTIONS:
In your Slow cooker, mix tapioca with milk, sugar, water and lemon zest, stir, cover, cook on Low for 1 hour, divide into cups and serve warm.

NUTRITION:
calories 200, fat 4, fiber 2, carbs 37, protein 3

Berries Salad

Preparation time: 10 minutes
Cooking time: 1 hour
Servings: 2

INGREDIENTS:
2 tablespoons brown sugar
1 tablespoon lime juice
1 tablespoon lime zest, grated
1 cup blueberries
½ cup cranberries
1 cup blackberries
1 cup strawberries
½ cup heavy cream

DIRECTIONS:
In your slow cooker, mix the berries with the sugar and the other ingredients, toss, put the lid on and cook on High for 1 hour. Divide the mix into bowls and serve.

NUTRITION:
calories 262, fat 7, fiber 2, carbs 5, protein 8

Fresh Cream Mix

Preparation time: 1 hour
Cooking time: 1 hour
Servings: 6

INGREDIENTS:
2 cups fresh cream
1 teaspoon cinnamon powder
6 egg yolks
5 tablespoons white sugar
Zest of 1 orange, grated
A pinch of nutmeg for serving
4 tablespoons sugar
2 cups water

DIRECTIONS:
In a bowl, mix cream, cinnamon and orange zest and stir. In another bowl, mix the egg yolks with white sugar and whisk well. Add this over the cream, stir, strain and divide into ramekins. Put ramekins in your Slow cooker, add 2 cups water to the slow cooker, cover, cook on Low for 1 hour, leave cream aside to cool down and serve.

NUTRITION:
calories 200, fat 4, fiber 5, carbs 15, protein 5

Pears and Apples Bowls

Preparation time: 10 minutes
Cooking time: 2 hours
Servings: 2

INGREDIENTS:
1 teaspoon vanilla extract
2 pears, cored and cut into wedges
2 apples, cored and cut into wedges
1 tablespoon walnuts, chopped
2 tablespoons brown sugar
½ cup coconut cream

DIRECTIONS:
In your slow cooker, mix the pears with the apples, nuts and the other ingredients, toss, put the lid on and cook on Low for 2 hours. Divide the mix into bowls and serve cold.

NUTRITION:
calories 120, fat 2, fiber 2, carbs 4, protein 3

Pears and Wine Sauce

Preparation time: 10 minutes
Cooking time: 1 hour and 30 minutes
Servings: 6

INGREDIENTS:
6 green pears
1 vanilla pod
1 cloves
A pinch of cinnamon
7 oz. sugar
1 glass red wine

DIRECTIONS:
In your Slow cooker, mix wine with sugar, vanilla and cinnamon. Add pears and clove, cover slow cooker and cook on High for 1 hour and 30 minutes. Transfer pears to bowls and serve with the wine sauce all over.

NUTRITION:
calories 162, fat 4, fiber 3, carbs 6, protein 3

Creamy Rhubarb and Plums Bowls
Preparation time: 10 minutes

Cooking time: 2 hours

Servings: 2

INGREDIENTS:
1 cup plums, pitted and halved
1 cup rhubarb, sliced
1 cup coconut cream
½ teaspoon vanilla extract
½ cup sugar
½ tablespoon lemon juice
1 teaspoon almond extract

DIRECTIONS:
In your slow cooker, mix the plums with the rhubarb, cream and the other ingredients, toss, put the lid on and cook on High for 2 hours. Divide the mix into bowls and serve.

NUTRITION:
calories 162, fat 2, fiber 2, carbs 4, protein 5

Pears and Grape Sauce
Preparation time: 10 minutes

Cooking time: 1 hour and 30 minutes

Servings: 4

INGREDIENTS:
4 pears
Juice and Zest of 1 lemon
26 ounces grape juice
11 ounces currant jelly
4 garlic cloves
½ vanilla bean
4 peppercorns
2 rosemary springs

DIRECTIONS:
Put the jelly, grape juice, lemon zest, lemon juice, vanilla, peppercorns, rosemary and pears in your Slow cooker, cover and cook on High for 1 hour and 30 minutes. Divide everything between plates and serve.

NUTRITION:
calories 152, fat 3, fiber 5, carbs 12, protein 4

Greek Cream Cheese Pudding
Preparation time: 5 minutes

Cooking time: 2 hours

Servings: 2

INGREDIENTS:
1 cup cream cheese, soft
½ cup Greek yogurt
2 eggs, whisked
½ teaspoon baking soda
1 cup almonds, chopped
1 tablespoon sugar
½ teaspoon almond extract
½ teaspoon cinnamon powder

DIRECTIONS:
In your slow cooker, mix the cream cheese with the yogurt, eggs and the other ingredients, whisk, put the lid on and cook on Low for 2 hours. Divide the pudding into bowls and serve.

NUTRITION:
calories 172, fat 2, fiber 3, carbs 4, protein 5

Rice Pudding
Preparation time: 10 minutes

Cooking time: 2 hours

Servings: 6

INGREDIENTS:
1 tablespoon butter
7 ounces long grain rice
4 ounces water
16 ounces milk
3 ounces sugar
1 egg
1 tablespoon cream
1 teaspoon vanilla extract

DIRECTIONS:
In your Slow cooker, mix butter with rice, water, milk, sugar, egg, cream and vanilla, stir, cover and cook on High for 2 hours. Stir pudding one more time, divide into bowls and serve.

NUTRITION:
calories 152, fat 4, fiber 4, carbs 6, protein 4

Greek Cream
Preparation time: 10 minutes

Cooking time: 1 hour

Servings: 2

INGREDIENTS:
1 cup heavy cream
1 cup Greek yogurt
2 tablespoons brown sugar
½ teaspoon vanilla extract
½ teaspoon ginger powder

DIRECTIONS:
In your slow cooker, mix the cream with the yogurt and the other ingredients, whisk, put the lid on and cook on High for 1 hour. Divide the cream into bowls and serve cold.

NUTRITION:
calories 200, fat 5, fiber 3, carbs 4, protein 5

Orange Marmalade

Preparation time: 10 minutes

Cooking time: 3 hours

Servings: 8

INGREDIENTS:
- Juice of 2 lemons
- 3 pounds sugar
- 1 pound oranges, peeled and cut into segments
- 1-pint water

DIRECTIONS:
In your Slow cooker, mix lemon juice with sugar, oranges and water, cover and cook on High for 3 hours. Stir one more time, divide into cups and serve cold.

NUTRITION:
calories 100, fat 4, fiber 4, carbs 12, protein 4

Ginger Cream

Preparation time: 10 minutes

Cooking time: 1 hour

Serving: 2

INGREDIENTS:
- 1 cup coconut cream
- 1 tablespoon ginger, grated
- 2 eggs, whisked
- 1 cup Greek yogurt
- 2 tablespoons brown sugar
- 1 tablespoon lemon juice

DIRECTIONS:
In your slow cooker, mix the cream with the ginger, eggs and the other ingredients, whisk, put the lid on and cook on High for 1 hour. Cool the cream down and serve.

NUTRITION:
calories 384, fat 33.2, fiber 3, carbs 17.9, protein 8.6

Berry Marmalade

Preparation time: 10 minutes

Cooking time: 3 hours

Servings: 12

INGREDIENTS:
- 1 pound cranberries
- 1 pound strawberries
- ½ pound blueberries
- 3.5 ounces black currant
- 2 pounds sugar
- Zest of 1 lemon
- 2 tablespoon water

DIRECTIONS:
In your Slow cooker, mix strawberries with cranberries, blueberries, currants, lemon zest, sugar and water, cover, cook on High for 3 hours, divide into jars and serve cold.

NUTRITION:
calories 100, fat 4, fiber 3, carbs 12, protein 3

Bread and Quinoa Pudding

Preparation time: 10 minutes

Cooking time: 3 hours

Servings: 2

INGREDIENTS:
- 1 cup quinoa
- 1 cup bread, cubed
- 2 cups almond milk
- 2 tablespoons honey
- 1 teaspoon cinnamon powder
- 1 teaspoon nutmeg, ground

DIRECTIONS:
In your slow cooker, mix the quinoa with the milk and the other ingredients, whisk, put the lid on and cook on Low for 3 hours. Divide the pudding into bowls and serve.

NUTRITION:
calories 981, fat 63.4, fiber 11.9, carbs 94.6, protein 19

Pears Jam

Preparation time: 10 minutes

Cooking time: 3 hours

Servings: 12

INGREDIENTS:
- 8 pears, cored and cut into quarters
- 2 apples, peeled, cored and cut into quarters
- ½ cup apple juice
- 1 teaspoon cinnamon, ground

DIRECTIONS:
In your Slow cooker, mix pears with apples, cinnamon and apple juice, stir, cover and cook on High for 3 hours. Blend using an immersion blender, divide jam into jars and keep in a cold place until you serve it.

NUTRITION:
calories 100, fat 1, fiber 2, carbs 20, protein 3

Melon Pudding

Preparation time: 10 minutes
Cooking time: 2 hours
Servings: 2

INGREDIENTS:
- 1 cup melon, peeled and cubed
- ½ cup white rice
- 1 cup coconut milk
- 2 tablespoons honey
- 1 teaspoon vanilla extract
- 1 teaspoon ginger powder
- ½ tablespoon lime zest, grated

DIRECTIONS:
In your slow cooker, mix the rice with the melon, milk and the other ingredients, whisk, put the lid on and cook on High for 2 hours. Divide the pudding into bowls and serve cold.

NUTRITION:
calories 545, fat 29.1, fiber 4.3, carbs 68.4, protein 6.9

Conclusion

Did you ever thought you could make so many wonderful and delicious meals using your Slow cooker?

Did you know that this is a very special kitchen appliance that helps you become a start in the kitchen?

More and more people all over the world chose to prepare their culinary feasts using this great tool.

So, what are you waiting for?

Get your hands on a copy of this amazing cookbook and start making the best dishes of your life!

Have fun!

Copyright © 2020 by Rosemary King

All rights reserved. No part of this publication may be reproduced, distributed, or transmitted in any form or by any means, including photocopying, recording, or other electronic or mechanical methods, without the prior written permission of the publisher, except in the case of brief quotations embodied in critical reviews and certain other noncommercial uses permitted by copyright law.

Disclaimer: The information presented is purely to svhare my experience and for entertainment purposes. As always, check with a doctor before making any fitness or nutrition changes. The author disclaims liability for any damage, mishap, or injury that may occur from engaging in any activities or ideas from this site. All information posted is merely for educational and informational purposes. It is not intended as a substitute for professional advice. Should you decide to act upon any information in this book, you do so at your own risk. The content displayed on the website is the intellectual property of the author. You may not reuse, republish, or reprint such content without our written consent.

Printed in Great Britain
by Amazon